New Spirits

D0204514

New Spirits

Americans in the "Gilded Age," 1865–1905

REBECCA EDWARDS
Vassar College

SECOND EDITION

New York   Oxford
OXFORD UNIVERSITY PRESS
2011

Oxford University Press, Inc., publishes works that further Oxford University's
objective of excellence in research, scholarship, and education.

Oxford   New York
Auckland   Cape Town   Dar es Salaam   Hong Kong   Karachi
Kuala Lumpur   Madrid   Melbourne   Mexico City   Nairobi
New Delhi   Shanghai   Taipei   Toronto

With offices in
Argentina   Austria   Brazil   Chile   Czech Republic   France   Greece
Guatemala   Hungary   Italy   Japan   Poland   Portugal   Singapore
South Korea   Switzerland   Thailand   Turkey   Ukraine   Vietnam

Copyright © 2011, 2006 by Oxford University Press, Inc.

Published by Oxford University Press, Inc.
198 Madison Avenue, New York, New York 10016
http:// www.oup.com

Oxford is a registered trademark of Oxford University Press

All rights reserved. No part of this publication may be reproduced,
stored in a retrieval system, or transmitted, in any form or by any means,
electronic, mechanical, photocopying, recording, or otherwise,
without the prior permission of Oxford University Press.

Library of Congress Cataloging-in-Publication Data
Edwards, Rebecca, 1966–
New spirits: Americans in the "Gilded Age"/Rebecca Edwards. —2nd ed.
    p. cm.
  Includes bibliographical references and index.
  ISBN 978-0-19-537670-8
1. United States—History—1865–1921. 2. United States—Social
conditions—1865–1918.   I. Title.
  E661. E27 2011
  973.8—dc22   2009053365

Printing number: 9   8   7   6   5   4   3

Printed in the United States of America
on acid-free paper

This is for Ben

Crees que la vida es incendio,
Que el progreso es erupción. . . .
Los Estados Unidos son potentes y grandes.
Cuando ellos se estremecen hay un
hondo temblor que pasa por las
vértebras enormes de los Andes.
　　　—RUBÉN DARÍO, "A ROOSEVELT"

You think that life is fire,
That progress is eruption. . . .
The United States are powerful and grand.
When they stir, an earthquake shudders
Down the Andes' great spine.

CONTENTS

For a comprehensive timeline and a collection of images and documents relating to *New Spirits*, go to http://www.rebeccaedwards.org.

INTRODUCTION

Democratic Vistas

Ach! America! From the other end of the earth from where I
came, America was a land of living hope, woven of dreams,
aflame with longing and desire.
— Anzia Yezierska, "America and I"

In the last half of the nineteenth century, a new United States emerged out of a
crucible of fire. Those fires were not just a figure of speech. Workers in Andrew
Carnegie's famous steel mills melted iron in Bessemer furnaces at 3,000 degrees.
Day and night, refineries in Ohio and Pennsylvania burned off tall plumes of gasoline, a by-product of kerosene that no one yet knew how to use. Coal fires stoked
the locomotives and steamships that began to dominate land and sea. Their flames
sometimes raged out of control: steamboat explosions scalded workers and passengers, while stray sparks from railroads ignited barns and homes. The explosive
energy of miners' blasting powder was also dangerous, trapping workers in underground infernos that killed as many as 200 in a single catastrophe.

Most dramatic of all were firestorms that raged around the Great Lakes, where
clear-cut logging left miles of dry brush. The holocausts of 1871, described by
terrified survivors as "tornadoes of fire," killed 1,500 people in Wisconsin alone.
The heat was so intense that a wooded island a half-mile offshore in Lake Michigan
burst into flames. Two decades later a similar firestorm in Minnesota incinerated
six towns in four hours. At Hinckley a heroic railroad crew saved 300 lives by running their train backward full-throttle to reach a pond beside the tracks. As roaring
flames cracked the train windows, an African-American porter paced the aisles
calming passengers and extinguishing sparks. When the engineer braked beside
the pond, everyone leaped from the cars and waded in. The engineer dragged with
him the train's unconscious fireman, who had shoveled coal frantically to stoke the
engine while his clothing burned. Neck-deep in water, the group waited for hours
until the flames passed by. Two Chinese immigrants, terrified and apparently
unable to understand English, stayed in their seats and burned with the train.

Americans in the growing cities suffered their own versions of such horrors.
Two dramatic fires marked the beginning and end of the era in Chicago, where the
Great Fire of 1871 destroyed most of the downtown and a 1903 blaze in the Iroquois
Theater, a modern "fireproof" building, trapped and killed more than 600.

Currier & Ives, *Night Scene at an American Railway Junction. Lightning Express, Flying Mail, and Owl Trains, "On Time,"* 1876. Currier & Ives were among the nation's most popular lithographers in the late nineteenth century. Many of their images celebrated technological progress, especially the speed and power of steamboats and railroads and their ability to run through the night. Courtesy Amon Carter Museum.

(Engineers hastily explained that the frame of a building could be made fireproof but its occupants could not.) A swath of central Boston burned in 1876; the same happened to large portions of Seattle in 1889 and Baltimore in 1904, while flames engulfed much of San Francisco after the infamous earthquake of 1906. Urban tenement fires became such a well-known phenomenon that amusement parks on New York's Coney Island staged live spectacles called "Fire and Flames." The parks hired off-duty firemen and actors to battle the blazes, scream from windows, and flee out the doors. (Real fire eventually touched Coney Island when all three of its famous parks—Dreamland, Luna Park, and Steeplechase—succumbed to accidental blazes.)

Some fires were set as intentional acts of protest in an era marked by sharp social and economic conflicts. A group of female convicts in Georgia reacted to sexual exploitation and abysmal living conditions by burning down the Chattahoochee brickyard where they had been sent for hard labor. Striking steel-workers at Homestead, Pennsylvania, lit up the night sky along the Monongahela River by torching the barges that had brought in an army of private detectives. White miners in Rock Springs, Wyoming, set fire to the cabins of Chinese workers; when the occupants fled they threw them back inside to burn, killing twenty-eight. And among 2,500 lynchings that occurred between 1885 and 1900, mobs burned at least twenty-three men and one woman at the stake. Civil War veteran Oliver Wendell Holmes famously wrote of his generation that "in our youth our hearts

The Rush for Life Over the Randolph Street Bridge. This dramatic image, drawn from a sketch by eyewitness John Chapin, shows Chicago residents fleeing from the immense October 1871 fire that ravaged the downtown and left almost 100,000 homeless. Currier & Ives adapted this image into a lithograph illustrating the disaster. *Harper's Weekly,* 28 October 1871. Courtesy Vassar College Library.

were touched with fire." The same was true for millions of Americans after the war's end—though their experiences were often less glorious than Holmes's memory of his war service. In fact, the postwar world was almost as lethal as the war itself. During four decades of clear-cut logging, more Americans died in forest fires than had been killed at the Battle of Antietam. The number of employees, passengers, and bystanders killed by railroads in the same years probably approached 200,000—a figure not far distant from the sum of battlefield deaths for the Union and Confederacy combined.

As significant as it was, the Civil War was thus part of broader, even more sweeping transformations. Confederate surrender did not so much restore the old nation as create a new one, reshaped by economic and political changes that had begun earlier and had helped precipitate the conflict. Industrialization, a mighty engine of transformation, gathered speed and expanded nationwide. The rise of corporate capitalism had been under way before the Civil War, but after 1865 it took on new scale and geographic reach. Steamships ferried wheat, cigarettes, rubber, missionaries, immigrants, and tourists all over the globe. Millions of people said farewell to friends and kin in China, Russia, Mexico, Italy, and other countries and sought their fortunes in America. Within the United States, individuals left the eastern seaboard for the frontier, the countryside for the towns, the towns for the cities, and together they made up mass migrations. Farmers' children headed to business school; the daughters and sons of slaves earned college diplomas and became teachers and insurance agents. Indian children left their parents' homes on reservations, entered boarding schools, and pursued careers as writers and doctors. The ideal of "separate spheres" for men and women began to fade; young women graduated from high school and even college, took jobs in the corporate world, and led great reform movements. If, as one historian writes, "the central dream of the modern world" is "the ability to escape the burden of the past," then Americans of the late nineteenth century embraced modernity with a passion.

Historians have long labeled the post–Civil War era "the Gilded Age," borrowing the title of an 1873 novel by Mark Twain and his friend Charles Dudley Warner. *The Gilded Age* satirized get-rich-quick schemes and corruption in Washington, and its title suggested that America glittered on the outside while it rotted at the core. Twain and his contemporaries saw much cause for cynicism and despair. One of the nation's most notorious scandals unfolded while Twain and Warner were writing *The Gilded Age*, as New York senator William "Boss" Tweed was put on trial. A member of Tweed's own party calculated that he and his Tammany Hall associates had bilked New York City out of at least $30 million. In the postwar years, lesser disgraces touched many city and state governments, not to mention Washington, D.C. They showed the temptations that arose with rapid economic growth and the entanglement of public and private interests. In his notes for the novel, Twain wrote that gold rushes and railroad speculation had been "the worst things that ever befell Amer[ica]; they created the hunger for wealth when the Gr[eat] Civ[ilization] had just completed its youth & its ennobling WAR—strong, pure, clean, ambitious, impressionable—ready to make choice of a life-course."

Meanwhile, a severe economic depression hit the United States just as *The Gilded Age* appeared. Fierce clashes between labor and capital broke out, while white workers in the West vented their prejudices against Chinese immigrants. Southern Reconstruction left even deeper scars. Portions of the South remained engulfed in violence, and idealistic Unionists began to grasp that they could not achieve full citizenship for freedmen and also reconcile ex-Confederates to Republicans' plans for the new nation. In fact, it increasingly seemed that they would achieve neither. Violence by southern white supremacists exposed northern indifference, as the public increasingly shrugged at the domestic terrorism of groups like the Ku Klux Klan.

Yet despite all this, the post–Civil War decades were also a time of enormous optimism. Walt Whitman suggested as much in his 1871 essay *Democratic Vistas*, capturing the hopes that arose in the wake of Union victory and Emancipation. Echoing Lincoln's call for a "new birth of freedom," Whitman proclaimed a "new spirit" in America's national experiment. Democracy, he argued, consisted of three related projects. First, it was a set of political structures vesting authority in the people; in this sense American democracy had begun with the Revolution and continued with the Fifteenth Amendment enfranchising all men, irrespective of race. (Whitman predicted that within a generation, women would also vote.) The second project was to advance "trade, finance, machinery, intercommunications," which Whitman hoped would provide broad-ranging benefits. The old poet loved tramping around New York City talking to peddlers, housekeepers, trolley conductors, and dockworkers, and he wanted enterprise to serve them all.

Whitman's third project, which he believed had just begun, was democratic culture. "Did you, too, O friend," he asked, "suppose democracy was only for elections, for politics, and for a party name? I say democracy is only of use there that it may pass on and come to its flower and fruits . . . in religion, literature, colleges, and schools—democracy in all public and private life." Whitman called for a new American culture to complement the nation's political forms. Its "genius" would lie in the popular, the spiritual, and the scientific, and its goals would be to help each individual find truth and self-expression while strengthening ties of community and love. In dreaming this grand dream, Whitman was in good company. Freedmen and freedwomen, immigrants, students, workers, artists, intellectuals, and grassroots reformers believed post–Civil War America offered a chance to start anew.

This optimistic, reform-minded spirit has not gotten its due from historians. On the whole, they tend to depict late nineteenth-century America as dominated by corruption and malaise. *New Spirits* approaches late nineteenth-century America from a different angle, exploring the many ways in which it was a starting point for modern America. Technological change was obvious: the era ushered in such familiar tools as telephones, electricity, bicycles, and cars. Such inventions as the modern cocktail were also products of the Gilded Age: in the 1880s Americans began to sip manhattans, and a decade later they were enjoying dry martinis. More seriously, today's military-industrial complex put down its roots in the late nineteenth century. The environmentalist movement did the same, as did many other modern initiatives and ideas.

Because most readers are familiar with the term, I have retained "the Gilded Age" in the subtitle of *New Spirits* (at least for this edition). But I hope to persuade you to think of these decades, instead, as the Early Progressive Era. Historians generally date the beginning of the Progressive Era—a period when citizens mobilized for reform—around 1900. Some have recently moved the starting date back to 1889, when Jane Addams founded Hull House in Chicago. The Progressives were people who worked to purify politics, regulate and restrict the extraordinary power of big business, and fight poverty and other social and economic injustices. *New Spirits* provides, I hope, ample evidence that these movements were well under way in the late nineteenth century. At the same time, many of the problems that plagued the so-called Gilded Age continued and even intensified after 1900.

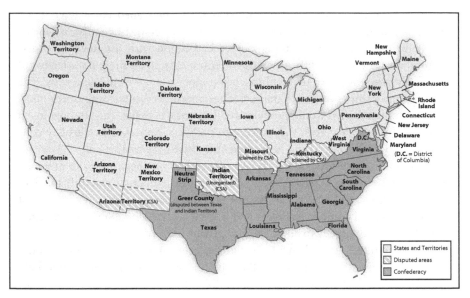

The United States in January 1865. The nation had expanded substantially between 1800 and 1850, through the Louisiana Purchase and the spoils of the Mexican-American War. But until the Union emerged victorious from the Civil War, its status as a continental nation remained in doubt. Portions of the West remained unmapped. Most land was not well connected to the eastern states, from which California could be reached only by ship or by an overland journey of several months.

Among the most critical developments were a burst of U.S. imperialism overseas and the rise of Jim Crow segregation and disfranchisement in the South. Both, in different ways, were products of Reconstruction and its demise.

The goal of *New Spirits* is to challenge historians' long-standing division between a corrupt, stagnant "Gilded Age" and a laudable, optimistic "Progressive Era." Instead, these pages describe the first four decades of a long Progressive Era that began with the myriad initiatives of Reconstruction and extended at least to 1920—perhaps 1932. These decades were characterized throughout by economic and political integration, the building of nationwide networks for reform and protest, and diverse experiments in the use of government for new ends. Americans felt the full impact of industrialization and its consequences, both positive and negative. A once-rural nation found its population crowding into immense cities, its society grappling with such diverse effects as militant new labor demands, transformations in the role of women, and the rise of consumer culture.

Americans had to adapt to these radically new conditions, and their political responses were particularly notable. At no point between 1865 and 1932 did the federal government achieve the scope and ambition of the New Deal that followed. Nonetheless, Civil War era Republicans ushered in a vastly stronger federal government than had existed in the antebellum years. The outlines of a modern state emerged, and the post–Civil War years served as a seedbed of progressive ideas and proposals. At the same time, the United States of America became a truly global society, incorporating immigrants from Latin America, Asia, and Eastern Europe as well as Western Europe and Africa. The global scope of multinational corporations began to present governments (including that of the United States) with new challenges to their power.

It is not surprising that such astute observers as Mark Twain and Walt Whitman expressed ambivalence about the wrenching changes they witnessed. Whitman, in particular, combined his irrepressible hope for the future of American democracy with a fear that it was messy and too frequently thwarted. He deplored his country's "hollowness at heart" and obsession with moneymaking. He worried about labor unrest and criticized Americans for fawning over European culture rather than celebrating the freshness and diversity of their own. He criticized American society as stuffy, overfed, self-righteous, and morally flabby. "In vain have we annex'd Texas, California, Alaska, and reached north for Canada and south for Cuba," he wrote. "It is as if we were somehow being endow'd with a vast and more and more thoroughly appointed body, and then left with little or no soul."

By rejecting the term "Gilded Age" and calling the years between 1865 and 1905 the Early Progressive Era, I do not want to undermine such eloquent critiques. Between 1865 and 1905, Americans witnessed the first march on Washington, the first federal welfare programs, the first elections in which women and black men voted for president, and the first national park in the world. But it would be folly to overlook other, grimmer and more foreboding events. By 1900 the fires of conflict that raged at home were igniting conflagrations overseas. These developments, and some of their consequences, are the subject of Part III of *New Spirits*.

In ways we often overlook, Americans today are heirs to the late nineteenth century. We live with the results of what Americans did in those decades, and also with the legacies of dreams they relinquished and paths they did not take. Now, as when Whitman and Twain wrote, we live in fiery, conflicted times—amid hardship and despair, and also vision and hope. *New Spirits* maps a crucial piece of our past. I have written it on behalf of all those who are now setting out, in Walt Whitman's words, to "write, as it were, upon things that exist not, and travel by maps yet unmade."

ACKNOWLEDGMENTS

New Spirits is a synthesis that seeks to weave together the work of dozens of historians into a single narrative. I am thus deeply indebted to the scholarship upon which I have drawn. Readers are encouraged to trace those sources in the Further Reading lists at the ends of chapters, as well as to explore opportunities for further reading in both primary and secondary sources at the New Spirits Web site. In addition to recent works mentioned earlier, previous overviews of the era include

The United States in January 1905. Just forty years later, the United States had expanded its influence far beyond North America. It had claimed territorial possessions in Alaska, Samoa, Hawai'i, Guam, Puerto Rico, and the Philippines. U.S. troops had joined a multinational force that enforced Western commercial interests in coastal China. Closer to home, the United States had set limits on Cuba's sovereignty; over the next decade it would open the Panama Canal and undertake military interventions and occupations in Mexico, Nicaragua, Haiti, and other nations in Central America and the Caribbean.

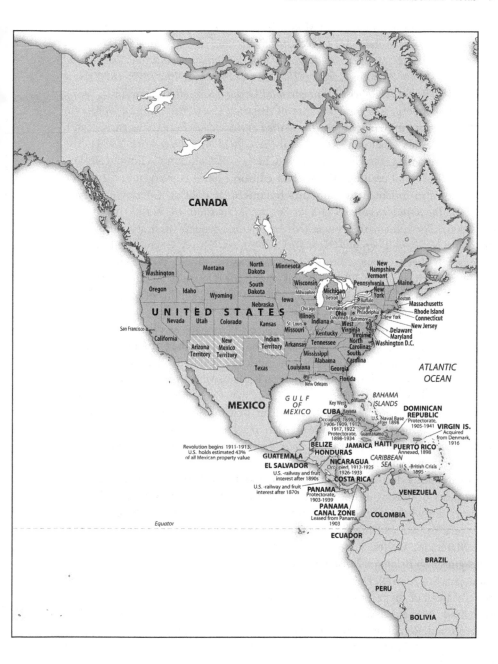

CANADA

Washington
Oregon
Idaho
Montana
Wyoming
Nevada
Utah
Colorado
California
San Francisco

North Dakota
South Dakota
Nebraska
Kansas
Arizona Territory
New Mexico Territory
Indian Territory
Texas

UNITED STATES

Minnesota
Wisconsin
Iowa
Milwaukee
Chicago
Illinois
Indiana
Missouri
St. Louis
Arkansas
Mississippi
Louisiana
New Orleans

Michigan
Detroit
Cleveland
Ohio
Cincinnati
Kentucky
Tennessee
Alabama
Georgia
Florida

New Hampshire
Vermont
Pennsylvania
New York
Buffalo
Pittsburgh
Philadelphia
Baltimore
New York
West Virginia
Virginia
North Carolina
South Carolina
Washington D.C.

Maine
Massachusetts
Rhode Island
Connecticut
New Jersey
Delaware
Maryland
Boston

ATLANTIC OCEAN

GULF OF MEXICO

MEXICO

Revolution begins 1911-1913,
U.S. holds estimated 43%
of all Mexican property value

GUATEMALA
EL SALVADOR
U.S. -railway and fruit
interest after 1890s
U.S. -railway and fruit
interest after 1870s

BAHAMA ISLANDS

Key West
Miami
CUBA Havana
Occupied, 1898, 1906,
1906-1909, 1912,
1917, 1922
Protectorate,
1898-1934
Guantánamo
U.S. Naval Base
after 1898

BELIZE JAMAICA HAITI
HONDURAS
NICARAGUA
Occupied, 1912-1925
1926-1933
COSTA RICA

DOMINICAN REPUBLIC
Protectorate,
1905-1941

VIRGIN IS.
Acquired
from Denmark,
1916

PUERTO RICO
Annexed, 1898

CARIBBEAN SEA

U.S.-British Crisis
1895

PANAMA
Protectorate,
1903-1939
PANAMA
CANAL ZONE
Leased from Panama,
1903

VENEZUELA

COLOMBIA

Equator

ECUADOR

BRAZIL

PERU

BOLIVIA

Thomas C. Cochran and William Miller, *The Age of Enterprise* (New York, 1942), Samuel P. Hays, *The Response to Industrialism, 1885–1914* (Chicago, 1957; 2nd ed., 1995), Carl N. Degler, *The Age of the Economic Revolution, 1876–1900* (Glenview, IL, 1967), John Garraty, *The New Commonwealth, 1877–1890* (New York, 1968), Robert H. Wiebe, *The Search for Order, 1877–1920* (New York, 1967), Alan Trachtenberg, *The Incorporation of America* (New York, 1982), Nell Irvin Painter, *Standing at Armageddon: The United States, 1877–1919* (New York, 1987), and Sean Dennis Cashman, *America in the Gilded Age* (New York, 1984). The excellent articles in *The Gilded Age*, ed. Charles W. Calhoun (Wilmington, DE, 1996), are essential reading. The second edition (2006) is even better than the first. I am also indebted to Calhoun's treatment of politics, *Conceiving a New Republic: The Republican Party and the Southern Question. 1869–1900* (Lawrence, KS, 2006). For information on noted Americans, readers' first stop should be *American National Biography* (New York, 1999), ed. John A. Garraty and Mark C. Carnes. Its twenty-four volumes are a treasure trove. Neil Harris, Alan Trachtenberg, Leon Fink, John D. Buenker, and most recently Janette Greenwood in *The Gilded Age* (New York, 2003) have edited fine collections of primary documents from the era.

On the theme of fire, treated in the introduction, see Stephen Pyne, *Fire in America* (Princeton, NJ, 1982). The quote about "escaping the burdens of the past" is from James M. Jasper in *Restless Nation* (Chicago, 2000), 5. On Mark Twain and Walt Whitman, see the biographies by Justin Kaplan, *Mr. Clemens and Mark Twain* (New York, 1966), *Mark Twain and His World* (New York, 1974), and *Walt Whitman, a Life* (New York, 1980), as well as Bryant Morey French, *Mark Twain and the Gilded Age* (Dallas, TX, 1965). Alan Trachtenberg also draws attention, in his book cited earlier, to Whitman's *Democratic Vistas*, though his reading of that text differs somewhat from mine.

I extend my deepest, most heartfelt thanks to all these scholars, as well as to the authors of dozens of books named in the Further Reading lists, and to the astute critics who gave me advice on the manuscript. In addition to anonymous reviewers for Oxford University Press, they include Cindy S. Aron, Richard John, Lisa Materson, Walter Nugent, Robert Prasch, Reuel Schiller, and my Vassar colleagues Bob Brigham, Miriam Cohen, Clyde Griffen, Wendy Graham, Michael Hanagan, Jim Merrell, Deborah Dash Moore, and Leslie Offutt. I am immensely grateful to all of them for correcting mistakes and suggesting improvements that have made *New Spirits* a much better book than it would have been without their generous aid. Remaining errors are, of course, my own responsibility.

I am grateful to Brian Wheel at Oxford, who has been a pleasure to work with. Deepest thanks go also to my Vassar research assistants, Michelle Cantos, Liz Fletcher, David Greenstein, Diana Hebron, Mary Joyce, and Kathleen Pierce. I want to acknowledge, with particular appreciation and affection, the supportive and friendly atmosphere of the Vassar College History Department. Thanks also to the dedicated staff of Vassar College Library for their help.

Last but not least, many thanks to my son Ben, to whom this book is dedicated with love. To my husband, Mark Seidl, I owe everything else, which is a great deal indeed. He offered patient and insightful readings of the manuscript (including at least five drafts of Chapter 2) while living with considerable burdens and distractions as a result of the writing process. He also provided invaluable aid with this second edition. His love and support and the joy of our life together continue to make it all worthwhile.

PART I

The Wedge

Three years after the Civil War, an itinerant journalist living in San Francisco ventured some predictions about the transcontinental rail line that would soon connect California to New York. In "What the Railroad Will Bring Us," Henry George developed the arguments he later presented in *Progress and Poverty*, a book that went through more than a hundred editions in the twenty years after its publication in 1879. *Progress and Poverty* shocked readers by challenging their belief in progress. The author observed that railroads, economic growth, and industrialization held out the hope of prosperity for everyone, but they delivered to only part of the population. George had watched rents escalate in San Francisco while more and more local people became wage workers in factory and service jobs. Unlike other observers, he saw that these were not temporary or marginal side effects but an integral part of the nation's economic transformation. "Widespread destitution is found in the midst of the greatest abundance," he observed. "Where population is densest, wealth greatest, and the machinery of production and exchange most highly developed—there we find the deepest poverty, the sharpest struggle for existence."

George hastened to note that economic growth *did* bring wealth to many Americans. The problem, he argued, was that the new forces "do not act upon the social fabric from underneath, as was for a long time hoped and believed, but strike it at a point intermediate between top and bottom. It is as though an immense wedge were being forced, not underneath society, but through society. Those who are above the point of separation are elevated, but those who are below are crushed down." George noted that these problems had arisen in monarchies and democracies, high-tariff and free-trade countries. He concluded that they were structural to capitalism, especially in its emerging corporate form. The new economy, George predicted, would destroy traditional agriculture, trades, and crafts and "make sharper the contrast between the House of Have and the House of Want."

The extent to which one accepts Henry George's critique depends on how one defines "Have" and "Want." Was the measure of "Have" the ability to put money in the bank? If so, then in George's lifetime the Wants far outnumbered the Haves. If the prospect of home ownership was the measure, then the numbers looked better, putting perhaps half above the wedge. Was it freedom from hard physical labor? More Americans rose above the wedge. Was it the ability to be one's own boss? Many more fell below it. The enjoyment of more consumer products, including more variety on the table? More above. In a global economy, though, poverty among workers overseas might need to be counted in the totals. And it was even more daunting to try to measure the development of democracy, cultural achievement, and spiritual growth. Capitalism promised *material* progress. Even if it delivered that to every person on the globe, other measures remained in question.

Part I of *New Spirits* turns first to the material, exploring the transformations wrought in the nineteenth-century United States by revolutions in technology, finance, and economic policy. Controversy over the role of government, especially in helping distribute economic risks and rewards, had helped precipitate the Civil War, and it remained a critical issue of the postwar decades. This, along with the many legacies of the war itself, is the subject of Chapter 1. Chapter 2 explores the speed and reach of telegraphs, railroads, and steamships and the more general impact of the rise of fossil fuels. Chapter 3 examines the world of work as experienced by those below and above Henry George's "wedge." Chapter 4 considers some of the ways in which Americans used, debated, deplored, and celebrated the power of money. Was the United States, as many critics charged, becoming a money-obsessed society? What were the benefits and pitfalls of rapid material progress? Were traditional values being displaced, and if so, was that a cause for celebration or for mourning?

CHAPTER 1

An Uneasy Peace

What is freedom? Is it the bare privilege of not being
chained? . . . If this is all, then freedom is a bitter mockery,
a cruel delusion.
—CONGRESSMAN JAMES A. GARFIELD

On New Year's Day, 1863, on a Union-controlled island off the coast of South
Carolina, Colonel Thomas W. Higginson bore witness to a great human
triumph. For weeks he had been drilling the First South Carolina Volunteers
(Colored) as they prepared to join the Union Army, but to recognize President
Lincoln's final Proclamation of Emancipation, which went into effect on January 1,
camp commanders declared a holiday. Former slaves gathered from miles around
to hear a local preacher read the executive order that made them officially free.
"The very moment the speaker had ceased," Higginson reported, "and just as I
took and waved the flag, . . . there suddenly arose close beside the platform a strong
male voice (but rather cracked and elderly) into which two women's voices instantly
blended." The assembly broke into an impassioned verse of "My country 'tis of
thee, sweet land of liberty, of thee I sing!" "I never saw anything so electric,"
Higginson wrote. "It made all other words cheap; it seemed the choked voice of a
race at last unloosed. . . . Art could not have dreamed of a tribute to the day of
jubilee that should be so affecting; history will not believe it." Against all odds, the
aspirations of a people in bondage and of the U.S. government had converged.
Higginson's soldiers would henceforth fight for a freedom President Lincoln had
ruled to be rightfully theirs.

Ironically, the men and women gathered at Camp Saxton were among only a
handful who were actually liberated by Lincoln's proclamation. Many thousands
had already escaped and freed themselves in the chaos of war; millions still lived
in parts of the Confederacy that U.S. forces had not conquered. Lincoln, in his
capacity as commander in chief, had issued the proclamation as a military measure to punish seceded states, and for the time being it left slavery intact in Union
border states such as Maryland and Kentucky. Not until 1865 did the Thirteenth
Amendment officially abolish slavery nation-wide and Union troops enforce that
measure with victory on the battlefield. Nonetheless, those who attended the celebration in South Carolina had good reason to hope that Lincoln's proclamation

marked the beginning of the end. When the United States fully ceased to practice slavery two years later, the trend toward New World abolition became unmistakable. Spain would sustain slavery in Cuba until 1886, while Brazil, the last holdout, abolished the institution two years later. In law, at least, four centuries of New World racial slavery had come to an end.

Immense as this transformation was, it was only one of several great revolutions, both national and global, carried forward by the American Civil War. A new United States, led by the victorious North and West, consolidated its boundaries from Atlantic to Pacific. The United States began to assert its power on the world stage while it continued to wrestle with domestic conflicts. Confederate general Robert E. Lee may have surrendered in April 1865, but in some ways the U.S. Civil War continued for decades afterward. So central was the war's legacy to American politics that the 1880 presidential campaign featured four ex-Union generals, running on the Republican, Democratic, Prohibition, and Greenback-Labor tickets. At each election, veterans in uniform marched in torchlight parades, and Republican candidates made pilgrimages to giant reunions organized by the powerful Union veterans' association, the Grand Army of the Republic. Even party symbols reflected the war: Cartoonist Thomas Nast began to draw the Democratic Party as a kicking donkey, symbol of the rebellious South; in 1876 he added the elephant, with its proverbially long memory, to represent Republicans' fixation on the Union.

While politics centered on war rhetoric and imagery, outright bloodshed continued sporadically throughout much of the 1870s. Parts of the South were accurately described as continuing war zones, with dozens of large-scale episodes of terror and many more local crimes carried out by loosely organized groups such as the Ku Klux Klan and Knights of the White Camellia. Freedmen's leaders were beaten, shot, or burned alive in their homes. There was little doubt of the motive when a woman in Henry County, Georgia—wife of a black Union veteran and Republican leader—was gang-raped at gunpoint by a group of Confederate veterans. The Republican governor of South Carolina testified in 1871 that an "actual state of war" existed in several counties. In 1880, at the end of his presidency, Rutherford B. Hayes observed, "I saw things done in the South which could only be accounted for on the theory that the war was not yet ended." Like his predecessor, Ulysses S. Grant, Hayes promised to "end the war and bring peace," which suggested how little peace had yet been accomplished.

THE SCARS OF WAR

When eighteen-year-old Isaac Moses Perski, a Russian Jew fleeing the czar's military draft, landed in New York in 1882, one of his first purchases was a picture book about the U.S. Civil War. Perski could see the war's legacy all around him in the city where he settled. Slavery was dead; African Americans in New York, as elsewhere, were building new institutions, founding churches and businesses, and creating nationwide networks of advocacy and mutual aid. The war had helped

Table 1.1 A Growing Urban Population

	1860	1870	1880	1890	1900
U.S. population	31,444,000	38,558,000	50,156,000	62,947,000	75,995,000
Urban population	6,217,000	9,902,000	14,130,000	22,106,000	30,160,000
Percent urban	19.8	25.7	28.2	35.1	39.7
Percent rural	80.2	74.3	71.8	64.9	60.3

While the majority of Americans still lived in rural areas (defined by the census as places with 2,500 or fewer inhabitants), the urban population increased spectacularly after the Civil War. By the turn of the century, thirty-eight American cities had passed the 100,000 mark of population, and more than 66 percent of northeasterners lived in urban areas. Note that during each decade, the U.S. population as a whole grew between 20 and 30 percent. Figures in the table above have been rounded to the nearest thousand.

Source: *Robert G. Barrows, "Urbanizing America," in* The Gilded Age, *ed. Charles W. Calhoun (Wilmington, DE, 1996), 93, 95.*

create New York's first millionaire class and fill the burgeoning tenement wards. In fact, the war had helped build New York itself. In all parts of the country, urbanization accelerated rapidly during the 1860s and 1870s. By the time Perski arrived, more than half of northeasterners lived in urban areas, and New York's population had recently surpassed one million. By 1900 it would double again.

While the former Confederacy remained in turmoil, Perski saw plenty of scars on the human landscape of the North. Thousands of veterans suffered lingering effects of wounds and wartime illnesses ranging from dysentery to syphilis. The Union alone counted more than 20,000 amputees. Contemporary testimony suggests that alcoholism rose sharply in both North and South after soldiers returned home. Confronted by an antiliquor reformer, one veteran scoffed that "we men of blood and iron, who have seen death in every shape and color without flinching, . . . we want something stronger than water, tea, or coffee." Many veterans dosed themselves with opiates, vast quantities of which had been administered in wartime hospitals. Morphine took the nickname "soldier's joy," while hypodermic drug use became known among pharmacists as "army disease."

Almost every aspect of American culture was reshaped by the Civil War. Veterans' writings brought a hard edge to journalism and literature in what one scholar calls "the chastening of American prose style." Colonel J. W. De Forest of Connecticut was still in the army when he published one of the first works of American realism, *Miss Ravenel's Conversion from Secession to Loyalty* (1867). The author bluntly depicted battlefield carnage, and he refused to punish bad characters and reward good ones, as Victorian convention required. Ambrose Bierce, a Union veteran who suffered recurring nightmares and trauma from his war experiences, also built his fiction around scenes he had witnessed: dead men's faces being eaten by pigs and a soldier writhing in the dirt after a shell removed the top of his skull. One of Bierce's favorite sayings was "nothing matters." His fellow

Union veteran Robert Ingersoll, who in 1863 had declined to reenlist because he could "bear no more bloodshed and mutilation," became the country's most prominent *agnostic*, a word that entered general usage after the war. Immense crowds flocked to hear Ingersoll hail Union victory and question the existence of God.

The war deaths of more than 1.5 percent of the nation's population—630,000 soldiers and perhaps 30,000 civilians—provoked major social upheavals. In the devastated war generation, thousands of young women gave up hope of marriage or remarriage. Thrown into desperation by the loss of a breadwinner, many war widows went looking for work, and their plight was so obvious that it helped establish women's right to earn a living by their own labor. Thousands of women pursued careers as teachers and nurses, while others went into reform and foreign mission work. "The exigencies and inspirations of the great civil war," wrote one missionary journal in 1879, "were the best of preparations. They evoked from the heart and brain of American women undertakings of national significance, and gave us, for the first time in our history, some adequate consciousness of our power."

The women's temperance campaign, one of the largest grassroots movements of the 1870s and 1880s, was partly a response to postwar conditions. The United States had seen considerable temperance activity before the war, but the plight of alcoholic veterans, as well as women's new prominence as reformers, intensified the campaign. Joining a wave of spontaneous local protests in the decade after the war, some women entered saloons to pray and sing; others circulated petitions asking officials to withhold licenses from liquor dealers. The national Woman's Christian Temperance Union (WCTU) coalesced in 1873, claiming more than a million members by its peak in the late 1880s. Under the guidance of its charismatic leader, Frances Willard, after 1879 WCTU members founded kindergartens, soup kitchens, free lunch rooms, and libraries; advocated prison reform and public health measures; endorsed an eight-hour day for workers; and denounced domestic violence. Willard also advocated women's suffrage, and when Republicans resisted the temperance agenda she persuaded the WCTU to back the Prohibition Party, taking women directly into partisan politics. In adopting this strategy, Willard drew on the legacy of antislavery. Her father had been a Wisconsin legislator whose Free-Soil Party had once, in the 1850s, "held the balance of power" on the question of slavery in the federal territories. For a decade Willard's party strove to win the same kind of power.

The war experiences of one woman, Clara Barton, helped prompt the United States to accept new international standards for human rights. Early in the war, forty-year-old Barton volunteered as a nurse in the Army's desperately understaffed field hospitals. She later remembered staunching wounds with corn husks when bandages ran out. At Fredericksburg, she recalled, she had to "wring the blood from the bottom of my clothing, before I could step, for the weight about my feet." After the war Barton traveled to Europe, where she met founders of the Red Cross and other humanitarian organizations. By 1881 she and her allies in the United States had established the American Red Cross, and a year later she won a related victory: due to Barton's almost single-handed lobbying, Congress ratified the 1864

Geneva Convention, agreeing to uphold international standards for treatment of wounded soldiers and prisoners of war. Through the Red Cross, Barton aided victims of natural and human-made disasters across the United States, including forest fires, floods, tornadoes, hurricanes, and yellow fever epidemics in the South. By the 1890s the American Red Cross began work overseas, supplying relief during a Russian famine and aiding refugees after the massacre of Armenians in Turkey. Barton became an outspoken leader of the international peace movement.

The Union and Confederacy had trained three million men to fight, and not all of them went home to live peacefully. The weapons of war were widely in evidence in the late 1860s and 1870s. With government permission, discharged veterans from both sides of the conflict took their sidearms home with them, and at the same time cheap handguns proliferated as patents expired on the famous Colt and Smith & Wesson revolvers. Shop windows displayed pistols with names such as Czar and Dictator, and in the decade after the war guns replaced knives and poison as the weapon of choice for both murder and suicide. Sensationalist newspapers exaggerated the threat posed by violent crime, but the headlines were right about the depredations of the country's most notorious ex-soldiers. Frank and Jesse James had been Confederate raiders in Missouri's vicious guerilla war. Using the railroads for mobility and surprise, they robbed a West Virginia bank in 1866, a Kentucky bank two years later, and a Missouri train in 1876. Jesse James, who never officially surrendered to the Union, was finally shot dead in 1882, the same year Russian immigrant Isaac Perski landed in New York.

RECONSTRUCTING THE SOUTH

The South's secession from the United States temporarily gave the North sweeping political control, just at the moment when the upstart Republican Party won national power. Republicans had a powerful vision of government activism, and in the decade after 1861 they implemented an ambitious array of new policies and programs. But at the same time, Unionists never formally acknowledged the Confederacy's existence. Throughout the secession crisis and the war, their chief aim was to reincorporate the South completely into the nation. Thus, ironically, the South's return to the Union undermined the program of the Republicans—who led the Union War effort. By the end of the long and grueling conflict, most Republicans hoped to transform the ex-Confederacy through Emancipation, free labor, economic development, and African-American citizenship. Democrats resisted that vision. Southern Democrats, in particular, fought to preserve as much as they could of the Old South's political, economic, and social order.

This result was not inevitable. After the surrender of their army, many former Confederates were prepared in 1865 for drastic changes in their society. "What new relations between us & our negroes will be established we cannot tell," wrote one Georgia planter in resignation, "but there is no doubt it will be a radical change. . . . We will be compelled to conform to the new conditions under which we are placed." He predicted optimistically that freedmen "will now have a choice where to labour.

This will ensure good treatment & the best terms. The most humane, the most energetic & the most judicious managers have the best chances in the race for success. I expect to see a revolution in the ownership of landed estates."

Such sentiments suggest that much could have been accomplished if policies toward the defeated South had been wisely planned and administered. But Abraham Lincoln's assassination in 1865 brought Vice President Andrew Johnson to the White House. Johnson proved to be a disaster. "He is obstinate without being firm, self-opinionated without being capable of systematic thinking, combative and pugnacious without being courageous," observed one disgusted Republican who had tried to work with the new president. "He is always *worse* than you expect." Johnson, a Tennessee Unionist Democrat, had been placed on the 1864 ticket to shore up support for Lincoln's reelection among Democrats and independent voters. As president he seemed, at first, to advocate vigorous reformation in the South, but in practice he was weak. Though he swore publicly to hang leading rebels, Johnson privately extended pardons to many wealthy Confederates and restored their lands. Presented with evidence of widespread murders and mob violence carried out by southern whites against blacks, he showed no interest in protecting freedmen.

Ex-Confederates read these signals and concluded that they could act with impunity. Within months of their military defeat, various former Confederate states enacted "Black Codes" that set terms for the subordination of former slaves. Under the Codes, freedmen and women could be forcibly indentured for long periods, beaten, deprived of pay if they protested, and have their children taken away to serve and work for whites. When southerners topped this by electing high-ranking ex-Confederates to state and federal positions, Johnson was shocked, though his own vacillation had precipitated the defiance. By the summer of 1866, when Johnson undertook a speaking tour to defend his policies, he was openly heckled in Cincinnati and other midwestern cities. General U. S. Grant privately dubbed him a "national disgrace."

Strengthened by sweeping victories in the midterm elections of 1866, Congressional Republicans seized the helm. They passed a series of new laws aimed at transforming southern society and protecting freedmen's rights. When Johnson vetoed their proposals and tried to punish Radicals by purging his cabinet, Congress impeached the president in February 1868. The showdown and trial wasted enormous political energy that, under better circumstances, could have been directed toward Reconstruction policy itself. Republicans ultimately failed, by one vote, to remove Johnson from office. Nonetheless, the impeachment forced Johnson to back down. From 1868 onward, Congressional Republicans salvaged Reconstruction as best they could. With the Reconstruction Act of 1867 they divided the former Confederacy into five military districts and outlined new requirements for states' readmission to the Union.

Union war hero Ulysses S. Grant, elected to the presidency in 1868, lent his stature to this Radical Reconstruction, which lasted from roughly 1868 to 1874. Among the Radicals' most enduring achievements were three landmark amendments

Group of freedpeople near the canal, Richmond, Virginia, April 1865. This informal portrait was taken by John Reekie (studio of Alexander Gardner) just after the Confederate capital fell to U.S. forces. Most African Americans were living in hardship amid the Confederacy's collapse, but their freedom was now secure. Courtesy Library of Congress.

to the U.S. Constitution, the first two of which had been passed earlier by Congress, and all of which won ratification between 1868 and 1870. The Thirteenth Amendment abolished slavery. The Fourteenth Amendment established the primacy of federal over state citizenship, declaring that no state could "deprive any person of life, liberty, or property without due process of law." For the first time, after this amendment's ratification, the U.S. Constitution asserted the federal government's authority to protect all Americans' rights from infringement by a state. The Fifteenth Amendment granted voting rights to men of all races, sending hundreds of thousands of freedmen to the polls. Republicans supported these amendments with enforcement apparatus, such as the creation of the cabinet-level Department of Justice in 1870. Faced with mounting violence by the Ku Klux Klan, whose members terrorized Republicans, Congress passed an 1871 law allowing the president to use both federal courts and the U.S. Army to put down conspiracies that deprived citizens of their rights. President Grant undertook vigorous enforcement, driving the Klan underground.

With the unprecedented expansion of U.S. citizenship, some Republicans even endorsed women's suffrage, which emerged during Reconstruction as a subject of serious national debate. In the campaigns to ratify the Fourteenth and Fifteenth amendments, suffragists pressed hard to include voting rights for women. Though the effort failed, a number of suffrage advocates tried to vote in the election of 1872, hoping to persuade judges that the language of the new Fourteenth Amendment included women as full citizens. In *Minor v. Happersett* (1875), the U.S. Supreme Court decisively rejected this interpretation. Women, they declared, could gain the ballot only when voters expressly chose to extend it to them. Voters in two territories had already done so: Wyoming in 1869 and Utah in 1870. Many Americans began to support such measures in the context of Reconstruction—not always because they took a positive view of the expanded franchise. "If we give

Atlanta University, graduating class of 1903, a portrait of achievement four decades after Emancipation. All the graduates in this picture were "Negro" according to prevailing racial definitions. Courtesy Robert W. Woodruff Library of the Atlanta University Center.

Negroes, and Chinamen, and everything else a right to vote," asked one disgruntled Californian, "why in the name of God don't you give [women] equal rights?" On the other hand, suffragist Olympia Brown argued that black women "need the ballot more than anyone in the world."

Meanwhile, Republican Reconstruction governments in the South undertook an array of activist measures. State legislatures sought to foster economic growth by building railroads and offering incentives to business. They established state-run asylums and orphanages, and they replaced gallows and whipping posts with penitentiaries. Most dramatically Republicans introduced public education, which had been virtually unknown for either blacks or whites before the war. Enrollments quadrupled in the space of a few years, and some schools—such as New Orleans' public schools and Kentucky's private Berea Literary Institute—were even racially integrated. Missouri's new public schools system enrolled more than 280,000 students by 1870 and won nationwide praise. At the same time, Republican city governments installed new amenities like streetlights and sewage systems. Many southern states created boards of health to combat yellow fever, and some provided free smallpox vaccinations.

It is difficult to mark one precise moment when all these various initiatives came to a close. In many ways, the greatest moments of opportunity had already been lost during Andrew Johnson's term. Republicans tried as late as 1890 to pass a new federal law to enforce fair elections in the South, and they almost succeeded. But in the shorter run, what most decisively ended Reconstruction was a severe economic depression that began in 1873, spreading hardship nationwide. Tax revenues dried up; state governments curtailed their ambitious new programs. As the Grant administration struggled to protect southern blacks, the northern public—and soon, federal courts—greeted these efforts with increasing hostility.

One turning point was a horrific episode in the village of Colfax, Louisiana. Louisiana's Republican Party had splintered into factions; white supremacist Democrats, who refused to accept the state government's legitimacy, operated with increasing boldness. One Republican was dragged from his bed and beheaded. Another opened a New Orleans newspaper and found his own obituary, printed by enemies as a warning. Faced with such threats, Republican leaders in Colfax Parish fled, abandoning local black farmers to a wage of vigilantism. Several dozen families trekked to town, dug trenches, and prepared to defend themselves. At dawn on Easter Sunday, armed Democrats gave the farmers thirty minutes to send their wives and children away. Then they attacked on horseback, supported by an artillery piece they had concealed across the river. When sixty men retreated inside the courthouse, the attackers set it ablaze and shot everyone who emerged. Then they marched forty prisoners into the woods and shot them dead. One elderly black man survived under the pile of bodies, to testify to what he had seen.

The Colfax Massacre provoked nationwide outrage, and federal investigators indicted ninety-eight men under a recent civil rights statute. But they could only secure three convictions. Then, in the case of *U.S. v. Cruikshank* (1876), the Supreme Court overturned even those three. The justices ruled that the Fourteenth Amendment could only prevent a *state* from violating citizens' rights; the federal government had no power over individuals, even those who organized themselves into private armies to seize political power. *Cruikshank* and a series of related decisions gutted almost all the postwar laws that Congress had designed to protect civil rights.

Most white northerners were becoming equally disinclined to intervene. Only a minority supported freedmen's rights, and the shock of a sudden economic depression made other issues seem far more urgent. A year and a half after Colfax, when President Grant sent troops to halt a Democratic coup in Louisiana, northern editors widely denounced the move. At a public meeting in Boston, leading abolitionists were booed when they spoke in favor of Grant's action. Such men, wrote the *New York Times* dismissively, "represent ideas in regard to the South which the majority of the Republican Party have outgrown."

The 1874 funeral of U.S. senator Charles Sumner, a passionate advocate of justice for freedmen, marked the eclipse of Republicans' progressive wing. In the midterm election of 1874, voters repudiated the whole Reconstruction program and chose Democrats in overwhelming numbers. With Democrats firmly in control of the House of Representatives, the chance for further Reconstruction legislation was dead. Violence and voter intimidation returned in parts of the South during the presidential election of 1876—so much so that it proved difficult to decide the extremely close race between Republican Rutherford B. Hayes and Democrat Samuel Tilden. Had the election been fair and free across the South, Hayes would have won. Ultimately, a special commission voted along party lines to recognize Republican electoral votes from parts of the fiercely contested South. Hayes took office; in exchange for Democrats' agreement not to resist his election, he removed the last federal troops from the South.

The consequences of political reaction were dramatic, as shown by the aftermath of an 1876 strike in coastal South Carolina. During the harvest season, freedmen walked off the job on big rice plantations, protesting sharp wage reductions and some employers' custom of paying in "scrip" that could only be used at the planter's own store. The black community united behind the protest with mass meetings and parades; employers were forced to pay higher wages or let rice rot in the field. The strike worked, in part, because South Carolina's Reconstruction government declined to intervene. When a delegation of planters demanded that the governor send for federal troops, he refused. Republicans simply allowed the power struggle to play out between workers and employers. Privately, some were amused at the spectacle of elite South Carolinians, who had just instigated a war to defend "states' rights," pleading for federal troops to police their plantations.

Though rice plantations extended farther down the coast into Georgia, the Combahee strike stopped abruptly at the state border. The reason was that in Georgia, ex-Confederate Democrats had seized power and largely excluded blacks from voting. When Georgia rice workers threatened to join the strike, planters informed them that "a company of soldiers was ready at a moment's notice in Savannah, to cross the river, and sweep out of the plantation all disaffected negroes." "This was strictly true," reported one planter, "and had the desired effect."

The lesson was not lost on elite South Carolinians. While the Combahee strike was still in progress, Democrat Wade Hampton, a wealthy planter and ex-Confederate general, launched his candidacy for the South Carolina governorship. During his campaign, vigilantes assassinated several Republican politicians, murdered thirty black militiamen in Aiken County, and assaulted would-be voters. Election results were nonetheless so close that they remained in dispute until March 1877, when the deadlock between U.S. presidential candidates Hayes and Tilden was resolved. South Carolina Democrats agreed to accept Hayes as president in exchange for Hampton as governor. Hampton implemented the kinds of policies that secured Georgia rice-growers' power: restrictions on black voting rights, steep cuts in landowners' taxes, and repeal of fair-labor laws.

Politicians like Wade Hampton often claimed that they sought to reduce the size and scope of government. To some extent this was true: southern Democrats did slash property taxes and cut an array of Reconstruction programs and services. But in other ways, southern state governments exercised far greater powers than they had before the war. Despite their attacks on Republican corruption, most continued to broker deals with railroads and other business interests. "You are mistaken," one Democrat wrote to a northern colleague, "if you suppose that all the evils ... result from the carpetbaggers and the negroes. The Democrats are leagued with them when anything is proposed that promises to pay."

The most notorious example was the convict lease system, a monstrous public/private hybrid that flourished across the South after 1880. Through it, legislatures authorized state courts to loan out thousands of convicts to private firms that paid a fee for their labor and promised to feed, clothe, and shelter them. Convicts were mostly African American, but they included poor whites and, in Texas, many Mexicans. The system grew to immense proportions: at its peak, Alabama received 73 percent of all state revenue from convict leasing. Set to work in mines and turpentine camps, leased convicts endured extraordinary brutality. In a typical Mississippi camp, they slaved from 4:30 A.M. until after sundown, "as long as it is light enough for a guard to see how to shoot." Before the 1890s, female convicts were often chained in bunks with male strangers. Beatings were routine; few inmates left without permanent scars, and overwork, scurvy, and typhoid killed as many as 5 percent of leased convicts each year, escalating to three times that level in disease-prone summers.

Convict leasing made a few insiders very rich. Among them was U.S. senator Joseph Brown, ex-Confederate governor of Georgia. Brown's Raccoon Mountain Coalmine employed convict laborers, courtesy of the state of Georgia, for $15 per year. Brown, who netted $98,000 annually from Raccoon Mountain alone, became a millionaire. His notorious mine inspired the black folk song "Joe Brown's Coal Mine": "Sez that's the train I leave here on, / Sez I'm bound to that sundown job."

Defenders of convict lease called it a small-government measure, one that saved taxpayer dollars by reducing the cost of prisons. But viewed from another angle, convict lease was an appropriation of government power for private ends on a scale few could have imagined in the days of slavery. Joe Brown's business in some ways mirrored the northern railroad industry. It used government subsidies to promote enterprise while helping private interests amass spectacular fortunes. Though public debate centered on the question of how big government should be, the underlying question was often "Whose interests should it serve?"

RECONSTRUCTING THE NATION

Though historians sometimes describe the late nineteenth century as an era of laissez-faire, when government was weak, that notion would have baffled both Unionists and ex-Confederates. Advocates of smaller government responded to what they saw, at the time, as a central government that was exercising extraordinary and unprecedented powers. Republicans set out, before and during the Civil War, to develop new initiatives that would help ordinary Americans. In doing so, they took an attitude toward government more like that of today's Democrats than today's Republicans. (We will explore, in Part III, how and why the parties began to change places in the late 1890s.)

Republicans used government power to promote economic development and industrialization. First and foremost, that meant railroads, which provided fast, powerful networks for travel and trade. Transcontinental railroads seemed crucial to Republicans, who believed these railroads would bind the nation together with ties of commerce and communication, discouraging future sectional conflicts. Since railroad building was expensive, policy makers offered aid. Between 1861 and 1872, Congress subsidized transcontinental railroads with grants of a staggering 100 million public acres and $64 million in tax incentives and direct aid. State and local governments vied to offer railroads their own subsidies. By the late 1890s, the United States boasted three transcontinental lines and a total of 183,601 miles of track, about 42 percent of the world's total. By then, the nation's roads were capitalized at $35 billion and employed almost 800,000 men.

Republicans undertook an array of other pro-business initiatives, notably high protective tariffs. First implemented in 1790 as a revenue measure, tariffs required overseas manufacturers to pay a tax for the privilege of selling goods in the United States. In the antebellum decades, northern mill owners had argued for much steeper "protective" tariffs to shield U.S. industries from foreign competition. Representatives from rural areas, especially the South, had blocked them, since tariffs on manufactured goods did not raise farmers' crop prices but cost them when they went shopping. After the South left the Union, Congress instituted higher tariffs and kept them in place for most of the rest of the century. Tariff rates were crafted to serve both economic and political goals, protecting textiles, steel, and iron and also sugar and wool, which were linked to critical constituencies in swing states. What the tariff did not cover was cotton and wheat, the great export crops so critical to southern and western farmers.

Tariffs brought in the bulk of federal revenue during the postwar decades, earning more than $2.1 billion in the 1880s alone. That income paid off the massive Union war debt with remarkable speed; two decades after the war, the U.S.

Treasury was accruing large surpluses. At the same time, American industries grew spectacularly behind the tariff barrier. Real gross domestic product rose an average of more than 4 percent a year for decades after the Civil War, and while many factors led to this high growth rate, tariffs played a key role. Such protected industries as sheep ranching and steel were among the fastest-growing parts of the economy. The western sugar beet industry was launched with the help of the sugar tariff. American-born cane planters in Hawai'i and Cuba, in fact, worked desperately for annexation so they could be classed as domestic producers and obtain the same advantage.

The United States emerged from the Civil War with far greater power to flex its economic and political muscle in places like Hawai'i and the Caribbean. During the war, leaders of both the Union and the Confederacy, like their forerunners in the early republic, fretted over the prospect of European intervention in the war. After Union victory the tables turned: British politicians listened anxiously as Congress debated whether to ask Britain to hand over Canada. Acknowledging that it owed reparations because Confederate raiders such as the CSS *Alabama* had been built in English shipyards, Britain submitted to international arbitration and paid the United States $15.5 million.

William Seward, secretary of state from 1861 to 1869 under presidents Lincoln and Johnson, developed a sweeping vision of global economic power. While European strategists believed that political conquests led to increased trade, Seward argued the reverse: if America achieved "commercial ascendancy," then political dominance would follow in its wake. In pursuit of this goal, Seward initiated talks with China to ensure an open market for American products and to arrange for Chinese immigrants, a source of cheap labor, to enter the United States. Seward advocated purchase of overseas sites for naval ports and coaling stations to strengthen trade. Faced with opposition at home, he won only two acquisitions, tiny Midway (an uninhabited Pacific island) and Alaska, purchased from Russia in 1867. Seward, however, accurately predicted that the United States would eventually control Hawai'i, the Philippines, and an isthmian (Panama) canal that American engineers would construct.

The most ambitious Republican proposals included measures to address the impact of war itself. A pension system for Union veterans, far more extensive than the programs provided in previous American wars, supported disabled veterans and widows, orphans, and dependent mothers and sisters of the Union dead. Branches of the U.S. National Soldiers' Home sprang up to care for the most disabled men. Showcases of Union pride, they featured libraries, telegraph offices, and the latest in medical care. Outside its gates, each home attracted a string of saloons—painful reminders of the war's psychic toll—but the homes' landscaped grounds became popular picnic sites for tourists. At the home outside Dayton, Ohio, visitors could stroll through acres of gardens and admire two scenic lakes and an aviary.

Public education was high on Republicans' agenda. In the immediate aftermath of war, the Freedmen's Bureau not only mediated legal disputes and provided food and shelter to destitute freedpeople in the former Confederacy; it also set up more than 2,500 schools. Bureau officials also played a central role in setting up freedmen's colleges like Fisk and Howard, both named for Bureau leaders. Through the wartime Morrill Act, Congress transferred thousands of federal acres to states for public universities, placing special emphasis on increasing access for women and working-class men. The act created or expanded an array of leading institutions, ranging from the University of California to Cornell University. Republicans created a federal Department of Education in 1867; though demoted to the status of "office" a few years later, it remained a national site for educational research and policy ideas.

Meanwhile, the Department of Agriculture, created during the war, set up a nationwide network of experiment stations and extension services to hybridize plants and advise farmers on crop rotation, fertilizer use, and control of insects and disease. U.S. Marine Hospital laboratories made advances in bacteriology. The National Weather Service began keeping systematic records and delivering public forecasts. The U.S. Geological Survey, founded in 1879, sent expeditions to map the far corners of the continent and precipitated discoveries in geology and paleontology. Americans were even prouder of the U.S. Life-Saving Service (LSS), whose heroic deeds won attention in the popular press. The service had existed before the Civil War but like many other federal agencies had been grossly underfunded, relying mainly on volunteers. In the 1870s Congress expanded and professionalized the service, ushering in its heyday. Stationed along the coasts, LSS employees warned navigators away from dangerous shores and staged dramatic rescues by lifeboat and towline. Between 1871 and 1915, when the LSS merged with the Coast Guard, its surfmen saved more than 178,000 lives.

Other revolutionary changes took place in the growing cities. Though rapid growth overwhelmed urban planners, most cities tried to enforce architectural safety, and many completed ambitious sanitary engineering projects. City dwellers began to expect paved sidewalks, where they could wait under gas or electric streetlights for trolleys that would carry them to and from the business districts and residential suburbs. One of the great questions of the Progressive Era was whether or not cities should contract with private companies for such services or inaugurate municipal ownership. (Like Congressional Republicans who subsidized the railroad, they usually opted for the former.) Mayors and city councils established thousands of public parks. New York's Central Park was the largest and most famous, but by the turn of the century Boston, Philadelphia, Chicago, and St. Louis each boasted more than 2,000 landscaped acres. An approving British visitor remarked that "no country in the world" had "such extensive and delightful public parks and pleasure-grounds."

As striking as such federal and municipal projects were, expansions of power by the states may have been even more significant. Almost all states recognized married women's right to claim their own wages, which had previously been the property of husbands. In many states, husbands and wives won broader access to divorce. Pressured by the WCTU and other temperance groups, many states

"Patience on a Monument," by cartoonist Thomas Nast, *Harper's Weekly*, 10 October 1868. In the early years of Reconstruction, Nast's cartoons offered powerful indictments of ex-Confederate violence. He appealed to northerners to sympathize with freedmen and support African-American voting rights. Courtesy Rutherford B. Hayes Presidential Center.

restricted the sale of liquor; several banned it outright. Some legislatures began to regulate key industries, appointing mine and factory inspectors and dairy boards. By 1883, four years before Congress created the Interstate Commerce Commission, fourteen states had established railroad commissions; fifteen had commissioners to oversee the insurance industry. Iowa, Illinois, Wisconsin, and Minnesota even regulated shipping rates. Many states (and municipalities, too) invested in public health projects. By the mid-1880s Massachusetts had capped the workday at ten hours for women and children, restricted unsafe food and drugs, and imposed state oversight of banks, insurance companies, and utilities. In the 1870s and 1880s, federal courts allowed most of these regulations to stand.

Such far-reaching initiatives, along with the bloody struggles of Reconstruction, prompted a backlash against rising government power. The term "Liberal Republican" was first made famous in Horace Greeley's presidential campaign against Republican U. S. Grant in 1872. Though Grant won overwhelmingly, liberal ideas were on the rise over the decade that followed. Influential proponents included editors such as E. L. Godkin of the *Nation* and George W. Curtis of *Harper's Weekly*. They were not "liberal" in the sense that the word is used today in the United States. Rather, they championed the virtues of laissez-faire and market economics. They mistrusted government power, critiquing Reconstruction policies in the South, high protective tariffs, and the "spoils system" of political appointments.

Liberal Republicans responded in the 1870s to what they saw as increasing corruption, and to new two challenges. First, wage workers' groups began to organize nationally in the late 1860s and called for laws limiting the workday to eight hours. Liberal Republicans argued that such laws would violate rights of contract and property (though they denied taking sides between labor and capital). Second, Liberal Republicans attacked southern Reconstruction governments as illegitimate, run by "trashy whites and ignorant negroes," as Godkin put it. Liberals cheered when white supremacist Democrats drove out southern Republicans, and they urged northerners to abandon freedmen's voting rights. Both North and South, they argued, should be governed by "the part of the community that embodies the intelligence and the capital."

Increasingly, in the 1870s, Liberal thinkers sided with Democrats in rejecting the Republican economic initiatives of the Civil War and Reconstruction. The excesses of lobbyists and corrupt legislators—not to mention machine grafters like Tammany's "Boss Tweed"—lent support to their arguments. Railroad building proved to be particularly subject to bribes and backroom deals, as dozens of railroad companies lobbied (and bribed) for government funds. The most notorious scandal of Reconstruction, the Crédit Mobilier affair, resulted from unsavory deals between legislators and railroad lobbyists. And it was not clear that the resulting transportation system served the public interest. Railroads outraged farmers with their complex rates, which discriminated against small shippers. Even worse, they built an array of competing and overextended lines, resulting in duplicate services, frequent bankruptcies, and fierce rivalries among the lines.

Controversy also ensued over who benefited from high protective tariffs. Republicans claimed tariffs helped workers, and high tariffs did in fact create new industries and protect jobs from moving overseas. But the argument that tariffs would keep American wages high proved false. By the 1880s economic reformers argued that most tariff benefits were going to major industrialists, who could mark up prices in the absence of foreign competition, hold wages low, and keep the profits. It gradually became clear that tariffs had helped create the giant corporations that were beginning to overshadow the economic landscape, while raising wages little, if at all.

"The Grand Old Party of Moral Ideas 'Keeping Up Appearances.' G.O.P. to W.R.: 'Hurry up and get my dress on; we must cover up this awful skirt.'" The Democratic-leaning humor journal *Puck* suggests how the Republican Party's fortunes have fallen. Her dress, bustle, and plume proclaim "political purity," "high moral ideals," and "war record." But a tariff "protection corset" gives the lady her shape; her patched petticoat records such scandals as Crédit Mobilier and the Navy and Whiskey Rings. The party's handmaid is Whitelaw Reid, editor of the staunchly Republican *New York Tribune*. *Puck,* 20 August 1884. Courtesy Rutherford B. Hayes Presidential Center.

Thus, as early as the mid-1880s, the stage was set for a protracted set of debates. Even high-tariff advocates, such as Pennsylvania congressman William "Pig Iron" Kelley, began to admit that Republican tariffs had not prevented industrial poverty in the United States. Kelley's daughter Florence, studying economics in Germany in 1884, wrote home arguing that laws to cap the workday at eight hours would help workers more than tariffs did. Politicians in the United States (like their German counterparts) were slow to accept such advice, but William Kelley read his daughter's letter into the *Congressional Record* and declared that he agreed.

Within a decade, Florence Kelley returned to the United States and launched a radical and creative career as an economic reformer.

FREEDMEN AND THE POSTWAR ECONOMY

One of the central challenges facing freedmen and freedwomen after Emancipation was shared by other Americans: how could one best get ahead in an economy that required mobility, flexibility, and very hard work? By any measure, freedmen's accomplishments in the decades after the war were impressive. In the Yazoo Delta of Mississippi, only a few years after slaves there had been tortured to death for conspiring to join the Union Army, freedmen were clearing forests, selling lumber, and saving money. Some learned to read and write, purchased land, and passed along prosperous farms to their sons and daughters. Freedman and Union veteran Isaiah Montgomery launched an even more ambitious project in the 1880s. When the railroad came through, he purchased 840 acres to create the town of Mound Bayou. Its African-American residents soon owned 30,000 acres surrounding the town, which supported a bank, railroad station, and cotton-oil mill. Mayor Montgomery proudly noted that in his town "a black man could run *for* sheriff instead of *from* the sheriff." Almost everyone could read and write, and the town later produced a number of distinguished civil rights advocates.

In rural areas compromises between the desires of landowners and freedmen led to the development of sharecropping, through which a landowner and a tenant family split the proceeds of the tenant's crop. Sharecropping was not exactly what anyone desired. Rather, it exposed divergent definitions of Emancipation. Former slaveholders wanted, of course, as much control over labor as possible. Most northern Republicans expected ex-slaves to become wage laborers on big plantations, so the South could continue to produce the export crops, especially cotton, that were so crucial to the nation's trade. But few former slaves saw gang labor on plantations as a full measure of freedom. They wanted autonomy and a life as different from slavery as possible. Many built cabins in the woods where they could hunt and fish, keep pigs or a cow, and grow crops for their own use. Yet because land ownership was elusive, most were eventually pushed into the cash economy, toiling for others (usually whites) at low wages. "A deep misunderstanding," historian Barbara Fields has observed, "caused the authors of Reconstruction to offer with a great flourish a gift that the freedmen did not want [that is, wage labor on plantations] and to interpret as perversity or racial incapacity the latter's refusal to accept the gift with gratitude."

Many tenant and sharecropping families were ambitious. A northern journalist reported from Alabama in 1880 that "I met a woman who lived a few miles from Talladega, and she showed me $98, the receipts from her own little cotton patch, and, said she, 'I plowed, and I sowed, and I hoed every lick of it myself, and I picked it, and got it baled and sold it too.' This is no extraordinary case. I met everywhere in the neighborhood of Talledega women not only able but willing to do more than a man's work, if by it they could send their children to school." But for rural blacks, economic success was achieved against enormous odds. They were barred by custom, if not law, from high-paying jobs, business loans, mortgages, and land purchases. In 1883 Mississippi counted 19 black-owned country stores, but this was out of a total of 2,248.

During the hard years between 1878 and 1881, as many as 50,000 southern African Americans moved west. About 68,000 went north in the 1870s, a figure that reached 185,000 by the 1890s and accelerated through the Great Migration of the 1910s. Before 1900, however, most journeys took place within the South. Mobility and dislocation, hallmarks of black life in America ever since African survivors of the Middle Passage had arrived in the British colonies, endured in new forms. Thousands of men and women undertook long journeys in search of work and to get back home to visit or care for kin. After Emancipation, Annie Burton, who began life as a slave on an Alabama plantation, moved into town with her mother and sisters to attend school. She cooked for families in Macon and Atlanta, Georgia, and then found a job in New England by responding to a magazine advertisement. She returned to the South frequently to care for ill relatives and to adopt her nephew after his mother died. At various times she operated restaurants in Massachusetts and Florida and a boardinghouse in Rhode Island.

A small, prosperous black elite emerged in the wake of the war: twenty-five black lawyers, real estate brokers, and other professionals began to serve their own communities. Even a single institution could make an enormous difference in the growth of the black middle class. The Freedmen's Hospital in Washington, D.C., for example, run by the Department of the Interior, was one of a tiny number of hospitals in the United States that trained African-American doctors; its interns went on to practice medicine all over the country. Dr. Daniel Hale Williams, the hospital's surgeon-in-chief, set up a nursing school and in 1893 performed the nation's first successful open-heart surgery.

Yet prosperous blacks felt, as keenly as the working class, the many impediments created by a race-conscious society. The prevailing code defined race both by color—brown, black, yellow, and white—and by nationality, and the consequences varied for groups designated by terms such as *Nordic* and *Hebrew*. The U.S. Immigration Commission, for example, designated southern Italians as an "Iberic" people. "Excitable, impulsive, highly imaginative, impracticable," they supposedly had trouble adapting "to highly organized society." But Italian immigrants were usually defined as white, permitted by both law and custom to live in white neighborhoods, attend white schools, and take jobs that blacks were denied. By contrast, prejudices of color and nationality worked in tandem against blacks: whether designated as Africans, Negroes, blacks, or "coloreds," they were assigned to the bottom tiers of the racial hierarchy.

Denied the right to locate in white neighborhoods, African Americans in southern cities often lived in cramped and filthy slums such as "the Bottoms" along polluted Cripple Creek in Knoxville, Tennessee, a neighborhood of "rickety shacks clustered on stilts." The vast majority of the post-Emancipation generation found themselves below the economic wedge described by Henry George, trapped in low-wage jobs or tenant contracts. Booker T. Washington, born a slave in Virginia in 1856 and educated at the Hampton Institute, spoke for millions of such farmers and laborers when he called for "industrial education," training that would help working-class youth get decent skilled jobs. In the two decades after 1881, when he assumed leadership of Alabama's Tuskegee Institute, Washington was the nation's most prominent black leader. He preached hard work, thrift, and respectability. "My experience," he wrote in his autobiography, "is that there is something in human nature which always makes an individual recognize and reward merit, no matter under what color of skin merit is found."

The career of African-American writer Charles Chesnutt offered a counterpoint to Washington's optimism. Chesnutt, a grocer's son who grew up in North Carolina, got a good education and began teaching at an early age. He reported the comment of an Anglo clerk when one of his friends called Chesnutt a gentleman: "With me a nigger is a nigger, and nothing in the world can make him anything else but a nigger." Very light-skinned, Chesnutt wrestled with the dilemma of whether he should pass himself as Anglo. "I am as white as any of them," he wrote angrily in his diary at age seventeen, but Chesnutt chose to identify himself as black. "I *will* live down the prejudice, I *will* crush it out," he vowed. "I *will* show to the world that a man may spring from a race of slaves, and yet far excel many of the boasted ruling race." For a decade Chesnutt produced subtle, accomplished fiction, but he was forced to give up writing in 1905 and return to law clerking, since demand for his fiction was insufficient to support his family. In that same year Thomas Dixon's pathologically racist novel *The Clansman*—basis for the later film *Birth of a Nation*—became a nationwide best-seller. It revised the history of Reconstruction to depict freedmen and their northern allies menacing white womanhood, while the Ku Klux Klan rode to the rescue as noble avengers.

Chesnutt captured some of the complexities of African Americans' struggles after Emancipation in his story "The Doll," told through the eyes of Tom Taylor, a barber who has moved north. When a political convention meets in town, one of Taylor's customers turns out to be an ex-Confederate colonel who long ago murdered Taylor's father. For decades the barber has dreamed of revenge, but with his razor at the colonel's throat, he looks around at the employees who depend on him. "One was sending a son to college; another was buying a home. The unmarried one was in his spare hours studying a profession." If he murders the colonel, all will be thrown into poverty. Tom himself will lose his access to prominent white citizens whom he has often asked for help on behalf of those in need. Still anguishing over what to do, Tom looks up and sees the doll his little daughter has asked him to repair, hanging beside his mirror. He decisively swallows his rage. "His own father had died in defense of his daughter; he must live to protect his own." Tom thus pins his dreams on the next generation, but to do so he has to let his father's murderer walk free. In describing the barber's dilemma, Chesnutt captured something essential about how African Americans entered the post-Reconstruction world, carrying burdens of justice denied.

Looking back from the vantage point of the 1930s, W. E. B. DuBois criticized Americans' tendency to think of Emancipation and southern Reconstruction as events segregated from the rest of U.S. history. "The most magnificent drama in the last thousand years," he wrote, "is the transportation of ten million human beings out of the dark beauty of their mother continent into the new-found Eldorado of the West. They descended into Hell; and in the third century they arose from the dead. . . . It was an upheaval of humanity like the Reformation and the French Revolution." The struggles of freedmen and freedwomen, DuBois argued, were central to the history of America's labor movement, its economic modernization, and its politics, culture, and religious faith. To claim otherwise was to be "blind and led by the blind."

African Americans shared with other Americans a postwar world of restlessness, mobility, and risk. Freedom itself brought the impulse to move along and seek new opportunities, to seek lost relatives or leave behind terrible memories. At the same time the postwar economy transformed the landscape of the South and the nation, pushing and pulling even those with the strongest ties to their old communities and to the land. Folk and blues ballads soon found in the railroad a symbol of restlessness and disconnection. "When a woman gets the blues," went one famous line, "she goes to her room and hides; When a man gets the blues, he catches a freight train and rides." Being on the railroad brought blues of its own: "I'm a broken-hearted bachelor, travelin' through this wide world all alone, It's the railroad for my pillow, this jungle is my happy home." Other songs spoke of the difficulties of traveling poor:

Mmmm—please help me win my fare,
Cause I'm a travelin' man, boys I can't stay here.

I said "Looka hyah engineer, can I ride your train?"
He said, "Look here you oughta know this train ain't mine an' you askin' me
in vain."

As such songs testified, a tremendous economic upheaval in the postwar years set the conditions not only for the hopes and struggles of freedmen and freedwomen, but for those of all Americans.

FOR FURTHER READING

Thomas Higginson's memoirs can be found in *Army Life in a Black Regiment* (New York, 1984 [1869]), and Isaac Perski's story is in Tony Horwitz, *Confederates in the Attic* (New York, 1998). On veterans see the Surgeon General's Office, *Medical and Surgical History of the War of the Rebellion* (Washington, DC, 1888), Richard Severo and Lewis Milford, *The Wages of War* (New York, 1989), Eric T. Dean, Jr., *Shook Over Hell* (Cambridge, MA, 1997), and T. J. Stiles, *Jesse James* (New York, 2002). On veterans' services see Patrick J. Kelly, *Creating a National Home* (Cambridge, MA, 1997), and Theda Skocpol, *Protecting Soldiers and Mothers* (Cambridge, MA, 1992), though I take a somewhat more optimistic view than Skocpol of the pension system's legacy. On guns and violence I rely on Donald B. Webster, Jr., *Suicide Specials* (Harrisburg, PA, 1958), and Eric H. Monkkonen, *Murder in New York City* (Berkeley, CA, 2001). Consider also the last chapter of Michael A. Bellesiles's provocative book, *Arming America* (New York, 2000).

On the war's cultural and religious impact see Edmund Wilson, *Patriotic Gore* (New York, 1962), and Susan Jacoby, *Freethinkers* (New York, 2004). For the impact on women see Jeannie Attie, *Patriotic Toil* (Ithaca, NY, 1998), Elizabeth B. Pryor, *Clara Barton* (Philadelphia, 1987), and for the WCTU, Ruth Bordin, *Woman and Temperance*, 2nd ed. (New Brunswick, NJ, 1990), and Barbara L. Epstein, *The Politics of Domesticity* (Middletown, CT, 1980). On suffrage see Ellen Carol DuBois, *Feminism and Suffrage* (Ithaca, NY, 1978), and in the West, Rebecca J. Mead, *How the Vote Was Won* (New York, 2004).

For Reconstruction in the South my main source is Eric Foner's *Reconstruction, 1863-1877* (New York, 1988). On the Combahee strike see Foner's *Nothing but Freedom* (Baton Rouge, LA, 1983), and on Colfax, Ted Tunnell, *Crucible of Reconstruction* (Baton Rouge, LA, 1984). Also helpful are Philip D. Curtin, *The Rise and Fall of the Plantation Complex* (Cambridge, MA, 1990), Howard N. Rabinowitz, *Race Relations in the Urban South, 1865-1890* (New York, 1978), and the essays in *Divided Houses*, ed. Catherine Clinton and Nina Silber (New York, 1992).

For politics and government at the national level, see Morton Keller's classic account *Affairs of State* (Cambridge, MA, 1977). On Reconstruction see Brooks D. Simpson, *The Recontruction Presidents* (Topeka, KS, 1998), and Michael Perman, *Emancipation and Reconstruction* (Arlington Heights, IL, 1987). On Seward see Walter LaFeber, *The American Search for Opportunity* (New York, 1993), which is volume 4 of the Cambridge History of American Foreign Relations. On partisan politics see H. Wayne Morgan's readable *From Hayes to McKinley* (Syracuse, NY, 1969), Robert W. Cherny, *American Politics in the Gilded Age, 1868-1900* (Wheeling, IL, 1997), and Charles W. Calhoun, *Conceiving a New Republic: The Republican Party and the Southern Question, 1869-1900* (Topeka, KS, 2006). For a broad view of Whig and Republican state-building see John Gerring, *Party Ideologies in America, 1828-1996* (Cambridge, 1998). On federal activism in the economy there are two immensely helpful books by Richard F. Bensel, *Yankee Leviathan* (New York, 1990), and *The Political Economy of American Industrialization, 1877-1900* (Cambridge, 2000). For an alternative perspective on protective tariffs see Alfred E. Eckes, Jr., *Opening America's Market* (Chapel Hill, NC, 1995), and Dana Frank, *Buy American* (Boston, 1999). On "Pig Iron" Kelley and his daughter see Kathryn Kish Sklar, *Florence Kelley and the Nation's Work* (New Haven, CT, 1995).

On new government powers see, in addition to Keller and Bensel, William R. Brock, *Investigation and Responsibility* (Cambridge, MA, 1984), Ballard C. Campbell, *The Growth of American Government* (Bloomington, IN, 1995), and Walter I. Trattner, *From Poor Law to Welfare State* (New York, 1974). Howard S. Miller discusses the USGS in "The Political Economy of Science," in *Nineteenth-Century American Science*, ed. George H. Daniels (Evanston, IL, 1972), 95-114, as does Thomas G. Manning in *Government in Science* (Lexington, KY, 1967). On the Freedmen's Bureau see Barry A. Crouch, *The Freedmen's Bureau and Black Texans* (Austin, TX, 1992), and *The Freedmen's Bureau and Reconstruction*, ed. Paul A. Cimbala and Randall M. Miller (New York, 1999). On city government see John C. Teaford, *The Unheralded Triumph: City Government in America, 1870-1900* (Baltimore, 1983), and Stanley K. Schultz, *Constructing Urban Cultures* (Philadelphia, 1989). As a starting point on urban machines see Terence J. McDonald's wonderful introduction to his edition of William L. Riordon's *Plunkitt of Tammany Hall* (Boston, 1994).

On northerners' fading support for Reconstruction see, in addition to Foner, David W. Blight, *Race and Reunion* (Cambridge, MA, 2001), Heather Cox Richardson, *The Death of Reconstruction* (Cambridge, MA, 2001), and Nancy Cohen, *The Reconstruction of American Liberalism, 1865–1914* (Chapel Hill, NC, 2002). Thomas A. Guglielmo offers a useful analysis of systems of racial categorization in *White on Arrival* (New York, 2003). On the South after Reconstruction see Edward L. Ayers, *The Promise of the New South* (New York, 1992), and Barbara Fields' brilliant essay, "Ideology and Race in American History," in *Region, Race, and Reconstruction*, ed. J. Morgan Kousser (New York, 1982). The quotation about the "deep misunderstanding" between Reconstruction policy makers and freedpeople is from Fields' essay, page 166.

On labor during Reconstruction see also Julie Saville, *The Work of Reconstruction* (New York, 1994). For Republican policies in one southern city see Lawrence L. Hartzell, "The Exploration of Freedom in Black Petersburg, Virginia, 1865–1902," in *The Edge of the South*, ed. Edward L. Ayers and John C. Willis (Charlottesville, VA, 1991), 134–156. There is a burgeoning literature on convict lease, including Alexander C. Lichtenstein, *Twice the Work of Free Labor* (London, 1996), Matthew J. Mancini, *One Dies, Get Another* (Columbia, SC, 1996), and Martha Myers, *Race, Labor, and Punishment in the New South* (Columbus, OH 1998). On Booker T. Washington's life and thought, Fitzhugh Brundage provides an excellent brief overview in his edition of Washington's autobiography, *Up from Slavery* (Boston, 2003).

On African-American experiences see also John Hope Franklin, *From Slavery to Freedom*, 8th ed. (New York, 2000), as well as Leon F. Litwack's two extraordinarily rich accounts, *Been in the Storm So Long* (New York, 1979) and *Trouble in Mind* (New York, 1998), and for a brief overview, Leslie H. Fishel, Jr., "The African-American Experience," in *The Gilded Age* ed. Charles W. Calhoun (Wilmington, DE, 1996). Also see Darlene Clark Hine et al., *The African-American Odyssey*, 2nd ed. (Upper Saddle River, NJ, 2003), Hine's *A Shining Thread of Hope* (New York, 1998), Dorothy Sterling, *We Are Your Sisters* (New York, 1984), and Tera Hunter, *To 'Joy My Freedom* (Cambridge, MA, 1998). On the Yazoo Delta see John C. Willis, *Forgotten Time* (Charlottesville, VA, 2000). Willard B. Gatewood examines the black elite in *Aristocrats of Color* (Bloomington, IN, 1990); on its rise in Washington, D.C., especially, see Jacqueline M. Moore, *Leading the Race* (Charlottesville, VA, 1999). W. E. B. DuBois reflected on African-American history in *Black Reconstruction in America, 1860–1880* (New York, 1935). On the blues see Paul Oliver, *Blues Fell This Morning*, 2nd ed. (New York, 1990), and Alan Lomax, *The Land Where the Blues Began* (New York, 1993).

CHAPTER 2

Reach

Corporation. n. An ingenious device for obtaining individual
profit without individual responsibility.
—AMBROSE BIERCE, *THE DEVIL'S DICTIONARY*

In the fall of 1883, dozens of buffalo hunters bought supplies for the season and
trekked out to the Dakotas and Montana to slaughter America's last great bison
herd. To their astonishment, it had vanished. In the previous three years, hunters
had already, without realizing it, exterminated so many bison that almost none
were left. Construction of the transcontinental railroad, had divided the Plains
buffalo into two great herds north and south of the tracks. The southern herd had
been hunted to near-extinction in the late 1870s; now the northern was gone as
well. Strips of tough, supple bison hide made excellent belts for eastern industrial
machines, and the slow animals were easy targets for modern weapons. Hunter
Orlando Brown killed 5,700 bison in the first two months of 1876 alone, firing his
.50-caliber rifle so many times that he went deaf in one ear. Taking only hides,
hunters such as Brown left skinned carcasses rotting across the Plains.

In one of the first pieces of legislation proposed to protect wildlife, Congress
tried in 1874 to prohibit the killing of female bison by non-Indians, hoping this
measure would allow the species to reproduce. But the Grant administration had
an incentive for extermination: removal of Plains Indians, who depended on bison
for tools, food, shelter, and clothing. In the 1867 Treaty of Medicine Lodge, for
example, the government had pledged that Comanche, Kiowa, Southern Cheyenne,
and Arapaho could hunt south of the Arkansas River "so long as the buffalo may
range thereon in such numbers as to justify the chase." Few officials openly said so,
but many agreed with an army officer who advised a visitor to "kill every buffalo
you can. Every buffalo dead is an Indian gone." Grant pocket-vetoed the bison
protection bill. In the next decade, six million bison vanished, with such horrific
speed that native peoples believed the animals had hidden themselves underground.

During the same winters when the last remnants of the northern herd fell,
shoppers in Chicago and New York City discovered fresh oranges at their grocery
stores. Chinese farmworkers in California had boxed the fruit in a much-admired
style called the China pack: "every wrapper smooth, not a wrinkle," as one citrus

grower described it, "and the tissue triangled to a point on top so that when the box was opened it was something to display." Fresh fruit in winter began as an expensive luxury, but boxcars soon arrived with larger cargoes, and Florida and California "sunshine fruit" became a national marvel. By 1891 California railroads were shipping out 302 million pounds of fruit a year.

The rotting bison carcasses in Montana and winter oranges in Chicago were twin manifestations of an economic revolution. In the name of progress, bison had to make way for railcars that could whisk products to customers across the continent. In the post–Civil War years, economic enterprise achieved new scale and reach, linking producers and consumers in a breathtaking set of transformations. Telegraphs, railroads, and steamships laid the foundations for this revolution. The process was a global one that disproportionately benefited the large and resource-rich United States. As the outlines of a modern global economy emerged, U.S. corporations exercised new and formidable power.

PALEOTECHNOLOGY

If any single factor brought this revolution, it was the development of fossil fuels. The energy of animals, humans, wood, and water came to be replaced by steam engines, petroleum, and then electricity. So essential was the shift that critic Lewis Mumford, looking back from the vantage point of the 1930s, characterized the mid- to late nineteenth century as the dawn of the "Paleotechnic Era." His phrase highlighted the use of coal and oil, two natural resources created in the distant geological past. (Mumford, an advocate of renewable energy, also hinted with the prefix "paleo-" that an economy based on fossil fuel was hopelessly retrograde.) By the 1850s steam engines were becoming more cost-effective than water in many applications. While as late as 1890 almost half of New England's manufacturing energy still came from water, steam engines could be taken to inland areas without prime sites along falling rivers and streams. Natural gas and artificial gas, extracted from coal, came into use by the 1850s for urban lighting. The development of kerosene from crude oil, which began in western Pennsylvania and Ohio just before the Civil War, soon offered a rival source of heat and light.

Paleotechnology wrought especially dramatic transformations in the Mid-Atlantic and Midwest. Before the Civil War, American manufacturing had been largely concentrated in New England's water-powered textile mills. Afterward an extensive industrial heartland arose. Rich coal deposits helped build the great steel mills of Pittsburgh, Buffalo, and Cleveland. Towns like Trenton, New Jersey, and Schenectady, New York, grew into busy manufacturing centers, while Ohio boasted major hubs such as Akron, Cincinnati, and Dayton. By 1900, industrial production in the United States exceeded the *combined* output of Britain, Germany, and France.

No place better exemplified the rise of paleotechnology than Chicago, which in the forty years after 1860 grew from a small city of 30,000 to a metropolis of two million. The city benefited from nearby deposits of bituminous coal, and while early Chicagoans relied largely on wood for heat and whale oil for light, these soon gave way to coal, coal gas, and kerosene. By the 1880s bright, steady, coal-fired electricity became a major energy source for streetlamps and commercial lighting. In 1893 tourists gasped at the sight of thousands of electric bulbs outlining the elegant buildings of the Chicago World's Fair against the evening sky. Electric trolleys ferried fair visitors and rush-hour commuters around the Loop and out to the suburbs. A decade later, the city's electric company had 30,000 private customers, and Chicago's inhabitants were using, per capita, 4.3 tons of coal per year.

Steam power had its most dramatic impact on transportation. In the 1830s the fastest form of inland transport had been the canal boat, pulled by plodding mules. Canals froze in winter, their walls collapsed in heavy rains, and they suffered frequent blockages from fallen trees. Furthermore, canals had to run near rivers or other water sources and could not extend into the arid regions of the West. Dirt roads were worse: rocky, muddy, and cratered, they were often impassable after spring rains. Steam locomotives not only moved goods and people much faster than canals and wagon paths, but engineers could also lay railroad tracks over rugged terrain, even deserts, and span wide rivers with bridges. Nimble small-gauge tracks soon carried passengers and freight through spectacular passes in the Rockies. Locomotives could run day and night, through searing heat, high winds, thunderstorms, droughts, and blizzards. They carried immense loads for long distances with no biological need for rest.

Railroads, then, facilitated commerce over vast geographic spaces. By 1905 a journey from New York to San Francisco—which a half-century earlier had required either months of overland trekking or a sail around Cape Horn—now took eighty-two hours. In order to support complex operations over broad swaths of territory, railroad companies pioneered many of the structures and practices of corporate capitalism. They organized their workforce into departments overseen by professional managers. They made creative use of engineers and accountants, whose specialized skills evolved to meet the companies' needs. Railroads dominated the New York Stock Exchange for decades, attracting the bulk of European investment in the United States. Everywhere, Americans acknowledged "the roads" as catalysts of geographic expansion and economic growth. An Illinois woman remarked that without a railroad her town would have "neither telegraph, nor schoolhouse, nor anything."

The power of fossil fuels depended to a large extent on political decisions. As we saw in Chapter 1, Union victory and Republican economic policies set the stage for industrialization. In an age of nationalism and empire-building, events in other nations worked toward similar ends. Canada attained dominion status within the British Empire in 1867, and in the same year France withdrew its claim over Mexico. Thus, America's two nearest neighbors gained an autonomy from Europe that brought them more tightly into the economic orbit of the United States. A year later advocates of modernization in Japan deposed the last shogun and set their country on the path toward industrial development. In 1870–1871 the crushing defeat of France by a combined army of German states reshaped Europe's

Guthrie Cotton Depot, Texas (undated). Workers pose atop immense bales of cotton, compressed in steam-powered cotton presses and loaded for shipment. While an array of raw materials and products traveled by rail and steamship, cotton remained the country's leading export in dollar value from the 1840s to the 1920s. Courtesy Library of Congress.

political landscape. Strong and unified, Germany would soon become the continent's leading empire, competing head-to-head with Britain around the globe. In all these countries a new generation of government leaders strove to harness paleotechnology and out-compete national rivals.

Meanwhile, observers around the world were shocked by the Paris Commune of 1871, in which French radicals protested government paralysis and the threatened return of monarchy. The Communards burned buildings and assassinated the archbishop of Paris; after the rebellion was suppressed the government ruthlessly executed 20,000 Parisians. The Commune raised a hysterical fear of "communism" that influenced for decades afterward political debate in every industrializing nation. It reinforced many Americans' conviction that, as Liberal Republicans argued, social order was a more urgent concern than social justice.

"Observation End of the *Pennsylvania Limited* on Horseshoe Curve" (detail), east slope of the Alleghenies, circa 1893. With the railroad revolution, people as well as goods moved from place to place more efficiently than ever before. William H. Rau, a photographer for the Pennsylvania Railroad, halted the train to take this publicity shot of elite passengers enjoying the view on the company's premier line. Courtesy American Premier Underwriters, Inc., and Library Company of Pennsylvania.

Government policies shaped the forms that paleotechnology took. The corporation itself, in the modern sense, was an invention of government. Over the course of the nineteenth century, state legislatures gradually gave up the task of chartering corporations only for special public purposes, and by the 1870s anyone could create a corporation for almost any purpose without a legislative act. At the same time, Congress and the federal courts worked to create an unimpeded nationwide market in goods, services, and labor. North Carolina, in an 1879 Supreme Court ruling, was not allowed to require out-of-state insurance companies to deposit funds with the state as security for residents who bought policies. A Virginia law that charged licensing fees to out-of-state manufacturers was struck down the following year. In *Munn v. Illinois* (1877) the Supreme Court did allow states to regulate grain-elevator operators (and by implication railroads) because those businesses were "clothed in the public interest," but in doing so the Court implied that any businesses *not* so clothed were out of bounds for regulation. Thus, as telegraphs and railroads bound the continent together, government policies not only facilitated their construction but also set sweeping new conditions for the business and trade they carried on.

The impact of paleotechnology was as apparent in traditional sectors such as agriculture as it was in heavy industry. Steam-powered grain threshers, corn huskers, sugar mills, cotton presses, and dairy cream separators appeared, manufactured by companies including McCormick and Deere in steam-powered plants and brought to the hinterlands by rail. In the 1830s growing twenty bushels of wheat had taken more than sixty hours of human labor; by the late 1880s and 1890s, the same yield took less than four hours. A midwestern farmer no longer bagged his wheat in burlap sacks clearly identifiable as his own product and liable to rot as it waited for shipment by wagon or barge. Instead, he sent it by rail to a steam-powered grain elevator in Chicago or another hub. The process rearranged economic re-lationships at every point along the path from farmer to consumer. It benefited large-scale processors such as the Pillsbury Company of Minneapolis, which bought great quantities of wheat at discount and shipped out mass-market products. Small-town mills could not compete. By the 1880s affluent shoppers began to think of Pillsbury and Gold Medal as synonymous with flour. Quaker Oats, Campbell's Soup, Hershey's Chocolate, and Heinz Ketchup arrived through similar large-scale manufacturing and marketing strategies.

Few industries showed more clearly than meatpacking the stunning reach of paleotechnical capitalism. Railroads began shipping live cattle and hogs to feedlots for fattening, then to centralized slaughtering facilities. (Frequent suffocation and injuries in these mass shipments prompted a long battle by the Humane Society against cruelty to livestock.) The ranching firm of Miller and Lux, which created a 1.25-million-acre empire in California, Nevada, and Oregon, sent its cattle to San Francisco's Butchertown. By the 1870s Chicago's Union Stockyards killed and processed more than a million hogs a year for pork and side products. Visiting British author Rudyard Kipling found the process disturbing. He described how on the slaughterhouse floor the hogs' "full-voiced shriek became a sputter, and then a fall as of heavy tropical rain." Hogs and cattle died at a rate of five per minute. "The blood ran in muttering gutters," Kipling reported. "There was no place for hand or foot that was not coated with thicknesses of dried blood, and the stench of it in the nostrils bred fear." While eastern shoppers were at first reluctant to purchase meat that had not been locally slaughtered, companies such as Swift and Armour ruthlessly undercut smaller competitors. In market after market they offered astonishingly cheap meat, pricing their products below cost if necessary until customers made the switch.

While paleotechnology standardized and mechanized the deaths of millions of animals, it also built up heavy industries, most prominently steel. The career of Andrew Carnegie suggested the complexities of this process. As a young immigrant from Scotland, Carnegie moved with his family to Pittsburgh, where he ingratiated himself with leaders of the Pennsylvania Railroad as an errand boy. Rising through the ranks, Carnegie worked his way into the steel industry by borrowing British technologies such as the Bessemer process as well as brokering deals for railroad rebates via his Pennsylvania connections. Carnegie shrewdly chose to enter the steel business just after policy makers erected a tariff barrier to block competing imports. Most of all, Carnegie watched the bottom line. He made innovative use of cost accounting to keep close track of expenses. He mercilessly slashed labor costs. On occasion, he tore down recently built factories and built them over, calculating that increased efficiency would make it worth his while. Carnegie maddened shareholders by refusing to pay dividends for years at a stretch, plowing profits back into the enterprise. He was fond of quoting his frugal Scottish mother: "Watch the pennies, and the pounds will take care of themselves."

John D. Rockefeller, whose Standard Oil Company dealt in fossil fuel itself, built an even bigger corporate empire. Like Swift and Armour, Rockefeller sold his products at below cost until he bankrupted competitors, a practice that became notorious as "predatory pricing." By 1880 Standard Oil controlled nine-tenths of the national market in refined oil, and its size allowed Rockefeller to demand deep rebates from railroads that shipped his oil. Former refiner George Rice told investigators that Standard Oil had driven him into bankruptcy through secret deals, predatory pricing, and collusion with the railroads. It was, Rice said, "a very sad, bitter, and ruinous experience for me." The scale of Rockefeller's empire can be measured by the companies that emerged from its court-ordered breakup after 1911: they included the roots of today's ExxonMobil, Amoco, Chevron, Sunoco, *and* Conoco.

As Rockefeller's maneuvers showed, powerful capitalists were no fans of marketplace competition; they gave only lip service to Liberal Republicans' ideal of laissez-faire. Instead, they strove to lessen and block rivalries by gobbling up competitors, and cooperating through secret financial deals. After experimenting for years with various unenforceable "gentlemen's agreements" and pools, corporations turned in the 1880s to the trust, a legal invention through which multiple firms deposited stock in an umbrella entity. The Standard Oil Trust led the way in 1882, followed within five years by trusts in linseed oil, sugar, whiskey, salt, and many other products. The resulting vast corporations began to dominate key sectors of the economy.

If in retrospect the transition appears orderly and inevitable, it was not. Though many Americans have seen photographs of the celebratory "golden spike" being driven in 1869 at the site of the first transcontinental link in Utah, few know the instructive story of the second transcontinental line, the Northern Pacific, which eventually ran from Minneapolis to Seattle. Despite a federal grant of sixty million acres—over half of all the land Congress gave to railroads before 1871—the line proved very difficult to build. Banking legend Jay Cooke, who had become a national hero by helping manage the Union's finances during the Civil War, over-extended himself selling risky bonds and illegally mortgaging government-granted property. The collapse of his firm in 1873 not only bankrupted the railroad but also helped trigger a severe depression. Cooke's successor, Henry Villard, completed the rail line a decade later, but the effort broke his health. He lost control of the Northern Pacific to rivals, who then competed ruinously with newer roads. Before Villard's death in 1900, the Northern Pacific had gone bankrupt a second time.

The replacement of Plains bison with millions of range cattle was an equally messy process. In the cattle bonanza of the early 1880s, giant ranching com-panies invested in ventures that stretched hundreds of miles. By 1884 they had turned loose twenty million cattle in the inland West. The cattle kings wanted large-scale, rationalized, efficient production, but they did not get it. Even the toughest cattle could not cope with the Great Plains' extremes of heat and cold, and a series of brutal winters on the Plains—so shocking that they introduced the term *blizzard* to Americans in its modern usage—starved and froze millions of cows and calves. As they migrated in search of food and warmth, the cattle bumped against barbed wire fences that marked property lines. Along fences where the bodies piled up, settlers later walked long distances on top of nothing but bones. Some cattlemen went bankrupt, while others were too revolted to stay in the busi-ness. "I wanted no more of it," a Montana rancher remembered later. "I never wanted to own again an animal that I could not feed or shelter."

Farming in the arid West proved equally problematic. In the immediate post-war years, the Great Plains had seemed well-watered. Not understanding the twenty-year cycle of rising and falling precipitation in Kansas, Nebraska, and the Dakotas, settlers concluded that their arrival was causing rainfall to increase. Both western promoters and scientific experts enthusiastically proclaimed that "rain follows the plow." Some believed sod-breaking itself released moisture into the air, while one Harvard professor proposed that steel railroad tracks had a magnetic effect on cloud formation. In the late 1880s the rain cycle shifted, and the resulting drought left thousands of farmers stranded. Homesteaders were not the only ones caught out. Large bonanza farms, similar in structure to the great cattle compa-nies, had set up operation in areas such as South Dakota's Red River Valley and planted thousands of acres of wheat. Drought and debt broke up most of these farms within a decade. Novelist O. E. Rolvaag, a Norwegian immigrant who worked for several years as a farmhand in the Dakotas, summed up his view of these disasters in his grim novel *Giants in the Earth*: "The Great Plain Drinks the Blood of Christian Men and Is Satisfied."

Despite catastrophic defeats, the incorporators forged ahead. Before railroad-builders had established themselves securely in the West, they were already reaching southward into Mexico. Railroads, again, served as catalysts for other forms of development, and in the early 1870s they demanded the same kinds of concessions from Mexico's government that they sought from their own. Mexico's Liberal leaders were, in fact, busily breaking up communal and church landholdings and seeking to modernize the economy, but President Sebastian Lerdo de Tejada thought U.S. railroad magnates asked too much, especially since they insisted on grants of land rather than bonds or cash. After Lerdo won reelection in 1875, private U.S. interests secretly sent weapons and $500,000 to the losing presidential candidate, Porfirio Díaz, who was so eager to promote development that his followers won the nickname "Railroaders." Díaz engineered a coup the following year.

Díaz's three decades of rule were some of the friendliest in Mexican history for U.S. corporate investment. The railroads that U.S. companies built and operated rarely served the interests of Mexican passengers or linked Mexican cities to one another. Rather, they were designed to ship raw materials from south to north and from the interior to the coasts. Each project solicited per-mile land concessions from Mexico—helpfully provided by the Díaz government—and each led investors to pursue further ventures south of the border. By 1896 American investors owned 80 percent of Mexico's railroad stocks and bonds. A decade later foreigners owned one-third of all the country's land, with Americans accounting for three-quarters of the total. Texas Oil had claimed four million acres for exploration and drilling. Phelps-Dodge oversaw a lucrative cross-border empire in copper mining, and the Guggenheim Company supervised mining and smelting operations in gold, iron, copper, and zinc. Around Monterrey U.S. companies vied with Italian and British competitors to exploit fabulous silver deposits. Other U.S. companies ran huge coffee, sugar, henequen, and rubber plantations.

These enterprises benefited from the policy, pursued by both Díaz and his predecessors, of dispossessing traditional Indian communities and breaking up landholdings for private sale. Many Mexicans uprooted by this process became wage laborers in corporate enterprises; for thousands, migration to northern Mexico and across the border in search of work became a way of life. Mexican workers faced relentless discrimination, as companies openly differentiated the "American wage" from the "Mexican wage" and reserved high-status jobs for U.S. nationals. At the Batopilas mine in the Sierra Madre, for example, an American supervisor earned $18,000 a year, an assistant electrician $1,500, and a Mexican miner about $75. Farmers forced from their land, however, had few options other than working on ranches, sugar beet farms, or railroad gangs. Northern Mexico developed a distinctive economy in the shadow of the United States. The people of Sonora, known as "Mexican Yankees" to their countrymen farther south, began to play baseball and incorporate words such as *picher* and *cacher* (as well as the curse *sanabich*) into their vocabulary.

Mexico became a model for American business expansion and corporate investment, in many parts of the world. Copper and rubber from Mexico joined the stream of commerce along with Montana cattle, Wisconsin ice, Georgia cotton,

Cuban sugar, and Brazilian coffee. By the 1890s dozens of U.S. corporations fit the modern definition of *multinational*. The pioneer was Singer Sewing Machine, which had exported its popular machines a decade before the Civil War, sent agents abroad during the war years, and by 1868 operated a factory in Scotland. A decade later Singer had sales headquarters in six European capitals, South Africa, and New Zealand. Singer managers experimented early with global marketing and sales. They advertised their sewing machine as "The Great Civilizer" and boasted of serving the "Hindoo mother," the "dark-eyed Mexican Senorita," and the "flaxen-haired Russian peasant girl." The company's foreign agents negotiated the complexities of the caste system in India, and in China they hosted free sewing schools, hoping students would become future customers.

Seeking markets abroad, companies often found it profitable (partly because of tariff barriers) to manufacture in those countries rather than at home. By the mid-1880s producers of farm machinery, locomotives, elevators, typewriters, and pharmaceuticals had substantial sales in Europe and elsewhere. Four dozen U.S. corporations had factories in Canada. Bell Telephone had subsidiaries in Europe, Latin America, and Asia. Edison was exporting electric lights to countries as far away as Chile and Japan. Standard Oil, the behemoth of them all, was competing head-to-head in foreign markets with refiners of Russian and Middle Eastern oil. George Eastman of Eastman Kodak, which by the end of the decade sold cameras from Shanghai to St. Petersburg, remarked that foreign sales cushioned the ups and downs of the U.S. marketplace: they helped "distribute our eggs and pad the basket." For Eastman and other corporate titans, the pile of eggs grew very high.

REDEFINING SPACE AND TIME

Railroads and steamships carried not only fruit, meat, and sewing machines, but also people with dreams of prosperity. Carlos Córdoba's journey began after his father's death, when he became an apprentice in his uncle's blacksmith shop near the border between Sonora and Arizona. There he learned to use the latest American machine tools, and at age fifteen he crossed the border and found a maintenance job at a copper mine. For Michael Daunis, a Lithuanian farmer's son, the journey began with letters from a cousin in the United States who reported (falsely, it turned out) that he was getting rich. The cousin sent a transatlantic ticket, and Michael left, expecting to return in a few years and buy "the biggest farm in the village." Ellen O'Grady's travels also began with kin: two sisters working in New York City paid her passage from Ireland. For Chen Yixi of Langmei village in southeast China, the journey began with famine and a ravaging civil war that left his family destitute. The teenaged Yixi headed for the United States, where he ended up in Seattle for almost four decades.

Like 40 percent of U.S. immigrants during the late nineteenth century, two of these migrants eventually went home. Carlos Córdoba returned to his childhood village with a sewing machine and stove for his mother. Chen Yixi returned triumphantly to China as a wealthy entrepreneur. Michael Daunis and

Ellen O'Grady, like the other three-fifths of new arrivals, ended up living and dying in the United States. Their journeys show how quickly global transportation became a direct consumer product, available to people abroad as well as within the United States. Paleotechnology made it far cheaper and quicker to cross an ocean or continent. With the advent of steamships the cost of a transatlantic or transpacific trip fell to $50 and sometimes half as much. At steamship offices in most major U.S. cities, workers could buy tickets to send back to family and friends. Labor recruiters also went abroad to offer contracts for work in the United States, with the cost of passage built in. Better communication provided incentives to go, since reliable mail and telegraph service allowed family and friends to keep in touch, wire money, and come home for visits.

The United States was by no means the sole destination for immigrants. Thousands of English and Welsh workers headed for Canada, Australia, and New Zealand, and many manual laborers left southern Italy for other parts of Europe and Argentina, with only a third choosing North America. Chinese migrants moved to Southeast Asia in large numbers before turning to the United States and Australia. But the United States was a major beneficiary whose arrivals came from every point on the compass. As one historian observes, "The American working class formed out of four great diasporas—from Europe, Africa, Asia, and Mexico." With Chinese and Latinos arriving in substantial numbers after the Civil War, Americans became a truly global people.

Not all migrants came willingly. Around the world, paleotechnology pushed people off the land and out of traditional trades, forcing them toward the industrial core. Small-scale farming proved vulnerable to capital intensification and consolidation of landholdings by powerful elites. European tailors and blacksmiths

Table 2.1 Sources of Immigrants to the United States, 1866–1900

COUNTRY OR REGION OF ORIGIN	NUMBER OF ARRIVALS	PERCENTAGE OF U.S. IMMIGRANTS
Germany	3,230,720	24.7
Ireland	1,720,188	13.0
Scandinavia	1,380,676	10.4
Britain	1,986,745	15.0
Austria-Hungary	1,026,296	7.7
Italy	1,023,238	7.7
Canada	900,103	6.8
Russia	759,739	5.7
China	239,730	1.8

Chinese immigrants are almost certainly undercounted. Most Mexicans in the United States were native born, but census takers did not ask citizens to identify themselves by Hispanic origin until 1930. The number of Americans who identified themselves as having been born in Latin America rose from 38,315 in 1860 to 137,458 in 1900; this number doubled by 1910.

Sources: *Roger Daniels, "The Immigrant Experience in the Gilded Age," in* The Gilded Age, *ed. Charles W. Calhoun (Wilmington, DE, 1996), 65–67; U.S. Census Bureau.*

found their crafts undermined by cheaper factory-made goods, while eastern European Jews, who had long held a distinctive place as artisans and middlemen, found their livelihoods undermined by urbanization and new networks of shipping and trade. In Poland the arrival of Singer sewing machines drew rural women into clothing factories well before they traveled to the United States to take up similar work. Government policies played a powerful role in these changes. By raising import duties, for example, the McKinley tariff of 1890 virtually destroyed the tin industry of Wales. U.S. manufacturers quickly recruited unemployed Welsh tin workers to emigrate and work for them.

Even migrants with noneconomic motives, such as Russian Jews seeking refuge from religious persecution, depended on the infrastructures of steam power: while railroads displaced Jews from their prescribed economic niche, railroads also enabled Jews to flee remote inland locations and reach Germany's ports, gateways to America. A Russian Jewish lullaby promised material plenty as well as religious freedom to those who undertook the journey:

> Your daddy's in America, little son of mine,
> But you are just a child now, so hush and go to sleep.
> America is for everyone, they say it's the greatest piece of luck
> For Jews, it's a garden of Eden, a rare and precious place.
> People there eat challah in the middle of the week.

As the song suggested, almost all immigrants came to America looking for economic opportunity. In doing so they changed their customs, languages, and sometimes even their names. At age twelve Spyridon Demopoulos was chosen by the elders of his Greek village to go to the United States; arriving in Maryland, he took the name Stephen Demas and worked his way up in the restaurant and laundry business, eventually bringing over three siblings. Min Chung of China became Billy Ford, a labor boss in the Nevada borax mines. He and his California-born wife, Loy Lee (Lily Sue), had seven children: Timothy, James, Rose, Bessie, Lillian, Alice, and George Washington.

On opposite sides of the globe, the factors that drove emigration in Ireland and southeast China were strikingly similar. Both were poverty-stricken agricultural regions swept up in Britain's expanding empire. Ireland had been a British colony for centuries, while China had recently been forced through gunboat diplomacy to trade with Britain on unfavorable terms. Both Ireland and South China suffered overcrowding on the land and massive crop failures. These catastrophes were exacerbated by British policies that dictated the export of grain from starving Ireland and the import of opium to China. Ireland's Great Famine left an estimated 1.1 to 1.5 million dead, and combined with the emigration of 2.1 million cut the island's population by a third. A decade later South China endured the extraordinary upheaval of the Taiping Rebellion, a civil war sparked by economic dislocation and exposure to Christian missionary ideas. The resulting struggle left twenty million people dead. Faced with such catastrophes, both the Irish and southern Chinese were drawn from their homelands into international manufacture and trade.

Having traveled halfway around the globe in opposite directions, Irish and Chinese railroad gangs met face to face in America when the Central Pacific (employing Chinese) and Union Pacific (employing Irish) joined up in 1869.

Millions of people took on transnational identities, viewing themselves as, for example, Chinese and American or Italian and Argentine. They subscribed to newspapers from their home countries and switched back and forth from English to their own languages. Their gamble was double or nothing. If they were lucky they might end up fitting in comfortably on two continents, sharing new prosperity with kin at home and abroad. The unlucky suffered poverty, illness, death, or prolonged separation. In California prominent Chinese merchants' wives told a visitor they were terrified that they would "die among strangers." Suey Hin, a successful San Francisco madam, had a more ambiguous view. She liked the United States but told a visitor she had returned to Hong Kong three times and hoped to go back permanently. "I am too old to be an American," she said. "If I were younger, I would be one."

Immigrants most often took jobs on the bottom rungs of the economic ladder. A few specialized in work they had done at home, but most, like the Chinese who started laundries and restaurants, carved out niches based on whatever work was available and allowed. Sweatshop garment production, so prominent in New York City, was already familiar to many European immigrants, but Syrians chose itinerant peddling simply because it required little overhead. In a pattern typical of many cities, Jewish men in Poughkeepsie, New York, tended to become tailors, an Old World holdover, while Irishmen found work as teamsters, carpenters, and policemen, jobs few had held at home. To a large extent immigrants settled in the Northeast, Midwest, and West, not the South. (In 1890 the populations of seven ex-Confederate states remained more than 98 percent native born.) In comparison to immigrants, though, Southern blacks had a more difficult struggle to purchase homes, move up the employment ladder, and secure better prospects for the next generation. Even in northern industrial cities, overt discrimination excluded blacks from most occupations and relegated them to the lowest-paying jobs as waiters, butlers, cooks, and maids.

Immigrants were an enormous asset to the American economy, which exercised its strongest pull during boom years. In effect, the United States skimmed off able-bodied and talented breadwinners from other countries, kept them during their peak productivity, and sent them home when they could no longer work. If the United States served as something of a safety valve for desperate immigrants, the reverse was also true. During severe depressions, millions of foreign-born workers returned to their homelands, exporting their poverty and easing unemployment pressures in the United States. Investigating in the early twentieth century, Italian officials were distressed to find that steamships were not only taking prime Italian workers to America but were also bringing home thousands with injuries and illnesses, including tuberculosis. Since the United States offered no social safety net, the elderly also tended to return home when they could no longer earn a living. Touring Greece in the twentieth century, the author

Wallace Stegner found coffeehouses filled with "gnarled, durable old men" who greeted American visitors in fluent English. "They tell you that they have spent many years in America. They wonder if you know their cousin Joe Kosmos in Joliet, Illinois, or if by chance you come from Paterson, New Jersey, or Denver, Colorado, places they have lived and have friends."

The benefits of migration were obvious: opportunities for migrants, cheap labor for employers, and flexibility and adaptability for both groups. Many of the costs fell into categories that economists tend not to measure. Most notable, perhaps, were the tremendous stresses on family life. Thousands of fathers never saw their newborn infants, meeting them only when they were older children or never at all. Occasionally a migrant husband just vanished, leaving a spouse who never knew whether she had been widowed or abandoned. Long years of loneliness sometimes contributed to prostitution, adultery, and divorce, and lack of proximity to kin brought an array of other problems. In Texas, where young Louisa Rollfing lived with her husband August, distance from her beloved mother in Germany contributed to tragedy. When her first baby was born prematurely, she had difficulty nursing and could not find an older woman to give her advice. "I did not have any experience," she later wrote. "Maybe he could have been saved if I had Mother near me." Instead, the baby died. Conversely, many women in South China counted themselves lucky to have a husband's income from overseas while they enjoyed extended periods of freedom from patriarchal control. The restless search for work and opportunity both strengthened women's rights and weakened family ties.

While immigrants journeyed to and fro in cheap, unpleasant steerage berths, affluent Americans enjoyed journeys of unprecedented luxury and speed. The New York Central, advertising a trip of only twenty hours from New York to Chicago, billed itself as the "fastest train in the world." On its premier service in the 1890s, the Pennsylvania Railroad featured not only mahogany dining cars and sleepers but also a library, barber, stenographer, and stock reports three times a day. Even before the Civil War railroads had begun to build and promote resorts, tempting well-to-do Americans to participate in a ritual newly described as "vacationing." In postwar decades the practice grew exponentially. Wealthy Manhattanites could get to the spa at White Sulphur Springs, Virginia, for $28, or to a great camp in the Adirondacks for $50. Philadelphians could reach Cape May, New Jersey, nonstop in three hours. Many of the great names of American travel— from Lake Tahoe to Palm Beach, Florida—became fashionable destinations. By 1900 railroads offered direct service to national parks in the West, which they played a role in developing. Even rural and working-class Americans shared some of the fun. Few had the money or leisure for extended tours, but through "excursion trains" an occasional summer Sunday at the state fair or the beach became accessible to millions.

Steamships allowed elite and middle-class travelers to venture overseas as travel to Europe and the Holy Land became cheaper, faster, safer, and more comfortable. Some travelers came home with their prejudices confirmed. "I felt as

"From Sicily," 1905. Cheaper, faster transportation led to more fluid patterns of immigration as well as increased numbers of migrants. Many, such as these new arrivals, came as single men or left wives and children at home, hoping to work in America for a few years and either send for their families or return home with their savings. Lewis Wickes Hine took this photograph as part of a series at Ellis Island in New York. Hine, who went on to a celebrated career as a photojournalist, hoped to instill in native-born Americans the same admiration for immigrants they had for the Pilgrims. SOURCE: George Eastman House, Rochester, New York.

never before," declared one visitor to England, "the unspeakable superiority of America." But ease of travel and communication also stimulated cross-fertilization of ideas. Jane Addams got the inspiration for Hull House in London; antilynching advocate Ida B. Wells funded her work through lectures to sympathetic Britons. Almost every major American artist sojourned in Paris, bringing the American art world fully into Europe's orbit. Scholars in many fields studied on the Continent or in England. Pioneer mathematician J. Willard Gibbs took his advanced degrees in Germany, and though his papers appeared in Connecticut, almost no Americans had the training to comprehend them. Major social thinkers such as Florence Kelley and W. E. B. DuBois also undertook postgraduate study in Germany. In a very different field of learning, Americans in London around 1870 first encountered the practice and the phrase "living in drag."

For Boston intellectual Henry Adams, son of the U.S. ambassador to Britain during the Civil War, extended travels in Europe prompted perceptive comparisons with conditions in his homeland. Having visited the great museums and cathedrals of Europe, Adams stood and pondered the operations of an electric

Mexican-American ranch family, Mora Valley, New Mexico Territory, 1895. Note the leather boots on the baby's feet: this ranching family appears to have aspirations for their young son. Courtesy Photographic Archives, Palace of the Governors, Museum of New Mexico.

dynamo at the 1900 Paris Exposition. The influence of Christianity, Adams wrote, was being eclipsed by American enterprise, powerful but bereft of spirituality. "At the Louvre and at Chartres," Adams wrote, speaking of religious faith, "was the highest energy ever known to man, the creator of four-fifths of his noblest art, exercising vastly more attraction over the human mind than all the steam-engines and dynamos ever dreamed of; and yet this energy was unknown to the American mind." Americans, Adams wrote with foreboding, "felt a railway train as power." Walt Whitman expressed a more optimistic version of the same view in "To a Locomotive in Winter":

> *Type of the modern—emblem of motion and power—pulse of the*
> *   continent . . .*
> *By day thy warning ringing bell to sound its notes,*
> *By night thy silent signal lamps to swing.*
> *Fierce-throated beauty!*
> *Roll through my chant with all thy lawless music, thy swinging lamps at night,*
> *Thy madly-whistled laughter, echoing, rumbling like an earthquake, rousing all,*
> *Law of thyself complete, thine own track firmly holding, . . .*
> *Thy trills of shrieks by rocks and hills return'd,*

Launch'd o'er the prairies wide, across the lakes,
To the free skies unpent and glad and strong.

Whitman's enthusiasm was widely shared. For the first time in human history, an ordinary person could cross an ocean in two weeks with reasonable safety, and the continent of North America in half that time. In 1889 millions of Americans followed the progress of twenty-two-year-old stunt reporter Nellie Bly, who set out to beat the fictional record set in Jules Verne's *Around the World in Eighty Days*. Bly traveled by rail and steamship from New York to London, Paris, and Italy; through the Suez Canal to Sri Lanka, Singapore, Hong Kong, and Yokohama; and across the Pacific. A special train dispatched by her sponsors at the *New York World* then whisked her from San Francisco to Manhattan for a record journey of seventy-two days, six hours, and eleven minutes. "Father Time Outdone!" trumpeted the *World*, proclaiming a "new age of lightning travel." The editors glossed over the inconvenient fact that Bly's achievement depended largely on British steamships, and ports. Instead, they hailed Bly as an American success story.

Bly's trip revealed as much about news as it did about transportation. The managers of the *World* funded her journey because she would write lively telegraph dispatches, fueling sales. Global communication had become, nearly instantaneous. Telegraph lines connected every continent; a reliable message could get from London to New York in only ten minutes and from Bombay in ninety. In 1871, in a stunt not unlike Bly's, the *New York Herald* had sent their reporter Henry Stanley to the Congo to "find" English explorer David Livingstone. (Livingstone was unaware that he was lost.) The significance of the trip had been again not so much the outcome but the search itself. Stanley's vivid dispatches made it to the coast to be telegraphed back for sensational headlines.

To a large extent the Civil War fostered Americans' insatiable demand for information, which papers like the *Herald* and *World* worked to sustain. "Each magazine and periodical," observed a reporter in 1893, "now runs a neck-and-neck race to capture the first and freshest news. . . . Priority in catching a current event is the overwhelming aim." Paper and printing costs fell steadily. Visitors to San Francisco could sample an array of ethnic newspapers, ranging from *União Portuguesa* to *Slavenska Čitaonica*. African-American "race papers" became a potent tool for discussion and organization, culminating by the turn of the century in papers of nationwide circulation and distinction such as the *Chicago Defender*. Meanwhile, mass-market papers boasted circulations in the hundreds of thousands. Like other corporations they sought profits on high volume and razor-thin margins, bolstering sales through celebrity coverage and aggressive advertising campaigns.

Information thus became a major industry in itself, just as critical as railroads to the expanding networks of administration and commerce. Western Union telegraph company, like Rockefeller's Standard Oil, succeeded in absorbing rival firms and establishing an effective nationwide monopoly. By 1900 it counted 22,900 offices in the United States and carried sixty-three million messages a year.

The telegraph helped transform financial markets, sending stock quotes and shipping news humming along the wires. Since before the Civil War most of America's major financiers, such as J. P. Morgan and J. and W. Seligman, had arrived with European connections, backed by substantial capital from Britain, Belgium, and other financial centers. In the postwar years rapid communication made it easier to sustain those connections and move money around the world.

Along with the telegraph, the postal service played a critical but underrecognized role in the transformation of news and commerce. Officials in the U.S. Railway Mail Service, created in 1869, found creative ways to deliver mail quickly using night trains and having workers sort in transit. While the expensive telegraph was used largely by businesses, almost all Americans benefited from cheap, reliable mail. "The post office is the visible form of the Federal Government to every community and to every citizen," declared the postmaster general in 1890. "Its hand is the only one that touches the local life, the social interests, and business concern of every neighborhood." Through Railway Mail, as well as subsidies to the railroads over which it traveled, the U.S. government gave a tremendous boost to economic growth. Banks, businesses, and customers mailed millions of checks, drafts, bills of exchange, and other instruments of credit, which by the 1880s made up more than 90 percent of all bank receipts. Cheap bulk mailing rates, introduced in the mid-1880s, stimulated the rise of mail-order catalogs and magazines.

By the 1880s one Michigan editor complained bitterly about the emerging global information age. There had been a severe forest fire nearby, he wrote, but nothing about it came over the wires; instead, the telegraph brought "a full account of the flood in Shanghai, a massacre in Calcutta, a sailor fight in Bombay, hard frosts in Siberia, a missionary banquet in Madagascar, [and] the price of kangaroo leather from Borneo." The editor, told readers he was canceling his telegraph service and would henceforth report only local news. Few followed his lead. Instead, further innovations quickened the pace. In 1899 the *New York Herald* followed the America's Cup race through a wireless radio broadcast, transmitted by inventor Enrico Marconi from steamships near the racing yachts. In 1903 Marconi opened the first commercial wireless service on Cape Cod, and the era of radio broadcasting was born.

Watching the hustle and bustle of information shipping, and shopping, many Americans experienced an accelerating rush in the pace of life. Newcomers shared the impression, especially when they disembarked in a metropolis such as New York. In his autobiographical novel *The Rise of David Levinsky*, Abraham Cahan described his character's disorientation after making the Atlantic voyage: "The active life of the great strange city made me feel like one abandoned in the midst of a jungle." Levinsky was struck by the "preoccupied faces and hurried step," "the scurry and hustle." One of the first English phrases he learned from his landlady was "hurry up." The noted pianist Ignace Paderewski, visiting from Poland in 1891, remembered in Chicago "an atmosphere of intense competition, of continuous effort, and of speed—speed, speed, even then."

Medical experts soon warned that the pace of information and travel was exerting great psychological pressure. They noted that it was much more stressful to receive stock market updates five times a day than it was to check them once a week. In *American Nervousness* (1881) Dr. George Beard warned of an epidemic of neurasthenia brought about by the need for punctuality. "We are under constant strain, mostly unconscious," Beard argued, "oftentimes in sleeping as well as in waking hours, to get somewhere or do something at some definite moment." He identified the five sources of neuresthenia as "steam power, the periodical press, the telegraph, the sciences, and the mental activity of women." Unfortunately, the exact symptoms of the malady remained unclear. Doctors suggested that neuresthenia might be implicated in almost every kind of complaint, including baldness, hay fever, headaches, insomnia, and sexual dysfunction. Authors such as Beard seemed proud of neuresthenia, a "distinguished" illness made "possible by a new and productive country." Others were not so sure. Writers such as Kate Chopin in *The Awakening* and Edith Wharton in *House of Mirth* used neuresthenic characters to critique American society and its money-centered values.

The illness Beard diagnosed was, he and many others assumed, a problem of the affluent classes. The drive for efficiency and speed was equally obvious, however, to railroad and telegraph workers and anyone whose job depended on those networks, including wholesalers and traveling salesmen. A Cincinnati paper worried that *commuters*—a new term in Americans' vocabulary—had to bend their lives to fit train schedules. Commuters enjoyed suburban life in more relaxing surroundings than the city could offer, but they lost much of that repose as they rushed to catch the 7:03. "The longer a man is a commuter," the editor worried, "the more he grows to be a living timetable."

Railroads altered the reckoning of time itself. Before the 1880s American cities and towns set their own local times. Savannah, Georgia, for example, operated a half-hour ahead of Atlanta time. This system wreaked havoc on railroad schedules and passengers—or, to put it another way, rapid intercity transit created confusion where before there had been little or none. At the behest of a zealous manager who advocated standard time, a group of major railroads announced in 1883 that they were dividing the nation into four zones—Eastern, Central, Mountain, and Pacific—and setting standard times for the operation of trains. Despite sporadic protests, usually from cities and towns that experienced a dramatic clock shift, most Americans accepted railroad time as a matter of convenience and progress. On Sunday, November 18, 1883, "the day of two noons," clock-keepers all over the country changed their clocks to reflect the new system. The *Washington Post* observed, with only slight exaggeration, that it was a revolution "scarcely second to the reformation of the calendar by Julius Caesar."

Even when the consequences of the new economy arrived at a precise moment—as they did at noon on that November Sunday—they often seemed unstoppable. The paleotechnical era, a creation of human invention and of myriad decisions by voters, policy makers, financiers, and businessmen, arrived like a mandate from nature itself. Andrew Carnegie perhaps expressed the attitude best in his famous essay "Wealth." "The conditions of human life have not only been changed, but revolutionized," he declared. "Whether the change be for good or for ill, it is upon us, beyond our power to alter, and therefore, to be accepted and made the best of. It is a waste of time," he added impatiently, "to criticize the inevitable."

Educational reformer John Dewey, writing in 1899, took an optimistic view of progress for reasons rather different from Carnegie's. In the economic revolution that was occurring, Dewey wrote, "the face of the earth is making over, even as to its physical forms; political boundaries are wiped out and moved about; . . . population is hurriedly gathered into cities from the ends of the earth; habits of living are altered with startling abruptness and thoroughness; the search for the truths of nature is infinitely stimulated." He observed that information, like wheat, now moved fluidly and in larger quantities than ever before. "Knowledge is no longer an immobile solid; it has been liquefied. It is actively moving in all the currents of society." Even morality and religious faith were undergoing change, and so were the values and skills that parents should teach their children. Just as Carnegie thought it a waste of time to lament the loss of traditions—in the modern world, after all, who wanted to light their homes with whale oil?—Dewey thought it "useless to bemoan the departure of the good old days of children's modesty, reverence and implicit obedience." Instead, Dewey identified other virtues that could make the new order serve the cause of democracy. "We must recognize our compensations," he wrote, "—the increase in toleration, in breadth of social judgment, the larger acquaintance with human nature, . . . greater accuracy of adaptation to differing personalities." Through his work at a model school attached to the University of Chicago, Dewey invented forms of education that would combine discipline with independence, manual skill with intellectual exploration. He hoped to imbue each student with "the spirit of service and . . . the instruments of effective self-direction."

Like many thinkers of his day, Dewey combined enthusiasm for progress with an attempt to preserve the best of what he saw fading away. He appreciated the ways in which children had traditionally learned from their parents, contributing to the productive work of the household while they mastered a skill such as carpentry or candle making. Dewey's model school thus engaged both boys and girls in sewing, cooking, and shop work, hoping to instill responsibility and love of craft. In this, Dewey's school was not so different from Booker T. Washington's Tuskegee Institute, which taught blacksmithing, tin making, sewing, and other industrial arts. They sought, in a world of coal-fired locomotives, Bessemer furnaces, and far-flung corporate enterprise, to sustain some of the virtues of local production and craftsmanship.

Dewey, Washington, and their counterparts recognized that they were preparing young Americans for revolutionary journeys—journeys from the farms to the big city, and from continent to continent, into a future world that would challenge the expectations of their grandparents' day. Dewey understood that the transformation of labor lay at the heart of the journeys his students would undertake.

But though he insisted that the corporate and industrial workplace depended, at root, on the old "household and neighborhood" systems of production, most of his students would enter employments of a very different type. The world of work was changing, both for the prosperous and for the struggling poor.

FOR FURTHER READING

On bison see Andrew C. Isenberg, *The Destruction of the Bison* (Cambridge, 2000), and Richard White, "Animals and Enterprise," in *The Oxford History of the American West*, ed. Clyde A. Milner II, et al. (New York, 1994), 237–74. On the citrus industry see Steven Stoll, *The Fruits of Natural Advantage* (Berkeley, CA, 1998), and Robert V. Hine and John Mack Faragher, *The American West* (New Haven, CT, 2000). Critical throughout this chapter is William Cronon's breathtaking exploration of Chicago's relationship to its western economic hinterlands, *Nature's Metropolis* (New York, 1991). For fossil fuel use see David Nye, *Consuming Power* (Cambridge, MA, 1998), and Harold Platt, *The Electric City* (Chicago, 1991). My analysis of Lewis Mumford's *Technics and Civilization* is indebted to Richard White, *The Organic Machine* (New York, 1995). For railroads I rely on another book by White, *"It's Your Misfortune and None of My Own"* (Norman, OK, 1991), and on Carlos A. Schwantes, *The Pacific Northwest*, 2nd ed. (Lincoln, NE, 1996), as well as John F. Stover, *American Railroads*, 2nd ed. (Chicago, 1997). For a history of Miller and Lux see David Igler, *Industrial Cowboys* (Berkeley, CA, 2001). On agriculture see Fred A. Shannon, *The Farmer's Last Frontier* (New York, 1945).

On consolidation of the infrastructure see George L. Anderson, "Banks, Mails, and Rails, 1880–1915," in *The Frontier Challenge*, ed. John G. Clark (Lawrence, KS, 1971), as well as Morton Keller, *Affairs of State*, Richard Bensel, *The Political Economy of American Industrialization*, and Edward L. Ayers, *Promise of the New South*, all cited in Chapter 1. On the information revolution see Richard R. John, "Recasting the Information Infrastructure for the Industrial Age," in *A Nation Transformed by Information*, ed. Alfred D. Chandler, Jr., and James W. Cortada (New York, 2000), 55–105; Wayne E. Fuller, "The Populists and the Post Office," *Agricultural History* 65 (1991): 1–16; Richard A. Schwarzlose, *The Nation's Newsbrokers* (Evanston, IL, 1989); Sally M. Miller, ed., *The Ethnic Press in the United States* (Westport, CT, 1987); Tom Standage, *The Victorian Internet* (New York, 1999); Susan J. Douglas, *Inventing American Broadcasting, 1899–1922* (Baltimore, 1987); and for a sweeping global perspective on technology, Daniel R. Headrick, *Tentacles of Progress* (New York, 1988). A helpful overview of industrialization and its impact in the United States is Walter Licht, *Industrializing America* (Baltimore, 1995).

The best biography of Carnegie is Joseph Frazier Wall, *Andrew Carnegie* (New York, 1970). For Rockefeller see Ron Chernow, *Titan* (New York, 1998). On the rise of corporate management the classic source is Alfred E. Chandler's *The Visible Hand* (Cambridge, MA, 1977). For an international perspective on these developments see E. J. Hobsbawm, *The Age of Empire, 1875–1914* (New York, 1987). On U.S. investment in Mexico I have drawn largely on John Mason Hart's study *Empire and Revolution* (Berkeley, CA, 2002). See also Ramón Eduardo Ruíz, *The People of Sonora and Yankee Capitalists* (Tucson, 1988), Matt S. Meier and Feliciano Ribera, *Mexican Americans/American Mexicans* (New York, 1993), and Linda S. Gordon, *The Great Arizona Orphan Abduction* (Cambridge, MA, 1999). The quote about the construction of the American working class out of "four great diasporas" comes from Gordon's book, p. 48. On the rise of multinational companies I have depended on

Emily S. Rosenberg, *Spreading the American Dream* (New York, 1982), and especially on Mira Wilkins, *The Emergence of Multinational Enterprise* (Cambridge, MA, 1970). On the Singer Company see Robert Bruce Davies, *Peacefully Working to Conquer the World* (New York, 1976).

The best overviews of immigration are Roger Daniels, *Coming to America* (New York, 1990), Walter T. K. Nugent, *Crossings* (Bloomington, IN, 1992), Mark Wyman, *Round-Trip to America* (Ithaca, NY, 1993), and Bruce M. Stave, *From the Old Country* (Hanover, NH, 1999). On specific immigrant groups see Donna R. Gabaccia, *Italy's Many Diasporas* (Seattle, 2000), Hasia R. Diner, *Erin's Daughters in America* (Baltimore, 1983), and Kerby A. Miller, *Emigrants and Exiles* (New York, 1985), both on the Irish; on Asian immigrants, Madeline Hsu, *Dreaming of Gold, Dreaming of Home* (Stanford, CA, 2000), Ronald Takaki, *Strangers from a Different Shore* (Boston, 1989), and Judy Yung, *Unbound Voices* (Berkeley, CA, 1999); on Jews, Hasia R. Diner, *A New Promised Land* (New York, 2003). Stegner's memoir of visiting Greece is in his introduction to Zeese Papanikolas, *Buried Unsung* (Salt Lake City, 1982). On Poughkeepsie see Clyde Griffen and Sally Griffen, *Natives and Newcomers* (Cambridge, MA, 1978).

Cindy S. Aron looks at tourism and vacations in *Working at Play* (New York, 1999); see also Earl Pomeroy, *In Search of the Golden West* (New York, 1957). On trans-Atlantic intellectual and political connections see Daniel T. Rodgers, *Atlantic Crossings* (Cambridge, MA, 1998). For neuresthenia I rely on Tom Lutz, *American Nervousness, 1903* (Ithaca, NY, 1991), and for railroad time on Ian R. Bartky, *Selling the True Time* (Stanford, CA, 2000). I am also grateful to David Greenstein for his research paper "From Sunshine to Smokestacks: Practicality and the Adoption of Railroad Standard Time," History 367, Vassar College, May 2003.

CHAPTER 3

Work

Go west, young man, and grow up with the country.
— Horace Greeley, 1853

Our young men can no longer go west; they must go up or down.
— Henry Demarest Lloyd, 1884

The most dangerous job on a nineteenth-century railroad belonged to the brakeman. Half a mile before a train reached its station, each brakeman climbed a ladder to the top of a car, turned a braking wheel, and crossed to another car to repeat the maneuver. Since no crew could do this in perfect unison, the cars jolted. Brakemen often suffered crushed hands and arms, especially in windy, rainy, or icy weather. Many fell to their deaths. On the Illinois Central Railroad between 1874 and 1884, one out of every twenty trainmen suffered death or disabling injury; among brakemen the rate was one in seven.

Management decisions had a great deal to do with these appalling odds. Railroad companies saw little incentive to improve safety; to cut costs they began in the 1870s to require brakemen to handle four, five, or six cars rather than two, upping the accident rate. State governments had trouble enforcing standards across state lines, and railroads worked strenuously to block safety bills in legislatures. Federal regulations were nonexistent until the Railroad Safety Appliance Act of 1893, which finally required the use of air brakes. George Westinghouse had invented these brakes back in 1869, after seeing the wreckage of a spectacular crash, but he had not been able to persuade many executives to adopt them. The act, by requiring use of the new brakes, promptly reduced the accident rate by 60 percent, bringing the U.S. industry in line with its European counterparts.

Thus, railroads mastered the business of *go* long before they committed themselves to *stop*. The same might be said of American enterprise generally in the late nineteenth century. The United States was a gambler's paradise, holding out the allure of jobs, money, and mobility but filled with mortal dangers for working-class women and men. Like the railroads that helped drive its growth, the country's economy astonished onlookers with its power and pace. Except during years of severe depression, manufacturers could boast faster production, higher outputs, and larger exports and domestic sales almost every year. Between 1870 and 1910, jobs in the chemical, oil, and rubber industries grew by an astounding 1,900 percent, in iron and steel by 1,200 percent, and in railroads sixfold. Service jobs also burgeoned, with the country counting five times more barbers and laundry workers by the end of the era than at the start. The dynamic economy drew not only men and women from abroad but also women from the domestic sphere. By the turn of the century, one of every five women in the country was working for pay.

Amid this extraordinary growth, business and political leaders put few brakes on the system. Like railroadmen, miners in the United States died at triple the rates of their European counterparts, who were protected by safety legislation. By one estimate, one-quarter of the immigrant men working the most dangerous jobs in Pennsylvania steel mills suffered death or disabling injuries. Other tasks killed men slowly. Well into the twentieth century blast furnace operators averaged a seventy-seven-hour workweek. Smelter workers—and everyone who lived downwind of their operations—endured constant exposure to sulfur fumes, arsenic, and lead.

Government activism did not extend to the provision of social safety nets. There was no legal minimum wage. Workmen's compensation, unemployment benefits, and Social Security (except for Union veterans' pensions) were unknown for the working class. Employer health coverage and paid vacations were rarities. Injuries on the job, unemployment, and chronic poverty were familiar problems to large swaths of the population. Industrialization left a human wreckage that affluent Americans tended to dismiss as the inevitable price of progress. Workers bore the consequences for the lack of regulatory brakes, just as brakemen paid the toll for employers' less-than-satisfactory control over their speeding trains.

Nowhere was the line between Henry George's "House of Have" and "House of Want" more clear than in the world of work. The divide between "blue collar" and "white collar" was to a large extent forged in the post–Civil War era. The new economy also excelled in creating middlemen (and middlewomen) of various kinds. Even groups of Americans who held the same job often did not agree on whether they worked in production, management, or service, much less on whether they should join a union. The hierarchical structure of the modern corporation encouraged many low-paid office workers to identify with management, while some independent merchants and businessmen, finding their autonomy threatened by voracious monopolies, forged ties with the labor movement. As it reorganized trade and finance, the economic revolution rearranged Americans' lives on the job.

BLUE COLLARS AND APRONS

The idea that most workers would earn a wage or salary, paid by an employer, was itself an innovation of the late nineteenth century. Pre–Civil War Americans had expected most men to become self-employed craftsmen, shopkeepers, or farmers,

Logger breaking a jam, upper Midwest. Loggers used river currents to carry lumber to the nearest trading centers, but huge piles of logs sometimes piled up, under pressure from the tons of lumber that lay behind. Breaking jams was dangerous business, and many loggers lost their lives. The wire in this picture may indicate that the logger is setting dynamite or attaching a line to a team of horses onshore, hoping to loosen the obstruction. Courtesy Wisconsin Historical Society.

an ideal that undergirded confidence in the independence of the citizenry. Permanent paid employment was widely derided as "wage slavery." In the post–Civil War decades, debate over the legitimacy of wage work faded. The key issue came to be not the existence of permanent wage earners but whether they enjoyed decent hours, working conditions, and pay.

Immigrants often remarked on the ruthless pace of labor in the United States. Young radical Emma Goldman, who had worked for a Russian glove manufacturer since age thirteen, found a New York factory "large, bright, and airy" by comparison, but she observed that "the work here was harder. . . . The iron discipline forbade free movement." Goldman was shocked to find that she could not use the bathroom without permission. Her workday, with no breaks except a half-hour lunch, seemed "endless." Watching an Italian railroad construction gang, which started each morning at 5 a.m., an observer wrote that "they work like bulls,

The Suffolk Mine, San Miguel County, Colorado. Workers pose with their tools at the opening to the mine shaft. Much industry, especially in the West, focused on the intensive harvesting and mining of natural resources. Courtesy Colorado Historical Society (20004574).

like slaves, like prisoners." "Here you do not have any free time!" exclaimed one recent arrival. "Everyone works like hell," reported an exhausted Finn. Paul Siu, a Chicago laundryman, recalled how thrilled he had been to leave southern China. "If I had known beforehand that this is the way I would have to toil, I would never have come here," he told an interviewer. "Now I am here, I begin to feel America is work, work, work."

In the making of everything from coffins to chocolates, traditions of craftsmanship eroded, and more and more workers repeated single, rote tasks. A light bulb maker might, for example, spend day after day inserting thousands of filaments into bulbs, while workers at adjacent tables used exhaust machines to create vacuums inside the bulbs and tested the finished product against a metal plate with electric current running through it, receiving a mild shock with each touch, at the rate of thirty-three bulbs per minute. Even at a brassworks in Connecticut, which relied on skilled brass molders, unskilled female operatives constituted half the workforce; they attached labels and packed products for shipping. Operatives did not necessarily work in factories. Many labored at home, where children could join them in piecework, paid by the item rather than the hour. Unskilled work required long days of concentrated effort in order to make a living. After touring a Chicago tenement, reformer Jane Addams was haunted by the memory of "a little girl of four who pulled out basting threads hour by hour, sitting on a stool at the feet of her Bohemian mother, a little bunch of human misery."

Women—notably African-American and immigrant women—did a great deal of the lowest-paid labor, and for most of them this work was not a particularly liberating experience. In the 1870s the most common employment was as a maid or housekeeper. Judging by domestic workers' high turnover rates and eagerness to enter other fields, it was a less-than-satisfying job. Live-in housekeepers, who remained on call twenty-four hours a day, found the demands placed on them especially relentless, and for black women reminiscent of slavery. Low pay and disrespectful or abusive treatment were common complaints. "I feel like a slave on account of the way I am treated," one housekeeper told an interviewer. In Kansas and Minnesota, female factory workers told the same story: they had left domestic work because it was "dirty," "nasty," and "degrading." The growing economy offered women alternatives. In 1870 about 1.5 million women worked for wages, 67 percent in domestic service; by 1910 a staggering 6.3 million women were earning wages, but less than 40 percent were domestics. Outside the South, where African-American women were excluded from nondomestic jobs, middle-class employers complained of a "servant problem." Servants, in other words, were finding better opportunities in other fields.

Jobs in manufacturing carried their own hardships. Employers knew that women, like non-English-speaking immigrants, could be isolated and intimidated more easily than men. Labor investigator Leonora Barry documented a host of abuses suffered by women in the textile industry, from starvation wages to sexual harassment. Many told her they would be fired if they complained, and they thought labor organizing was futile. "Through long years of endurance," Barry wrote, "they have acquired, as a sort of second nature, the habit of submission and acceptance without question of any terms offered them, with the pessimistic view of life in which they see no hope."

Mechanized steam laundries, which employed 125,000 people by the turn of the century, became a focus of journalistic exposés because they embodied all that was wrong with industrialism. Laundry employees, most of whom were black and immigrant women and Chinese men, endured extreme heat and harsh chemicals. Foul wash-water pouring over arms and legs caused swelling and skin ulcers. In *The Long Day* (1905), undercover journalist Dorothy Richardson described her forays into housekeeping, box making, and crafting artificial flowers, but she found laundry work worst of all. Richardson's protagonist (a stand-in for herself) is horrified to find that during the summer rush, with heaps of sheets and towels coming in from hotels, her crew works on Saturdays till 1 a.m. A coworker tells the story of her missing hand:

> I was clean done out, one Saturday night, and I jist couldn't see no more; and first thing I know—Wo-o-ow! And that hand went right straight clean into the rollers. And I was jist tired, that's all. I didn't have nothing to drink all that day,

excepting pop; but the boss he swore I was drunk, and he made the foreman swear the same thing, and so I didn't try to get no damages. They sent me to the horspital, and they offered me my old job back again; but I jist got up my spunk and says if they can't pay me some damages, and goes and swears I was drunk when I didn't have nothing but rotten pop, I says, I can up and go someplace else and get my four dollars a week.

Richardson's heroine sticks to the job for several weeks and wins a promotion, but a foreman warns her not to take the new job because the boss reserves it for his sexual prey.

As Richardson discovered to her dismay, the American workforce was ruthlessly sex-segregated. Women earned half or less of men's wages on the widespread supposition that as wives or daughters, women only needed pocket money while men provided the "real" income for their families. Except among African Americans, the majority of female workers outside the home were unmarried, but many were breadwinners, and the wages of many independent women could not keep them above the poverty line. Investigator Helen Campbell reviewed the budget of one widow and her daughter in New York who had fallen on hard times after the death of the husband and father. The widow had suffered a debilitating fever, and now the two were scraping by on the daughter's pay of $23 a month. After $10 rent and the cost of coal and transportation to and from work, mother and daughter were living on 24¢ a day. "I've had no shoes in two years," the mother told Campbell. "I patch the ones I got then with one of my husband's old coats, and keep along."

Urban areas offered a gamut of wage work. Cincinnati, a typically diverse city, boasted more than 1,600 different small and medium-sized firms that processed meat, lumber, and tobacco and manufactured beer, liquor, baked goods, clothing, books, carriages, clothes, and tools. Though workers in some of these enterprises enjoyed relative freedom to practice a craft, even they were vulnerable to seasonal slumps. The factories of Haverhill, Massachusetts, made only women's summer shoes, purchased by consumers in the spring. "January, February, March and April we are rushed to death," a local worker reported, but summer and fall brought waves of layoffs. Furniture workers in Grand Rapids, Michigan, worked seventy-hour weeks in the high season but faced months of unemployment with little saved from wages of $1.75 a day. Thus, even skilled workers in boom times experienced a paradox: as a business prospered, its workers often did not. Managers resorted to deskilling and cyclical layoffs to slash costs while pressuring workers to increase their pace.

Low as urban wages were, they exceeded those in rural areas. Western cowboys, for example, despite their mythic status as rugged frontier individualists, were for the most part poorly paid wage-workers for cattle corporations. Cowboys in the Texas Panhandle struck for higher wages in 1883, though employers moved quickly to suppress the revolt. In the same state, skilled *tasinques* came over from Mexico in spring and late summer for two rounds of sheep-shearing; a Mexican-born *pastor* (shepherd), working in isolation in the mountains, might tend 2,000

Table 3.1 Two Household Budgets in New York City, 1905

SEAMSTRESS

INCOME

Mrs. M., sewing, 14 weeks, avg. $5.00 a week	$70.00
Mrs. M., sewing, 38 weeks, avg. $3.00 a week	114.00
Girl, 13, earned in summer	14.00
Mother, extra work	20.50
St. Vincent de Paul Society, grocery tickets	26.00
St. Vincent de Paul Society, shoes	4.00
Charity Organization Society, for rent	11.50
Total income:	$260.00

EXPENDITURES

Food	$130.00
Rent	92.75
Clothing	18.00
Fuel	13.00
Medicine	1.00
Moving expenses	3.00
Sundries	2.25
Total expenditures:	$260.00

GLASSWORKER

INCOME

Man, 51 1/2 weeks at $14.00 (3 holidays deducted)	$721.00
Woman, for janitor services	132.00
Boy (15), 22 weeks at $3.50, 25 weeks at $4.00	177.00
Gift from landlord at Christmas	10.00
Total income:	$1,040.00

EXPENDITURES

Food, $10 a week, including lunch money	$520.00
Rent	132.00
Clothing	85.00
Light and fuel	48.50
Insurance, .60 a week	31.20
Newspapers, .11 a week	5.72
Union dues	6.00
Drink for man, $3 a week	156.00
Medical attendance	27.00
Church	13.00
Recreation for father and oldest boy	10.00
Sundries	5.58
Total expenditures:	$1,040.00

The seamstress and her daughter lived in dire circumstances, though the mother did manage to keep her child in school. They scraped by with aid from two charitable organizations, which required the mother as an independent woman to show proof that she was "respectable" and deserving of aid. The glassworker and his family enjoyed a considerably higher standard of living (note that the main breadwinner belonged to a trade union). But Louise Bolard More, the researcher who compiled these data, was clearly aware of the unequal distribution of rewards between men and women in the glassworker's household.

Source: *Thomas J. Schlereth,* Victorian America *(New York, 1991), 80–81.*

sheep for as little as $8 a month. Three million people worked for hire on farms, including more than 600,000 women, most of whom were black southerners. A South Carolina plowhand might earn as little as 20¢ a day, paid partly in corn-meal, bacon, and credit at an employer's store. In California, by contrast, Chinese wheelbarrow crews earned up to $4 a day reclaiming farmland from the swamps of the Sacramento–San Joaquin Delta. But the work was so brutal and dangerous that employers testified no white person would do it. Some survivors became tenant farmers on the reclaimed land. By 1900 two-thirds of all Americans in agriculture were not the yeoman landowners of Thomas Jefferson's dream but sharecroppers, tenants, or workers for hire.

Faced with high risks, farmers and workmen in many industries formed mutual benefit associations (*mutualistas* for Latinos) that pooled members' contributions and used them to support the widows and orphans of any who died. Other forms of solidarity skirted the law: hard-rock miners looked the other way when fellow workers tucked ore into their boots, and investigators in Cripple

"The Champion Chinese Hose Team that Won the Great Hub-and-Hub Race at Deadwood, Dakota Territory, July 4, 1888." Chinese workers played critical roles in the West. Due to hostility and legal restrictions, they most often worked as wage laborers or tenants, finding it difficult to obtain their own land. This group proudly participates in one of the great rituals of nineteenth-century American manhood: organized to protect public safety and property, fire companies excelled in athletic feats and martial drills. Courtesy Library of Congress. John C. H. Grabill Collection.

Ole Johnson Family, Round Valley, Custer County, Nebraska, 1886. Only immigrants who arrived with significant savings, like this Norwegian family, could pay for rail tickets to the inland West and purchase land and farm equipment. But despite their relative advantages, those who sought to farm the Plains often endured prolonged periods of deprivation and hardship. Solomon D. Butcher, who recorded this image, returned in 1904 to photograph the same family in front of their new white two-story clapboard farmhouse. Like many Plains families, the Johnsons probably converted their old sod house into a barn. Courtesy Nebraska Historical Society.

Creek, Colorado, guessed that a quarter of all miners engaged in this practice of "high-grading." Employers considered it theft, but miners argued that they were just closing the gap between what they were owed and what the company paid. On a less militant level, textile workers sometimes chipped in coins when a woman's pay was docked for breaking a needle or talking on the job. Department store clerks developed informal systems to distribute commissions fairly. Once a worker made her daily "stint"—an agreed-upon income from commissions—she would move to a corner to clean shelves or fold clothes, giving others a chance to make their share. Clerks who tried to grab all the commissions found themselves shunned.

More organized resistance to deskilling, low wages, and bad working conditions proved to be an uphill battle. Labor unions tried two strategies in the late nineteenth century. The first was broad-based organizing to unite workers in different jobs and trades, sometimes even across lines of gender and race, into associations such as the Knights of Labor. The second strategy was to build craft-based trade unions, usually limited to skilled men in a single job, such as carpenters or brakemen. Neither avenue proved fully successful. Among the structural problems faced by unions were the sheer size of the United States, the scale of enterprise, and the diversity of the workforce. As we shall see in Chapter 9, ethnic, religious, and racial animosities among workers, and especially antagonism toward Chinese immigrants and African Americans, proved particularly divisive. At peak in 1886 the Knights of Labor unionized almost 10 percent of the nation's nonagricultural workers, an achievement that collapsed due in part to problems of scale and organization. Craft unions, reaching a later peak around the turn of the century through the leadership of the American Federation of Labor, counted about two million members. But they did so, in part, by excluding unskilled workers and women.

Skilled craftsmen had good reason to organize on their own, since they had much to lose. Traditionally proud and independent, craftsmen had once asserted their right to frequent holidays and leisurely lunches over a pint of beer, alternating periods of intense work with spells of relaxation. The post–Civil War era brought less leisure, less control over workplace conditions, and fewer skilled jobs. A major defeat occurred in 1892 at Homestead, Pennsylvania, the last union hold-out in Andrew Carnegie's steel empire. At issue was not so much wages or hours but the very existence of the Amalgamated Association of Iron and Steel Workers, with whom Carnegie officials refused to negotiate a new contract. In one of the most infamous and bitter lock-outs of the century, Carnegie's deputy, Henry Clay Frick (with the aid of 300 Pinkerton detectives and the Pennsylvania militia), succeeded in crushing the union. Carnegie was then free to bring in new technologies that shunted aside craftsmen.

Professional ballplayers found themselves as stymied at the bargaining table as the Amalgamated was at Homestead. With baseball flourishing in the 1880s, team owners of the dominant National League (NL) introduced a $2,000 salary cap, ensuring that owners rather than star players kept most of the game's profits. They followed this with an infamous "reserve clause" under which players had no control over their contracts and no chance to achieve what is now called free agency. Like many factories of the day, the NL introduced a complex system of fines against players' salaries for offenses ranging from absence caused by injuries to "lacking zeal." For players the last straw was the establishment of salary categories designed to slash pay even more. As a spokesman for the players put it, the issue was whether they were skilled craftsmen or team owners' "chattel."

Already organized in a secret Brotherhood of Professional Base Ball Players, a majority of aggrieved players refused to sign for the 1890 season. Instead, they found financial backers for their own Players' League, with eight teams of top talent. In the Players' League there was no reserve clause or "sale" of players. It was a grand experiment in player-managed baseball, but it did not last.

Though Players' League attendance was higher, both leagues lost money in the first year. Faced with uncertain financial backing and intimidation from NL owners, the new league collapsed after one season. The National League emerged from this conflict with virtually absolute control over wages and working conditions.

The rise and fall of the Players' League highlighted the challenges facing workers in the post–Civil War economy. Whole new industries arose in which the rules of employment were fluid and contested. With managers slashing costs and pressing advantage, many employees yearned, like the baseball Brotherhood, to assert their independence and resist being robbed of power and pride on the job. Yet in the complex new economy, it was hard for many workers to become their own bosses. Just as unions disappeared from Homestead's steel mills for decades, baseball owners and players went back to occupying different realms, and the reserve clause remained in place for more than a century.

WHITE COLLARS AND SHIRTWAISTS

By no means all workers lost ground in the post–Civil War years. Thousands of rural Americans got off the farm and earned better pay in the growing towns and cities. Unmarried women took up opportunities in teaching and clerical work, and thousands of working-class men found a place as salesmen, middlemen, and managers. Their experiences raised questions about which jobs lay above and below Henry George's wedge. Many emerging forms of employment were not managerial or supervisory, but they also required no hard physical labor. A stenographer might spend her day doing tasks as routinized as the average factory worker's, and she was just as unlikely to move up the corporate ladder. But men and women who dressed smartly in the morning and came home clean at the end of the day could count themselves upwardly mobile. "All want to crowd into employments deemed genteel," Massachusetts reformer Lydia Child observed, "that do not soil the clothes or the hands." After interviewing telegraph operators, one writer described what they liked about their job: it did not "soil their dresses" or "keep them in a standing posture," and it placed them in "a social position not inferior to that of a teacher or governess." Telegraphers also earned $10 a week, the equivalent of better-paid nurses and teachers and four times more than a factory operative.

The contrasts among emerging forms of work were nowhere sharper than in Troy, New York, which by the 1880s carried the proud name of Collar City U.S.A. The nation's leading producer of cuffs and collars for men's shirts, Troy employed 8,000 female operatives who ran collar-making machines and washed, starched, and ironed the products for sale. Thousands of other women took in collars as piecework to sew details such as buttonholes and trim. The products manufactured by Troy women served men of a different class. Crisp detachable collars were becoming standard wear for businessmen and professionals, who earned sufficient income to afford a fresh collar each morning, attaching it to the same shirt several days in a row to save on laundry. In contrast to denim-shirted workers who sweated for their bread, these were "white-collar" men.

Servers and customers at a Chicago restaurant, 1895. Many sectors of the service industry moved from the domestic space of the private home into public venues ranging from steam laundries to commercial boardinghouses. In the burgeoning cities, restaurants like this one catered to increasing numbers of single men and those with no place to cook at home.
Courtesy Chicago Historical Society.

Such workers began to coalesce as a recognized class, albeit one with many layers and complications. The term *middle class* first appeared in the *Century Dictionary* in 1889, and men of that class began to speak of making a career rather than finding a job. Most often native-born white Protestants, they lived in towns or suburbs outside the burgeoning cities. C. W. Post marketed his famous breakfast drink, Postum, to these "brainworkers." Post, addressing widespread anxieties, advertised that drinking coffee would "reduce your work time, kill your energy, push you into the big crowd of mongrels, deaden what thoroughbred blood you may have and neutralize all your efforts to make money and fame." He recommended that middle-class men and women choose Postum instead. (Despite his warnings, Post himself was often seen sipping coffee.)

Some of the most dramatic areas of growth were in professional occupations. Lawyers had traditionally trained by reading in a law office, like apprentices to a craft, but the increasing need for specialized training, notably in high-status fields such as corporate law, was reflected in the rapid proliferation of law schools. In medicine, lay healers and midwives found themselves marginalized or banned from practice altogether by state legislatures, as male doctors with M.D. degrees and state licenses became the norm. New professional societies brought together specialists in such fields as neurology, dermatology, orthopedics, and pediatrics. By 1900 the nation had thirty-eight schools of pharmacy and forty-seven of dentistry. In the 1880s professionals could already join national associations of chemists, foresters, geologists, and statisticians. The number of engineers rose 586 percent between 1870 and 1900, forcing U.S. census-takers to begin differentiating civil engineers, electrical engineers, and those in other fields. New professional groups vigorously defended their privileges. The American Medical Association, for example, fought various plans to provide free government medical care in the 1890s, arguing that only doctors in private practice could give quality care. For many years the association refused to admit women, even if they had graduated from an accredited medical school.

A far larger number of Americans entered white-collar ranks as business managers and corporate employees. Traveling salesmen, or "drummers" (who drummed up sales), became familiar figures in small towns and country stores, where they tried to persuade merchants to carry their companies' products. By the 1880s John Patterson, the founder of National Cash Register, provided salesmen with handbooks explaining how to approach customers "scientifically" and close a deal. Arch Trawick, a young Tennessee drummer in the 1890s, recalled years later the thrill of his first tour. "I am traveling on the railroad," he wrote. "I buy a new suit; have grown a full set of whiskers, very imposing. I have a derby hat, a white vest, an ascot tie and patent leather shoes; carry a neatly folded umbrella, ride the bus [electric streetcar] from the depot to the hotel, 25 cents round trip, the hotel porter handles my bags. I am now a full fledged Commercial Traveler."

Among the elite and professional classes there was considerable doubt as to whether a drummer, clerk, or typist counted as "one of us." These workers, however, generally saw the class wedge as falling below them. Tens of thousands of successful men now earned salaries in complex bureaucracies, hoping to climb through the ranks. They ranged from insurance agents to wholesalers and included, in the higher ranks, experts in the developing fields of corporate accounting, finance, and advertising. At the same time, "management" came to be defined as a standard set of skills, irrespective of any particular service or product. The Wharton School at the University of Pennsylvania offered the first undergraduate business degrees in the 1880s, and other universities soon followed suit, while in the first decade of the twentieth century, Harvard pioneered the M.B.A.

Corporate managers expected blue-collar workers to provide the hands and themselves the heads. In comparison to their counterparts in Europe, U.S. companies developed an especially wide gap between the work of white-collar managers and that of employees on the shop floor. America's distinctive corporate pattern emerged over several decades, and it was both a result and a cause of the weakness of labor unions. In the pre–Civil War era, for instance, U.S. cotton-spinning companies faced less pressure than did their English counterparts to preserve jobs; they were therefore freer to cut labor costs by using high-quality cotton that broke less often. That choice led, in turn, to further mechanization and greater management power. Industrial workers often complained that they were merely "an appendage of a machine." This was especially true in the United States, and in tandem with the benefits of the immense domestic market, it helped build the country's industries into some of the largest in the world. But it also created a management class notably insulated from those beneath them in the hierarchy, less sensitive to employees' needs and experiences. In later eras, as a result, many U.S. corporations proved to be less adaptable to changing circumstances than their rivals overseas.

The drive to professionalize had a different effect on government than on private business. In one of the major achievements of the late nineteenth century, Liberal Republican reformers succeeded in beginning to replace the "spoils system" of appointments with civil service. They launched the process after President James Garfield was shot to death in 1881, allegedly by a disappointed office-seeker. (In fact, the killer was mentally ill, but reformers made shrewd use of the tragedy to promote legislation.) The Pendleton Act, passed two years later, established a basic structure for civil service and applied it to 10 percent of federal jobs. By 1897 civil service rules applied to half of federal positions, and many state and local governments had followed suit. Some politicians protested, with justification, that the system took jobs from working-class men and handed them to the college-educated elite. But over time the civil service increased fairness and expertise in administration. Both were sorely needed. The cost of collecting tariff revenues at U.S. customs houses, a notorious site of corruption and spoils, was four or five times higher than that of European equivalents.

The growth of public schools was a crucial source of jobs for women. By 1900 the country's schools employed almost half a million teachers, more than 70 percent of them female. Teaching had become women's work, so much so that a third of all native-born American women in this era may at some point have taught school. Teaching was one of the few jobs open to educated African-American women, and black teachers served as distinguished community leaders and spokeswomen for the race. Along with teaching, nursing joined the trend toward professionalization, though female nurses struggled to win respect and decent pay.

Other women struck out on their own. A visitor to Tampa, Florida, in the late 1880s could meet the female editors of both the *Guardian* and *Daily Times*, patronize a female-owned bookstore and grocery, and visit more traditional women's enterprises such as millinery shops and boardinghouses. Tampa residents could refresh themselves at Mrs. Hirst's Ice Cream Parlor and transact business with a female teller at the local bank. All these jobs were reserved for white native-born women, with African-American and Afro-Cuban women segregated in domestic service, laundry, and the higher-paid but grueling jobs in Tampa's cigar factories.

The corporate office symbolized many of the innovations of the age, and it had from the start both male and female employees. By 1900 more than a quarter of a million women worked as typists, stenographers, filing clerks, and

Telephone linesmen, Black River Falls, Wisconsin, circa 1899–1903. Tools and work uniforms often appear in studio portraits from the era, as well as in photographs taken on the job.
Photograph by Charles Van Schaick. Courtesy Wisconsin Historical Society.

switchboard operators. Like telegraphy, such employment was "respectable" and offered relatively good pay. Typists and clerks handled burgeoning stacks of paperwork with the aid of such recent inventions as typewriters, dictation machines, mimeographs, and vertical filing cabinets. The definitions of *clerk* and *secretary* changed. Such employees were no longer young men just starting out who expected to move up into management after a few years. Instead, women, who could be paid half as much as men began to seem "naturally" suited for dead-end secretarial jobs, allegedly because they were more patient than men and had more dextrous fingers. The "typewriter girl," dressed in a crisp shirtwaist and dark skirt, became a fixture on the corporate landscape.

Young clerical workers reported mixed experiences on the job. Effie Jones, who moved from Iowa to Chicago in 1890, took stenography courses and obtained work with an import company. She found the job not onerous and Chicago's downtown exhilarating. "[My] office is very nice," she wrote home, "and I have a nice desk right by the window. We are opposite the Post Office and I amuse myself looking at the people who are always around." On the other hand, typists at Sears Roebuck worked in vast rooms of 150 employees and received their assignments through impersonal graphaphone cylinders. Though the Illinois Bureau of Labor Statistics calculated a young woman's minimal living cost at $312 a year in 1892, Sears started its typists at $208. To add insult to injury, Sears employees were evaluated on manners and deportment, and entering a saloon was grounds for dismissal. Thus, Chicago clerical workers who typed and filed for Sears had much in common with blue-collar employees, also subject to low wages and strict workplace discipline.

In a famous speech in 1892, suffragist Elizabeth Cady Stanton appealed for women's voting rights on the basis of women's paid labor. "Machinery has taken the labors of woman as well as man on its tireless shoulders," she observed. "The loom and the spinning wheel are but dreams of the past; the pen, the brush, the easel, the chisel, have taken their places, while the hopes and ambitions of women are essentially changed." Women needed equal rights, Stanton argued, because the economy's liberating power was accompanied by great risks. "The talk of sheltering woman from the fierce storms of life is the sheerest mockery. They beat on her from every point of the compass, just as they do on man, and with more fatal results, for he has been trained to protect himself, to resist, to conquer." Stanton argued that each woman should be "arbiter of her own destiny," raised to "use all her faculties for her own safety and happiness." Such an appeal would have been almost inconceivable a century earlier, but by the turn of the twentieth century, women's paid employment persuaded increasing numbers of Americans that women needed equal rights.

The spectacle of men and women working in the same office disturbed some observers. As late as 1900 the *Ladies' Home Journal* warned that secretarial jobs put too much stress on the female brain and could result in nervous collapse. In a perhaps subconscious effort to ease fears of the unfamiliar, corporate offices took on many of the trappings of the middle-class home. Executive suites featured fireplaces, chandeliers, expensive carpets, and other markers of domesticity. But these offices echoed the decor of exclusive gentlemen's clubs even more than that of the home, reflecting and perpetuating divisions of both gender and class.

The grandest enterprises housed white-collar employees in skyscrapers whose design celebrated the "vertical vision" of the emerging professional class. With the nine-story Montauk Block (1882) and the Home Insurance Building two years later, Chicago launched a national trend toward multistory offices. The city's most famous architect, Louis Sullivan, incorporated large windows into his designs, providing office workers with much-needed light. He explained his architectural decisions with the famous dictum "form follows function." Reacting to the flowery excesses of Victorian decor, he called for "manliness" in commercial design.

The appeal of a steel-framed skyscraper, Sullivan suggested, lay in its "suggestion of slenderness and aspiration." Its builder's message was, "I shall do as I please with my own." (Though hailed for his innovations, Sullivan became disillusioned with his corporate clientele, whose priority was not architectural purity but efficiency and rental income.)

The lives of men at the top of the corporate hierarchy, who implemented their "vertical vision", seem at first glance to have been worlds away from that of immigrant and working-class employees. Yet for both groups, in different ways, "America was work, work, work." John D. Rockefeller, Sr., made it a point to arrive first at his workplace each to morning and leave last at night. He worked all morning on his wedding day (as did President Grover Cleveland) and even after retirement was noted for his restlessness and attention to detail. J. P. Morgan lamented "the wear and tear" on his body and psyche of his compulsion to "do everything myself or personally supervise everything done." Morgan exhausted everyone around him and eventually worked himself into a nervous breakdown. Henry Clay Frick of Carnegie Steel, when he was stabbed in the chest by a would-be assassin, famously wrapped the wound in a bandage and stayed at his desk until the end of the day. Of course, most of the titans eventually bought yachts, joined country clubs, and enjoyed substantial leisure (to the extent their hard-driving personalities allowed them to relax). But they understood the importance of continuing to *appear* to work hard. Even at the pinnacle of achievement, men flaunted the national work ethic at their peril. Andrew Carnegie endured enormous public criticism and damage to his reputation when he went fishing in Scotland during the clash at Homestead. George Pullman, who had flamboyant tastes, met the same storm of outrage when he skipped out of Chicago during a strike against his company. (Public anger redoubled when a judge, improperly influenced by Pullman's allies, imposed no fine for the magnate's failure to answer a subpoena.)

Men such as Frick and Rockefeller, on the other hand, understood that hard work was one of the few accepted bases for the legitimacy of wealth. The fundamental insight of reformers such as Henry George, in fact, was to question whether it was really "industry" and "good habits" that got some men to the top while others sweated and failed.

Why did Americans work so hard and accept such risks and dangers in the marketplace? Each individual was, of course, constrained by the opportunities available, and those who made it to the top, from Carnegie to P. T. Barnum, were only too happy to write books crediting their own hard work for their success. In a mobile, boom-and-bust economy, many a laborer wiped the sweat from his brow and hoped fervently that things would get better next month or next year, when he had saved enough to move on. Hamlin Garland captured this dogged faith in his short story "Under the Lion's Paw," about a midwestern farmer and his wife. "Haskins worked like a fiend, and his wife, like the heroic woman that she was, bore also uncomplainingly the most terrible burdens," Garland wrote. "They rose early and toiled without intermission till the darkness fell on the plain. . . . No slave in the Roman galleys could have toiled so frightfully and lived, for this man thought himself a free man." Farmer Haskins and John D. Rockefeller, Sr., might have recognized each other as kindred American souls.

Americans' hard work was driven not only by material necessity but also by a host of less tangible desires and perceptions. The workforce included former slaves and desperately poor immigrants; their work, however difficult, could look better than the hardships of the past. At the same time, urban young people could use their spare hours to revel in the pleasures of amusement parks and baseball games. An expanding array of mass-market goods offered the promise of "material progress" in concrete forms. Consumer culture held out enticements that promised—or seemed to promise—that the sweat, risk, and long hours on the job might all be worthwhile.

FOR FURTHER READING

On the changing structures of American business, see Walter Licht, *Industrializing America* (Baltimore, 1995), influential throughout this chapter, and also William Lazonick, *Competitive Advantage on the Shop Floor* (Cambridge, MA, 1990), Philip Scranton, *Endless Novelty* (Princeton, NJ, 1997), and Alfred Chandler's *Visible Hand*, cited in Chapter 2. On the dangers of work, see Licht's *Working for the Railroad* (Princeton, NJ, 1983), and John Stover, *American Railroads*, 2nd ed. (Chicago, 1997). Lawrence B. Glickman traces debates over "wage slavery" in *A Living Wage* (Ithaca, NY, 1997).

On the working class two key books by David Montgomery are *The Fall of the House of Labor* (Cambridge, 1987), and *Citizen Worker* (Cambridge, MA, 1993). For an overview, the American Social History Project's *Who Built America?* (New York, 1989) is broad-ranging and readable. On mining and steel I depend on, respectively, Mark Wyman, *Hard Rock Epic* (Berkeley, CA, 1979), and David Brody, *Steelworkers in America* (Cambridge, MA, 1960). On dockworkers see Eric Arnesen, *Waterfront Workers of New Orleans* (New York, 1991). On Homestead see Paul Krause, *The Battle for Homestead, 1880–1892* (Pittsburgh, 1992), and David P. Demarest, ed., *The River Ran Red* (Pittsburgh, 1992). On Latinos see Richard G. del Castillo, *La Familia* (Notre Dame, IN, 1984), and Arnoldo DeLeón, *The Tejano Community, 1836–1900* (Albuquerque, NM, 1982). On immigrant experiences see the books on immigration cited in Chapter 2.

For women's employment a key source is Julie A. Matthaei, *An Economic History of Women in America* (New York, 1982). See also Arwen P. Mohun, *Steam Laundries* (Baltimore, 1999); on Italian immigrant women, Miriam Cohen, *Workshop to Office* (Ithaca, NY, 1992); and on domestic service, three books: David M. Katzman, *Seven Days a Week* (New York, 1978), Faye Dudden, *Serving Women* (Middletown, CT, 1983), and Susan Strasser, *Never Done* (New York, 1982). On Eva McDonald's investigation of factory conditions see Elizabeth Faue, *Writing the Wrongs* (Ithaca, NY, 2002). On store clerking see Susan Porter Benson, *Counter Cultures* (Urbana, IL, 1986), and on Troy, New York, Carole Turbin, *Working Women of Collar City* (Urbana, IL, 1992).

On ranching and farming see Richard White, "Animals and Enterprise," cited in Chapter 2; Fred A. Shannon, *The Farmer's Last Frontier* (New York, 1945), and for the Chinese in California, Suchen Chan, *This Bittersweet Soil* (Berkeley, CA, 1986). Baseball and football are covered in Steven A. Riess, *Sport in Industrial America, 1850–1920*

(Wheeling, IL, 1995). For the baseball Players' League I have relied in addition on Michael Dimmitt Magidson, "'The Greatest Move in the History of the National Game': The Players' League of 1890," senior history thesis, Vassar College, 2000.

For white-collar workers see Barton J. Bledstein, *The Culture of Professionalism* (New York, 1976), Stuart M. Blumin, *The Emergence of the Middle Class* (Cambridge, MA, 1989), and on the culture of salesmanship Walter A. Friedman's *Birth of a Salesman* (Cambridge, MA, 2004). For women's work in key industries see Thomas C. Jepsen, *My Sisters Telegraphic* (Athens, OH, 2000), Lisa M. Fine, *The Souls of the Skyscraper* (Philadelphia, 1990), Venus Green, *Race on the Line* (Durham, NC, 2001), and Stephen H. Norwood, *Labor's Flaming Youth* (Urbana, IL, 1990).

For civil service and government work see Ari S. Hoogenboom, "Spoilsmen and Reformers," in *The Gilded Age*, ed. H. Wayne Morgan (Syracuse, NY, 1963), 69–90, and Cindy S. Aron, *Ladies and Gentlemen of the Civil Service* (New York, 1987). Nancy A. Hewitt covers women's work in Tampa in *Southern Discomfort* (Urbana, IL, 2001), and Angel Kwolek-Folland analyzes the corporate office in *Engendering Business* (Baltimore, 1994). A discussion of "vertical vision" appears in David Shi, *Facing Facts* (New York, 1994), a book helpful to me here and elsewhere in its coverage of the rise of realism and modernism in the arts.

CHAPTER 4

Money

As I know them, there are few millionaires, very few indeed,
who are clear of the sin of having made beggars.
—ANDREW CARNEGIE, "WEALTH"

For the Lakota Sioux, the Black Hills are the world's sacred center, the heart of lands their great-grandfathers fought for and won. As early as the 1840s some Lakota knew that the hills' streams glittered with a mineral that newcomers eagerly sought. They kept the secret for decades, but in the 1870s rumors spread nationwide about "gold in the hills." Prospectors invaded Dakota Territory, encouraged by boosters and driven by desperation in the midst of a severe economic depression. The army, upholding a U.S. treaty with the Lakota, forcibly removed as many prospectors as it could, but more and more arrived. Some came in the middle of winter, hoping blizzards and subzero temperatures would hamper the army's efforts to police Indian lands. One persistent gold seeker was ejected five times in seven months.

While temporarily protecting treaty rights, the Grant administration pressured the Lakota to sell the Black Hills, arguing that it could not stop the hordes for long. Indian leaders refused. Chief Sitting Bull contemptuously proposed getting a scale and digging up soil to "sell it by the pound"—which, he knew, was exactly what prospectors were doing. When negotiations broke off in 1875, federal officials instructed the army to stop defending Sioux lands. Prospectors surged in to stake claims and build the mining camps of Deadwood and Lead. The Lakota angrily withdrew northward; on isolated claims dead miners were found with arrows through their hearts. Sitting Bull and other chiefs declined to relocate to a proposed reservation, pointing out that less than a decade earlier the United States had promised they could live forever in the Black Hills. A few Lakota who settled on the new reservation found conditions so wretched that they abandoned it. The resulting stand-off led to the Battle of the Little Big Horn in 1876, the death of George Armstrong Custer, and the Lakota's dispossession from their land.

In the meantime, prospectors found what they came for, but few of them got rich. A man working alone could pan flakes from the streambeds, but these were just the eroded edges of an immense 480-foot-wide underground vein of gold. Extracting that wealth required advanced equipment and engineering. Investors from California and elsewhere, led by railroad magnate George Hearst, were the ones who built and profited from the Black Hills' gigantic Homestake Mine. By 1880 it produced more than a million dollars worth of gold per year, enabling the lead investor to pass on a stupendous fortune to his son William Randolph Hearst. The 2,200 men who actually mined Homestake—immigrants from Britain, Ireland, Scandinavia, Serbia, Turkey, Russia, and elsewhere—worked seven days a week for less than $3 a day.

The seizure of the Black Hills was one of a long series of nineteenth-century gold rushes, starting in California with the " '49ers" and ending with the Klondike strike of 1898. Other minerals also provoked rushes. Copper and zinc, for example, came into great demand for industrial applications, and Nevada's Comstock Lode yielded such a flood of silver that it altered world silver prices and helped keep the Union afloat during the Civil War. But gold was the great bonanza prize, a metal of extraordinary economic and political significance. With the United States on the gold standard, it underpinned the nation's money supply. In a literal sense Homestake miners dug money out of the ground.

The fabulous and corrupting power of money was late nineteenth-century Americans' great obsession. Women who tried to woo wealthy men were "golddiggers." A person with a gold tooth had a "California smile." In a broader sense, from the icy streams of Dakota Territory to the plush executive offices of Standard Oil, men bent their energies to the search for dollars. Government monetary policy, finance, enterprise, speculation, and new extremes of wealth and poverty all proved critical topics of national debate.

WALL STREET AND WASHINGTON

The gold standard established key conditions of the nineteenth-century economy. To pay the enormous cost of the Civil War, the Union printed paper dollars, popularly known as greenbacks, that could not be exchanged for a fixed amount of gold from the Treasury. In addition, Republicans set up a system of designated national banks whose notes also circulated, backed by U.S. bonds that the banks purchased and on which they received interest (at a hefty profit). This system, skillfully managed during the war, played a significant role in Union victory. But hard-money Republicans viewed the circulation of millions of greenbacks, unsupported by equal reserves of gold, as inflationary and "unnatural," a temporary expedient that ought to end after the war. After intense debates in the 1870s, Congress resumed specie payments in 1879. This meant that, at the federal subtreasury window in New York, anyone could exchange a greenback dollar for its equivalent in gold. Western and southern congressmen forced some concessions to silver, which was monetized during parts of the postwar era. But in 1897, the hardest of hard-money advocates won out and put the United States fully on the gold standard.

This system had critical flaws. Republicans failed to expand the money supply at a time when the economy was growing rapidly, a policy few economists today would endorse. The national banks, privately owned and run for profit, enjoyed special privileges but were under no obligation to issue notes. They often had little incentive to do so, and between 1882 and 1891 the number of banknotes in circulation declined by half. Lack of money kept interest rates high, wreaking tremendous hardship. Money was tight for ordinary people, especially in the West and South, because bank reserves remained concentrated in the northeastern industrial core. Interest rates on farm and home mortgages, for example, averaged below 5 percent on the island of Manhattan, 8 percent in Louisiana, and more than 12 percent in western Kansas.

In the South, where the Confederacy's collapse destroyed old banking networks, cotton farmers could go years without seeing a dollar. Many owed the entire value of each crop to landlords and local store owners, whose extensions of credit often forced them, in turn, to do without much cash. The shrinking money supply placed severe pressure on debtors. A farmer, merchant, or home buyer who borrowed $500 had to pay back that loan plus interest in dollars that were worth more and more. In the same decades, industrial workers experienced sharp, repeated wage cuts. Not surprisingly, many protested a monetary system that enriched bankers and investors at the expense of those who grew wheat and cotton and crafted steel and textiles. Republican policies, they argued, impoverished these producers while rewarding men who shuffled papers or lived on accumulated wealth.

During the depression of the 1870s, midwestern critics organized the Greenback Labor Party, which at peak won more than a million votes and fourteen seats in Congress. Greenbackers sought a return to the Civil War system of unhitching paper dollars from the gold supply. They denied that gold had any special value: government, they asserted, had the right to define money as it chose. As one argued, "Gold is not money until coined, and made money according to the law. . . . Paper is equally money, when conditioned and issued according to the law." Paper dollars, by this view, could be issued on the nation's whole wealth— land, labor, and capital—rather than reserves of one metal. An increased money supply would create wealth in turn by giving borrowers access to cash and loans on easier terms.

In the twentieth century, the federal government accepted Greenbackers' central idea, and today Americans use paper dollars marked "United States of America—This Note Is Legal Tender for All Debts" without expecting to exchange them for gold at a government window. During economic crises the Federal Reserve lowers interest rates in an attempt to make credit (that is, money) easier to obtain and to stimulate economic activity, a policy Greenbackers would have understood and approved. At the time, however, Greenbackism was viewed as heresy by the financial and political establishment.

Ironically, financiers and officials in Washington had an acute understanding of the perils of the existing system. The Treasury faced the daunting task of

Thomas Nast, "New York in a few years from now. View from the harbor." With rapid urban growth, property owners began to build up as well as out, aided by technological innovations like elevators and structural steel beams. Chicago played a leading role in this trend, with architect Louis Sullivan designing some of the first acclaimed "skyscrapers." Sullivan became disillusioned with the priorities of his corporate clients, whose key interest was not architectural purity but increased rental income from their valuable downtown real estate. *Harper's Weekly*, 27 August 1881. Courtesy Vassar College Library.

keeping a "safe" level of at least $100 million in gold coin and bullion on hand at all times, in case a panic caused thousands of note-holders to suddenly demand gold. But European investors were a powerful force in the U.S. economy: interest on their loans flowed steadily out of the United States, often in the form of gold. During periodic depressions European lenders called in as much gold as they could get to stabilize their own finances, and ships filled with gold left New York for London and the Continent. During such moments of economic pressure, the U.S. financial system became virtually unmanageable.

Most spectacular was the crisis of 1893, when the nation's gold reserves dropped sharply and kept on dropping. Banks failed, depositors lost their savings, the Treasury's gold reserve plunged, and it took President Grover Cleveland three years to stabilize the situation with extensive help from J. P. Morgan and August Belmont. These private financiers sold the government $65.1 million worth of gold coin in exchange for $62.3 million in bonds, which they resold through their extensive personal networks at a profit of $1.5 million (not counting interest on the bonds). The deal was risky, but as the dominant American financier, Morgan was forced to act, since collapse of the gold standard would have been catastrophic

"The Buckeye Lawn Mower." This trade card advertises the suburban ideal, complete with a lawn mower that is allegedly so easy to operate, middle-class women and girls can use it for a bit of healthy exercise. Author's collection.

for the whole U.S. economy. Watching maneuvers like this, foreigners marveled that the United States managed to stay afloat. "God is good to his little children, to drunken men, and to the people of the United States," said one observer, "or they would have gone to eternal smash long ere this."

The country maintained its unwieldy and unfair monetary system for two main reasons. The first was financial: all of western Europe was on the gold standard, and until 1900 the United States was a net borrower of European money. British and Dutch investors who bought railroad stock and western land did not want currency fluctuations to devalue their holdings. Keeping the United States tied to gold stabilized the dollar in relation to pounds, francs, and marks (or so everyone thought until the crisis of World War I, but that is a story for another book). The post–Civil War financial system brought much-needed capital into the

United States, but at a high price for American wage workers and farmers. During the depressions of the 1870s and 1890s, unemployment soared and wages plunged. Even in boom periods farmers struggled to make mortgage payments due to deflation and falling crop prices, and thousands watched as homes and land they had partly paid for were seized by lenders for nonpayment. The system operated much like those of many Latin American and African nations today, where governments enforce domestic misery in order to meet the demands of foreign investors and the World Bank. The United States' immense domestic market and diverse economy, however, to some extent helped offset the disadvantages.

The second reason the United States clung to gold was political. Soft-money advocates like the Greenbackers did not have enough power to change the monetary system, but they looked threatening enough that even doubtful conservatives rallied to defend the status quo. The climactic fight was the presidential campaign of 1896. Democrat William Jennings Bryan was the first major-party candidate to run against the gold standard, though he advocated not greenback dollars but the more limited goal of coining silver as well as gold, fixing the ratio at sixteen to one. Bryan's opponent, Republican William McKinley, had remarked in the past on the advantages of bimetallism, but as a candidate backed by northeastern capital he toed the gold-standard line. Gold, Republicans claimed, was the only sound and honorable form of money, and they labeled advocates of "free silver" as anarchists and thieves.

In retrospect, it seems unlikely that Democrats' cautious proposal for a bimetallic system would have produced the desired effect. And since most financiers and businessmen backed the gold standard, Republicans' promise to restore business confidence when they took office was something of a self-fulfilling prophecy. But Bryan eloquently expressed the grievances of millions of Americans disadvantaged by the gold standard, especially rural people in the South and West who had come to hate the northeastern "money power." In a famous speech, Bryan reminded urban middle-class voters where true value lay:

> You come to us and tell us that the great cities are in favor of the gold standard; we reply that the great cities rest upon our broad and fertile prairies. Burn down your cities and leave our farms, and your cities will spring up again as if by magic; but destroy our farms and the grass will grow in the streets of every city in the country.... We answer the demand for a gold standard by saying ...: You shall not press down upon the brow of labor this crown of thorns, you shall not crucify mankind upon a cross of gold.

In the midst of a severe depression that had begun on the Democrats' watch, McKinley won. The currency issue then faded through an accident of fate most fortunate for the Republicans: immense gold strikes in the Klondike, South Africa, and Australia boosted the world's gold supply and saved the system for another forty years.

Republicans may have clung to their gold creed in part because other financial assets were becoming less and less tangible. Capital, traditionally held in the form of land and slaves, took on a new array of abstract forms, prompting an exuberant era of risk and speculation. Stocks, which had once held a fixed par value, now fluctuated in price. On the New York Stock Exchange, which had settled into its permanent home in 1865, an investor with inside connections could buy $50,000 worth of stock on margin for a down payment of only $5,000. He might end up either rich or ruined, owing the remaining $45,000 of the price and more besides. Unscrupulous corporate directors created and manipulated secret hoards of stock, diluting the value of the certificates in general circulation. Brokers peddled stocks for nonexistent mines, while ranching companies listed as assets the theoretical offspring of uncounted cattle wandering on the Plains. Even an honest chief executive could rarely tell how much he or his company was worth on any given day. The scale and complexity of the financial system made simple answers obsolete.

Thus, the line between investment and speculation blurred, and the success of a new class of financiers and corporate managers came to depend on shrewd manipulations of numbers. Successful men (and a very few women) had to master cost accounting and excel at deal making on a grand scale. Many importers profited by grossly undervaluing products such as bananas to get them through foreign and U.S. customs barriers at minimal cost and then revaluing them far higher for sale in the United States. Theodore Dreiser described some of the new financial maneuvers in his novel *The Financier*, based on the life of streetcar magnate Charles Yerkes. "He knew instinctively what could be done with a given sum of money," Dreiser wrote, "how as cash it could be deposited in one place, and yet as credit and the basis of moving checks, used in not one but many other places at the same time." Often such transactions were illegal but secret; sometimes there were no laws on the books that could be applied.

Most bewildering to many observers was the growing trade in commodity futures, in which buyers purchased contracts for cotton or hogs to be delivered at an agreed-upon date. Futures were designed to help companies manage and predict costs. Cereal manufacturers such as Kellogg's and Post could, for example, buy wheat, oat, and barley futures in January for crops that would mature in September. They then knew in advance what they would pay for key ingredients in Grape-Nuts and Shredded Wheat. Companies paid a premium for this guarantee, but they preferred predictability over lower cost. Designed for such uses, futures markets quickly took on a speculative life of their own. By the mid-1880s brokers on Chicago's Board of Trade were exchanging contracts for twenty times more wheat than actually passed through the city in a given year. Savvy dealers "cornered" markets, secretly buying up contracts until they controlled a product and could command exorbitant prices. As early as 1868 a Chicago observer reported "three [corners] on wheat, two on corn, one on oats, and one attempted on rye." The novelist Frank Norris used the famous Leiter Corner of 1896 as the basis for his novel *The Pit*. With each corner grain prices fluctuated wildly, and prices ceased to bear any relation to quality or supply. The spectacle outraged farmers, who with falling crop prices saw their own fortunes fail. Why, they asked, should farmers fall deep into debt while brokers gambled and got rich on a crop they never saw? Even the railroad magnate James J. Hill complained that the nation's financial markets focused not on building tangible wealth but on "selling sheaves of printed securities."

In their novel *The Gilded Age,* Mark Twain and Charles Dudley Warner poked fun at Americans' speculative urges through the character of Colonel Mulberry Sellers, a hapless Kentuckian who tried to make money by raising mules, lobbying for a railroad to run through his property, and selling a patent medicine called The Infallible Imperial Oriental Optic Liniment and Salvation for Sore Eyes. Despite repeated failures, Sellers greeted each new idea and swindle with the exclamation, "There's millions in it!" (A group of Colorado prospectors honored the character by naming their Leadville site the Colonel Sellers Mine. It turned out, remarkably, to have millions in it.) Sellers, with his fatal ability to draw others into disastrous schemes, was instantly recognizable to Americans in 1873. "Everyone knows Mulberry Sellers at once," wrote the *New York Tribune,* "and recognizes in him his next door neighbor, his chum at college, his wife's uncle—the one that ruined the family." Twain and Warner were hardly alone in criticizing Americans' attitude toward money. Ministers warned of the perils of greed. Advice books cautioned (somewhat in the face of facts) that only hard work made men rich. Reformers denounced government's lack of control over speculation, and after the crisis of the 1890s, many Americans looked back on the previous decades with a critical eye. No less conservative a figure than Republican president William Howard Taft remarked in the 1910s that "for thirty years we had an enormous material expansion in this country, in which we all forgot ourselves in the enthusiasm of expanding our natural resources and in making ourselves the richest nation on earth."

At the time, however, critics seemed outnumbered by those seeking to strike it rich. Immigrants from China and Poland came looking for what they called "Gold Mountain." Gambling houses in San Francisco's Chinatown posted large signs promising "riches ever flowing." An African-American author argued that freedom would come "when we [blacks] have more bank and railroad stock." Boys read Horatio Alger's stories about urchins who worked their way up from rags to riches, and young men studied success manuals called *Pushing to the Front* and *The Way to Win.* Crowds flocked to hear Baptist minister Russell Conwell give his famous address "Acres of Diamonds," which he supposedly delivered more than 5,000 times. "I say you ought to be rich; you have no right to be poor," Conwell thundered. "Money is power; money has power, and for a man to say 'I do not want money,' is to say, 'I do not wish to do any good to my fellow man.'" "There is not a poor person in the United States," Conwell claimed, "who was not made poor by his own shortcomings."

Like Conwell, many commentators argued that if a man suffered financial ruin, it was the result of his own flaws, even as they acknowledged steep odds against success. The author of *Onward to Fame and Fortune* warned readers that only three out of every hundred American business ventures succeeded. But despite this daunting estimate, he told those who failed they could blame only themselves; they were "lacking in tact, economy, judgment and persistence." Samuel Smiles echoed the sentiment in four books that sold more than one million copies each, with the titles *Self-Help, Character, Thrift,* and *Duty.* Published between 1860 and 1881, they promised to guide young men through the competitive world of work, which Smiles and other authors described as a violent "battle of life." A man of insufficient boldness, authors advised, "must expect not only to be outstripped but knocked, crushed, and trampled underfoot in the rush and roar of the nineteenth century."

Following this creed to its conclusion, some unemployed and bankrupt men deserted their families in shame or committed suicide. Tens of thousands who were desperate to overcome a debilitating addiction to alcohol chose a more positive course of action, but one that aptly represented Americans' obsession with money and especially gold. The famous Keeley Cure, promoted by former Civil War surgeon Leslie Keeley, consisted of doses of a mysterious compound called Bichloride of Gold. The drink contained little or no gold, but it had powerful symbolic appeal. Its name was a "concession," one observer remarked, "to the prevailing materialism." Bichloride of Gold supposedly purged the body and ended alcohol cravings. It apparently did help some patients, though whether this was due to secret ingredients or the power of optimism only the inventor knew. In any case, the product proved valuable for Keeley himself. He made bundles of money on the Keeley Cure and retired to a mansion in Los Angeles, where he died a millionaire.

CONSUMER APPETITES

With the rise of mass consumer culture, Americans devoted themselves to spending money as well as making it. One of the things they bought most frequently was information, including reams of advertisements and advice about what they should buy. With developments in printing and chromolithography as well as new bulk mailing rates, newspapers and magazines found that advertisements could subsidize much of their production cost, enabling them to lower subscription prices and achieve mass circulations. The 10¢ magazines *Munsey's* and *McClure's* became so famous for the appeal of their illustrations and ads that writers complained they were just filling gaps between the pictures. The magazine that innovated most brilliantly was *Ladies' Home Journal*, which in the 1880s built an unheard-of circulation of more than 500,000 at a price of 5¢ and in 1903 became the first magazine to reach a million subscribers. *Journal* readers eagerly awaited columns such as "Heart to Heart Talks" as well as diet and fashion news, sheet music, and glimpses into the homes of the famous. The diary of Mary Dodge Woodward, a widow homesteading with two grown sons and a daughter in Dakota Territory, suggested how important such publications became. "We have all been reading nearly the whole day long," she recorded one winter Saturday. "I have read *Harper's Monthly*, 'Easy Chair' and all. Walter takes the Fargo papers and the *Weekly Wisconsin*; I take the *Examiner*; Katie, the *Ladies' Home Journal*; and Fred, my baby, the *Police Gazette* [a racy sports and 'true crime' magazine]." She added that "without material to read we could not live here."

Advances in printing also brought an array of illustrated books, posters, and trade cards at decreasing prices, and by the 1890s Sunday color comics. The Irish tenement boy featured in one of the most popular comics, F. J. Outcault's "Yellow

Kid," was a special hit with working-class readers. There was a national craze for stereographs, in which viewers placed a double-image card in a stereoscope and got a three-dimensional effect. Stereograph sets offered photographs of world landmarks, steamships and engineering marvels. "Do you wish to travel around the world and not leave your own household?" asked the president of the National Photographic Association as early as 1871. "Photography will give you hill, valley, mountain, plain and river, city and hamlet, and the inhabitants, too, of every nation, placing all before you for your examination."

Like advertisers, wholesalers used the rail and telegraph networks to build nationwide marketing networks. "Commercial travelers are more numerous today than ever before," noted a candy-makers' trade journal in 1875. "No firm can get along without them." By the early 1890s America's traveling sales force had expanded to more than 60,000, with top sellers earning $2,000 or more per year. Barnum & Bailey's Circus used the railroads to build a sophisticated multimillion-dollar enterprise. Special trains transported lions, elephants, and circus performers, and advance cars crisscrossed the nation on a carefully orchestrated schedule. Employees on the advance cars contracted for supplies, took out advertisements in local newspapers, created handbills, and arranged "excursion trains" to bring folks from outlying areas. The company spent as much as $128,000 a year just on its brightly colored posters.

With their pace of life accelerating, Americans were captivated by a host of convenience products. After 1889 Eastman Kodak offered hand-held cameras loaded with film that could be mailed intact for processing. "You press the button," Kodak promised, "we do the rest." The Gillette safety razor with disposable blades arrived in 1895. Meanwhile, James Buchanan Duke had pioneered the 5¢ cigarette pack. Though wealthy men still savored hand-rolled cigars and rural folk chewed tobacco, time-pressed urban consumers chose premade cigarettes, easy to carry and quick to smoke. By the 1890s housekeepers opened their pantry doors and reached for Jell-O, while Aunt Jemima mixes offered tempting shortcuts at breakfast time. Aunt Jemima herself made an appearance at the Chicago World's Fair. The company hired Nancy Green, a freedwoman working as the cook for an elite Chicago family, to dress in a bandanna and apron and dispense pancakes to fairgoers, showing how good they tasted "right out of the box." In creating the character of Aunt Jemima, the company harked back to the mythic values of the antebellum South: a slower pace of life, rural hospitality, and attentive service by allegedly cheerful slaves. In this and many areas of consumer culture, manufacturers evoked nostalgia in order to persuade customers to accept the new.

Aunt Jemima won quick success because customers were accustomed by this point to other processed foods. Even poor tenants in the rural South used canned meat, vegetables, and fruit. Condensed milk, invented in the 1850s, had been a staple of Union soldiers' rations, giving veterans a taste for it in their coffee. Out on the range, cowboys celebrated the product with a witty song:

Carnation milk, best in the land,
Comes to the table in a little red can;

No teats to pull, no hay to pitch,
Just punch a hole in the son of a bitch.

By the 1890s some products succeeded largely on the basis of clever packaging. Uneeda Biscuit sold ten million packages a month not by claiming their cracker tasted good but by touting its humorous name and portable airtight package. The company's slogan, "Lest you forget, we say it yet, Uneeda Biscuit," proved so popular that a host of less successful imitators followed, including Uwanta Beer and *Ureada Magazine*.

Some of the most popular products offered consumers energy to compete in the economy. With Americans' hurried, striving attitude, the use of depressants such as alcohol was widely frowned on, but stimulants of all kinds gained favor. By 1900 the United States bought almost half the world's coffee crop; the average American used almost twelve pounds a year. Both industrial operatives and "brain-workers" found that coffee allowed them to work longer and harder on fewer calories, especially with sugar added. Sharecroppers were as likely to drink it as Pittsburgh steel executives. "Families whose aggregate incomes do not amount to three dollars a week," wrote one southern observer, "will rather let their youngsters run barefoot" than give up coffee. Living with her traditional Dakota mother on the Yankton reservation, young Zitkala-Sa remembered making coffee over an open fire as a key ritual of hospitality.

Sugar also took on mass-market forms with the introduction of such all-American treats as chewing gum, Cracker Jack, and Tootsie Rolls. Chocolate, once an elite indulgence, became a popular mainstay. At the 1893 World's Fair, caramel magnate Milton Hershey purchased a collection of German chocolate-making machines and soon introduced Americans to the nickel chocolate bar. One of Hershey's by-products, cocoa bean shells, was rich in the stimulant theobromine, and he began selling it to the makers of another famous pick-me-up, Coca-Cola. Invented by an Atlanta doctor and licensed for bottling in the 1890s, Coca-Cola was touted for its stimulating effects as a "Brain Tonic" that would "Renew and Refresh."

Thus, the economic transformations that hurt many Americans as workers helped them as consumers: deflation and mass production slashed prices and delivered an ever larger and more enticing range of consumer goods. The cost of food dropped, and on the whole Americans enjoyed wider variety on the table than they had in the past. One undercover journalist working in a Chicago department store was astonished at how a low-paid clerk comforted herself when she had a headache. Fed up with weeks of scrimping, the young woman marched to the department store's restaurant and splurged on 25¢ worth of Swiss cheese sandwiches, coffee, chocolate ice cream, and plum pudding with wine sauce. Observing such exuberant purchases—especially the popularity of cheap beef shipped in from the West—German sociologist Werner Sombart famously wrote that "on roast beef and apple pie, all socialist utopias founder." In other words, Americans identified themselves increasingly as consumers rather than as workers. Struggling families put up with loss of craft pride, grueling hours, and risky conditions on the job in order to sit down for steak on Saturday night.

Mass consumer culture had clear democratic tendencies, offering the promise of material comfort and pleasure to anyone who could raise the cash. Macy's advertisements promised "goods suitable for the millionaire at prices in reach of the millions," and many former luxury items did drop in price and become widely available. At the 1876 Philadelphia Exposition, wealthy tourists bought individual bananas as expensive curiosities; two decades later a dime bought a large bunch at new chain groceries such as A&P, Grand Union, and Kroger. (One family of poor immigrants played a prank on a greenhorn relative by serving her a banana, which she had never seen before. After watching her struggle to eat it with a knife and fork, the onlookers burst out laughing and showed her how to remove the peel.) Similarly, the tradition of Christmas cards—inspired by an antebellum craze for St. Valentine's Day cards—began in the 1880s with expensive and fashionable cards

"Let the advertising agents take charge of the Bartholdi Business, and the money will be raised without delay." In the early 1880s, French citizens raised money to present to the United States *Liberty Enlightening the World*, the immense sculpture by Frederic-Auguste Bartholdi. American fund-raising to build the pedestal took considerably longer, proving something of an embarrassment until publisher Joseph Pulitzer ran a high-profile campaign in the *New York World* and secured the needed $100,000. While fund-raising efforts were still struggling, cartoonist Frederick Opper offered this wry suggestion. *Puck*, 1 April 1885. Courtesy Vassar College Library.

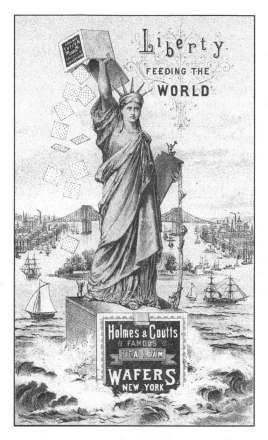

"Liberty Feeding the World," trade card for Sea Foam Wafers printed by Holmes & Coutts, circa 1890. Many companies, selling products that ranged from kerosene to sewing thread, used the Statue of Liberty in their advertisements. Courtesy Winterthur Library. Joseph Downs Collection of Manuscripts and Printed Ephemera.

offered by the lithographer Louis Prang. By the 1890s cheap imported cards enabled many Americans to take up the custom.

In fact, holidays and special occasions were a major focus of consumer culture. Births and weddings acquired long lists of consumer "must-haves" for the properly outfitted baby or bride. Funeral rituals were increasingly complex, involving the purchase of fancy caskets, memory books, mourning clothes, and stationery. Christmas became more and more a celebration of material abundance, marked by trees, stockings, and gifts. The cartoonist Thomas Nast drew the first modern Santa Claus during the Civil War, and Macy's introduced its famous Christmas display windows in 1874. Within a decade, Santa's arrival with presents defined the holiday for millions of American children. At the same time Easter became an important time to buy new ready-made clothes, carrying forward in new ways the traditions summed up by the old Irish adage, "for Christmas, food and drink; for

Easter, new clothes." In New York by the 1880s, afternoon parades of churchgoers in their spring dresses and bonnets became an urban public spectacle, a sort of informal fashion show. Clothing retailers quickly incorporated it into a preholiday marketing blitz.

Mass consumer culture did not prompt Americans to reshape their identities completely, but instead to interpret old traditions in new ways. While many Christians feared rising commercialism was undermining faith, others saw no contradiction. "Went to town looking for Easter cards and buying myself a dress," wrote one New York woman in 1881, "and then went to Bible class and heard a lovely lecture from Dr. Hall on the resurrection." Networks of trade and advertising might even advance the gospel cause. One religious writer urged "the Christian business men of America" to "make the marketplace as sacred as the church." Christian retailing was on its way to becoming a major industry by the 1880s. Customers could choose an increasing array of Bibles, filled with color illustrations and informative articles about the coins, plants, and customs of Bible times. The Gospel Trumpet Company of Indiana (precursor to today's Warner Press) offered postcards, tracts, and inspirational mottoes for sale through independent agents.

Consumer culture could reinforce other traditional identities, for example, the affirmation of manhood. Attending sports events became an important form of male bonding across class lines. And while saloons and taverns were increasingly owned by large commercial breweries, they nonetheless carried on the tradition of the tavern, serving as informal working men's clubs. Surrounded by colorful advertisements as they enjoyed mass-market Budweisers, working men confirmed bonds of class and masculinity. Saloons also sustained the ethnic identities of Irish, Germans, Italians, Russian Jews, and other recent immigrants. In large cities merchants and grocers competed to help immigrants maintain and celebrate their distinctive cultures, offering everything from kosher and ethnic foods to fireworks for the Chinese New Year.

While saloons and Chinese groceries looked disreputable to native-born Protestants, urban department stores became celebrated sites for the fulfillment of middle-class material desires. A. T. Stewart began the trend during the Civil War with his large New York emporium. The Philadelphia merchant John Wanamaker learned a great deal from the 1876 exposition in his city, winning customers through museumlike exhibits, concerts, and lectures as well as fantastic window displays. (Frank Baum, the author of *The Wizard of Oz*, was a professional display artist in Chicago whose belief that people loved to be deceived helped to inspire the novel.) Department stores offered personal services ranging from credit accounts to free delivery. Stores in New York's department store district, christened the Ladies' Mile, vied to attract middle-class women by offering ladies' lounges, tea rooms, and indoor playgrounds, encouraging women to bring friends and children and linger all day. Macy's, Wanamaker's, and Marshall Fields installed elevators and electric lights when they were still novelties. This fascinated the public and gave stores an aura of public service. In theory, at least, any American could walk in and stroll the aisles, enjoying a store's amenities without spending a dime.

But the commercial space of department stores was not quite like a public park or town hall. Managers quickly realized that their profits came from consumers who made multiple purchases, and they discouraged the poor from entering while avidly seeking customers with discretionary income. A tasteful mannequin or window tableau encouraged such women and men to buy on impulse once they had entered the magical world of the store. Managers also quickly comprehended the "Diderot effect," in which buying one item precipitates further purchases. The acquisition of a suburban home, for example, required not only furniture and carpets but also drapes, linens, lithographs to decorate the walls, bookcases (which needed books and knickknacks to cover their shelves), and perhaps a gazebo and croquet set for the backyard.

Merchants and advertisers, then, made it their specific goal to entice people to buy products they did not need or had not thought they needed. Department stores experimented with dazzling displays through the use of vibrant colors and glittering lights. They placed items on open tables to be touched and admired, and they suggested that particular items were not just products but affirmations of a buyer's respectability, religious faith, or love of home and children. The big retailers did this so effectively that a few respectable middle-class women, lost in the fantasy world of the department store, began to steal. In a series of well-publicized trials, women from prosperous families confessed that they could not stop themselves from roaming department stores and engaging in repeated shoplifting. The phenomenon seemed to have no precedent. Why should a well-to-do woman choose to shoplift? Puzzled by the impulse, doctors labeled it *kleptomania*.

Well before 1900, then, the supposedly natural laws of supply and demand were turned on their head in the consumer marketplace, just as they were in the abstract world of futures markets and stock exchanges. "The time to advertise is all the time," declared John Wanamaker. "Without advertising," wrote Frank Baum, "the modern merchant sinks into oblivion." Advertisers launched sophisticated campaigns to familiarize Americans with such products as the W. L. Douglas $3 Shoe for Gentlemen, the $8 American Typewriter, and medicines such as Lydia Pinkham's Vegetable Compound ("for female complaints—from a woman who knows"). Ads plastered city sidewalks, buildings, and barns. Edward Bellamy commented on the phenomenon in his famous utopian novel *Looking Backward*. Waking up back in 1887 after dreaming of a pristine ad-free future in the year 2000, Bellamy's protagonist is revolted by all the ads he sees on a Boston street. "The walls of the buildings, the windows, the broadsides of the newspapers in every hand, the very pavements, everything in fact in sight, except the sky, were covered with the appeals."

While products begged to get bought through advertising, one journalist observed in 1876 that money was "shouting itself hoarse in the effort to get itself loaned." "On credit" became a more and more common way to buy, whether one was a farmer assembling bare necessities or an urban lady choosing to splurge. Though commentators constantly warned Americans about the dangers of going into debt, no admonishment stemmed the tide of loans and installment purchases. Asked how she balanced her family's meager budget, one German-American woman wrote in 1882 that "I buy everything on credit until I get no more, then I go to another store and do the same there." "Borax stores," so named because they could clean you out, offered high-interest purchases to the urban poor, and pawn shops and loan sharks did a thriving business. "We Trust the People" was the motto of Bell's Easy Payment Store in Chicago, though it accompanied its expression of faith in humanity with very high interest rates.

By the late 1880s the level of private debt in the United States became a political issue, though no attempt had yet been made to measure it statistically. In response, Congress directed census-takers to collect data for the first time on private debt. Robert Porter, the 1890 census director, warned in his final report that he had probably missed billions of dollars in informal loans, but the figure he produced was stunning: at minimum, private debt in the United States totaled more than $11 billion. It was a dramatic example of the direction in which Americans were heading in the new economy.

THE PROBLEM OF PECUNIARY STANDARDS

The total of $11 billion worth of private debt flew in the face of some of Americans' most deeply held convictions in the 1890s. Many commentators continued to declare that debt was shameful and should be avoided at any cost. They linked thrift and savings to the much-admired traits of hard work and self-control, without which no man could succeed. At the same time, women's highest calling was said to be the nurturance of noncommercial values: domesticity, faith, self-sacrifice, and charity. Among the many things Americans were buying were millions of copies of books such as Louisa May Alcott's *Little Women*, published in 1869, with its story of how frugal, benevolent Marmee and her four daughters spend Christmas morning sharing their gifts and holiday breakfast with poorer neighbors. Catherine Beecher and Harriet Beecher Stowe's best-selling guide *The American Woman's Home*, published one year later, urged Christian women to practice "self-denying benevolence." Beecher and Stowe condemned the "mind that is worldly, living mainly to seek its own pleasures instead of living to please God." As late as 1875 Abraham Lincoln's son Robert managed to get his mother, Mary Todd Lincoln, committed to an insane asylum in part by demonstrating that she purchased things she did not need.

If this was the standard of sanity, then Americans' mental health was in serious trouble. In his brilliant book *The Theory of the Leisure Class*, published in 1899, Wisconsin-born sociologist Thorstein Veblen satirized Americans' acquisitive practices. Practitioners of "pecuniary emulation," he argued, spent money to mimic the habits of wealthier people. A "pecuniary standard of living" promoted sheer waste rather than taste, comfort, education, or moral improvement. Veblen observed that people often suffered great discomfort and inconvenience to vacation in the "right" way or hold the "right" social event. The beauty of a silver spoon or a manicured lawn, Veblen proposed, lay in what it signified: the power to command someone else's labor to keep the spoon polished and the lawn mowed.

Most famous was Veblen's concept of "conspicuous consumption." He argued that particular types of carriages, clothing, or even diseases (such as gout from rich eating) served to demonstrate social position. They enabled people to establish "invidious distinctions" between themselves and those lower on the social scale. Veblen observed that fashionable dresses were heavy and restrictive, hampering the ability of women who wore them to move around or even breathe. Their design, he concluded, "showed the wearer's exemption from or incapacity for all vulgarly productive employment." In other words, ultratight corsets and heavy brocades advertised a woman's status as a lady of leisure and by extension her husband's or father's ability to pay for her to do nothing.

No one exemplified Veblen's analysis more clearly than Alva Smith Vanderbilt, an Alabama belle who married the heir to a great shipping fortune. Alva had a burning ambition for social glory, but she and her family were shunned as "new money" by Caroline Astor, arbiter of the New York elite. Alva took revenge by engaging famous architect Richard Morris Hunt to design an extravagant mansion on Fifth Avenue, complete with turrets and flying buttresses. With all New York curious to peek inside, Alva announced that a housewarming costume ball would be held on a Monday evening—the night Mrs. Astor traditionally received callers at her home. The Astors' daughter, who loved to dance, pleaded desperately with her parents to recognize the Vanderbilts so she would receive an invitation. Her mother relented, paid a social call to the Vanderbilts, and promptly received her daughter's wish. Alva had broken the power of Mrs. Astor's "Four Hundred" (supposedly the number of people who could fit in the Astor ballroom) and opened New York society to money, old or new.

The party that followed astounded the nation. Having spent $3 million on the house (roughly $43 million today), the Vanderbilts lavished another quarter-million on food, music, and decorations for the ball. Among the guests was Alva's sister-in-law Alice, dressed as The Electric Light in an evening gown fitted with gas jets that periodically spouted flames. Other guests appeared as famous royal figures, including Elizabeth I of England and Louis XV of France. The host and hostess dressed as the duc de Guise and a Venetian princess, and their mansion featured bronze sculptures that had once belonged to Marie Antoinette. Clearly, among the most flamboyant faction of America's rich, democratic pride was giving way to "pecuniary emulation" of European monarchs and aristocrats.

The getting and spending of money became a central theme in the work of American fiction writers as well as a topic of research for social scientists such as Thorstein Veblen. The relationship of women to money was especially fascinating, as writers made the transition from romanticism to more realistic treatments of American life. William Dean Howells's *The Rise of Silas Lapham* described the efforts of a Vermont paint manufacturer and his wife and daughters to break into Boston society. The Laphams shed their country virtues of honesty and compassion as they attempt to rise—thus, in fact, sinking morally until they come to their senses. Henry James's *Portrait of a Lady* told the story of Isabel Archer, an heiress who travels through Europe with her sophisticated aunt and becomes entangled in others' financial intrigues. Lily Bart, the heroine of Edith Wharton's *The House of Mirth*, is a "hothouse flower" from a wealthy family who is devoted to material comfort and unable to prioritize love over money. American writers also explored the underside of the class structure. Stephen Crane's *Maggie, a Girl of the Streets* offered a landmark portrait of life in New York's slums, tracing the descent of a young girl from abuse and seduction into prostitution and suicide. Theodore Dreiser's *Sister Carrie* was even more controversial because its heroine does not die. Instead, young Carrie Meeber conducts a lucrative affair and ends up a Broadway star.

Material standards posed many moral problems. The very goals of capitalism seemed at odds with human decency and the collective good. Grain speculators rejoiced in bad harvests. Speculators on the volatile New York Coffee Exchange were thrilled in 1899 when Brazil went under quarantine during an outbreak of bubonic plague. Anger mounted at the way individuals and corporations used great wealth to purchase influence, and many writers explored money's impact on civic life as well as individual character. Twain and Warner's *The Gilded Age* launched a cottage industry in novels about Washington corruption, including Henry Adams's *Democracy* and Hamlin Garland's *A Spoil of Office*. The machinations of streetcar companies inspired such diverse treatments as Howells's *A Hazard of New Fortunes* and Dreiser's *The Financier*. "The misapplication of public money has become the great crime of the age," intones a judge in Dreiser's novel. "If not promptly and firmly checked, it will ultimately destroy our institutions. When a republic becomes honeycombed with corruption its vitality is gone." But the judge himself is an appointee of Philadelphia's Republican ring, and he reaches the verdict his bosses demand.

Novelists produced an array of broad critiques of industrialization, ranging from Rebecca Harding Davis's *Life in the Iron Mills* in 1861 to Upton Sinclair's indictment of Chicago meatpacking companies, *The Jungle*, in 1906. Frank Norris's *The Octopus* condemned the stranglehold railroads maintained over California's economy, a theme María Amparo Ruiz de Burton had explored years earlier in *The Squatter and the Don*. By the 1890s nonfiction treatments also gained prominence. Henry Demarest Lloyd's *Wealth Against Commonwealth* pointed out that assets were concentrating in the hands of a few. Ida Tarbell offered a scathing account of Rockefeller's rise to power in *The History of the Standard Oil Company*, while Lincoln Steffens condemned urban machines in his famous tract *The Shame of the Cities*. Magazines such as *Arena* and *McClure's* made their reputations on article-length investigations. By the turn of the century, critiquing American business had become an industry itself.

Some powerful titans dismissed the Vanderbilts as nouveau riche and strove to give away large sums of money—while simultaneously defending how they had gotten it. Even before he created his famous charitable foundations, John D. Rockefeller, Sr., gave great sums to the Baptist Church, the temperance movement, and projects for medicine and education. Rockefeller kept his pocket full of dimes to give away to children, keenly aware of the public relations value of largesse. Most overt in his efforts to develop an ethics of wealth was Andrew Carnegie, who was tormented as a young man by the belief that he had sacrificed religious principles for financial gain. Carnegie tried to reconcile the two, arguing that a rich man's money was a public trust he must spend for the common good. Such a man, Carnegie wrote, should strive to "set an example of modest, unostentatious living, shunning display or extravagance; to provide moderately for the legitimate wants of those dependent on him; and after doing so, to consider all surplus revenues . . . simply as trust funds." He must spend his riches in the way "best calculated to produce the most beneficial results for the community." If a wealthy man failed to follow such a course, Carnegie proposed that the government levy a 100 percent estate tax. He followed his own advice by founding an array of charitable and reform institutions.

While one of the country's richest men mulled over the proper disposition of money, commentators lamented what they saw as dramatic new extremes of wealth and poverty. Amid furious debate over inequalities of wealth, few hard facts were available until the 1890 census, which on this as on other questions unleashed a storm of controversy. The economist George K. Holmes summarized what census-takers found: 71 percent of the nation's private wealth belonged to 9 percent of the population, while 91 percent of the population held the other 29 percent. Conditioned, like most Americans of his day, to believe that industrialization was promoting widespread prosperity, Holmes could scarcely believe these numbers. "This result seems almost incredible," he wrote. He reluctantly concluded that "the concentration of wealth has probably gone too far" and warned that "the problem that is to vex the coming ages of the republic is already clearly manifest."

Holmes's figures roughly matched those of historians today, who estimate that in the post–Civil War decades, roughly 27 percent of America's private wealth belonged to the top 1 percent of households and 49 percent to the top 5 percent. Expressed in quintiles (dividing the entire population into five groups of equal size), this meant that 87 percent of private wealth belonged to the richest fifth, 11 percent to the next fifth, 2 percent to the next fifth, and virtually none to the rest. Wealth had, in fact, been highly concentrated since the colonial era; the greatest increase in inequality occurred in the three decades before the Civil War, when industrialization began. A study of Massachusetts suggests that during the severe depression of the 1870s, middle-class wealth did erode and the richest 5 percent got substantially richer. Equally important, extremes of wealth and poverty were increasingly noticeable to Americans in the late nineteenth century, as wealth took new forms (stocks and bonds rather than land and slaves) and a new class of multimillionaires became highly visible. This tiny group constituted less than one-third of 1 percent of the U.S. population in 1900, but they owned about one-sixth of the nation's private wealth.

At the same time Americans could see all around them signs of economic desperation, even starvation. In towns and cities across the country, women's relief organizations geared up each winter to feed and shelter the destitute. In the depression of 1873, one Massachusetts editor reported the "pitiful and miserable sight which we have seen night after night in front of the fruit and vegetable stands .... A drove of poverty-stricken children, often girls, clad only in one or two ragged and dirty garments down on their hands and knees in the gutters, greedily picking out of the mud and dirt and eating the bits of spoiled and decaying fruit which have been thrown away." Visiting New York, the Chinese diplomat Lin Shu was shocked by juxtapositions of luxury and homelessness. They reminded him of a line by the classical poet Du Fu: "'Crimson mansions reek of wine and meat, while on the road lie frozen bones. Rich and poor but a foot apart; sorrows too hard to relate.'" "New York is the most prosperous city in the world, and also the bleakest," Lin Shu wrote. "I look at the slums of New York and think with a sigh that socialism cannot be avoided."

The pain of poverty was made all the keener by lavish displays in grocery and department stores and mail-order catalogs. It was bad enough to be poor while millions in the professional and business classes prospered; it was even worse to see what they had, temptingly laid out in the pages of the Sears catalog and in Macy's windows. The ultimate insult was a grotesque display like Alva Vanderbilt's party. During the terrible 1870s, financier August Belmont threw his daughter a debutante ball "more splendid than the famous one given the previous year in London by the Prince of Wales." American heiresses began to marry European noblemen. The years between 1874 and 1911 brought 115 such weddings. For noblemen such marriages brought a much-needed financial lift. For heiresses these unions were the logical result of the quest for status: in the United States a title was the only thing money could *not* buy.

American onlookers were fascinated and outraged. "Of what account is it," demanded *Life* in 1889, "that Thomas Jefferson perspired, and our forefathers fought and bled in the Revolution to be quit of titles and class distinctions?" Populist orator Mary Lease accused the elite of auctioning off their daughters: "Once we made it our boast that this nation was not founded upon any class distinction," she declared, but now the super-rich were "selling our children to titled debauchees." Newspapers anxiously calculated the sums flowing overseas with every match between a daughter of Goulds or Pfizers and a British duke or earl. "American Dollars the Prop of Europe's Tottering Aristocracy," blared the *New York World*. "The millions belong in America," declared the *New York Journal*, which printed caricatures of puny British fops marrying tall, athletic American brides.

The phenomenon of the titled match reached its apex with the infamous wedding of eighteen-year-old Consuelo Vanderbilt, daughter of the ambitious Alva who had bested Mrs. Astor. Alva had named her daughter in honor of a friend, an heiress of Cuban-American descent who married Britain's Viscount Mandeville. Little Consuelo was groomed to marry a nobleman as well, and though she longed to go to college and inconveniently fell in love with a plebian suitor, her mother got her way. In November 1895 Consuelo Vanderbilt, her eyes red from hours of crying, married the ninth duke of Marlborough. The fashionable Fifth Avenue church was buried in roses and orchids. *Vogue* devoted pages to describing Consuelo's wedding dress, diamond tiara, and trousseau. In a move that appalled arbiters of taste, wedding gifts were put on display at the reception, accompanied by social cards so guests could see who had spent what. (Consuelo eventually got the last laugh. After her husband cheated on her repeatedly and ridiculed the charities to which she devoted herself, she separated from him in 1906, won a divorce in 1920, and remarried happily to a Frenchman. In a lively memoir, *The Glitter and the Gold*, she later depicted her unhappy life in England.)

Ten years after Consuelo boarded a steamship for London as the new duchess of Marlborough, novelist Henry James returned to the United States at age sixty-two following two decades as a European exile. James, like Consuelo, was struck by the contrasts between cultures on either side of the Atlantic, and he struggled to come to terms with the new United States in an extended essay called *The American Scene*. Sitting in a theater in New York's Bowery district, James concentrated less on the melodrama than on people in the audience—Americans of many ethnic and national backgrounds, sitting together in a way, James recognized, that "we had not dreamed of in my day." Pondering the presence of Greeks, Italians, Germans, Irish, and many other European immigrants, James reflected that he had toured their home countries and knew the beautiful landscapes and rich legacies of literature and culture that flourished there. Why, then, had these people come to America? What did they find here? He watched peddlers moving up and down the aisles selling treats to the audience. He pondered the variety of candies that many in the audience (including himself) were happily munching. "These almost 'high-class' luxuries," he observed, "circulating in such a company, were sort of a supreme symbol of the promoted state of the aspirant to American conditions." Immigrants, James suggested, had "been promoted, more or less at a bound, to the habitual use of chocolate creams."

James captured in this brilliant passage many of the ironies of American consumer culture. For the past twenty years, while he had been admiring London, Berlin, and Florence, working-class Europeans had been streaming into the United States. All hoped to partake of what James called "a sense of material ease"—the goods Werner Sombart referred to when he described great reefs of beef dashing the little ship of socialism. Having come to a place where money was the measure, immigrants would earn it, save it, spend it. But, James wondered, would they keep their religious faith? What would they remember from the cultures of their childhood? Would they build a great civilization in America? Would they pass down any values other than material ones? In other countries, James observed, "the wage-earners, the toilers of old . . . were known by the wealth of their songs." "Has it been given to the American people," he wondered, "to be known by the number of their candies?"

FOR FURTHER READING

On gold rushes see William S. Greever, *The Bonanza West* (Norman, OK, 1963). In addition to key works cited in previous chapters, especially Bensel's *Political Economy* and

Cronon's *Nature's Metropolis*, three books are central to this chapter. They are William Leach's sweeping history of the rise of consumer culture, *Land of Desire* (New York, 1993), Judy Hilkey's study of success manuals, *Character Is Capital* (Chapel Hill, NC, 1997), and Thomas J. Schlereth's overview of daily life and material culture, *Victorian America* (New York, 1991). On consumerism and domesticity Ellen Garvey, *The Adman in the Parlor* (New York, 1996) is also helpful. See also the essays in *Consuming Visions*, ed. Simon J. Bronner (New York, 1989). On money questions in politics see, in addition to Bensel's book cited earlier, Walter T. K. Nugent, *Money and American Society, 1865–1880* (New York, 1968), Gretchen Ritter, *Goldbugs and Greenbacks* (Cambridge, MA, 1997), Milton Friedman, "The Crime of 1873," *Journal of Political Economy* 98 (1990): 1159–94, and Stanley L. Jones, *The Presidential Election of 1896* (Madison, WI, 1964).

An enduring overview of the social impact of industrialization is Thomas C. Cochran and William Miller, *The Age of Enterprise* (New York, 1942); see also Walter Licht, *Industrializing America*, cited in Chapter 2. On Barnum & Bailey's business strategy see Janet M. Davis, *The Circus Age* (Chapel Hill, NC, 2002), and on the selling of Aunt Jemima, Grace Hale, *Making Whiteness* (New York, 1998). On stereographs and photography see Peter Bacon Hales, "American Views and the Romance of Modernization," in *Photography in Nineteenth Century America*, ed. Martha A. Sandweiss (Fort Worth, TX, 1991). Leigh Eric Schmidt looks at holidays in *Consumer Rites* (Princeton, NJ, 1995); on religion and consumer culture see Colleen McDannell, *Material Christianity* (New Haven, CT, 1995), and on the saloon, Madelon Powers, *Faces Along the Bar* (Chicago, 1998). H. Wayne Morgan discusses the Keeley cure in *Drugs in America* (Syracuse, NY, 1981). For Americans' diverse experiences with consumer culture see also passages from David S. Cohen, ed., *America, The Dream of My Life* (New Brunswick, NJ, 1990), Daniel S. Boorstin, *The Americans* (New York, 1973), and Elaine S. Abelson's wonderful study of department store shoplifting, *When Ladies Go A-Thieving* (New York, 1989). Histories of two peppy products are Pendergrast, *Uncommon Grounds* (New York, 1999—on coffee, of course), and Joël G. Brenner, *The Emperors of Chocolate* (New York, 2000).

On the super-rich, Gail MacColl and Carol McD. Wallace's book *To Marry an English Lord* (New York, 1989) is both well researched and fun. For more scholarly treatments see Eric Homberger, *Mrs. Astor's New York* (New Haven, CT, 2002), and Sven Beckert, *The Monied Metropolis* (Cambridge, MA, 2001). I rely also here on Ellen Adams, "'Noble Husbands and Republican Wives': American Perceptions of International Marriages, 1874–1911," senior history thesis, Vassar College, 1998. On broader critiques of consumption see Michael Barton, "The Victorian Jeremiad," in *Consuming Visions*, cited earlier, 55–71. On Werner Sombart see, in addition to Glickman's *A Living Wage*, cited earlier, Eric Foner, "Why Is There No Socialism in the United States?" *History Workshop* 17 (Spring 1984): 57–80.

On debt and credit I am, well, very much indebted to Lendol G. Calder's detailed history, *Financing the American Dream* (Princeton, NJ, 1999). On measures of wealth I depend on Richard H. Steckel and Carolyn M. Moehling, "Rising Inequality: Trends in the Distribution of Wealth in Industrializing New England," *Journal of Economic History* 61 (March 2001): 160–83, Carole Shammas, "A New Look at Long-Term Trends in Wealth Inequality in the United States," *American Historical Review* 98 (1993): 412–31, and Jeffrey G. Williamson and Peter H. Lindert, *American Inequality* (New York, 1980). The views of Chinese visitors to the United States are documented in *Land Without Ghosts*, ed. R. David Arkush and Leo O. Lee (Berkeley, CA, 1989).

PART II

The Exchange

For a young woman of the 1880s who needed a job, one of the best opportunities was to become a telephone operator—a "hello girl." The pay was fairly good, up to $6 a week, and working conditions were not dangerous. Hello girls wore big headsets and sat side by side facing the walls of the exchange room, scanning panels that held operating keys, connecting holes, transmitters, and receivers. Each operator served a specific set of subscribers (in the 1880s usually between fifty and eighty). Whenever one rang, a metal flap dropped to indicate service was desired. The operator connected to the line in question, asked whom the caller wanted to speak to, and routed the call. After 1900 operators began to handle much higher volumes of calls, making their work frantic and stressful. But in the early years, the pace was manageable as long as a worker kept her attention focused on her panel and refrained from talking to others in the room.

We can think of the telephone exchange as a metaphor for the rearrangement of Americans' identities in the late nineteenth century. Sitting elbow to elbow with fellow operators wearing their headphones, a hello girl had less connection to them than she did to subscribers sitting in their homes several miles away. The transformed economy disconnected and reconnected individuals. Mass-market magazines, products, and associations created new communities made up not of people in a particular town or county but of bicyclists, ragtime aficionados, baseball fans, and users of Pear's Soap. Political interest groups, from wildlife defenders to women's rights advocates, developed extensive national networks, as did young people who developed an exuberant sense of generational identity. Even Americans' sense of geography got rearranged. Villagers with a railroad station might find themselves more connected to stations down the line, reachable in fifteen minutes, than they were to nearer towns accessible only by dirt roads. With Chicago newspapers arriving on the morning train, residents of Davenport, Iowa, might know more about doings in that city than in their own state capital.

Economic growth and dislocation, especially the "reach" of transportation and communication lines, disrupted old identities and encouraged Americans to reshape their ideas and beliefs. Part II of *New Spirits* examines four realms in which these sweeping rearrangements occurred. Chapter 5 looks at the lives of young

Americans, born during and after the Civil War, who grew up in a world sharply different from that of their parents. Chapter 6 considers sexuality and family life, while Chapter 7 outlines developments in science and medicine. Chapter 8 looks at changing institutions and ideas in the world of religious faith. In all these realms, Americans adapted old ways to accommodate the new.

CHAPTER 5

Youth

The form of the dreams for beauty and righteousness changes
with each generation, . . . and it is always difficult for the
fathers to understand the sons.
—JANE ADDAMS, *THE SPIRIT OF YOUTH*
AND THE CITY STREETS

Between 1853 and 1893 the New York Children's Aid Society shipped more
than 84,000 working-class children out of New York City and placed them
with small-town and farm families across America. The society's famous "Orphan
Trains" were misnamed, since most of the resettled children had at least one living
parent and many had two. Some had been born out of wedlock. The parents of
thousands of others faced unemployment, prolonged illness, desertion, the death
of a spouse, or another family catastrophe that led them to give up children to
prevent them from starving. Organizers of the Orphan Trains expressed utter
confidence in their mission. They believed that big cities exercised a corrupting
influence, especially in poor immigrant wards, and that rural life was wholesome.
They assumed Protestants had a right (even a duty) to convert immigrant Catholic
children, and they argued that hard work on a farm would benefit "orphans" as
much as it did the families who took them in.

Thus, at rail depots across the country, excited crowds gathered to watch
agents disembark with children ranging from toddlers to teens. The society asked
civic leaders to find families with good reputations and keep track of new arrivals,
but hundreds of children were handed off to bystanders on impulse. In the absence
of paperwork some changed hands multiple times. Efforts to check on the children's welfare were haphazard. Pressured by critics, society officers acknowledged
in the 1890s that in parts of the country they had no clue as to the whereabouts of
one of every ten children they had placed.

The outcomes of these placements varied wildly. Hundreds, perhaps thousands, of children endured abuse and cruelty. One teenager placed in Missouri
found herself virtually enslaved, as her foster "mother" conspired to get her
pregnant by one of the family sons, hoping shame would keep the girl in her power.
A much larger number of children were clothed and fed but received little

affection, finding themselves treated like hired hands. "They never touched me or said they loved me," one man remembered of his adoptive parents. "Think what that does to you. . . . They weren't mean, they were cold." Many children tried secretly to keep in touch with their birth families. Some ran away. Others became beloved members of their new families. When birth parents tracked down children and came to claim them, some refused to go. After being forcibly returned to her birth father, one nine-year-old girl wrote wistfully of the Nebraska farm where she had been placed. "I had a nice room, good meals, taking lunch out to the men out in the fields. . . . For three short years, I had love." Many children who stayed in their placements got a good education and grew up to be teachers, civic leaders, and even a governor of Colorado. One of the luckiest, a boy raised in Indiana who went on to attend Yale, wrote that he would "ever acknowledge with gratitude that the Children's Aid Society has been the instrument of my elevation."

Children on the Orphan Trains were apt representatives of their generation, young Americans born between about 1860 and 1900. Millions of these young people ended up far from the world of their parents, swept up in a vast lottery with high risks and potential rewards. Americans had always been a young, restless, and mobile people, and this was strikingly true after the Civil War. The war itself divided Americans into three loose age groups: one that had parented the war generation, one that fought the war, and one that came of age or arrived in the country after it was over. The war profoundly marked survivors of the middle generation. Those who came afterward were shaped in turn by the sense of having missed a great revolution, yet it was they who grew up wrestling most directly with its consequences.

Whether by choice or necessity, young Americans of the late nineteenth century proved notably mobile and independent minded. Many who lived with their parents wrestled over what kind of work they should pursue, how much education they needed, and, if they were female, whether they should work outside the home. Participants in an exuberant mass consumer culture, young Americans began to enjoy a range of activities and institutions—from basketball teams to urban dance halls—designed largely for them. In an era of wrenching discontinuities, young people were often best positioned to adapt.

OUTSIDERS

Young people from the working classes took some of the most dramatic journeys of the post–Civil War era. A common strategy for advancement was for parents to invest in the next generation, selecting a promising child and paying for education or, in the case of immigrants, passage to America. Parents and siblings accepted a future of hardship and pinned their hopes on these children, sisters, and brothers. Those left at home sometimes resented their lot; those singled out for opportunity could feel guilt and intense pressure to succeed. At best, adaptation created chasms between the experiences of young and old. In a Lower East Side theater, one

Yiddish-speaking woman confided to a stranger that " 'I like to talk about the old country, . . . and some day I think I go back; but my children make fun of me and call me 'Dutchman.' Here the father chirped in: 'Yes,' they say, 'What hell good the old country? This here the United States.' "

Hamlin Garland was one of thousands of farm boys, who made the trek to cities in search of opportunity. Born in Wisconsin in 1860, Garland did years of backbreaking agricultural work in Iowa and the Dakotas while becoming angry at the hardships of rural life. He grieved for his mother, worn from toil. "I bled, inwardly, every time I looked at her," he recalled. "Why should this suffering be?" Garland got a college education and moved east to become a teacher and writer. His early fiction captured the grim realities of midwestern farm life, most powerfully in the 1891 collection *Main-Traveled Roads*. With his income Garland bought his parents a comfortable cottage in a Wisconsin town so they could abandon their bleak farm on the Plains. He reported proudly that the effect on his mother was "almost miraculous."

African-American youths faced perhaps the sharpest gap between dreams and realities. Those born after about 1860 were the first free generation, with little or no memory of slavery, and their elders hoped they would enjoy previously unimagined opportunities. Young freedmen and freedwomen poured into schools founded by philanthropists, Reconstruction governments, and literate freedmen, while dedicated northerners journeyed South to serve as teachers. Ohio-born Lucie Stanton Day, who in 1850 had become the first black woman to graduate from an American college, headed to Mississippi. She wrote simply, "I desire the elevation of my race." Day taught in the South for the next thirty-two years.

The spirit of emancipation manifested itself in the lives of young people such as Ella Shepherd, whose mother had once nearly drowned herself and her baby in despair over their bondage. In the early 1870s Shepherd made her way to Fisk University in Nashville, Tennessee, but by the time she arrived the school faced closure from lack of funds. Advised by an abolitionist teacher, a group of students created the Jubilee Singers to raise money through concert tours. Transcribing slave music in ways white audiences could appreciate, Ella Shepherd created the first nationally recognized versions of such spirituals as "Swing Low, Sweet Chariot" and "Steal Away." The Jubilee Singers toured the Northeast, finishing with a triumphant concert for President Grant in Washington. Over the next five years they traveled twice to Europe, sightseeing in Geneva and performing before Queen Victoria in London. Their income saved Fisk and built the university's imposing Jubilee Hall.

By the 1890s the postwar generation began to exercise broad leadership, and their activism culminated, as we shall see in Chapter 10, with the creation of twentieth-century civil rights groups. W. E. B. DuBois, born in Massachusetts in 1868 and educated at Harvard, predicted in 1903 that "the problem of the twentieth century would be the problem of the color line." He urged African Americans who had gained education and material prosperity to use their influence on behalf of the race as a whole. DuBois described this group as the "talented tenth."

The challenges they faced were revealed by the fraction DuBois chose. Far less than 10 percent of black teenagers completed high school, while native-born whites educated a "talented fourth" to this level. The wealth of whites was also vastly greater. In 1890 one African-American editor estimated that the twenty richest black men in Baltimore, many of whom had started out as caulkers and stevedores, were together worth about $500,000. The wealthiest handful of black families in the District of Columbia were worth about $100,000 each. They were successful, yes, but by the standards of the new super-rich, such fortunes were modest.

For poor blacks living in rural parts of the South, the legacies of slavery proved to be a powerful obstacle even to the most ambitious. Ned Cobb, a son of Alabama sharecroppers, grew up determined to escape poverty and live differently than his abusive father. "Slavery just taught the colored man to take what come and live for today," Cobb observed. "My daddy was a free man but in his acts he was a slave. Didn't look ahead to profit hisself in nothing that he done." Cobb had watched white men cheat his father out of his land and savings, twice. He guessed that his father's reasoning was "it weren't no use in climbing, . . . if they was going to take everything you worked for when you got too high." Cobb himself worked his way up from hauling logs and loading fertilizer to tenant farming and eventually land ownership. He was not alone: the 1900 census estimated that one-fifth of black farmers in the former Confederacy owned their land. Yet later in life, when Cobb defended Alabama sharecroppers' right to form a union, he was convicted on trumped-up charges and spent twelve years in jail.

Young men like Cobb found that most whites expected subservience and refused to sell them land or hire them for better-paying jobs. Grossly unequal segregated schools also hindered advancement. After the fading of Reconstruction, the best most black youngsters in the South could hope for was the basic "three Rs" in a poorly funded, understaffed primary school. Over and over, white editors and politicians declared that "education spoiled a good field hand" and that "what the Negro needed" was not books but "manual toil." Asked why black education roused such opposition, a professor at the University of Mississippi gave a frank response: "because the white people want to 'keep the negro in his place,' and educated people have a way of making their own places and their own terms." The level of state funding for education bore out his point. In 1900 the seventeen ex-Confederate and border states had an average of six black high schools. Despite such obstacles, illiteracy had dropped from 85 percent among African Americans over age sixty-five to about 30 percent among young teenagers.

The nation undertook an enthusiastic burst of school building. Before the Civil War, public education had been sparse in much of the South and West. Even in the Northeast, funding had been contentious and limited. By 1900, 80 percent of children between ages ten and fourteen—over 6.4 million—were in school. Developments in North Carolina exemplified broader trends. Before the Civil

War, only half of white children attended any school. In 1868, during Reconstruction, the state began to require all localities to offer at least a four-month school session, including segregated schools for black children. Progressive North Carolina districts began to adopt graded education, which by the 1880s spread across the state. Students were organized by class year and tested annually in specific subjects, with the names of honor students listed in local newspapers.

At the same time, teachers were encouraged to abandon harsh punishments and rote memorization of lessons, which one reformer dismissed as producing "blind obedience" and "dead results." Instead, teachers should try to engage students' interest, "enkindling in their minds the power of seeking truth for themselves." More and more teachers were exposed to such ideas in "normal schools," or teaching-training institutions. Before the Civil War, the United States had counted 30 public normal schools, all in the Northeast and upper Midwest; by 1900 there were 170 of them, located in almost every state.

Black southerners were not the only ones who had to overcome segregation, both informal and formal, in public education. From 1860 onward California schools were segregated, with the state legislature authorizing school boards to deny funds to any school that admitted "non-white" students, whether black, Indian, Asian, or in some cases Mexican. Segregation was a special affront to assimilated Americans such as Mary Tape, who had been raised by missionaries in China and married a Chinese-American teamster. When their daughter was denied entry to San Francisco's public schools, Tape wrote to a local paper. "It seems no matter how a Chinese may live and dress so long as you know they [are] Chinese. Then they are hated as one. There is not any right or justice for them." In rural parts of the state, education for Mexican children was virtually nonexistent until the 1880s. Growers then found they needed to form community schools in order to attract and keep laborers. The practice spread, suggesting that Mexican farmworkers placed a high value on education for their children.

For American Indians, school carried distinctive meanings, as reformers engaged in an unprecedented campaign to enroll reservation children in federally funded boarding schools. By the late 1880s Congress appropriated more than a million dollars a year to Indian education, turning over much of the money to private missionary groups. Whether public or private, almost all Indian schools had the same goal: to obliterate "barbaric" cultures and languages and turn the rising generation into English-speaking Christians. Boarding schools were the favored option, since day schools did not remove students from kin and traditional ways. The most famous was Pennsylvania's Carlisle School, founded by the U.S. Army lieutenant Richard H. Pratt. Pratt began his educational career teaching Cheyenne and Kiowa military prisoners; when he sought placements after his students' release, state universities refused to admit them. Pratt persuaded the federal government to fund his school. By 1895 Carlisle was one of 157 Indian boarding schools operating in the United States, with a total attendance of more than 15,000.

Like the New York children shipped out on Orphan Trains, Indian students took bewildering journeys. (In fact, many of the Indians *were* orphans, often the first selected when reluctant tribes faced pressure to enroll.) Going to school required considerable courage. "When I had reached young manhood the warpath for the Lakota was a thing of the past," recalled a man named Ota K'te. "So I could not prove that I was a brave and would fight to protect my home and land. . . . When I went East to Carlisle School, I thought I was going there to die. . . . I could think of white people wanting little Lakota children for no other reason than to kill them, but I thought, here is my chance to prove that I can die bravely." Boarding school began traumatically, with harsh scrubbing, uncomfortable new clothes, and the symbolic cutting of long hair. Language differences were a painful barrier. Much of the daily routine focused on farm tasks for boys and sewing and laundry for girls. Lessons were, by design, completely disconnected from Indian history and life ways. Use of corporal punishment was a shock, since most Indians thought it both cruel and cowardly to strike a child. Zitkala-Sa described boarding school as an "iron routine" that transformed her into a "dumb sick brute . . . one of many little animals driven by a herder."

Yet Zitkala-Sa's reaction to school, like that of many students, was complex. Having begged her widowed mother to let her go away in the first place, she found herself equally restless after coming home. She returned to school, eventually graduated from college, and became a teacher and writer in English. Apache student Asa Daklugie denounced Carlisle as "a vicious and hostile world that we both hated and feared," yet he met his future wife and many friends there and reported moments of intense intellectual excitement. He remembered when one of his favorite teachers "opened a big book to show me Arizona, and for the first time in my life I saw a map. I was fascinated. When she showed me mountains and rivers I could tell their names in my language. . . . She let me take that geography book to the dormitory and Frank Mangus and I almost wore it out." One Carlisle graduate, Reginald Oshkosh, went home and used his education to help his Menominee people defend their lands from government encroachment. Two other Menominee children, desperate to escape a Wisconsin boarding school, ran away and froze to death in a blizzard.

For those who survived, boarding school offered tools for self-defense. While he was still at Carlisle, Patrick Miguel, son of a Quechan chief in Arizona, wrote back to the Indian agent in English, warning that he knew about the agent's abuses and would report him if he did not stop. When he returned to Arizona, Miguel helped his people win limited self-rule. Other graduates filed suits over land rights, petroleum rights, and treaty violations. Having studied with students from many different tribes, some built upon those networks to create cross-tribal advocacy groups. In doing so they laid the foundations for a native renaissance in the twentieth century, in which Indians would forcefully defy the assumption that they were "a vanishing race" unfit to adapt to the modern world.

One of the most celebrated voices of the rising generation was Ohiyesa, a Santee Sioux born in 1858, who earned a medical degree and became Dr. Charles Eastman.

Young Ohiyesa struggled to resolve a conflict between generations of his elders. His grandmother maintained the old ways and warned against white education, but his father, a Protestant convert, wanted for his son "the wisdom of the white man." "We have entered upon this life, and there is no going back," he advised the boy. "All of the white man's children must go to school, but those who study best and longest need not work with their hands after that, for they can work with their minds." Ohiyesa took the observation to heart. After graduating from Boston University's School of Medicine, he took a post at Pine Ridge, South Dakota, one of the poorest reservations in the country. Eastman never accepted the claim that traditional Indian ways were inferior. At Pine Ridge he worked side by side with elder healers, winning their trust and respect.

Eastman married a white woman, Elaine Goodale, a teacher who had come to Pine Ridge in 1886 to serve the Oglala Sioux and had published several essays on Indian rights. A few years later, when they exposed a scandal that had defrauded Pine Ridge residents of more than $10,000, the Eastmans were forced out by the corrupt local agent. Charles wrote later that he was "disillusioned and disgusted" by the incident, which made him realize "the helplessness of the best-equipped Indians to secure a fair deal for their people. Later experience, both my own and that of others, has confirmed me in this view." Charles carried his medical practice to St. Paul and New England while Elaine raised their six children, but the couple did not give up their advocacy. They spent two years in Washington, where Charles lobbied for recognition of Indian land claims. Charles wrote a series of acclaimed memoirs, beginning with *An Indian Boyhood*. On the frontispiece of some of his books, Charles chose to appear as Ohiyesa, in traditional native dress.

The life of Anzia Yezierska reflected similar creativity in new circumstances. Born in a Polish village in 1885, Yezierska immigrated with her family to New York's Lower East Side when she was a young teenager. In her autobiographical novel *Bread Givers,* she described her stormy conflicts with her Old World father, a Talmudic scholar who, unlike most immigrant Jews, clung to the old ways, expecting to be supported by his wife and daughters so he could devote himself to prayer and study. "Heaven and the next world were only for men," as his daughter summarized his views. "Women had no brains for the study of God's Torah, but they could be the servants of men who studied the Torah. Only if they cooked for the men, and washed for the men, and didn't nag or curse . . . then, maybe, they could push themselves into Heaven with the men, to wait on them there." The fiercely independent Anzia rejected this role. She left home at seventeen and supported herself as a garment worker.

Inflecting her prose with the rhythms of Yiddish, Yezierska vividly described the experiences of young immigrants caught between their parents' traditions and the novelties of American life. In "When Lovers Dream" she told the story of an immigrant girl who falls in love with a second-generation Jewish medical student but loses him because his family despises her poverty. In perhaps her greatest story, "Children of Loneliness," Yezierska related the torments of Rachel Ravinsky, a college-educated immigrant who returns to her parents' cramped, filthy East Side apartment and finds herself torn between love and shame. "I have broken away from the old world; I'm through with it," Rachel thinks. "I must hope for no help. . . . [I am] wandering between worlds that are at once too old and too new to live in."

Yezierska described her fiction as an effort to "build a bridge of understanding between the American-born and myself," a project carried on by other immigrants in less public ways. One of them was Suey Hin, born in Shandong in northern China and sold by her family at age five. "My people were poor," she said. "Two baby girls had been left exposed—that is, to die, you know. They were born after me and my father said often, 'She is too many.'" Brought from Hong Kong to San Francisco, Suey Hin was raised with a half-dozen other girls and at age twelve sold into prostitution. A local laundryman fell in love with her, and for eight years both saved to buy her freedom. But soon after they succeeded and married, the husband died. Suey Hin returned to prostitution, becoming by the 1890s a prosperous madam. She resolved to return to her hometown in China—but not to contact her parents. Instead, poignantly, she sought out the place where baby girls were left to die. There she found an infant whom she brought back to California and raised as her daughter. Suey Hin told an interviewer that her daughter was a "good girl": she would never work as a prostitute. She would grow up as a proud American, living the respectable life that Suey Hin herself had not been able to achieve.

INSIDERS

While working-class and immigrant youth were crossing great divides, the world of white privilege was also rapidly changing. Outsider Anzia Yezierska vividly described her encounter with affluent young people when she won a scholarship to a small-town college:

> What light-hearted laughing youth met my eyes! All the young people I had ever seen were shut up in factories. But here were young girls and young men enjoying life, free from the worry of living. . . . Societies, dances, letters from home, packages of food, midnight spreads and even birthday parties. I never knew that there were people glad enough of life to celebrate the day they were born.

Unbeknownst to Anzia, these students' parents may have looked on them with a similar sense of wonder. The late nineteenth century was an extraordinary period of opportunity. High school and college enrollments boomed, while the stresses of standardized testing and College Boards (first administered on an experimental basis in 1901) still lay in the future. In comparison with their fathers and grandfathers, young men had an expansive choice of professions with few formal requirements to get in the door. Many entered business or finance with a high school education or less. A study of New Jersey lawyers practicing in 1912 found that 86 percent of those born after 1881 had begun practicing law by age twenty-four and some as early as eighteen. College professors—much in demand with the growth of higher education—had not always gone to college, much less obtained a Ph.D. Careers in pharmacy, journalism, and advertising were even more accessible.

In this loosely credentialed world the purpose of a high school education was rather vague, and for most Americans it remained an unaffordable luxury. In a pattern typical of other groups, young Italian immigrants in New York tended to go to school until age ten or twelve, after which half the boys and three-quarters of girls dropped out and went to work. In 1870 about 2 percent of Americans over seventeen had completed high school. By 1900 the percentage had risen to only 6.4. Yet this percentage was rising much faster among Americans under twenty-five, and for an elite group of mostly native-born youth, high school became a defining experience. In age-graded, coeducational high schools, these students began to identify themselves by class year. With the advent of cheap printing presses they published student newspapers and built lively networks of gossip and debate. Male students studied classical subjects that would prepare them for college; they joined debate clubs and even high school fraternities. In sports, female students were at first recruited to cheer the boys (and fund-raise for their clubs), but by the turn of the century they began to win basketball, field hockey, and other teams of their own.

Tensions over competitive sports were part of a larger pattern of gender rivalry. From the 1870s onward, girls outnumbered boys at almost all public high schools. This happened in large part because young women received lower pay and fewer job opportunities, and parents could more easily give up girls' income in the teenage years. Many hoped a high school degree would enable their daughters to "marry up," while lessons in typing and math provided an emergency income plan in case of future need. High school commencement became a rite of passage and a striking sign of the opportunities opening up for young women. *Ladies' Home Journal*, the voice of an older generation, argued that the chief task of graduating girls was "to look their prettiest," not engage in "mental calisthenics." But female valedictorians, ignoring such advice, addressed audiences on such questions as "The Negro and His Right to Vote" and "Some Factors of the Labor Problem." Girls swept the honors and prizes so thoroughly that some schools created separate awards for girls and boys to protect the latter from embarrassment. In an 1898 survey 2,000 schoolgirls in Massachusetts said they hoped to teach, become stenographers or bookkeepers, establish businesses, and even become doctors and lawyers. "It was an extraordinary period of awakening," recalled Maritcha Lyons, a black assistant principal in a New York City public school, when young women began "to select their own life plans instead of tacitly accepting those arranged for them."

Leaving both public high schools and private academies, the luckiest young women could choose from a growing number of colleges and universities that admitted women. In the 1860s Vassar became the first women's college to offer a curriculum equivalent to that of men's institutions, rather than a "ladies' seminary" emphasizing domestic arts. Wellesley and Smith followed in 1875, and Bryn Mawr in 1884. Even more important were coeducational colleges and universities, which constituted almost half of the country's degree-granting institutions by 1890. Among state universities only the University of Iowa admitted women before the Civil War, but during Reconstruction the universities of Wisconsin, Kansas, Indiana, Minnesota, Missouri, Michigan, and California followed suit.

Even young women from prosperous families had to overcome obstacles to gain higher education. Many parents feared college would "unsex" their daughters or waste prime courtship years and leave them spinsters. Young Cleo Martínez, from an elite New Mexico family, longed for "a year at one of those fine colleges I saw advertised in my *Home Journal* magazine." She sent back a suitor's engagement ring, but her anxious mother warned, "you will never find another boy like Venceslao." Cleo accepted the proposal and gave up her college dream. Those who made it to college faced further impediments. At Oberlin Mary Church Terrell was discouraged from taking the challenging classical track. She was told that "Greek was hard; that it was unnecessary, if not positively unwomanly, for girls to study that 'old, dead language,' . . . and worst of all it might ruin my chances of getting a husband." Church ignored them, graduated with high marks, and went on to become a leader of the National Association of Colored Women—as well as to marry Robert Terrell, a prominent lawyer unfazed by the intellect of his bride.

The dramatic entry of young women into high schools and colleges prompted a backlash. Medical experts warned that too much education would channel young women's energies into their brains instead of their ovaries, leading to infertility, sickly babies, and the "decline of the race." "Identical education of the two sexes," intoned Dr. Edward Clarke, who had served on the medical faculty at Harvard, "is a crime before God and humanity, that physiology protests against, and that experience weeps over." But experience did not weep. Female college graduates proved healthy and talented, especially when colleges such as Vassar required exercise, naps, and nutritious diets to reassure nervous parents of their daughters' well-being. Graduates of schools such as Wellesley, Iowa, and Michigan were soon becoming anthropologists, writers, and reformers. The "coed," depicted in her dorm room studying chemistry or elegantly boating on the college lake, became a prominent role model for American girls.

By the 1890s commentators were describing the arrival of a so-called New Woman, embodied in figures such as Charles Dana Gibson's sketches in leading magazines of his "Gibson Girl." In her purest form the New Woman was a daughter of the white elite, fashionable and rich, who made men swoon at charity balls as she spoke fluently in French about her recent Continental tour. The New Woman enjoyed croquet, archery, tennis, golf, and swimming; perhaps she even tried mountain climbing or the exotic sport of skiing that Scandinavians were introducing in the West. On a more ominous note, she subscribed to a new cult of thinness, and she knew—unlike women of her mother's generation—what dress size she wore and the exact weight of her body. At Baylor College for Women in Texas during the 1880s, Gertrude Osterhout was already worrying about these matters in a modern way. Out shopping with classmates in the spring of her freshman year, she agreed to be weighed. She "stepped on the scales as lightly as possible," she reported, "hoping it would balance at one hundred and twenty pounds. But what was my astonishment when the merchant said 'one hundred and forty three.' . . . [I] stepped off with a little more force than I got on with remarking that 'I knew those scales were not right.'" By the 1890s "diet" had taken on new usage as a verb, and doctors had begun to diagnose anorexia nervosa and other eating disorders.

Nothing marked the new physicality of youth more clearly than the bicycle craze, which swept the United States after manufacturers began to sell modern-style bikes. By 1890 U.S. firms were selling ten million bicycles a year. The bicycle foreshadowed the motorcycle and the automobile in giving riders a sense of freedom and personal mobility. Girls' bicycling, generated considerable controversy. For decades doctors had warned parents that their daughters should never sit astride hobby-horses or seesaws, since this might stimulate them sexually and compromise their innocence. Within a decade, bicycles destroyed the taboo. Reformers such as Frances Willard of the Woman's Christian Temperance Union made a point of appearing publicly on their bikes to persuade parents that cycling for girls was healthy and fun.

Metallurgical/Chemical Lab Crew baseball team, Jones and Laughlin Steel Company (undated). After the Civil War, baseball took off as America's national sport. Businesses of all kinds, from neighborhood bars to giant corporations, fielded teams like this one.
Courtesy Historical Society of Western Pennsylvania.

Not coincidentally, at the same time women began riding bikes and going to college, elite male educators took pains to assert that men were men. "Training for manhood" in school and athletics emerged as a clear response to women's entry into higher education, outdoor pastimes, and the public sphere. Of course, other reasons accounted for why men's education changed with the times. In a country increasingly driven by commerce, elites expressed hope that centers of higher education would remain sanctuaries from what novelist Henry James called "the poison plant of the money-passion," a place where ideas could flourish without relentless subjection to marketplace demands. In "The Social Value of the College-Bred," Henry's brother, William James, expressed a similar desire for liberal arts graduates to serve as a "saving remnant," an intellectual class that could think widely and deeply, in contrast to narrowly trained recipients of technical and business degrees. James highlighted the centrality of manhood to this vision when he described the most important lesson of his college mentor: "Stop your sniveling complaints, and your equally sniveling raptures! Leave off your general emotional tomfoolery, and get to WORK like men!"

The James brothers were products of Harvard, which became in this era America's most influential college. Harvard's dynamic president Charles Eliot, arriving in 1869, revolutionized the curriculum and essentially created what we know today as the liberal arts. He abolished mandatory chapel, slashed the number of student regulations, and placed new emphasis on "the pure and applied sciences, the living European languages, and mathematics" rather than Latin and Greek. Eliot also created electives, arguing that each individual needed to develop his own unique talents and strengths. The Harvard system spread to many other schools. It did so despite critics' observations that choice might mean a decline in standards: a 1903 study found that Harvard students studied far less than in the past, and more than half the class of 1898 graduated with only entry-level coursework on their transcripts. "The wisdom of the ages is to be as naught," quipped one Harvard professor, "compared with the inclination of a sophomore."

Yet to Eliot and his followers, such critiques were beside the point. Harvard dedicated itself in this era less to knowledge than to strengthening *masculinity*, a word just coming into general use. A Harvard education came to mean the development of manly character and rugged physicality more than excellence in the classroom. Harvard philosopher Josiah Royce proposed that athletics rather than study provided the best source of character development. Across the nation, flourishing campus sports began to include track, rowing, wrestling, and boxing.

The manly sport par excellence was American football, which spread from the Ivy Leagues (over the vehement but futile objections of President Eliot) to universities nationwide. Its rules remained alarmingly loose. Yale's 1905 team captain was twenty-seven years old and received for his services free tuition, a vacation in Cuba, and exclusive rights to sell American Tobacco products on campus. Players wore no helmets and little padding. Punching opposing linemen was a popular strategy. Charles Eastman, chosen to lead his class squad at Dartmouth on the assumption that he was a fierce Indian warrior from the West, observed wryly that

Vassar Resolutes baseball team, 1870s. Not long after Vassar College opened its doors to give young women an education equivalent to that offered to young men at Harvard and Yale, Vassar students made a bid for equality on the baseball diamond as well as in the classroom. Female baseball playing proved too controversial, however; teams like the Resolutes faded by the end of the 1870s, yielding to other athletic pursuits.
Courtesy Archives and Special Collections, Vassar College Library.

on the football field, he had "most of my savage gentleness and native refinement knocked out of me." Intercollegiate competition was fiercer. In a notorious Harvard-Yale match in 1894, two players' eyes were gouged, another's collarbone was deliberately stomped on and broken, and a fourth player ended up comatose. That same year a Georgetown quarterback died from injuries inflicted on the field. Nationwide, twenty-one deaths were reported during the 1904 season.

Football's supporters gloried in this violence, claiming it cultivated "vitality" and a "manly spirit." Reform bills presented to state legislatures failed again and again. William Harper, president of the University of Chicago, defended deaths on the field: "If the world can afford to sacrifice lives for commercial gain," he said, "it can more easily afford to make similar sacrifices on the altar of vigorous and unsullied manhood." Like the era's industrial and financial titans, football players did not so much break rules as fiercely resist the creation of them. When successful reformers came along they cited, in fact, economic regulation as a precedent for their work. Purdue University's president took the lead in 1894, organizing the Western Conference (known today as the Big Ten) and pointing to the Interstate Commerce Act passed by Congress five years earlier. Like governments, he argued, schools had the right and obligation to set rules and insist on fairness and safety. But football heroes such as Yale's Walter Camp (who went on to become president of the New Haven Clock Company) disagreed. "American business has found in American college football the epitomization of present day business methods," he wrote without apparent irony. He called football "the best school for instilling into the young man those attributes which business desires and demands."

Meanwhile, Austrian bodybuilder Eugen Sandow took America by storm in the 1890s, prompting young men to take up weight lifting. Sandow, the son of a Königsberg vegetable peddler, shrewdly hid his origins and presented himself as a product of the middle class, speaking to the American audience most anxious about its self-definition (and most able to pay for admission to Sandow's shows). At least one of Sandow's admirers absorbed the point: a sixteen-year-old named Angelo Siciliano changed his name to Charles Atlas before launching his bodybuilding empire. In the meantime, crowds of well-to-do New Yorkers packed Madison Square Garden to watch six-day bicycle marathons, modeled on earlier working-class footraces. Six-day racers tried to get as far as they could in six days without stopping for rest or food. So many severe injuries and even deaths resulted that New York City officials stepped in to regulate the sport in 1898.

As early as the 1850s, a few American authors had begun to stress that a rugged physique was a mark of character. Oliver Wendell Holmes, Sr., who ran and rowed, complained in 1858 that "such a set of stiff-jointed, soft-muscled, paste-complexioned youth as we can boast in our Atlantic cities never before sprang from the loins of Anglo-Saxon lineage." By the 1890s his son Oliver, Jr., a Supreme Court justice, was urging American boys "to pray not for comfort but for combat; . . . to love glory more than the temptations of wallowing at ease." Harvard psychology professor G. Stanley Hall fueled such attitudes with his influential book *Adolescence*, published in 1904. Hall argued that each boy retraced stages of racial development as he grew up. Early childhood corresponded to "primitive" society, when men had played with sticks and rocks; adolescence re-created an era of questing. Differences between the sexes, Hall argued, "ought to be pushed to the very uttermost and everything should be welcomed that makes men more manly and women more womanly." New groups such as the Boy Scouts leaned heavily on Hall's analysis, seeking to help boys cultivate and channel "primitive" skills so they could mature to the highest level. The boys most in need of such guidance were whites, of course, because they were said to be the most highly evolved. Bernard

Berenson, a Jewish Lithuanian immigrant who graduated from Harvard in 1887, satirized this line of thought by dubbing its authors the "Angry Saxons."

Theodore Roosevelt, one of Harvard's most famous graduates, summed up the creed in his speech "The Strenuous Life." He equated peace with inaction and denigrated both in comparison with "those virile qualities" that marked "stern men with empires in their brains." He denounced "weaklings" who thought only of commerce, and he told women that if they did not embrace motherhood and domesticity, the nation "trembled on the brink of doom." When Roosevelt became a war hero in Cuba in 1898, his brand of masculinity veered into a militarism that earned the disdain of his Harvard mentor, William James. James complained that Roosevelt "swamps everything together in one flood of abstract bellicose emotion" and diagnosed his former student as "still mentally in the Sturm und Drang period of early adolescence."

Public opinion, however, ran more with Roosevelt than with James. Masculinity by this point translated into militarism, and the new creed of combative manhood played no small part in justifying the war of 1898 and other imperial undertakings. In this context it was not only elite but also explicitly racial. As Roosevelt put it, a "stronger, manlier power" had to step up and rescue the "wretched" men of Cuba, the Philippines, and other unfit races from themselves. Overseas expansion, one author claimed, would prevent America from deteriorating "toward Chinese immobility and decay." Implicit in such claims was an uneasy awareness that white men no longer had a monopoly on political, economic, and cultural power in the United States. In fact, the new creed of masculinity depended, as in Hall's *Adolescence*, on conscious borrowings from "primitive," working-class, and non-white traditions. The most "civilized" men, as Theodore Roosevelt wrote, needed to combine "barbarian virtues" like physical strength with their own presumed superiority in intellect and culture.

A MODERN YOUTH CULTURE

Before the Civil War, America's bourgeoisie had set the cultural tone, and strivers in the working classes were expected to emulate middle-class piety, respectability, and self-cultivation. But by 1900 leisure and mass consumer culture were undermining older norms. As one critic observed, America had entered the era of the vaudeville theater, the baseball game, the amusement park ride, and the department store display window. All of these appealed "to the individual who wants to be diverted but doesn't want to think." The country was producing "a kind of lunch-counter art," he concluded. "But then art is so vague, and lunch is so real."

Vaudeville drew on such working-class traditions as minstrel shows, concert saloons, and variety theater, remaking them for audiences that crossed class and ethnic lines. Vaudeville managers offered something for everyone in a never-ending parade of short acts: banjo players, comedians, jugglers, yodelers, animal trainers, and magicians. Vaudeville began in New York but spread across the country in the 1880s and 1890s. Its long-term impact on the American entertainment industry can hardly be overstated. Stand-up comedy and the variety-show format, both of which vaudeville popularized, would eventually shape radio and television.

Vaudeville also helped give birth to one of America's most popular and lucrative businesses—the movies. After years of experimentation with motion picture photography, inventors introduced large-screen projection in 1896. They quickly found that movies appealed to working-class audiences, tired from a long day's work and eager to stop in for fifteen minutes of light entertainment. Producers obliged these viewers with vaudeville-type skits, risqué scenes, and footage of cockfights and boxing matches. At first vaudeville managers used movies to close their shows, but films proved so popular that separate nickel theaters arose to meet demand. By 1906 hundreds of these theaters had opened in cities from New York to San Francisco, almost always on busy commercial streets in working-class neighborhoods.

The working class also flocked to beer gardens, boardwalks, and "10–20–30s"— cheap theaters nicknamed for the price range of their seats—while trolley companies discovered the lure of amusement parks. The most famous parks were on Coney Island, which New Yorkers could reach for 5¢. Numerous imitators such as Ohio's Cedar Point and Chicago's Riverview sprang up; soon almost every big city in America had a trolley park. Drawing on the popularity of the great world's fairs, parks offered "scientific" exhibits such as reenactments of naval battles and replicas of exotic sites. But the most popular attractions were Ferris wheels and fun houses. Some rides lifted women's skirts, while others tossed men and women against one another and invited them to cling. "Will she throw her arms around your neck and yell?" advertised Coney Island's Cannon Coaster. "Well, I guess, yes!" A replica of the canals of Venice, popular with young lovers, prompted the introduction of tunnels of love.

Proper middle-class adults avoided amusement parks, and reformers denounced the shocking things that went on there, but to no avail. In the summer of 1904, four million visitors came to Luna Park alone. By this point, city youth were upsetting their elders by patronizing an even bolder institution, the dance hall. "Dance madness" swept America, and syncopated ragtime became the rage after it emerged out of vaudeville. In cities from Seattle to Boston, young men and women took up dance styles that brought a couple's bodies and legs in close contact. By 1905 they were "tough dancing," borrowing styles that originated in San Francisco brothels.

Like the movies, the dance craze marked a great divide between nineteenth- and twentieth-century cultures. The dance hall started off as a working-class institution, but middle-class youths quickly joined the fun. They bought ragtime sheet music, followed the latest hits, and went out to clubs to practice the two-step and bunnyhop. Ragtime drew directly from black musical traditions and brought them into the cultural mainstream. The process, like acceptance of "tough dancing," was gradual and accompanied by vigorous disapproval from older generations. In part this was because of ragtime's racial imagery and lyrics. Sheet music covers

Students in a typing class, Broken Bow Business College, Nebraska, 1903. Thousands of young women and men trained for clerical positions through classes at public schools and business colleges. Photographer Solomon D. Butcher recorded this class at work. Note the high ratio of female to male students. Courtesy Nebraska State Historical Society.

projected a stereotype of fast living and promiscuity. Big hits included "Coontown Ball" and "All Coons Look Alike to Me," which won its author, black musician Ernest Hogan, considerable criticism. Soon, though, overt racist slurs began to fade, and ragtime lovers popularized "African Reverie" and "African Smile." By 1899 pianist Scott Joplin was composing complex and lovely hits such as "Maple Leaf Rag," one of 124 piano rags published in that year alone. The American popular music industry was born in modern form, paving the way for such hybrid inventions as jazz, rock and roll, and hip-hop.

The rise of mass sports also represented a break with old restraints. In parks that had been designed four or five decades earlier for strolling and carriage riding, city governments installed tennis courts, ice-skating rinks, and baseball diamonds. By 1892 the nation boasted 348 Young Men's Christian Associations (YMCAs), whose quarter-million members practiced football, calisthenics, swimming, weight lifting, and bowling. Looking for indoor sports to promote teamwork and health in the winter months, YMCA leaders invented basketball in 1891 and volleyball four years later. Newspapers boosted circulation by meeting the avid demand for sports scores, while a moving-picture recording of an 1897 heavyweight boxing match became one of the first commercially successful film releases.

The Beach at Santa Monica, 1890. Saturday at the beach became a summer rite around the United States as trolley companies and railroads offered cheap excursion fares. The possibility of ocean breezes and a cool dip drew people of all ages; the short skirts on young ladies' "bathing costumes" had attractions of their own. Courtesy Los Angeles Public Library. Security Pacific National Bank Photo Collection.

Americans who were not riding bicycles, hiking, or playing team sports seemed to be out rooting for their favorites at the racetrack or stadium.

Baseball won the widest and most enthusiastic following. Labor union picnics featured baseball games; companies sponsored teams for employees; empty lots in every town and village sprouted after-school stickball. Urban streetcar companies found that professional ball stadiums were, like amusement parks, a lucrative draw. On Saturday afternoons their cars ferried hordes of young men and boys out to root for the Brooklyn Trolley Dodgers, Louisville Colonels, and Cleveland Spiders. Those who could not afford the 25¢ ticket to a game could track their team's progress in the papers. For sons of immigrant Jews, Poles, and Italians, following the home team became a marker of American identity. (New York's socialist *Jewish Daily Forward* occasionally tried to explain the game to bewildered Russian-born parents, who found it a mystifying waste of time and physical energy.) A striking number of African-American and Native American players entered the new professional leagues, which between the 1870s and the 1890s were not yet segregated. Even a few women asserted their right to play, though only pitcher Lizzie Arlington, daughter of a Pennsylvania coal miner, made it briefly as far as the minor leagues.

America's vibrant youth culture looked modern because it was consumer oriented, and in theory accessible to all. It was largely secular—notwithstanding the YMCA's promotion of "muscular Christianity"—and in the realm of sports it relied on forms of standardization that echoed those of the emerging corporate world, from complex team hierarchies to stopwatches and statistics. Leisure softened some of the cultural boundaries among ethnic groups and between the elite and working class. On a summer Saturday an Italian-born cook, a Jewish tailor, and a white insurance agent might cross paths at the beach or stadium; while few struck up close friendships, all recognized something mutual in their quest for a Red Sox victory or a dip in the ocean. A certain cultural hybridity resulted. By 1900 the traveling chautauquas, which for decades had provided scientific and cultural programs for middle-class self-improvement, interspersed Chopin etudes and astronomy lectures with jugglers and magic acts borrowed from vaudeville.

It was hard for an old-fashioned American to know which way was up. Men and women in the generation that had fought the Civil War often suggested that the mighty purposes of *their* youth had given way to shallow materialism. They, in fact, urged young men to cultivate courage and rugged physicality—even undertake overseas military conquest—to reject commercial values and prove their fitness to rule. But more and more, Americans gave themselves permission for leisure and fun. The impact of these cultural shifts ranged far beyond the movie theater and dance hall. Makers of mass culture had already learned that "sex sells," and from insinuating ragtime lyrics to Coney Island's tunnel of love, many of the new consumer pleasures were overtly erotic. As Americans refashioned their ideas about their bodies, morality, and respectability, they renegotiated their beliefs about sex itself.

FOR FURTHER READING

On the orphan trains see Marilyn Irvin Holt's *The Orphan Trains* (Lincoln, NE, 1992) and Linda S. Gordon, *The Great Arizona Orphan Abduction* (Cambridge, MA, 1999). On African Americans, in addition to works listed in earlier chapters, I have used Andrew Ward, *Dark Midnight When I Rise* (New York, 2000) on the Jubilee Singers, and Theodore Rosengarten, *All God's Dangers* (New York, 1974). On Asian immigrants, in addition to works cited earlier, see K. Scott Wong and Suchen Chan, *Claiming America* (Philadelphia, 1998), Charles J. McClain, *In Search of Equality* (Berkeley, CA, 1994), and Sue Fawn Chung, "Ah Cum Kee and Loy Lee Ford: Between Two Worlds," in *Ordinary Women, Extraordinary Lives*, ed. Kriste Lindenmeyer (Wilmington, DE, 2000), 179–96. Suey Hin's story is in Judy Yung, *Unbound Voices* (Berkeley, CA, 1999).

On Mexicans see Arnoldo De León, *The Tejano Community*, cited in Chapter 3, and Martha Menchaca, *The Mexican Outsiders* (Austin, TX, 1995). There is a rich vein of work on young Indians' experiences in boarding schools; see especially David Wallace Adams, *Education for Extinction* (Lawrence, KS, 1995), Michael C. Coleman, *American Indian Children at School, 1850–1930* (Jackson, MS, 1993), and two books by Frederick E. Hoxie, *A Final Promise* (Lincoln, NE, 1984) and *Talking Back to Civilization* (Boston, 2001). I also rely broadly on Hoxie's article "Exploring a Cultural Borderland: Native American Journeys of Discovery in the Early Twentieth Century," *Journal of American History* 79 (1992): 969–95. For individual reminiscences see *Our Hearts Fell to the Ground*, ed. Colin G. Calloway (Boston, 1996), and Theda Perdue, *Nations Remembered* (Westport, CT, 1980).

On childhood and education among the professional classes, see Karin Calvert, *Children in the House* (Boston, 1992), Joseph F. Kett, *Rites of Passage* (New York, 1977), Barton Bledstein's *The Culture of Professionalism*, cited earlier, Jane H. Hunter, *How Young Ladies Became Girls* (New Haven, CT, 2002), Barbara Miller Solomon, *In the Company of Educated Women* (New Haven, CT, 1985), Rosalind Rosenberg, *Beyond Separate Spheres* (New Haven, CT, 1982), James L. Leloudis, *Schooling the New South: Pedagogy, Self, and Society in North Carolina, 1880–1920* (Chapel Hill, NC, 1996), David B. Tyack, *The One Best System: A History of American Urban Education* (Cambridge, MA, 1974), and on women in the South, Laura F. Edwards, *Scarlett Doesn't Live Here Anymore* (Urbana, IL, 2000). On young women's body images see two books by Joan Jacobs Brumberg, *Fasting Girls* (Cambridge, MA, 1988) and *The Body Project* (New York, 1997), though I use evidence that locates the arrival of dieting and weight-consciousness a bit earlier than Brumberg proposes.

A key source on elite masculinity and education is Kim Townsend's wonderful book *Manhood at Harvard* (New York, 1996). On sports see also John Sayle Watterson, *College Football* (Baltimore, 2000), Elliot Gorn and Warren Goldstein, *A Brief History of American Sports* (New York, 1993), and Stephen Riess's *Sport in Industrial America*, cited in an earlier chapter. I also rely on Michael Attie, "The Gentrification of the Six-Day Bicycle Race," senior history thesis, Vassar College, 1999. On bodybuilding and changing standards of male physicality, see John E. Kasson, *Houdini, Tarzan, and the Perfect Man* (New York, 2001). On political and military ramifications of the "new masculinity," see Kristin L. Hoganson, *Fighting for American Manhood* (New Haven, CT, 1998). General overviews of changing male roles are E. Anthony Rotundo, *American Manhood* (New York, 1993), and the essays in *Meanings for Manhood*, ed. Mark C. Carnes and Clyde Griffen (Chicago, 1990).

Three histories of consumer amusements in this era are Robert W. Snyder, *The Voice of the City* (New York, 1989), John E. Kasson, *Amusing the Million* (New York, 1978), and David Nasaw, *Going Out* (Cambridge, MA, 1993). On the birth of motion pictures see Robert Sklar, *Movie-Made America*, 2nd ed. (New York, 1994), and on dance halls and "charity girls," Kathy Peiss, *Cheap Amusements* (Philadelphia, 1986). An insightful examination of class relations and culture in these decades is Lawrence Levine, *Highbrow/Lowbrow* (Cambridge, MA, 1988). On ragtime see Edward A. Berlin, *Ragtime* (Berkeley, CA, 1980), and David A. Jasen and Gene Jones, *That American Rag* (New York, 2000).

CHAPTER 6

Sex

The strongest motive power in the world is the attraction
between the sexes. It even exceeds the desire for gain.
—MRS. E. B. DUFFEY, *WHAT WOMEN SHOULD KNOW*

In the early decades of Queen Victoria's reign (1837–1901), Anglo Americans so closely followed Britain's cultural lead that society on both sides of the Atlantic was described as "Victorian." The word conjures up parasols and bustles, over-stuffed parlor furniture, and sexual prudery. According to legend, Victorian etiquette books advised housekeepers to place covers over the immodestly exposed legs of their pianos and to keep books by male and female authors on separate shelves. Sex outside wedlock was supposed to be shocking, and respectable women too pure to feel any sexual desire. Ideas like these did hold considerable influence in the 1800s. Unmarried girls and courting couples were usually chaperoned. Many young women learned little about sex, being told only that doctors brought babies in their medical kits. Experts warned that too much sexual activity caused mental and physical weakness, and one infamous advice book instructed married couples to schedule sexual intercourse once every three years, between the hours of 11 A.M and noon. The author even made recommendations on what to eat that day for breakfast.

But today's caricature of Victorian primness would have looked alien to Americans in the decades after the Civil War. For one thing, it describes little of the experience of working-class people, including millions from non-Anglo back-grounds. The barrelhouse dance music of the black South was famously explicit ("squat low, mama, let your daddy see / You got somethin' that's worryin' me") but many rural and frontier whites shared non-Victorian mores. Farming couples in the Ozarks planted spring crops and then went out before sunrise to make love in the field, which supposedly ensured a good harvest. Arkansas fiddle tunes had names such as "Take Your Fingers Out of My Pants" and "Grease My Pecker, Sally Ann," while a square-dance lyric moved from the suggestive to the specific:

Lead the ace and trump the king,
Let me feel that pretty little thing,
Up and at 'em, everybody dance,
Goose that gal and watch her prance.

Ladies do the shimmy, down goes her britches,
In goes a little thing about six inches.

Though historians as yet know little about the sex lives of working-class Americans in this era, customs like these hardly suggest a "Victorian" mentality. Even among the elite, many married couples enjoyed passionate sexual relations. One respectable lady asked her husband to write her a naughty letter, "for it makes me want you a lot to read one." The wife of an army officer teased her husband for having once courted another girl; that woman, she wrote in a letter, could never have handled "your long Tom!!!" While they cautioned against excessive lust, most advice books told husbands they had a conjugal duty to satisfy their wives in bed.

To the extent it existed, sexual Victorianism was on the wane by the post–Civil War years. By the 1890s even young women from the elite stepped out on "dates" without chaperones, and the diaries of high school students record considerable flirting and sex games. Claude Bowers, president of his class at Indianapolis High School, reported after one party that he had enjoyed "50 kisses, 3 girls on lap, 25 embraces. . . . Ye Gods!" Married women also began to challenge Victorian restrictions on their conduct. In the 1880s a furor erupted in one Iowa town when Methodist ladies appeared in a local production of Gilbert and Sullivan's *Pirates of Penzance* wearing costumes that revealed their legs. The minister denounced them the following Sunday with a sermon drawn from Revelation 19:2: "He hath judged the great whore which did corrupt the earth with her fornications." The amateur actresses blushed angrily, and one got up and walked out of church.

While definitions of respectability shifted, a flourishing world of commercialized sex and sexual crime contradicted supposed Victorian norms. Prostitution probably reached an all-time national per capita peak in the 1870s. New York's vice district was the most notorious, occupying many blocks along Broadway and offering every imaginable performance and service. But across the country, luxurious brothels served elite men in privacy and comfort, while prostitutes in "cribs" worked in horrific, degraded conditions, sometimes servicing dozens of partners per night. At least 2,500 prostitutes, half of them Chinese, worked in San Francisco by 1870. Officials counted 517 brothels in Philadelphia. Lumber and mining camps were as notorious as big cities.

For most prostitutes, life held little glamour. Virtually every prostitute in Virginia City, Nevada, dealt with the physical and emotional pain of the job by abusing alcohol, cocaine, opiates, or all three at once. Venereal disease was rampant and suicide by morphine so common that newspapers often just reported that "another unfortunate" had "ended her life by the usual means." A high percentage of prostitutes suffered rapes, beatings, and knife attacks. A study of Chinese prostitutes in California found they were vulnerable to kidnapping and extortion by Chinese bosses and racially motivated assaults by non-Chinese customers.

What worried respectable Americans most about the sex trade, in addition to the plight of its victims, was the challenge of drawing a clear boundary between themselves and what was politely called the demimonde (a "half-world" of doubtful morality). Red-light districts often abutted downtown businesses and working-class residences. Predation at work was a constant danger for wage-earning women. Leonora Barry, an investigator for the Knights of Labor, documented an array of complaints by female workers ranging from demands for sexual favors to outright rape on the factory floor. In an 1888 Minnesota strike female garment workers demanded, as a condition for returning to the job, that male clerks stop "trying to mash us when we go to and from work." One journalist, working undercover at a Chicago department store, was shocked by the dangers she confronted after her shift ended at 10 P.M. "There were always men on the street corners," she reported. "Almost every morning the girls had some story to tell of encounters with men of that class." One night a menacing man stalked her as she made her way home. Terrified, she sprinted the last two blocks to her apartment building and slammed the door just before the man could force his way in.

Sexual exploitation was a notorious danger for women in domestic service. This was especially true in the South, where as a legacy of slavery many male employers expected sexual access to black women who worked in their households. Echoing the sentiments of many parents, one African-American woman wrote that "there is no sacrifice I would not make, no hardship I would not undergo rather than allow my daughters to go in service where they would be thrown constantly in contact with Southern white men, for they consider the colored girl their special prey." In northern cities, as well, investigators found that a high percentage of prostitutes were former domestic workers who had been raped or seduced by employers. (If one was going to be forced into sex on the job, some women reasoned, why not earn the high wages of a prostitute rather than the pittance of a maid?) Reformers were as distressed by such discoveries as they were by the fact that some respectable women contracted syphilis from husbands who visited brothels.

Marriage did not always provide women with physical security and sexual respect. Women wrote sadly in their diaries about acquaintances who were married to alcoholic or abusive men and suffered "hell on earth," often with the specific implication of marital rape. Domestic violence was nothing new, but it became a topic of public alarm as women won legal redress and the problem came out in the open. Newspapers began to report cases of women who secured divorces after extreme sexual abuse. "[He] would force me to submit to him," testified one petitioner, "so that often I could not get out of bed. . . . I would beg him not to do it as I was so very sick. The only answer he gave me was 'you damned bitch, you have no business being a woman.'" One frontier husband told a judge "he would not give two cents and a half for a wife like [his own], who did not give a man all he wanted. . . . It did not seem to hurt whores to be treated in that way and he did not see why it should hurt his wife." In Sacramento a married man with two young children greeted a coworker with this story: "You ought to have been with me last night. I went to Lafferty's stable and got me a buggy and took a ride out aways and met a young cunt, and I took her over the levee and fucked her three times and made her suck my cock." The statement emerged in his trial for rape, of which he was duly convicted.

Much more common than such gross brutality was a set of widespread, stubbornly un-Victorian assumptions about male sexual privilege. After a painful divorce, Rheta Dorr moved from Seattle to New York and found that as a divorcée she attracted scores of "game-hunters" who plied her with drinks and told lewd stories to try to get her into bed. Male college students wrote cheerfully to classmates about girls they had managed to "screw." When in the 1880s middle-class women campaigned to raise the age of consent for girls (which most states set at ten or twelve), numerous legislators opposed this. One Nebraska lawmaker dismissed it as "a measure built on sickly sentimentalism." A Texan predicted the law would allow "working girls" to "blackmail their employers," while a Kentucky legislator, in an even more telling objection, claimed it would put black women "on the same plane as the white female." Writing in the midst of the debate, one medical authority claimed *all* laws against rape were superfluous because no virtuous woman could possibly be raped as long as she was conscious—and if she lost consciousness, she could not testify accurately. Such attitudes suggest a certain thinness to men's veneer of Victorian respectability.

Even the highest circles of society and finance—perhaps especially these—underwent a parade of sex scandals in the post–Civil War decades. One of the most famous involved Congregational minister Henry Ward Beecher of New York, whose love affair with the wife of a parishioner was exposed in 1874. U.S. senator Roscoe Conkling had a famous liaison with Kate Chase Sprague, the married daughter of Lincoln's secretary of the Treasury. Conkling's Senate colleague from Kentucky, W. C. P. Breckenridge, was convicted of seducing and abandoning an unmarried girl. New Yorkers followed the misdeeds of financier Jim Fisk, who was shot to death by his mistress's new lover, and shipping titan Commodore Vanderbilt, whose affairs included simultaneous flings with women's rights advocate Victoria Woodhull and her sister Tennessee Claflin. Philadelphia's elite was shocked by the adultery of streetcar magnate Charles Yerkes, who divorced his wife to marry his ambitious lover. If anything made the Gilded Age "gilded," it was a sense that sexual intimacy, the last refuge of noncommercial relations, was being polluted by money and greed. To some extent, "Victorianism" itself was a response to seismic shifts in both economic and sexual relations. When people worked for "home protection," they sought to preserve marriage, family, and religious faith from what seemed to be all-consuming material values.

WIVES AND HUSBANDS

During his first term as president, Grover Cleveland undertook one overwhelmingly popular act: he got married. His fiancée, Frances Folsom, was the daughter of a deceased colleague, and at the time of their White House wedding in 1886, she had just turned twenty-two. (Her husband was forty-nine.) Americans went wild for "Frankie," who combined a boyish nickname with an elite education that had begun at a newfangled French kindergarten and ended at Wells College in upstate New York. Newspapers reported so avidly on the couple's honeymoon that the

groom complained about lack of privacy. Cleveland Democrats churned out celebratory books such as *The Bride of the White House*, while even the Republican
New York Tribune admitted that "no American wedding has attracted such general
and amiable attention." Advertisers borrowed the first lady's face (over the
Clevelands' objections) to sell everything from soap to thread. In the next presidential campaign, young women formed Frankie Cleveland clubs to march in
Democratic parades.

The Cleveland wedding bestowed political benefits on the groom. It domes-
ticated the Democratic Party, which had nominated a striking number of
bachelors in the previous three decades, while Republicans had celebrated
the moral influence of mothers and wives. Americans who remembered the lingering death of President James Garfield, welcomed the wedding as a joyful
counterpoint to that moment of national mourning. Most of all, the wedding reassured Americans about the intentions of a rising generation of college-educated
women. Instead of reform work or a professional career, Frances Cleveland chose
domestic life with a portly older husband. In fact, she largely disappeared from
public view after the wedding, though the birth of the couple's first child, "Baby
Ruth," sparked another round of feverish publicity and the marketing of a new
candy bar.

Americans at the time found themselves anxious and uncertain about marriage. After the Civil War, in keeping with other reforms, divorce became legal
everywhere in the United States. (On the eve of the war, abolitionist Massachusetts
had had some of the country's most liberal divorce laws, while secessionist South
Carolina had been the only state where no divorce could be obtained for any
reason. Divorce reform and Emancipation—which removed slaves from the legal
"family unit"—thus went hand in hand.) Divorce advocates hoped that the reform
would end bad matches and keep the institution of marriage purer and healthier
than in the past. A "good marriage law is prevention," as one sociologist put it,
"whereas a good divorce law is cure." The number of divorces skyrocketed in the
1870s and 1880s, and a few states, such as Indiana, became virtual divorce mills.
Americans at the same time faced, more than ever before, the uncomfortable fact
that marriage was a kind of contract in an era when contracts (and the ability to
make and break them) reigned supreme in law.

Idealists saw marriage as the ultimate expression of the romantic self. Some
argued that every individual had a single divinely ordained partner somewhere in
the world, and only with that person could his or her soul achieve fullest development. But for many immigrants and rural folk, marriage arose from more pragmatic
concerns. A southern Italian man, working as a railroad boss in New Jersey,
remarked to friends that he "could be happily married on my present salary."
"I didn't do anything about it," he remembered, "but my friends did, for in about a
month's time I had received several photographs of girls of my hometown and
other towns adjoining; so that I was not long in selecting one which appealed to
me." Soon after her arrival, his wife was contributing to the household income by
cooking and washing for two dozen men.

Table 6.1 Estimated Fertility Rates for the White U.S. Population, 1850–1910

YEAR	ESTIMATED FERTILITY RATE
1850	5.24
1860	5.21
1870	4.47
1880	4.24
1890	3.87
1900	3.56
1910	3.42

A long, precipitous decline in the birthrate resulted in the average adult white woman bearing roughly three children by the early twentieth century, down from an average of about seven children a century earlier. Historians still debate how this was accomplished, but it appears that contraceptives were widely used (though little mentioned). The decline was most dramatic for the urban middle classes; their children were not "assets" on the family balance sheet at an early age, as in rural and working-class households, but instead were expensive to raise and educate, with the goal of longer-term prosperity in mind.

Source: *Ansley J. Coale and Melvin Zelnik,* New Estimates of Fertility and Population in the United States *(Princeton, NJ, 1963).*

Middle-class Americans, uncomfortable with such matter-of-fact calculations, were even more disturbed by lurid tales of sin and lust in high society, such as Charles Reade's 1871 best-seller *A Terrible Temptation*. Some members of the elite quietly deplored the decline of morals among their own class. Edith Wharton, a daughter of New York's upper crust, structured her story "New Year's Day" around whispers of adultery. A matron in Wharton's *House of Mirth* laments "what society is coming to. Some one said the other day that there was a divorce and a case of appendicitis in every family one knows."

Interracial marriage was an explosive issue in all parts of the country, especially in the South. Such marriages were legalized in many states during Reconstruction, but only briefly; as early as 1877 a white Alabama woman, Julia Green, spent two years in prison for the crime of marrying a black man. The rise of formal segregation was linked to fears over cross-racial sexual contact, with segregation laws designed largely to separate white women from black men. Spaces designed for men only, such as racetracks and saloons (not to mention brothels), remained largely unsegregated. So did private homes where black women, working as cooks, nursemaids, and housekeepers, worked intimately with white women and children. In the meantime, cross-racial marriages in other regions became more stigmatized in the 1890s. Western states exceeded the South in passing laws that forbade the marriage of whites to blacks, Asians, and American Indians.

In a positive development, rapidly growing urban populations stimulated creative ideas for modernizing marriage and family life. Utopian writers envisioned cooperative kitchens and laundries, whose efficiency and convenience would rescue women from isolation in the home. Charlotte Perkins Gilman drew on her own unhappy experience in *Women and Economics*, a landmark feminist analysis

"The Latest Nobleman. 'Girls, girls, don't press his Grace! He can only take one of you, and with him it is purely a matter of business.'" In the 1890s, the "Gibson Girl" became a model of female sophistication and beauty. Charles Dana Gibson often depicted his slim-waisted young women golfing or walking outdoors. Here he depicts them in high society, commenting on the phenomenon of "titled matches" between American heiresses and English aristocrats. Charles Dana Gibson, *Sketches and Cartoons* (New York, 1898).

published in 1898. Gilman argued that the problem with marriage was women's economic dependency. The wife's role was "over-sex-specialized": all wives were expected to keep house and raise children even though many found themselves (as Gilman had) painfully unsuited to these tasks. Gilman suggested that isolating children in the home with a miserable mother might be bad for everyone involved, and she proposed cooperative day care centers that would provide expert, professional care while freeing many women for other pursuits.

Gilman's ideas were radical for the 1890s, but one project she endorsed, day care for the children of working mothers, already existed in experimental form. By 1892 urban reformers had opened ninety day nurseries in the United States, a number that grew exponentially over the next two decades. Philadelphia Sunday School teacher Hannah Biddle, who developed one of the nation's first day nurseries in 1863, was motivated by the experience of finding working-class children locked into apartments alone while their mothers were at work. "I was moved with pity for the forlorn children who were left all day," she later wrote, "either shut up in their homes, or allowed to wander about the streets. . . . I thought of the Creche I had seen in Paris and was sure that was the best way to brighten the lives of these children." Early child care centers focused on strict schedules and discipline; they lacked toys, and some mothers urged that their children get more outdoor playtime.

CHOICE OF A LIFE TIME

Advertisement for "The Rambler Bicycle," American Bicycle Company. "Many of the first wheels made in the great Rambler factories, twenty-one years ago," read the accompanying text, "were ridden by boys whose whole families to-day ride." This image reflects the growing popularity of family entertainment, vigorous exercise for all, and male domesticity: the husband and father enjoys riding bicycles with his family on the weekend, rather than getting together with other men. *Harper's Weekly*, 14 April, 1900, 352. Courtesy Vassar College Library.

But day nursery founders acknowledged that some women worked as breadwinners. From 1898 onward, the National Federation of Day Nurseries provided opportunities for research and advocacy of child care and family welfare needs.

Along with shifting expectations for wives and mothers, husbands' obligation to provide necessities for their wives and children also came into question. In one turn-of-the-century case, Wanamaker's Department Store sued the husband of a customer who ran up substantial debts buying toys, shoes, and linens. The store argued that a husband was legally responsible for his wife's purchase of "necessities . . . in view of her position in life." New York courts reversed themselves twice before making a final ruling against Wanamaker's. The old rule did not apply, they decided, when a woman bought tablecloths and napkins without telling her husband. A wife, in other words, might be supported financially by her husband, but when she shopped she acquired debts on her own.

Almost every major policy debate touched in some way upon marriage. Was the Freedmen's Bureau helping to model proper marital relations for former slaves?

Did Union widows' pensions, which ended when the recipients remarried, encourage immoral cohabitation? Did the Republican tariff enable wives to stay out of the workplace and elevate home life for their husbands and children, or did it force them to pay more when they went shopping? The Woman's Christian Temperance Union shrewdly chose the name *Home Protection* for its women's suffrage campaign, arguing that wives and mothers needed the temperance ballot to shield their families from the ravages of liquor.

Another home protection battle was fought over Mormon plural marriage, a practice that had begun in the 1840s. Politicians, especially Republicans, denounced polygamy as dreadful. Diaries and letters by plural wives suggest that their experiences varied greatly. Patty Bartlett Sessions, a successful Utah midwife, wrote that she "felt as though her heart would break" when her husband took a second wife, a woman Sessions judged to be self-centered and lazy. But other "sister wives" became close friends, and some felt closer to each other than to their husbands. Annie Clark Tanner, a second wife, named her baby Jennie in honor of the first wife, who had been unable to bear a child.

Ignoring such evidence, reformers and Republicans insisted that Mormon women were degraded creatures trapped in "harems" on American soil. Until the Mormon hierarchy officially abolished plural marriage in 1890, the practice was under continuous attack. Missionaries set up a "rescue home" in Salt Lake City to lure plural wives away from their families and offer them training for paid employment. (Very few took up the offer.) In the name of protecting womanhood, Congress even disfranchised Utah women in 1887, after Utah became the second federal territory to give women the vote. The bill's sponsors argued that Mormon women's votes were helping to sustain polygamy.

Indian agents and missionaries sought to suppress polygamy among native peoples who practiced it. Under pressure from government agents, a Northern Cheyenne named Wooden Leg agreed after much anguish to send away his second wife, who had not yet borne a child. Tormented by the decision, he was relieved to hear a few years later that she had found a loving husband. The directive shocked older men of the tribe. "Who will be the father to the children?" asked one, outraged at the command to cast part of his family adrift. Wooden Leg, appointed by the United States as a tribal judge, insisted that each man send away one wife but refused to follow up with enforcement. "My heart sympathized with them," he said later. "From time to time somebody would tell me about some man living a part of the time at one place with one wife and a part of the time at another place with another wife. I just listened, said nothing, and did nothing."

While stamping out marriages that did not correspond to Christian norms, reformers also undertook sweeping campaigns to protect women and children from dangerous information. Here was Victorianism in its most obvious form, driven by fears that commercialism and sexual license were spinning out of control. Pornography proved an especially troubling phenomenon. Union and Confederate soldiers created an avid market for sexually stimulating materials, and after the war the efficient new networks of mail and trade carried a lively national trade in pornographic photographs, lithographs, books, and magazines. Wrapped in unmarked brown paper, these publications proved difficult to intercept, and they provoked anxiety over information that children might obtain without parents' knowledge. Antivice crusader Anthony Comstock, making the case for federal action, submitted as evidence dozens of requests for pornography sent by students at boarding schools.

Comstock persuaded Congress to ban from the mails all "obscene literature," including information about birth control. (At the time the law passed in 1873, Republicans were reeling from financial scandals; they apparently hoped a vote for sexual purity would bolster their party's reputation.) Making citizen arrests as leader of the New York Society for the Suppression of Vice, Comstock became a controversial figure. Many of the convictions he won were later overturned, and for those who were convicted officials quietly issued a number of pardons, ruling that Comstock had overstepped the bounds of law. Female reformers in the WCTU and other groups, who had supported Comstock at first, broke with him when he began to attack the women's suffrage campaign as a symptom of modern evil.

The results of Comstock's campaigns were ambiguous. There is ample evidence that many Americans continued to manufacture, buy, and use birth control, including diaphragms, condoms, and sponges (often purchased through the mail). But federal anticontraception provisions remained in effect until the 1930s, and parts of the law lingered three decades more. Comstock's work had a chilling effect on information and public debate, much as the rants of Senator Joseph McCarthy did in a later era. Several writers who challenged Comstock lost their lives to the fight. Ida Craddock, an author of advice books for married women, committed suicide after being hounded by Comstock for years. Radical editor Ezra Heywood had mixed results in defending his work. In 1877, under the Comstock Law, Heywood was convicted of circulating obscene material but secured a presidential pardon after supporters organized a petition campaign. In a second case concerning ads for a birth control device that Heywood wickedly dubbed "the Comstock Syringe for Preventing Conception," a jury dismissed all charges. But Comstock won the final battle when Heywood was convicted in Massachusetts of circulating obscene literature. He was sentenced to two years of hard labor and emerged from prison in 1892 with his health broken, dying soon afterward. His wife, Angela Heywood, also a women's rights advocate, had to raise their four children alone.

Following the lead of courageous men and women such as Ezra and Angela Heywood, more mainstream commentators began to speak publicly about sex and marriage. Many condemned the assumption that a wife's body belonged to her husband. The forcible deflowering of a bride on her wedding night, one author wrote, constituted "rape and torture." Dr. John Kellogg, in an 1895 health guide for women, addressed husbands as well. "The most heroic battle which many a man can fight," he wrote, "is to protect his wife from his own lustful passions." Warning of the health risks when women were forced to submit to unwanted sex, Kellogg wrote that "every young wife should know that it is her duty as well as her privilege to protect herself. . . . It is no woman's duty to surrender herself soul and body to her husband." Some judges began to agree. While marital rape was not a recognized crime until a century later, it became harder by the 1880s and 1890s for a husband to win divorce on grounds that his wife did not provide him with adequate sexual services. Conversely, it became easier for spouses (overwhelmingly women) to obtain divorce when constant sexual demands impaired their physical and mental health.

Assuming women were less sexual than men, reformers began to call for two sweeping changes in marital relations. The first was "free love," which for most advocates meant wives' freedom to choose when they would engage in sex with their husbands. The closely related movement for "voluntary motherhood" advocated women's right to choose whether and when to bear children. Most reformers expected these choices to be made within marriage, ideally by both partners in a spirit of mutual respect. Doctors, health reformers, and women's rights advocates all condemned marital rape and the dangers of unlimited childbearing. Women, they argued, risked their lives in pregnancy and were expected to raise the resulting children. Husbands should not have unilateral power to force wives to submit to intercourse and potentially assume these burdens.

A few radicals went even further in their definitions of free love. The colorful Victoria Woodhull famously announced in an 1871 speech that "I have an inalienable, constitutional and natural right to love whom I may; to love as long or as short a period as I can; to change that love every day if I please." In the novel *Hagar Lyndon*, published in 1893, women's rights advocate Lizzie Holmes told the story of a heroine who earned economic independence and then chose motherhood out of wedlock with the help of a male friend who sympathized with her views. In the novel Hagar endures both the disapproval of those around her and a change of heart by her friend, who decides that she and her child need a protector and Hagar ought to marry him. But the heroine maintains her independence and raises her beloved son by herself. Such ideas remained scandalous in the late nineteenth century, but they extended the Victorian ideal of motherhood in directions that presaged the twentieth-century movement for women's rights. As radical reformer Moses Harman phrased it, families would be happiest and most harmonious when women chose "motherhood in freedom."

BACHELORS AND INDEPENDENT WOMEN

In the late nineteenth century, more and more Americans chose a single life. Some women chose professional and reform careers and never married, while divorced women also increased in numbers. By 1890 more than 10 percent of adult wage-earning women in major cities were unmarried and not living with family members. (The percentage rose to one-fifth in Chicago and one-third in St. Paul.) Such women, roughly half immigrants and half native born, came from all walks of life and ranged from elites to those below the poverty line. They included businesswomen, seamstresses, artists, social workers, and factory operatives.

Adult men escaped the bonds of matrimony in even larger numbers than women. The reasons so many chose bachelorhood were hotly debated. Many male immigrants came to the United States alone; others, immigrant or not, needed to work for a decade or more to save enough to support a family. But some chose permanent bachelorhood. Three years after the Civil War, a writer for the *Nation* was already noting that "the city is the habitat of the single." "By the general diffusion of education and culture, by the new inventions and discoveries of the age, by the increase in commerce," he observed, "the tastes of men and women have become widened, their desires multiplied, new gratifications and pleasures have been supplied to them.... The domestic circle does not fill so large a place in life as formerly.... Married life has lost in some measure its advantage over single life."

Single men and women not only enjoyed urban amenities ranging from diners to movie theaters; some also built on a Victorian tradition of same-sex friendship and companionship whose meaning was slowly changing. Men and women, both married and single, had long shared homosocial bonds that the culture at large viewed as innocent and praiseworthy. Many such relationships seem to have been erotically charged "romantic friendships" that fulfilled a need for companionship but were not physically sexual. Close female bonds, in particular, were considered natural, and parents and husbands thought little of it when girls or adult women held hands, took walks with their arms around each other, or shared a bed when visiting each other's homes. One doctor commented in 1896 that only very recently would anyone have suggested "there could be anything improper in the intimate relations of two women."

But by the time this doctor wrote, medical experts were using the terms *homosexuality* and *lesbianism* to describe what they now saw as unnatural relationships (establishing, in the process, *heterosexuality* as a presumed norm). For both men and women, homosexuality was coming to be recognized as an orientation rather than a sexual act that people might engage in without re-shaping their identities. The transition could be traced at women's colleges, where in the 1870s and 1880s students engaged in a practice called "smashing": sending each other love notes and poems, sharing beds, and pursuing all the other rituals of love affairs, including tumultuous breakups. Girls cheerfully reported the details of their latest "smashes" to parents and professors, and unless it interfered with a student's academic work, the custom was widely accepted as innocent. But by the 1890s and early 1900s, statistics showed that almost half of Bryn Mawr, Wellesley, Vassar, and Radcliffe graduates were choosing not to marry after they left school. Instead, they launched careers, often continued to live with other women, and sometimes forged lifelong female bonds. In light of these developments, "smashing" came to seem more subversive.

Homosexual relationships were not new in the late nineteenth century. The American sculptor Emma Stebbins and the actress Charlotte Cushman, for example, lived openly as lovers before the Civil War (though they did so as expatriates in Rome). In the 1850s Walt Whitman's "Calamus" poems celebrated, among other things, the physical pleasures of male love. Jason Chamberlain and John Chafee, two prospectors who traveled to California in the '49 gold rush, could still be found living there together in the 1890s. Visitors called them the "wedded bachelors." After fifty-four years together, John died in the summer of 1903; three months later Jason spent the day picking apples and then, bereft of his life partner, went into the house and committed suicide.

The recognition of homosexuality emerged in indirect and hidden ways. Many women entered "Boston marriages" that did not necessarily have a sexual dimension, and some saw their relationship with a woman as a second-best substitute for marriage. Mary Woolley and Jeanette Marks, two educators who began their relationship at Wellesley in 1895, lived together for decades afterward, yet Marks insisted in her public writings that only a male-female relationship could be "complete." New England writer Mary E. Wilkins lived from 1883 onward with a close female companion but left her to enter a difficult marriage to an alcoholic. Novelist Sarah Orne Jewett, who never married, had a deep romantic friendship with Annie Fields, the widow of leading publisher James T. Fields, but neither woman ever defined herself as a lesbian. Years later, in fact, Jewett seemed perplexed that her young literary protégé, Willa Cather, masked her passion for women by creating male narrators in her novels whose romantic feelings spoke in certain ways for Cather herself. Cather, twenty-four years younger, lived in a world that viewed homosexuality as a defined orientation; she knew her lesbianism was stigmatized in ways the older Jewett did not seem to understand.

Doctors were not the only ones beginning to see homosexuality as something different from Victorian romantic friendships. In 1892 in Memphis, Tennessee, nineteen-year-old Alice Mitchell slit the throat of her seventeen-year-old lover, Freda Ward, in a murder that shocked the nation. Alice testified that she had begged Freda to marry her and offered to dress as a man so they could escape and live together in St. Louis. Alice had killed Freda after she refused. Judged insane and committed to an asylum, the "girl lover" died of tuberculosis a few years later. The case distressed Americans, in part, because of a marked increase in the number of women who were cross-dressing and living with female lovers, as Alice had intended to do. Cases of this phenomenon surfaced all over the country. Even a Tammany ward boss in New York named Murray Hall turned out in 1901 to have been a woman who had lived as a man for a quarter-century. As in this case, women's identities were often discovered only after their deaths.

A remarkable memoir published by thirty-year-old Claude Hartland in 1901 offers an even more intimate picture of the emergence of homosexual identity. Hartland, born in 1871 in a southern railroad town, realized at age eleven that he felt desire for men. A few years later a visitor shared a bed with him, as was general practice:

> We had not been in bed five minutes, when he turned toward me and boldly placed his hand upon my sexual organ, which was already erected. . . . He then unfastened my clothing and his own and brought his organs and body in close contact with mine. I was simply wild with passion. All the pent-up desire of years burst forth at that moment. I threw my arms around him, kissed his lips, face,

and neck. . . . The intense animal heat and the friction between our organs soon produced a simultaneous ejaculation, which overstepped my wildest dream of sexual pleasure.

Thereafter Hartland experienced both anticipation and anxiety when he shared a bed with other men. Several seemed unapproachable; one gave him a fatherly hug and said, "God bless this boy"; others (including one visiting minister) responded with passion when Hartland caressed them. Several times Hartland sought medical advice, and on the instructions of one doctor he slept with a prostitute, making it through the unpleasant encounter by focusing his thoughts on "a very handsome man." After years of teaching in rural areas, he moved to a big city, probably Baltimore, and later to St. Louis. In the process he discovered to his relief that "many others were suffering from a disease similar to my own." At the time he wrote his memoir, Hartland had not reconciled himself to his sexual orientation. He viewed it, however, not as a sin but, in a more modern way, as an incurable disease. It is difficult to estimate how many Americans had such homosexual experiences, much less how they understood them. It is clear, though, that a gay male subculture was flourishing in many cities by the 1880s and 1890s.

One can trace simultaneous shifts in heterosexual practices. Sentimental songs such as "Sweet Genevieve" and "Molly and I and the Baby" gave way to more flirtatious lyrics, often celebrating brief affairs rather than enduring love. "My Best Girl's a Corker" and "A Hot Time in the Old Town Tonight" fell into this genre; many ragtime songs appropriated a lusty celebration of sex outside wedlock, projecting it onto blacks but popularizing it among Americans of all races and classes. On a humorous note Americans sang "You've Been a Good Old Wagon But You've Done Broke Down," as well as the 1891 smash hit "Ta-ra-ra-boom-de-re," borrowed, like much of the new music and dance, from a red-light district. A decade later Americans were singing about a couple who drank beer together and made out "Under the Anheuser Busch." In the same years increasing evidence came to light of premarital sexual play, heavy petting, and explicit talk—an especially striking change for young women. For young men such practices were not so much new as more open and accepted—something your father might have sought out in a brothel but which you might engage in with a girl from a respectable family. Whether you saw the young woman herself as respectable was another question. The double standard that Victorian reformers had lamented by no means died.

These shifts went along with a larger emphasis on physicality and the body, which encompassed far more than the "discovery" of homosexuality. In this as in many other aspects of the emerging youth culture, middle-class adolescents took their lead from working-class contemporaries. By the 1890s working-class young people spoke of going on a "date": rather than stopping by a young woman's home for a visit, a young man expected to take her out to a public venue such as a restaurant, theater, or amusement park. There the young man paid for consumer pleasures such as ice cream or carnival rides, and the couple enjoyed themselves without adult supervision. This practice quickly affected middle-class courtship. By 1904

Frank Eugene, "Adam and Eve." Photographer Frank Eugene, who studied in Europe before returning to the United States for a successful career, blended the techniques of photography and painting. He created this image in 1898 by photographing nude models and then scratching and marking the negative. This image appeared in *Camera Work*, 30 (April 1910). Courtesy Frances Lehman Loeb Art Center, Vassar College.

even the stodgy *Ladies' Home Journal* was ruling that respectable girls needed to have only one chaperoned home visit, so that parents could meet a young man and assess his character; subsequent dates could be out on the town.

Dating opened a new world of nightlife to young men and women who previously would have courted on their parents' front porches. Like many enticements of consumer culture, it brought pressures along with pleasures. Young men were expected to spend plenty of money to impress their dates, a process antithetical to the steady saving that prior generations had advised for husbands-in-the-making. For women, the "treat" or "date" began as a way for working-class girls to enjoy excursions that their meager salaries did not allow them, since most made far lower wages than did men. But the adventure came with a price: men often expected sexual favors in proportion to the amount spent. This expectation was not, of course, respectable. New York working girls who participated in it won the nickname "charity girls," an ironic play on the fact that they were not quite prostitutes but instead sold their favors for drinks or dance hall admission. Nonetheless, the assumption that young women should deliver sex in exchange for male spending marked a transformation of courtship that eventually affected all levels of the

Elvira Virginia Mugarrieta, known as "Babe Bean." Mugarrieta had been living as a man for some years when her identity was discovered in 1897. "Jack," who had run away at age fifteen from the convent her mother had chosen for her education, told reporters she disguised herself so she could "travel freely, feel protected, and find work." After much publicity surrounding her case, "Jack" disappeared and fought in the Spanish-American War, afterward living in San Francisco under the name Jack Garland. Jack, who was much admired for providing food and volunteer medical aid to the destitute, died in 1936 at age sixty-six. In the decades after the Civil War, unknown numbers of women chose to cross-dress, often for the same reasons given by "Babe Bean": freedom, safety, and work opportunities. The phenomenon was frequent enough to unsettle Americans and garner attention in the press. This image is from the *Stockton Evening Mail*, California, 9 October 1897. Mugarrieta's story is in the San Francisco Lesbian and Gay History Project article, "She Even Chewed Tobacco': A Pictorial Narrative of Passing Women in America," in *Hidden from History*, ed. Martin B. Duberman et al. (New York, 1989), 183–94.

social scale. In exchange for freedom from parental oversight and the exhilaration of amusement parks and movie theaters, young women assumed a new set of risks.

Dating, like other aspects of youth culture, opened up a host of conflicts between young women and men and their anxious and disapproving parents. A New York reformer reported that many working girls asserted their right as wage earners to come and go as they pleased: "there was no law but their own will." Authoritarian parents did not necessarily win the fight. "If I went out," remarked a young dance hall fan named Maureen Connelly, "and I knew I'd get hit if I came in at twelve . . . I'd stay out till one." To some extent, though, a zest for independence and sexual experimentation emerged even far from the cities, among young men and women who still trysted in their parents' parlors. Rolf Johnson, a Swedish-born farmhand in rural Nebraska, enjoyed a torrid affair with his neighbor Thilda Danielson. Thilda let Rolf know her feelings directly and invited him over for an evening when her family was away. "We played 'love in the dark,'" Rolf reported, "as we lighted no lamp not wishing to be watched from without through the window. When I heard her folks drive into the yard I tried to slip from the house unobserved, as I knew there would be hell to pay if they found us together with no lamps lit." Thilda's father had a "stormy session" with his daughter, calling her a prostitute and warning that Rolf had no intention of marrying her. Thilda angrily declared her right to love Rolf if she chose.

In the end Thilda and her father were both partly right and partly wrong. Rolf did not propose. "I couldn't see it," he wrote. "I am not quite prepared to leave the state of single blessedness for that of double misery." He broke off the relationship and went off to wander and work odd jobs for three years in South Dakota, Colorado, and New Mexico. But when he returned, he found that the dire warnings of his girlfriend's father had proven false: instead of suffering a ruined reputation, Thilda had happily married someone else.

Thilda and Rolf lived in a world in which adults said one thing about premarital sex and a powerful peer culture was beginning to say something else. Even in rural Nebraska they enjoyed more freedoms than their parents had had to follow their own inclinations. In some ways they returned to older, pre-Victorian customs. Two centuries earlier, in colonial New England, a third of all brides had been pregnant on their wedding day; in the Victorian era that percentage had dropped, but by 1900 active adolescent sexuality was reemerging. Newly added to the mix was a consumer culture that emphasized flirtation, physicality, and fun.

As to sex itself, respectable adults were still Victorian enough to give young people little guidance about it, and therein lay some of the power of peers and consumer culture. When WCTU officials ran a nationwide campaign promoting a "white life for two," they hoped it would encourage more equal marriages. "The law of purity," the WCTU wrote, should be "equally binding upon men and women." Prospective brides were to tell their husbands, "you must be as pure and true as you require me to be, ere I give you my hand." But the WCTU instructed that the specific meaning of the phrase "a white life" (no sex before or outside of marriage) be explained *only* to boys; girls should not hear this information. In the face of such ambivalence and confusion, men and women explored on their own the meanings of sexuality. For a few that meant creating a family of two women or two men; for others it meant seeking anonymous sexual encounters in the exciting urban underworld. For much larger numbers of young Americans, it meant playing "love in the dark" like Thilda and Rolf or heading out to the amusement park for a ride through the tunnel of love.

FOR FURTHER READING

Two books important throughout this chapter are Karen Lystra, *Searching the Heart* (New York, 1989), a history of romantic love in the nineteenth century, and John D'Emilio and Estelle B. Freedman, *Intimate Matters* (New York, 1988), a history of sexuality. On the emergence of modern public sexuality, see Sharon R. Ullman, *Sex Seen* (Berkeley, CA, 1997).

On prostitution see Benson Tong, *Unsubmissive Women* (Norman, OK, 1994), Joel Best, *Controlling Vice* (Columbus, OH, 1998), Marion S. Goldman, *Gold Diggers and Silver Miners* (Ann Arbor, MI, 1981), and Roger D. McGrath, *Gunfighters, Highwaymen, and Vigilantes* (Berkeley, CA, 1984). On domestic violence see Elizabeth H. Pleck, *Domestic Tyranny* (New York, 1987). Sexual exploitation of domestic servants is documented in the histories of female domestic service cited in Chapter 3. Age-of-consent campaigns are covered in David J. Pivar, *Purity Crusade* (Westport, CT, 1973), and a more nuanced update is provided by Mary E. Odem, *Delinquent Daughters* (Chapel Hill, NC, 1995). On women's moral uplift campaigns in the West see Peggy Pascoe, *Relations of Rescue* (New York, 1990), and on pornography Wayne E. Fuller, *Morality and the Mail in Nineteenth-Century America* (Urbana, IL, 2003). For a brilliant exploration of the Beecher-Tilton affair see Richard Wightman Fox, *Trials of Intimacy* (Chicago, 1999). The quotation about home as haven comes from the title of Christopher Lasch's book *Haven in a Heartless World* (New York, 1977).

On the Cleveland wedding see Rebecca Edwards, "Frances Folsom Cleveland," in *American First Ladies*, 2nd ed., ed. Lewis L. Gould (New York, 2001), 161–69, and on "family values politics" generally, Rebecca Edwards, *Angels in the Machinery* (New York, 1997), and "Domesticity versus Manhood Rights," in *The Democratic Experiment*, ed. by Meg Jacobs, William J. Novak, and Julian E. Zelizer (Princeton, NJ, 2003), 175–97. On the pension issue see Megan J. McClintock, "Civil War Pensions and the Reconstruction of Union Families," *Journal of American History* 83 (1996): 456–80, and on polygamy debates, Joan Iverson, *The Antipolygamy Controversy in US Women's Movements, 1880–1925* (New York, 1997), as well as Sarah Barringer Gordon, *The Mormon Question* (Chapel Hill, NC, 2002). On Mormon women's lives I rely also on Lorraine Bellard's study of Patty Bartlett Sessions, "Living Her Faith on the Mormon Frontier," senior history thesis, Vassar College, 1998.

On marriage law see Michael Grossberg, *Governing the Hearth* (Chapel Hill, NC, 1985), Nancy F. Cott, *Public Vows* (Cambridge, MA, 2000), and Amy Dru Stanley, *From Bondage to Contract* (New York, 1998). On judges' changing attitudes toward sex in marriage see Jill Elaine Hasday, "Contest and Consent: A Legal History of Marital Rape," *California Law Review* 88 (Oct. 2000): 1375–505. On tensions over commerce and domesticity see Ellen Garvey, *The Adman in the Parlor,* Elaine Abelson, *When Ladies Go A-Thieving,* and William Leach, *Land of Desire,* all cited in Chapter 4. On day nurseries see Elizabeth Rose, *A Mother's Job: The History of Day Care, 1890–1960* (New York, 1999).

On contraception and sex radicalism, respectively, see Andrea Tone, *Devices and Desires* (New York, 2001), and Joanne E. Passet, *Sex Radicals and the Quest for Women's Equality* (Urbana, IL, 2003). On Angela and Ezra Heywood I am also indebted to Ben Holtzman, "'Saying Naughty Words and Shocking the Whole World,'" senior history thesis, Vassar College, 2003. On Charlotte Perkins Gilman see Ann J. Lane, *To Herland and Beyond* (New York, 1990). On single life in the cities see Joanne J. Meyerowitz, *Women Adrift* (Chicago, 1988), and Howard P. Chudacoff, *The Age of the Bachelor* (Princeton, NJ, 1999). On romantic friendships and the emergence of homosexuality I draw on Lillian Faderman, *Surpassing the Love of Men* (New York, 1981), George Chauncey, *Gay New York* (New York, 1994), and Leila Rupp, *A Desired Past* (Chicago, 1999), as well as works on early women's colleges, cited earlier. Individual stories of gays and lesbians recounted here appear in Susan

Lee Johnson, *Roaring Camp* (New York, 2000), Lisa Duggan, *Sapphic Slashers* (Durham, NC, 2000), and Jonathan Katz, *Love Stories* (Chicago, 2001). On sex in popular music see Nicholas E. Tawa, *The Way to Tin Pan Alley* (New York, 1990), and on the origins of modern dating, Beth L. Bailey, *From Front Porch to Back Seat* (Baltimore, 1988). Rolf and Thilda's story unfolds in Rolf Johnson's diary, published as *Happy as a Big Sunflower*, ed. Richard E. Jensen (Lincoln, NE, 2000).

CHAPTER 7

Science

Man . . . translated himself into a new universe which had no
common scale of measurement with the old.
— HENRY ADAMS, "THE DYNAMO AND THE VIRGIN"

In the summer of 1877, a Union Pacific section foreman and a station agent in Wyoming sent a confidential query to paleontologist Othniel Marsh. Would the professor, they asked, be interested in some enormous fossils of unknown animals, including a thirty-inch vertebra and a five-foot shoulder blade? If so, how much would he pay? "You are well known as an enthusiastic geologist and a man of means," the men wrote slyly, "both of which we are desirous of finding, especially the latter." Marsh rushed an assistant to the site and received a stunning report. The fossil beds were seven miles long and lay in easy-to-dig sandstone, so close to Union Pacific tracks that workers could load them directly from wheelbarrows onto railcars bound for Marsh's Yale laboratory.

The excavation at Como Bluffs, Wyoming, became one of the most famous in all paleontology. It uncovered the Jurassic dinosaurs, many of which still carry Marsh's names for them, including *Stegasaurus* with its plated spine, sauropods *Diplodocus* and *Brachiosaurus*, and toothy predator *Allosaurus*. Marsh's lab reconstructed whole skeletons and presented them at museums such as the Smithsonian, where the displays helped revolutionize Americans' understanding of natural history. More than a century earlier, British geologist James Hutton had shocked scientists by proposing that Earth was more than sixty million years old. That estimate gained increasing acceptance over the course of the nineteenth century. Charles Darwin's theories, first published in 1859 in *The Origin of Species*, depended on Hutton's geological estimates to conceive of evolution as a process taking millions of years; Darwin's ideas, in turn, revolutionized biology. By the 1870s scientists studying fossil oysters and horseshoe crabs spoke confidently of the Triassic and Cambrian eras.

While English scientists conducted the crucial early investigations, in the late nineteenth century the western United States became the font of paleontology. Its alkaline soils preserved bones beautifully, while eroded buttes and canyons made fossils easy to find and dig. Fossil hunts took on aspects of a gold rush. Othniel Marsh and his bitter rival, Edward D. Cope, staked out secret claims and hired spies to report on each other's finds. Their haste to claim discoveries left a trail of confusion that lingered for decades. The primate *Notharctus* received seven different names. Skulls got attached to the tails of skeletons or the wrong bodies altogether. Marsh ridiculed Cope for such mistakes, but he himself invented the now-discredited *Brontosaurus* from bones of two different species. The legacy of the two men's feud was not unlike that of the era's corporate titans, who left others to clean up the mess from their reckless careers. A leading paleontologist of the next generation wrote that he and his colleagues spent "the best years of our lives" sorting out the chaos left by Marsh and Cope.

For the public, unaware of these difficulties, dinosaurs opened a new window on prehistory and undermined the long-standing assumption that God had created the earth in 4004 BC. Though some clung to the hope that human and dinosaur bones would be found together, dating both to the biblical era before the Flood, they waited in vain. The fossil lode at Como Bluffs confirmed that dinosaurs had had their own great age. Even more spectacular revelations lay ahead, as astronomers offered evidence for a new understanding of space and time. In 1878 young Albert Michelson, teaching physics at the U.S. Naval Academy, accurately measured the speed of light and that there was no "luminiferous ether" between the stars. His work paved the way for a series of breakthroughs in physics that led to Albert Einstein's theory of relativity three decades later. In the meantime, photographers began to offer clear images of the Milky Way, proving it was made up of myriad distant suns. In 1885 observers of the Andromeda nebula witnessed the birth of a star. Scientists were measuring what one naturalist has called "deep time": the true immensity of the geological and astronomical record. As they did, they began to suggest humans' insignificant place in cosmic history.

The late nineteenth century thus brought intellectual as well as economic and social turmoil to the United States. A popular cult of science arose, and the tools of science, from spectroscopes to X-ray machines, offered compelling advancements in knowledge and human welfare. Science promised progress and delivered on that promise in tangible ways. Medicine, especially, began to hold out the hope of curing diseases that caused incalculable suffering and grief. "There has never been in the history of civilization," declared one observer in 1891, "a period, or a place, or a section of the earth in which science and invention have worked such progress . . . as in these United States in the period since the end of the Civil War."

EVOLUTION

Science by no means displaced religion in American thought. Not until 1895 did the National Education Association begin to suggest textbooks based on evolutionary principles, and battles over the teaching of evolution did not begin for two decades more. In the meantime, biologists and paleontologists reached no consensus on how evolution worked. In one of his greatest achievements, Othniel Marsh traced the fossil record from ancient *Eohippus* to the modern horse, which, he said, proved Darwin's theory of natural selection by random mutation.

Marsh, however, was in the minority. Others looked at the same evidence and drew the opposite conclusion: the progression of species was too regularly spaced to be the result of accidental mutations. They argued, in the tradition of French biologist Jean Baptiste Lamarck, that animals developed new traits during their lifetimes and passed them to offspring. This Lamarckian idea of "acquired traits" dominated evolutionary science for decades. The idea that evolution was driven by random mutations, including painful and fatal ones, seemed utterly cruel. Surely the Creator had developed life by more humane and orderly means.

The struggle between Lamarckian and Darwinian views also translated into a debate over whether human societies and economies evolved, and if so, how. For many, evolution was synonymous with progress. Anthropologist Lewis Henry Morgan, writing in the 1870s, proposed that human family structures evolved over time, and he set up a system of classification whose legacy endures in popular thought. Primitive societies, he argued, were "promiscuous"; humanity then rose through matriarchy and patriarchy to the pinnacle of civilized family life, which not surprisingly turned out to be Victorian-style monogamy. Morgan believed this pattern of progress to be universal. Ethnologists could study the kinship system of any culture and rank it above or below others on his scale.

Others looked at the world of commerce and saw a clear application of evolutionary ideas. "The growth of a large business is merely a survival of the fittest," declared John D. Rockefeller in a statement typical of the genre. "This is not an evil tendency of business. It is merely the working out of a law of nature and a law of God." This "social Darwinism" drew on the influential work of English author Herbert Spencer. It was Spencer, not Darwin, who coined the phrase *survival of the fittest*. His most prominent American adherents included steel manufacturer Andrew Carnegie and Harvard sociologist William Graham Sumner. The latter's view of humanity was especially grim, because he feared that well-intentioned busybodies had interfered for centuries with nature by feeding the hungry and unemployed. Instead, Sumner argued, humans must stop "sentimentalists" and allow unfit people to die, or at least not reproduce. Accused of wishing to kill off a large portion of humanity, Sumner denied the charge. But, he added, "as to a great many persons and classes, it would have been better for society, and would have involved no pain to them, if they had never been born."

A more innovative response to Darwin's theory was the American philosophy that came to be known as pragmatism. Philosophers such as William James and John Dewey began to question whether there was such a thing as universal truth. Instead, they suggested that human ideas operated like genetic mutations: some worked and some did not, and the only way one could judge the difference was through experience and experimentation. All knowledge, James and Dewey proposed, was local, provisional, and constantly shifting, just as biological species were not fixed over time. Such ideas were out of the mainstream, but in the twentieth century they would shape new ways of thinking in many fields. William James laid the foundation for modern psychology as a "natural science of the mind." Among other things, James suggested that biological processes might trigger emotions rather than the other way around. He also observed that thought flows like "a stream ... of consciousness," an insight that influenced modernist writers.

In the near term, a more widespread response to evolutionary theory was to take an optimistic Lamarckian view. If people could acquire strength, wisdom, and moral goodness and transmit them to their children biologically, then education and uplift would magnify a hundredfold. Reformers spoke of furthering human evolution by cooperation, especially through collective institutions such as government, schools, and churches. Books such as *The Evolution of Christianity*, in which reform minister Lyman Abbott explored changes in Protestant theology, won broad readership. Sociologist Lester Frank Ward observed that a thorough application of William Graham Sumner's views would require humans to dispense with all medicine, government, law, emergency rescue from floods and hurricanes, and anything else that might interfere with the "natural" processes of life and death. The lesson to Ward was clear: "if nature progresses through the destruction of the weak, man progresses through the *protection* of the weak."

Experts in the rising fields of Egyptology and Assyriology—the latter focusing on the biblical Babylon, or today's Iraq—sought to confirm the truth of Old Testament stories. Linguists looked for clues to the location of the Tower of Babel, while wealthy patrons funded archaeological excavations in the Near East through American Palestine Exploration Societies. Between 1888 and 1900 the Babylonian Expedition Fund, based at Philadelphia's University Museum, sent four expeditions to Nippur, south of Baghdad. Both of the Assyriologists who led these expeditions were Protestant ministers, and one edited the national *Sunday School Times*. A participant described their mission as a blend of spiritual and scientific goals. The expedition worked, he wrote, "in the spirit of Christian enlightenment and scientific inquiry to bring forth from its ancestral home, now desolate and forsaken, the heritage of forgotten ages."

Since scientific knowledge was presumed to arise from classification, museums were the era's great institutions of scientific education and study. Institutions such as the Smithsonian displayed ranks and ranks of stuffed birds and animals, mineral specimens, and pottery and spears in glass cases, expecting visitors (including professional scientists as well as the public) to grasp the essence of each species or culture by examining representative objects. Schools and colleges boasted of the quality of their geological and botanical "cabinets." Genteel families transformed their parlors into little museums, cramming into one room all the functions of a science display and an aristocratic drawing room, music room, and art gallery. A collection of seashells might sit side by side with a globe, a specimen case of stuffed songbirds, and a terrarium filled with different types of ferns. Embracing the cult of collection and display, one decorating expert assured readers that "there is hardly likely to be too much in a room."

Similar assumptions underlay the era's influential world's fairs. Starting with Philadelphia's Centennial Exposition in 1876, these fairs introduced millions of Americans to the latest advances in technology and science along with art and artifacts from around the world. The grandest of them all, the Chicago World's

Columbian Exposition of 1893, attracted 27.5 million visitors. Its White City displayed the wonders of American industry, housed in steel frame structures such as the Palace of Mechanic Arts, the Horticulture Building, and a dozen others. The centerpiece of the Electricity Building was a Tower of Light, featuring an enormous dynamo from General Electric. The Transportation Building displayed the latest rail technology, sponsored by companies such as the Baltimore and Ohio Railroad. Dominating all was the immense Manufactures Building, which had a fifty-foot-wide avenue running through its interior. Here visitors could marvel at the latest innovations in pharmaceuticals, ready-made clothing, clocks, elevators, and thousands of other products. The Remington Company, for example, displayed dozens of its typewriters, adapted to various languages and to specialized tasks such as weather reporting.

In keeping with the mania for classification, human beings from various tribal cultures went on display in Chicago. Anthropologist Franz Boas of the American Museum of Natural History in New York organized these exhibits, which ranged from North American Penobscot Indians to "little Javanese people." They included some people who were brought to Chicago under false pretenses and held virtually

Mary Cassatt, "Young Women Plucking the Fruits of Knowledge and Science," detail from the center panel of a mural commissioned for the Women's Building at the Chicago World's Columbian Exposition, 1893. Cassatt, a leading American impressionist painter living in Paris, inverted the biblical story of Eve and the apple to celebrate women's achievements in science, the arts, and professional life. The original mural has been lost. This reproduction appeared in *Harper's New Monthly Magazine* 86 (May 1893), 837. Courtesy Vassar College Library.

as slaves. The exhibited villagers built samples of their housing and crafts and per-formed traditional dances for fairgoers. Guidebooks ranked them, according to Lewis Henry Morgan's theory, from the "savage" to the most "civilized." At the same time, along the fair's midway, male visitors lined up to see Syrian-born belly dancer Fahreda Mahzar, billed by the stage name "Little Egypt." Mahzar's "genuine native muscle dance," popularly known as the hootchy-kootchy, afterward became a staple at amusement parks such as Coney Island. This "scientific" display of foreign culture capitulated entirely to the commercial and sexual.

Science and education mingled with for-profit entertainment in a variety of ways. Showmen such as Buffalo Bill laid great stress on the authenticity and instructional value of their offerings. Bill, for example, never called his produc-tion a "show," but simply "Buffalo Bill's Wild West." By 1893, when Bill set up shop near the Columbian Exposition in Chicago, his horsemen included Russian Cossacks, Mexicans, Arabs, and Syrians, whom he advertised as an "Ethnological Congress." By 1894 the Barnum and Bailey Circus was also marketed as a "Grand

Laboratory at the Tuskegee Institute, Tuskegee, Alabama, 1902. African Americans, as well as women, challenged the prevailing assumption that scientific research and discovery was a white men's realm, as well as "scientific" claims about the limited intellectual capacity of women and "lower races" of men. Booker T. Washington's showcase for his goal of industrial education, Tuskegee featured by this time a $2 million endowment, a faculty of nearly 200, and an extensive, well-equipped campus. Courtesy Library of Congress.

Ethnological Congress." Promoters suggested that its famous chimpanzees, Chiko and Johanna, belonged on an evolutionary continuum beside "strange and savage tribes" from around the globe. Meanwhile, objects amassed for the Chicago exposition became the foundation for the city's new Field Museum, launched with a million-dollar donation from department store magnate Marshall Field.

The rage to build distinguished collections led to competition not unlike the fossil-hunting frenzy unleashed by Marsh and Cope. Edward Thompson, a Harvard professor serving as consul to Mexico in 1901, used a crude mechanical bucket to dredge the sacred well at the ancient Mayan site of Chichen Itza, obtaining (and irreparably damaging) superb gold and jade artifacts that he smuggled illegally to the United States. Even more disturbing were the activities of bone hunters, who robbed American Indian graves and shipped home skeletons of native people killed in conflicts over western land. The Army Medical Museum in Washington amassed hundreds of skulls, including those of Cheyenne people killed in Colorado's Sand Creek massacre and Pawnee killed by Kansas vigilantes. In response, many native people began to bury relatives beside their homes in order to guard the bodies.

TECHNOLOGY AND CORPORATE CAPITALISM

Though American anthropologists won acclaim for studies of native peoples whom they could easily reach by railroad, the United States remained in some ways a scientific backwater. Many of its leading scientists were émigrés trained in Europe, and those born in the United States went abroad to get advanced training. As enthusiasm for science swept the country in the early 1870s, a Dartmouth student confirmed the dominance of England. "Ten or fifteen years ago," he reported, "the staple subject here for reading and talk, outside study hours, was English poetry and fiction. Now it is English science. Herbert Spencer, John Stuart Mill, Huxley, Darwin, Tyndall have usurped the place of Tennyson and Browning, and Matthew Arnold and Dickens."

Americans excelled in applied fields such as engineering and materials science, and their efforts tended toward the pragmatic and profitable. Railroads hired metallurgists who designed more powerful and safer steam engines, and chemists developed creosote treatments to extend the life of wooden cross ties. Other industries followed suit, and by 1899 almost 150 American corporations had created research laboratories. Steel magnate Andrew Carnegie summed up the benefits when he described the work of a German chemist he employed. "Great secrets did the doctor open up to us," Carnegie wrote. "Mines that had a high reputation were now found to contain ten, fifteen, and even twenty percent less iron than [they] had been credited with. Mines that hitherto had a poor reputation we found to be now yielding superior ore. . . . Nine-tenths of all the uncertainties of pig-iron making were dispelled under the burning sun of chemical knowledge. What fools we had been! But then there was this consolation: we were not as great fools as our competitors, [who] said they could not afford to employ a chemist."

Discoveries in industrial laboratories were proprietary, and corporate scientists and engineers engaged in a constant race for patents. The managers of Bell Telephone, for example, learned that every patent strengthened their control over earlier inventions whose patents had run their seventeen-year course. When competitors could copy an old telephone design but were barred from using a reworked, newly patented receiver, Bell retained the advantage. As one adviser to the company noted, the drive to maintain market dominance pushed Bell to "organize a corps of inventive engineers." In the emerging electric power industry, Westinghouse and General Electric (GE) followed a similar strategy. When necessary they bought rival patents and squelched them rather than allow new products to compete with their own.

The innovations of Bell and GE engineers were spectacular in a different way than were Marsh's sketch of *Stegasaurus* and the excavations at Chichen Itza and Nippur. Stronger, more flexible steel brought better and cheaper typewriters, bicycles, and eventually automobiles. The invention of reinforced concrete allowed architects and engineers to construct such modern marvels as skyscrapers and the Brooklyn Bridge. The largest piece of steel forged in the United States before 1893 was created for entertainment: it became the forty-six-ton axle of the celebrated Ferris wheel at the 1893 world's fair, which lifted 1.5 million riders to vistas above Chicago. Other innovations reshaped the geographic landscape. Minneapolis flour-milling corporations developed steel rollers that could handle spring wheat, previously too hard-kernelled for efficient milling. Great swaths of Minnesota, the Dakotas, and Montana, whose climate permitted the cultivation of only spring wheat, became open to farming.

The post–Civil War surge of innovation sent so many applications and models to the U.S. Patent Office that it ran out of space to store them all. Corporations held a large and growing percentage of these patents, but it was not their engineers and chemists who captured the public imagination. Instead, the popular heroes of American technology were independent inventors such as Thomas Edison, whose New Jersey laboratory produced an astonishing series of products between the late 1860s and the early twentieth century. Starting off as a humble telegraph worker in the Midwest, Edison moved east at age twenty-one and presented a new telegraph design that enabled operators to send multiple messages at the same time. He went on to produce stock tickers, the phonograph, the incandescent light bulb, improved electric generators, storage batteries, motion picture technology, and even Portland cement. Edison was the consummate entrepreneur, skilled at pitching ideas in the marketplace. He chose to concentrate on electric light, for example, because he knew it would make money, based on his study of the enormously profitable gaslight industry. Edison shrewdly demonstrated his product by lighting up the headquarters of J. P. Morgan and the adjacent *New York Times* building, ensuring both publicity and investor attention.

In the 1880s Edison became embroiled in a controversy with his corporate challenger, George Westinghouse, who advocated alternating current (AC) rather than Edison's direct current (DC). Their furious public relations battle revealed some of the pitfalls of corporate science, and it tarnished both inventors' reputations. Westinghouse, with the aid of Croatian-born physicist Nikola Tesla, made false claims about the safety of his AC system, asserting that the electricity entering users' homes would be entirely harmless. Meanwhile, in his effort to discredit AC, Edison electrocuted animals in his laboratory and encouraged New York State to test the electric chair on AC current in 1889, hoping it would not work. The first execution by electric chair was, in fact, terribly botched, but Edison lost the long-term battle. His financial backers saw alternating current as the better bet and wrested control of his company from him. By 1892 Edison's leading enterprise was no longer Edison General Electric but simply General Electric, led by J. P. Morgan. While Americans continued to celebrate Edison as the "Wizard of Menlo Park," for many years the embittered inventor never set foot inside a GE building. In scientific innovation, as in mining and other sectors of the economy, pioneers were often not the ones who reaped the big rewards.

THE PROMISE OF MEDICINE

In the late nineteenth century, Americans lived in the shadow of death. Yellow fever and typhoid wreaked periodic devastation, especially in the South. Future labor leader Mary (Mother) Jones, living in Memphis, lost her husband and all four children to yellow fever in 1867. "All around my house," she recalled, "I could hear weeping. . . . I sat alone through nights of grief. No one came to me. No one could. Other houses were as stricken as mine." A decade later, in a yellow fever outbreak that claimed 10,000 lives, future antilynching investigator Ida B. Wells lost both parents. She received the news while staying with her grandmother in Mississippi and immediately boarded a freight train headed to Memphis. She remembered that "no passenger trains were running or needed. The caboose in which I rode was draped in black for two previous conductors who had fallen victim." By the time Wells reached home, her infant brother had also died. At the age of sixteen, Wells became sole caretaker for her five surviving brothers and sisters.

Among nonepidemic diseases the greatest scourge was tuberculosis, responsible for perhaps one of every five deaths in America. Millions of parents also agonized over the risk of measles, mumps, whooping cough, scarlet fever, diphtheria, and other diseases that struck young children. No parent could rest when a child was ill. Typical were the meditations of Laura Hamilton Murray, a young African-American mother living near Washington, D.C. "Baby sick today, poor little fellow," she wrote of her young son Raymond. "I wonder if we will raise him. There is something that I think that a Christian should not think." Few parents saw all their children reach adulthood.

Among poor and minority populations, death rates were staggering. American Indians suffered severely, as the viral and bacteriological assault that had begun in the sixteenth century entered its closing phase. In 1900, Atlanta's board of health reported that the death rate among the city's black population was 69 percent higher than that of whites; almost *half* of all black children died before their first birthday.

Mortality rates at New York City's public infant orphanages ranged somewhere between 60 and 75 percent, largely from diarrhea caused by contaminated milk. An alternative hospital for abandoned babies, run by the Catholic Sisters of Charity, won praise for reducing mortality to 19 percent. The sisters did so largely by encouraging new mothers to stay and nurse their own babies—and others if they could—through the perilous first months of life.

Wealth and status offered no guarantees of protection from disease. On a single day in 1884, young Theodore Roosevelt lost both his young wife Alice to a post-childbirth kidney ailment and his mother to typhoid fever. First Lady Caroline Harrison died of tuberculosis while living in the White House. "Baby Ruth," the adored daughter of President Grover Cleveland and his wife Frances, died of the same illness at age eleven. Her mother was so distraught that friends feared she would die. Any parent who visited a lovingly tended Mexican cemetery in the Southwest would have identified with the toys and handcrafted cradles left on tiny graves, along with crosses bearing the words *Bebita Mia* (my baby).

Even access to the best doctors often did not help. One of the nation's first female medical researchers, Dr. Mary Putnam Jacobi, lost her seven-year-old son

Photograph of infant after death, Ohio, circa 1890–1910. Children's deaths were frequent occurrences, and families often took photographs like this one, at the casket, to remember the deceased. Courtesy Ohio Historical Society. Nathan R. Skipper Audiovisual Collection.

to diphtheria. Cleofas Jaramillo, a well-to-do young wife in New Mexico, went to Denver's finest hospital to give birth to her first child. But the baby's bladder function was blocked; in attempting to fix the problem, the specialist cut a blood vessel and the five-day-old boy bled to death. For her second delivery, Jaramillo turned to a local hospital and the advice of old-fashioned *medicas* in her community. This time all went well, but at fifteen months the child died of cholera infantum (bacterial diarrhea), after an eighteen-day vigil during which her mother prayed by her crib night and day. The little girl's death, her mother wrote, "tore her out of our hearts." Cleofas's husband died soon afterward of yet another illness, and she was left widowed and childless.

Such tragedies had plagued humans for thousands of years, and physicians could do little but make patients comfortable and counsel the grief-stricken to accept God's will. In the late nineteenth century, that began to change. Thanks to the discoveries of British surgeon Joseph Lister, for example, doctors began to grasp the role of bacteria in post-surgical infection. They adopted the use of sterilized bandages and tools; surgeons, their practice boosted by better anesthesia, began to work in antiseptic conditions. Results were dramatic: more and more patients survived. By 1900 the surgeons in one leading Philadelphia hospital were performing more operations in a single year than they had ventured in the entire first half of the century. Urban hospitals, no longer viewed as death houses, advertised their modern equipment to well-to-do clients. "*All germs are destroyed*," promised Memorial Hospital in Richmond, Virginia, "by the best and most scientific means."

Building on earlier developments in microscopy and chemistry, researchers applied germ theory to specific ailments. French doctor Louis Pasteur developed a technique to kill germs in milk—called pasteurization in his honor. Germany's Robert Koch identified the cause of anthrax in 1876 and began research on tuberculosis, work that German scientist Emil Behring and his Japanese colleague Shibasaburo Kitasato soon refined. Americans hailed these advances. Newspapers trumpeted Pasteur's successful treatment of rabies, a fatal disease contracted from animal bites. In 1885 three children from Newark, New Jersey, made headlines for several months after a rabid dog bit them. Through a massive newspaper campaign, funds were raised to rush the children to Pasteur's clinic in Paris, where he injected an antitoxin and probably saved their lives. Equally celebrated was Koch's 1890 announcement that he had found a cure for the dreaded tuberculosis (a claim that turned out to be premature) as well as 1894 trials of a diphtheria antitoxin. American doctors were soon using the latter, and the *New York Herald* led a high-profile movement to distribute the drug free to at-risk children.

Vaccines and antibiotics were not, however, the first or primary tools against disease. What proved most effective were broad-based public health campaigns. As early as 1866, Americans began to get an inkling that science offered hope. When an arriving ship brought cholera from Germany, New York City faced the possibility of an epidemic. Back in 1832, when the disease first ravaged New York, doctors had believed that some kind of atmospheric disturbance was causing the illness.

"A Hint to Boards of Health—How Our Cities Invite the Cholera." Frank Leslie's Illustrated Newspaper, 2 August 1884. By the 1880s, Americans understood the causes of some diseases; they recognized that urban poverty and crowding made cities especially vulnerable, and they expected state and municipal boards of health to tackle these problems. Here, used clothing and tainted food are cited as causes of cholera, amid a New York investigation of milk dealers in the slums who watered down milk and added chemicals like borax. Courtesy Rutherford B. Hayes Presidential Center.

But an English doctor had proven that good sanitation would prevent it, and in 1866 New York leaped into action. Professional medical men were appointed to a Board of Health with sweeping powers to order clean streets, garbage removal, building evacuations, and the burning of infected clothes and bedding. To everyone's amazement, the outbreak stopped. Though New York's population had grown immensely since the Civil War, the deaths in 1866 totaled only 591, one-tenth the number that had died in a cholera outbreak seventeen years before.

New York's attack on cholera prompted a nationwide crusade for public health. With an ambitious project to provide clean water in the 1870s, Massachusetts demonstrated that it could conquer typhoid fever. Soon afterward, Memphis, Tennessee, constructed a sewage system that cut the city's mortality rate in half. Other cities and states followed suit. Housekeepers learned to boil milk and water to combat diphtheria and infant diseases. Urban environmentalists tackled dirt and waste. Female volunteers and professional nurses undertook the bulk of such work. In New Orleans, for example, male scientists led by Dr. Walter Reed curtailed the city's last yellow fever outbreak in 1905, but equal credit for longer life spans should go to the New Orleans Woman's Drainage and Sewerage League, which in 1899 did the unglamorous work of collecting taxpayer signatures and funding bonds for a better drainage system.

By 1904 the National Tuberculosis Association mobilized a nationwide network of volunteers for a prevention campaign. The first disease-specific effort, it provided the model for an array of later campaigns against diseases such as cancer, diabetes, and AIDS. Since germ theory was still poorly understood, any speck of dirt came to be suspected of harboring disease, and educators urged housekeepers to strive for almost surgical cleanliness. The last decade of the century thus marked a shift toward more spare and simple interiors, inspired by a rejection of unhealthy dust on heavy drapes and carpets (as well as all those collections of stuffed birds). Carpets and wooden cabinetry had been the style in bathrooms, but by the 1890s sanitary educators promoted glistening germ-free surfaces. In children's nurseries and kitchens, tile and hardwood floors and fresh paint replaced carpets and brocaded wallpaper. "Scientific hygiene" also influenced personal grooming. Shorter skirts for women were justified as a health measure, since long skirts gathered dirt, and by 1903 *Harper's Weekly* commented on the demise of the male beard in the years since tuberculosis had been ruled "not hereditary but infectious." A clean-shaven face, unusual in the nineteenth century, became the norm.

Public health measures had their ironies and complications, including the circulation of myths such as the idea that germs lingered forever on a sick child's toys. One of the most successful projects of the WCTU was its campaign for Scientific Temperance Instruction, which promoted a long list of dubious "facts." Mandated in every state by 1901, Scientific Temperance probably reached half of all school-children with textbooks endorsed by the WCTU. The authors claimed that alcohol was a poison whose use, even in small amounts, destroyed the liver, brain, skin, eyes, and bones. Alarming charts and sketches showed the alleged toll on the body of even one glass of wine per day. By the 1890s Scientific Temperance had provoked major controversies in the emerging fields of chemistry, psychiatry, and clinical medicine. WCTU leaders shrewdly quoted European allies who hinted that American research was not on the cutting edge. Opponents of the program insisted the reverse. "Let us not palm off on innocent minds," wrote one outraged doctor, "pseudo-chemistry and inaccurate physiology." Nonetheless, Scientific Temperance Instruction endured in many schools until after World War I.

Among the saddest unintended consequences of public health campaigns was a new epidemic. In the 1890s polio suddenly emerged as a dreaded childhood disease. Unbeknownst to people at the time, children had traditionally been exposed to polio virus in infancy when they were biologically equipped to combat it. Now, with more hygienic water supplies, the virus reached children at a later age and found them vulnerable. Polio devastated families for a half-century before researchers found an effective vaccine. Even setting aside this tragedy, it must be noted that Americans' enthusiasm for medical advancements outran immediate results. Infant mortality rates did not begin to drop significantly until after 1900. In fact, as new hardships and urban concentration bred disease, the average man born during or after the Civil War could actually expect a life span ten years *shorter* than that of a free American man born a century earlier—forty-five to fifty-five years, rather than fifty-five to sixty-five.

At the same time, sweeping advances in science led to arrogance and overconfidence. "If the cause of degradation and ignorance, of poverty, of contagious disease, or of any of the miseries which make a nation wretched, can be pointed out by scientific methods," declared one researcher, "then it is the stern duty of science to step in." But scientists' recommendations were rarely as objective as they hoped. Growing support for "scientific racial hygiene" was a notorious example. As early as 1875 Richard Dugdale's *The Jukes* proposed that crime and alcoholism ran in families, which by the turn of the century was widely interpreted as meaning that heredity caused most social problems. Legislators were already proposing laws that forbade alcoholics to marry. In 1899 a state asylum in Indiana began sterilizing "mental defectives" for the good of society, a practice later upheld by the courts. By the 1920s half the states were experimenting with forced sterilization of those deemed unfit to reproduce.

The treatment of venereal disease showed how racial prejudices informed and could be reinforced by medicine. Many southern whites believed venereal disease was a "Negro problem"; when infected with such diseases, white men (and sometimes women) avoided stigma by seeking treatment from black physicians, who they assumed had expertise in the field. White doctors thus saw relatively few cases of syphilis and gonorrhea, while some African-American doctors built lucrative practices treating them. The fact that cases were largely hidden from the view of whites reinforced myths about who suffered from these diseases.

Meanwhile, a notorious case of racialized decision making occurred in San Francisco in 1900, when bubonic plague was discovered in Chinatown. City police and health authorities decided to quarantine the area, but they first went through the neighborhood and urged all non-Chinese to leave. A federal health inspector, working at a bacteriological laboratory in the city, claimed Asians were vulnerable to the plague because they ate too much rice. His antiplague measures, including turning Asian homes and businesses upside down in a mass disinfection campaign, proved not to work. He then proposed forcible experimental inoculations of every Asian person in San Francisco. Attorneys for a coalition of Chinese organizations took the matter to court and were vindicated. It took health authorities four more years to fully eradicate the disease in the city by focusing on the rats that carried the plague to Asians and non-Asians alike.

Medicine was not the only branch of science freighted with prejudice. After 1898, when the Weather Bureau set up operations in U.S.-occupied Cuba, its officers resented competition from local forecasters who were Catholic priests at Havana's Belen Observatory. The priests had developed a series of excellent forecasting techniques over the previous thirty years, but to professionally trained

Weather Bureau officials they were amateur "cranks"—and even worse, excitable Hispanics who damaged business confidence by predicting too many hurricanes. To the outrage of Cubans, the bureau banned Belen forecasts from being transmitted over U.S.-controlled telegraph wires. The result was far more damaging to Americans than to Cubans. In 1900 Belen forecasters accurately described the scope and path of a rising hurricane, which Weather Bureau experts dismissed as a light tropical storm that would head for the Atlantic. The hurricane, the deadliest ever to hit the United States, crossed the Gulf of Mexico and obliterated the city of Galveston, Texas. Survivors buried the uncounted dead—somewhere between 6,000 and 10,000—in huge pyres on the streets of the wrecked downtown. Galveston never regained its position as a leading Gulf port.

PROGRESS OR APOCALYPSE?

Scientists, then, were hardly free of the larger prejudices of their culture, and their inquiries were shaped by the economic, social, and political contexts in which they worked. We can imagine late nineteenth-century American science as located in the middle of a square, pressured on four sides and exercising its own influence in those four directions. On one side were widely held prejudices about race, ethnicity, and gender. On another was the profound power of religious faith, especially Protestant Christianity. On the third side was the voracious economy of corporate capitalism, whose private for-profit laboratories became a key venue in which careers were made and scientific questions asked (or not asked). On the fourth side was government, which affected science through funding provided by the U.S. Geological Survey, agricultural experiment stations, and the new land-grant universities. Connections were already beginning to emerge between these last two sides. After England began to produce steel-hulled naval vessels in the 1870s, the race was on for armor that could resist bombardment. The American inventor August Harvey solved the problem in 1890, and in the next decade Andrew Carnegie's Homestead mill retooled to create nickel-plated "harveyized" steel in open-hearth furnaces. Carnegie's main customer for this steel was the U.S. Navy.

In their enthusiasm, observers overlooked the ways in which science replicated or magnified problems in the society that produced it. In the emerging genre of science fiction, American writers imagined every kind of future luxury and marvel, from time travel to vast underwater cities. King Camp Gillette, soon to be a famous manufacturer of razors, proposed that Americans would live in a single metropolis of sixty million people, powered by Niagara Falls, while the rest of the country became a vast parkland. Popular dime novels such as *Edison's Conquest of Mars*, by Garrett Serviss, offered spectacular visions of the triumphs of American ingenuity. Writer Anna Bowman Dodd, predicting the ruin of the world by women's liberation, nonetheless took time to describe the technological marvels she envisioned for AD 2050, such as an electric pneumatic tube that carried passengers under the Atlantic at 300 miles an hour while they enjoyed saunas and Turkish baths along the way.

Yet other writers emphasized the dark side of technological progress. Cosmic disasters figured largely in the era's imaginative fiction—speaking, perhaps, to the disturbing links between science and the destruction wrought by the new corporate order. Popular novels featured comets and meteors destroying large portions of the planet; in one novel a giant earthquake released poisonous clouds of gas from beneath the earth's crust. In *Caesar's Column*, a science fiction protest novel, Minnesota Populist Ignatius Donnelly envisioned a future America of cruel aristocrats and "great, dark, writhing masses"—an authoritarian hell on earth.

Bleakest of all, perhaps, was Mark Twain's 1889 book *A Connecticut Yankee in King Arthur's Court*, one of the first American novels to feature time travel. Twain's Yankee was Hank Morgan, a superintendent at the Colt firearms factory who found himself accidentally whisked back to sixth-century England. There he became known as The Boss and won almost unlimited power through his shrewd negotiations and technological know-how. Twain used the book to satirize monarchy and organized religion, the cult of Arthurian chivalry, and nineteenth-century Americans' belief in progress. In doing so he managed to offend an array of readers on both sides of the Atlantic. "A book that tries to deface our moral and literary currency by bruising and soiling the image of KING ARTHUR," huffed a British reviewer, "is a very unworthy production of the great humourist's pen." More perceptive critics saw that the novel's brilliance lay in its suggestion that industrial technology and militarism were wreaking as much havoc on the modern world as Hank Morgan did on King Arthur's England.

In Twain's climactic passage, which a critic called "one of the most distressing passages in American literature," Hank Morgan kills 25,000 of King Arthur's knights in an apocalyptic battle. Many die in an artificial flood engineered by the vengeful Yankee. Others are burned alive in a great explosion of dynamite. ("As to destruction of life, it was amazing," Morgan comments. "Of course we could not *count* the dead, because they did not exist as individuals, but merely as homogeneous protoplasm, with alloys of iron and buttons.") The rest of the knights, advancing across a field at night, walk into a series of electric fences. "Our current was so tremendous," Morgan observes, "that it killed before the victim could cry out. . . . One terrible thing about this was the absence of human voices; there were no cheers, no war cries." As the last contingent of knights crosses between the wires, Morgan flips a switch and electrocutes them all. His Gatling gun, an early form of machine gun, mows down the few survivors.

In the same year that *Connecticut Yankee* was published, a catastrophic flood in Johnstown, Pennsylvania, was brought on by the failure of a dam at an elite country club in the nearby hills. (The wealthy Pittsburgh industrialists who owned the property were never held liable.) The same year, 1889, witnessed America's first botched execution by electric chair. Twain's point about the dark uses of science and power seemed even more prescient with the arrival of the twentieth century. Little more than a decade after 1889, wars around the globe were being waged with Gatling guns manufactured in Morgan's hometown of Hartford, Connecticut, as well as barbed wire concentration camps, steel battleships, and dynamite and other new explosives. The gravity of these developments perhaps explains the tone that so unsettled Twain's contemporaries. "I have always preached," Twain remarked. "If the humor came of its own accord and uninvited I have allowed it a place in my sermon, but I was not writing the sermon for the sake of the humor." The final pages of *Connecticut Yankee* were, in fact, a grim sermon about the ominous bent of modern technology. Hank Morgan's flaw was not his scientific knowledge, but the fact that he wielded it with serene confidence in his own goodness and wisdom.

FOR FURTHER READING

On the dinosaur hunts see David R. Wallace, *The Bonehunters' Revenge* (Boston, 1999); John McPhee writes about "deep time" in *Annals of the Former World* (New York, 1998). On scientific thought more generally see Paul F. Boller, Jr., "New Men and New Ideas," in *The Gilded Age* ed. H. Wayne Morgan (Syracuse, NY, 1963), 221–44, Richard Hofstadter, *Social Darwinism in American Thought*, 2nd ed. (New York, 1955), and on pragmatism, Louis Menand, *The Metaphysical Club* (New York, 2001). Two sources that proved immensely useful in shaping this chapter are Peter J. Bowler, *The Eclipse of Darwinism* (Baltimore, 1983), and Steven Conn, *Museums and American Cultural Life* (Chicago, 1988).

On parlor collections see Katherine C. Grier, "The Decline of the Memory Palace," in *American Home Life, 1880–1930* ed. Jessica H. Foy and Thomas J. Schlereth (Knoxville, TN, 1992), 49–74. On grave-robbing in the West see David H. Thomas's *Skull Wars* (New York, 2000), and on anthropology in the Near East, Bruce Kuklick's fascinating study, *Puritans in Babylon* (Princeton, NJ, 1996). Thomas R. Trautmann, *Lewis Henry Morgan and the Invention of Kinship* (Berkeley, CA, 1987), is helpful on this leading anthropologist. On the world's fairs see Norman Bolotin and Christine Laing, *The World's Columbian Exposition* (Urbana, IL, 2002), Robert W. Rydell, *All the World's a Fair* (Chicago, 1984), and Alan Trachtenberg, *Incorporating America* (New York, 1982); on the "ethnologies" marketed by Buffalo Bill and Barnum and Bailey see Janet M. Davis, *The Circus Age*, cited in Chapter 4.

On technology and business see Nathan Rosenberg's thorough article, "The Commercial Exploitation of Science by American Industry," in *The Uneasy Alliance*, ed. Kim B. Clark, Robert H. Hayes, and Christopher Lorenz (Boston, 1985), 19–51, and on corporate laboratories, David F. Noble, *America By Design* (New York, 1977). Two excellent introductions to famous inventors are Theresa M. Collins and Lisa Gitelman, *Thomas Edison and Modern America* (Boston, 2002), and on the battle between Edison and Westinghouse, Jill Jonnes, *Empires of Light* (New York, 2003).

On the conquest of cholera see Charles E. Rosenbery *The Cholera Years: The United States in 1832, 1849, and 1866* (Chicago, 1962). On medicine more broadly see W. F. Bynum, *Science and the Practice of Medicine in the Nineteenth Century* (Cambridge, MA, 1994), and Paul Starr, *The Social Transformation of American Medicine* (New York, 1982); on hospitals I have drawn on Charles E. Rosenberg, *The Care of Strangers* (New York, 1987). For lively histories of antigerm campaigns see Nancy Tomes, *The Gospel of Germs* (Cambridge, MA, 1998) and Suellen Hoy, *Chasing Dirt: The American Pursuit of Cleanliness* (New York, 1995). On popular reception of medical advancements see also two articles by Bert Hansen, "America's First Medical Breakthrough," *American Historical Review* 103 (1998): 373–418, and "New Images of a New Medicine," *Bulletin of the History of Medicine* 73 (1999): 629–78.

On demographics see Michael Haines, "Life Expectancy," in *The Oxford Companion to United States History* (New York, 2001), 444–47. Scientific Temperance education is treated in Jonathan Zimmerman, *Distilling Democracy* (Lawrence, KS, 1999). On racial prejudice in medicine see Daniel J. Kevles, *In the Name of Eugenics* (New York, 1985), and Donald K. Pickens, *Eugenics and the Progressives* (Nashville, TN, 1968), as well as Leon F. Litwack's *Trouble in Mind* and Charles J. McClain's *In Search of Equality*, both cited earlier. On the gendered aspects of eugenics and related campaigns (such as "better baby contests") see Laura L. Lovett, *Conceiving the Future: Pronatalism, Reproduction, and the Family in the United States, 1890–1938* (Chapel Hill, NC, 2007). On the Galveston disaster see Erik Larson, *Isaac's Storm* (New York, 1999). For a detailed look at the emerging military-industrial complex see B. Franklin Cooling, *Gray Steel and Blue Water Navy* (Hamden, CT, 1979), on Johnstown, David G. McCullough, *The Johnstown Flood* (New York, 1968), and on science fiction Dolores Hayden, *The Grand Domestic Revolution* (Cambridge, MA, 1981). For helpful guides to *Connecticut Yankee* see the books on Twain by Justin Kaplan and Bryant Morey French, cited in the introduction. The quotation about the "distressing passages" at the novel's end, from Henry Nash Smith, is in Kaplan's *Mark Twain and His World*, 144.

CHAPTER 8

Faith

The great task of modern times [is] to solve, on the basis of
justice and righteousness, the problems presented by the
contrasts and evils of the present organization of society.
            —RABBI EMIL G. HIRSCH, CHICAGO

In September 1893 an ambitious conference took place on the grounds of the
Columbian Exposition in Chicago. The World's Parliament of Religions
attempted to bring representatives from every "great faith" into conversation. In
attendance were not only delegates from many Protestant denominations, Roman
Catholics, and Jews, but also Muslims, Hindus, Confucians, Jainists, Zoroastrians,
and Buddhists from around the globe. Scholars lectured on comparative world
religions, while reformers touched on such topics as "Human Brotherhood" and
"The Role of Spiritual Matters in Human Progress." One organizer declared in the
closing session that "what men deemed impossible, God has finally wrought. The
religions of the world . . . have conferred together on the vital questions of life and
immortality in a frank and friendly spirit, and now they part in peace, with many
warm expressions of mutual affection and respect."

The World's Parliament was not the first interfaith conversation in the United
States, much less in the world. The rise of ecumenical groups such as the Sunday
school movement and the YMCA had already strengthened ties among different
Protestant denominations, as had cooperative efforts in foreign missions. Some
liberal Protestants, Catholics, and Jews were already working together in the cause
of social reform. More radically, followers of Theosophy had been trying for a
decade to reconcile Christian and Buddhist principles into a universal faith. They
had presented this program to several Asian Buddhist leaders who were themselves responding to the threat of Christian missions with tentative efforts at
cooperation. Anagarika Dharmapala of Ceylon (now Sri Lanka), a prominent delegate to the Parliament, was a friend of elite Bostonian Henry Olcott, who some
years earlier had moved to Ceylon to study Buddhism and promote Theosophy.

Such delegates came to Chicago, in part, to offer pointed critiques of Western
imperialism. A number of Hindu and Buddhist speakers described Christian missionaries as arrogant and bigoted. Pung Kwang Yu, a Chinese representative,
denounced the entanglement of foreign missions with Western economic and

political designs. Jesus, he observed sharply, had not advised his followers to league themselves with "the foreign masters that were exercising supreme political control over his own country at the time." Even Asians who accepted Christianity warned against chauvinism. "We do not want the Christianity of England nor the Christianity of America," declared Japanese Protestant Nobuta Kishimoto. "We want the Christianity of Japan." An Armenian Protestant, Herant Kiretchijian, likewise identified himself with "the Orient" and informed Westerners that "you have unwittingly called together a council of your creditors. . . . We have given you science, philosophy, theology, music and poetry, and have made history for you at tremendous expense. . . . With that rich capital you have amassed a stupendous fortune, so that your assets hide away from your eyes your liabilities."

These sophisticated messages shocked Americans who had come to the Parliament to meet and convert heathens. "The people expected pagans. And pagans, they thought, were ignorant and impotent of mind," wrote one Methodist. "The Parliament was a stunning revelation." Protestants found to their dismay that others had come to Chicago to convert *them*. One delegate, a former U.S. diplomat named Mohammed Webb who had adopted Islam in Turkey, created a stir by announcing the foundation of a Muslim mission in New York City. Hindu Swami Vivekananda undertook a national lecture tour after the Parliament ended, and his followers created the American Vedanta Society. After hearing a speech by the charismatic Anagarika Dharmapala, a journalist reported that "one trembled to know that such a figure stood at the head of the movement to consolidate all the disciples of Buddha and 'spread the light of Asia' throughout the civilized world."

Christians, in the meantime, negotiated painful differences among themselves. One Protestant speaker dismissed Catholicism as an "ethnic faith" and its rites as mere superstition. Catholic representatives fired back, deploring Protestant laxity and "the shame and mischief of the divorce evil." Conflict surfaced within religious groups as well as among them: Jewish women were outraged when rabbis excluded them from the speaker's platform, and in response they organized a separate Jewish Women's Congress that led to the foundation of the National Council of Jewish Women. The Parliament's very existence provoked angry responses. Sultan Abdul Hamid II refused to allow anyone from the Ottoman Empire to participate, and Islam was thus poorly represented. So was the Church of England, after the archbishop of Canterbury condemned the idea of meeting with non-Christians in a spirit of mutual inquiry. The Presbyterian Church of the USA declined to participate, while one Protestant missionary wrote from Hong Kong to accuse conference organizers of planning "treason against Christ." A U.S. Catholic bishop who attended the Parliament endured fierce criticism for allegedly violating the principle of *communicatio in sacris*, which forbade Catholics from participating in any non-Catholic service.

At the same time, ironically, the Parliament planners overlooked some of the most creative religious movements emerging in the United States. The vibrant African-American denominations were grossly underrepresented. No delegates spoke from the Mormon church, the Holiness movement, or the growing ranks of

Christian Scientists. The Native American peyote faith, taking hold in Indian Territory during the early 1890s, might have been of great interest to scholars of comparative religion, since it blended the use of peyote spirit medicine with hymn singing, prayers to Jesus, and use of eagle feathers. Similarly, the Ghost Dance religion of native peoples greatly interested anthropologists such as James Mooney. Originating with a Paiute shaman, the Ghost Dance was a pan-Indian movement that strove to bring back bison and drive invaders from the land. Its rituals were so little understood by non-Indians that a tense standoff between Ghost Dancers and a U.S. cavalry unit at Wounded Knee, just three years before the Parliament, ended in the massacre of more than 200 Sioux men, women, and children. Parliament leaders, reflecting prevailing prejudice, found Indian beliefs and practices too alien for inclusion.

Despite its limitations and failings, though, the Parliament did open a tentative interfaith dialogue. Well before Americans grasped all the implications of their nation's rising political and economic power, they were debating pluralism, cultural differences, and foreign relations in the arena of religious faith. In doing so they raised issues that would haunt future American society and politics. Anglo-American Protestants still largely presumed that the United States was a Christian nation and that Protestants spoke for the best interests of their country and even the world. But their provincialism met spirited challenges both at home and abroad.

GLOBAL MISSIONS

Protestant foreign missions reached new heights of ambition in the 1890s. Steamships carried U.S. missionaries abroad in record numbers, with more than 5,000 serving by the turn of the century. Missionaries could now reach remote sites with relative case, bring extensive supplies, and return regularly to the United States for fund-raising tours. They enjoyed support from the largest grassroots American movement of the era, the Protestant missionary societies, whose combined membership in 1900 totaled more than one million.

Though foreign mission work had decidedly mixed results for "heathens," it offered bracing challenges for Americans. It drew especially on young people's idealism and desire for adventure and self-testing. Missionaries often discovered their calling in emotional revival meetings. Many were swept up in the Student Volunteer Movement, an offshoot of the YMCA that recruited idealistic college graduates for the mission field, hoping to achieve "the evangelization of the world in this generation." George Campbell and Jennie Wortman, two students at an Illinois college, separately reached the conclusion that they should go into mission work. "Oh, how I want to *do* something," Jennie wrote in her diary. With the mission board pressing George to find a wife, the two arranged to meet, conduct a quick courtship, and marry—a not uncommon strategy for women to find their way into overseas service.

A decade later more women went into foreign missions by themselves, as part of a bold expansion of female authority. By 1903 more than 60 percent of foreign

Table 8.1 Largest Religious Denominations in the United States, 1895

DENOMINATION	ESTIMATED NUMBER OF COMMUNICANTS
Roman Catholic	7,988,322
Methodist Episcopal	2,629,985
Southern Baptist	1,448,570
Methodist Episcopal, South	1,379,928
Colored Baptist	1,343,530
Northern Baptist	985,752
Disciples of Christ	923,663
Presbyterian, North	902,757
Protestant Episcopal	616,843
Congregational	600,000
African Methodist Episcopal	594,776
Lutheran Synodical Conference	479,221

H. K. Carroll, who compiled these statistics, reflected contemporary prejudices when he lumped together as "pagan" all Buddhists, Theosophists, followers of the Ethical Culture movement, and communal utopian societies. He did count, however, 182 Chinese temples and religious organizations.

Source: *H. K. Carroll, The Religious Forces of the United States (New York, 1898).*

Protestant missionaries were women, a number that did not include many missionary wives who assisted unpaid in their husbands' work. Women argued that they were indispensable to the mission project, since uplifting "degraded" women and modeling Christian family life were central goals. Sarah Goodrich, who went to China as a single female missionary, explained her choice as one of selfless faith: "Sometimes I feel as if a woman could comprehend the Christ, this utter sacrifice of self, as no man can." "Among uncivilized people woman is a slave, nude, filthy, her life by a degree above the brute," declared the president of the Congregational Woman's Board of Missions. "Only a woman can teach her purity, delicacy, and the divine art of home-making."

Despite such condescension, many missionaries reacted to the cultures they encountered with a mixture of fascination and respect. Many came to understand the havoc wrought by Western imperialism and commercial interests, and some became openly critical of European and U.S. designs. Those who expected to encounter "barbarism" often came to appreciate the worldviews of people they served. Others shifted in the opposite direction, finding that a custom such as Chinese foot binding turned them into critics of the societies they hoped to alter. Jean Kenyon Mackenzie, who served as a Presbyterian missionary in West Africa, began her service expressing great sensitivity to African customs, but after a year in the field she wrote home, "Polygamy is terrible. I had too open a mind about it when I came to Africa—and now I have so many sad thoughts of it." Mackenzie came to believe that she had a special mission to comfort African women who suffered "superstition and blame" because they could not bear children. Wielding scientific explanations as well as a gospel message, Mackenzie wrote, "I am coming to be a kind of doctor to the hearts of childless women."

As Mackenzie's account suggested, foreign missionaries found that medicine and education were among the most effective tools they carried with them. Earlier in the century Protestants had emphasized straightforward preaching in foreign lands, without much attempt to shape customs or cultures. Now they recognized that science was useful to those who were enduring political and economic upheaval. Missionaries thus shaped and fostered modernization, especially by bringing medical training and support for women's rights and female education. Ida Scudder, born in South India, was a granddaughter of American missionaries and daughter of a missionary doctor. She grew up expecting to move to the United States and marry, but local men began asking her to serve as a midwife, since her father, as a man, was not permitted to fulfill this role. Ida was untrained in medicine and refused, but her conscience was seared after three women died in childbirth. Ida headed back to the United States for a medical degree from Cornell and then returned to India, where she worked as a traveling doctor for half a century in rural areas around Vellore. Among other achievements, she helped found a hospital, a nursing school, and a women's medical college.

Other missionaries advanced far more dubious projects. Violence against Protestant missionaries in China provided the chief justification for Western military intervention around the turn of the century, which forced an open door to business interests. One of the first Protestants to begin work in Korea, Presbyterian Horace Allen had become by the mid-1880s the United States' key diplomat there. Lending his influence to a promodernization faction, Allen also helped Secretary of State James Blaine and the Wall Street firm of Morton Bliss obtain large tracts of Korean real estate and access to rich gold mines. Allen ended up quite wealthy himself, while his business and diplomatic maneuvers helped leave Korea weak. When the peninsula fell under Japanese control, Allen protested bitterly, but partly due to Allen's own actions, Japan's power over Korea was by then a fait accompli.

Home missions, undertaken within the boundaries of the United States, could also have troubling consequences. From Reconstruction onward, Christian reform groups such as the Indian Rights Association played major roles in developing federal Indian policy, working to convert native peoples and "kill the Indian to save the man." Women's mission groups throughout the West raised money to convert American Indians, Chinese immigrants, and even Mormons. Such efforts were viewed suspiciously by those being proselytized, but missionaries were not always unwelcome. San Francisco's Presbyterian Mission Home, run by the energetic Donaldina Cameron, became popular with Chinese prostitutes who arranged to escape from brothels and meet Chinese-American husbands-to-be inside the mission's sheltering space, away from employers who sought to hold them in virtual slavery. Cameron, who supervised the home for almost forty years, argued that this validated her work, and she strove to win conversions among those who asked for her aid. At the same time she defended Chinese Americans against what she saw as racist stereotypes in the larger culture. She studied Chinese literature and history, often wore traditional Asian clothing, and worked side by side with

Chinese-American "native helpers" such as Ah Tsun Wing and Tien Fu Wu, converts who, like the missionaries, negotiated between the expectations of different worlds.

African-American Protestants found themselves in a position very different from that of their white counterparts. Participating in the extraordinary growth of black religious institutions after Emancipation, members of the Baptist, African Methodist Episcopal (AME), and other churches focused much of their attention on pressing problems near at hand. Church members helped their communities by providing adult education, aid to the unemployed, and care for children, orphans, and the elderly. Black churches also became vehicles for temperance, racial justice campaigns, and other expressions of African-American identity. Black women carved out key roles in the churches, using Christian respectability as a bridge between themselves and white women interested in reform. As churches became expressions of race pride, they served as vehicles for drawing a line between the respectable and the unchurched. Mindful of white stereotypes, some black ministers condemned not only gambling and fast living but also loud talk, bright clothes, and Sunday baseball games.

Overseas, white Protestant denominations increasingly refused to sponsor black missionaries, even in Africa, where European colonial governments discouraged almost all educational projects on the grounds that they might cause unrest. Thus Africa, unlike Asia, saw the creation of very few Christian schools founded by Western donors. In 1899 AME missionaries from the United States were stymied when they undertook an outreach campaign in what is today South Africa. A leader of the project, Bishop Henry McNeal Turner of Georgia, advocated education and collective action for racial justice. His lectures on "The Unity of the Race" frightened British and Afrikaner authorities. AME representatives were denied permits to travel in rural areas and for decades afterward had to offer financial and legal aid from afar.

Foreign missions, then, had the capacity to carry Protestants far beyond their provincial worldview, but at the same time missionary work could reflect and even magnify existing prejudices. Some missionaries offered vocal and enthusiastic support for the World's Parliament of Religions. One minister in southern India, writing to endorse the plan, reported that he and local Brahmins were "continually comparing Christianity with Hinduism" and "having conferences with the representatives of Islam." Criticized by Asian delegates, some missionaries at the Parliament freely acknowledged the shortcomings of European and American policy and expressed hope that Christianity might provide colonized peoples with tools to defend their rights. Yet missionaries retained a persistent tone of chauvinism, and those who brought home news of their exploits often reinforced the condescension of American audiences. One speaker at the Parliament, having returned from a trip around the world, attacked Islamic "superstition and bigotry" and dismissed Asia as a "stagnant pool of heathenism." In the worst cases, such as that of Horace Allen in Korea, missionaries facilitated bold grabs for imperial power and enjoyed the fruits of that power themselves.

ROOTS OF FUNDAMENTALISM AND LIBERALISM

In Harold Frederic's wonderful novel *The Damnation of Theron Ware*, published in 1896, a young Methodist minister named Theron Ware finds himself posted in the imaginary town of Octavius, New York. Reverend Ware is supremely confident in his beliefs, but he has not reckoned on the forces of modernity and pluralism. Theron first meets a Catholic priest who studies anthropology and speaks casually of "this Christ-myth of ours." Then he encounters a doctor who endorses Darwin's theory of evolution. Last Theron is swept away by the beautiful Celia Madden, a wealthy Catholic girl. Celia is a leisured, freethinking music lover with the ambition to do what she pleases. Hearing Celia sing and play Chopin, Theron is smitten. He contemplates adultery while becoming ever more cruel and patronizing toward his devoted wife. At the end of the novel, Theron receives an intellectual and spiritual comeuppance. The author leaves him in limbo- no longer satisfied by the old ways, but woefully unsuited to the new.

Through Theron Ware, Harold Frederic explored the forces that were eroding mainstream Protestantism in the last decades of the nineteenth century: materialism, science, and the growth of Catholicism and other competing faiths. But Frederic suggested that new ideas held their power because Protestantism was rotting from the inside. The elders in Theron's church are mean and narrow-minded. They forbid the minister's wife to wear flowers in her bonnet, and they force Theron to pay the parsonage gas bill from his skimpy salary. Meanwhile, two elders are profiting from high-interest loans they made to the church. When the congregation hires a professional evangelist for a fund-raising campaign, she corrupts Theron far more thoroughly than the priest, the doctor, and Celia do. She tells him he must manipulate people to get what he wants, and her successful revival suggests that her strategy works. Protestantism, in this light, was becoming another venue for marketing and commercial empire-building. "You simply *can't* get along," the evangelist tells Theron, "without some of the wisdom of the serpent."

At the time *Theron Ware* appeared, Protestants faced an array of profound challenges. Old denominational barriers were weakening, and conflicting attitudes toward modernity pushed Protestants down divergent paths. By 1900 the rough outlines of two emerging camps were discernable. Fundamentalists, though they did not yet go by that name, denounced modern secularism and defended the literal truth of the Bible, while adopting marketing techniques that helped them build Gospel empires. Liberal Protestants, on the other hand, made common cause with one another and occasionally with Jews and Catholics in the work of the Social Gospel. They challenged Americans to leave their comfortable Sunday pews and take their faith into the world, fighting the poverty, degradation, and despair that industrialization had wrought.

The United States in these years was evangelized as well as evangelizing. That fact was dramatically illustrated one May afternoon in 1880 when eight English men and women marched off a steamship in New York and reenacted Columbus's discovery of America. To the bewilderment of onlookers, they hoisted a "Blood and Fire" flag and, on behalf of the Salvation Army, claimed the United States in the name of God. It was the first wave of an invasion launched by William and Evangeline Booth, founders of the Salvation Army in England. The army's early efforts met ridicule (especially when a banner informed New Yorkers by mistake that the army would "Attract the Kingdom of the Devil" rather than "Attack" it). But within a decade, Salvation Army street ministers and rescue workers had become a familiar sight across the United States.

The Salvation Army focused on action—saving souls for Christ. Its founders were not so much theological innovators as brilliant publicists who adopted mass marketing to serve their cause. "ATTRACT ATTENTION," advised William Booth, an early proponent of the idea that there is no such thing as bad publicity. "If the people are in danger of the damnation of Hell, and asleep in the danger, awaken them," he wrote. Salvationists alerted bystanders through music, bell-ringing, pageants, dramatic readings, and personal testimony. Many were drawn from the working class or had once been "down and out," and they took their movement to people they thought needed it most. Salvation Army bands played and preached on the streets and at parks where people gathered to relax. Most of all, they marched into slums and skid rows to offer food and shelter to the destitute. Advancing no systemic critique of poverty and avoiding most political issues (though they denounced lynching in 1895), Salvation Army leaders offered, instead, "heart religion" and direct material aid.

The Army's American branch evolved into a sophisticated social welfare agency with conversion as its core goal. In 1891 it opened the New York Lighthouse, a shelter for men in Greenwich Village. Those who needed a bed could stay for 7¢ a night, and the penniless could sweep or chop wood to cover the fee. Unlike most charitable agencies, the Salvation Army made no judgments about a person's past or whether he or she "deserved" aid, a strategy crucial to its success. At the height of the depression of the 1890s, the New York branch housed as many as 3,000 homeless men per night, as well as providing day care for working mothers and a "rescue home" for women who wanted to stop working as prostitutes. Aggressive evangelical campaigns could be dangerous, and workers who preached in rough neighborhoods were frequently beaten up and sometimes even killed. Like foreign mission work, though, the Salvation Army held out great spiritual rewards.

The Army's founders emphasized emotional passion and individual salvation, hallmarks of emerging fundamentalism, but like proponents of the Social Gospel, they advanced a public mission. The Army was unusual in bridging both camps, which may explain why it has endured so long. Doctrinally, the Booths and their followers emerged from Holiness, a cross-Atlantic spiritual revival movement. Holiness thinkers stressed the ability of the Holy Spirit to fill a person with direct, ecstatic power. Army followers spread that gospel in an atmosphere of warmth and festivity. When the movement arrived in Kingston, North Carolina, one local woman dismissed it at first as "a minstrel or comic show," but she changed her mind, reporting that "I never saw such a happy set of people before and I soon became convinced that they were a very different set of Christians."

Pillar of Salt, circa 1880s. A Kansas salt company uses the biblical story of Lot's wife—along with sketches of adorable children—in a trade card advertising its "R.S.V.P. Table Salt." The strategy of using religious themes in advertisements may not have been successful, since religious images like this became less frequent in later ads. Author's collection.

Holiness, a radical outgrowth of Methodism, attracted people from many backgrounds by encouraging believers to celebrate a personal experience of Christ's power. Holiness teachings broke down barriers of all kinds. In Arkansas the widow of one Holiness preacher was asked to speak before 500 men at a penitentiary. Terrified, she felt a spiritual "loosening" that helped her testify to God's love, launching her on her own preaching career. By the turn of the century, Holiness had produced cross-racial congregations in all parts of the country, during a decade when racial lines were hardening. Outside Houston, Charles Fox Parham preached Holiness ideas and faith healing in his new Apostolic Faith Movement. One of his disciples, a former slave from Louisiana named William Seymour, took this gospel to Los Angeles, where he shared the gifts of faith healing and speaking in tongues. Parham and Seymour's followers created a faith soon known as Pentecostalism. Intensely personal and emotional, it would exert a profound influence on twentieth-century Protestantism.

Salvation Army, "Cathedral of the Open Air." This cartoon shows that Christians could envision crowded urban squares, as well as rural landscapes, as sacred spaces for the faithful. *War Cry*, 7 October 1893.

Even more influential was the preaching of Dwight Moody, the era's most famous evangelist. Born in 1837, Moody drew his faith not from a traditional denomination but from service to the ecumenical YMCA. By the end of the Civil War, Moody had given up work as a shoe salesman to build a street church in Chicago. He soon embarked on international preaching tours, and after winning mass conversions in England and Scotland in 1873, he came home a celebrity. Appealing to audiences through his rugged physique and friendly, colloquial style, Moody departed sharply from "perfectionism," the optimistic belief that Christians could bring about the millennium through good works. Moody instead argued that the world was preordained by God to fall further and further into sin and wretchedness. When humanity had reached the nadir, Christ would resurrect the righteous and consign sinners to hell. "I look upon this world as a wrecked vessel,"

Moody declared. "God has given me a lifeboat and said to me, 'Moody, save all you can.'" This pessimistic view suggested that humanitarian and reform projects were a useless distraction from the business of filling the lifeboat. Moody told Christians to look beyond this world to the next. Yet he was a transitional figure who did not call himself a fundamentalist—as his successors would by the 1920s—and refrained from attacking those who held different theological views.

Other Protestants were less willing than Moody to consign the world to doom. Proponents of the Social Gospel urged Christians to respond directly to the evils of industrialization, as they had to slavery and other national sins. Charles Sheldon's novel *In His Steps*, which originated the phrase "What would Jesus do?" perhaps captured the essence of the Social Gospel more fully than any other text. Sheldon's story, published in 1896, was set in Raymond, a fictional midwestern railroad hub that looked suspiciously like the author's own Topeka. At the start of the book, a visiting tramp enters the First Church of Raymond and asks the congregation about their faith. "Somehow I get puzzled," he says,

> when I see so many Christians living in luxury and singing "Jesus, I my cross have taken, all to leave and follow Thee," and remember how my wife died in a tenement in New York City, gasping for air and asking God to take the little girl too. Of course I don't expect you people can prevent every one from dying of starvation, lack of proper nourishment and tenement air, but what does following Jesus mean? . . . It seems to me there's an awful lot of trouble in the world that somehow wouldn't exist if all the people who sing such songs went and lived them out.

Moved by the tramp's speech and subsequent death, the minister of First Church invites members of his congregation to join him in a pledge: for a year they will ask themselves before taking any action, "What would Jesus do?" The results revolutionize the congregation and the city of Raymond. A number of church members quit their ethically compromising jobs. A department store magnate begins paying higher wages to his employees, and a railroad superintendent submits evidence of his company's illegal activities to the Interstate Commerce Commission. Professors at the local college take part in a temperance campaign, even though they hate the rough-and-tumble world of politics. A young heiress and her brother endow a newspaper, whose editor finds that in order to stick to principles rather than money, he must operate the *Raymond Daily News* as a nonprofit venture. The minister himself finds that following Jesus requires him to practice more "self-denial and suffering." He gives up his comfortable position at First Church and moves to the slums to work with the poor.

Though few acknowledged the connection, Social Gospelers sought many of the same goals as did Holiness and Pentecostal Christians. Both turned in different ways to the history of the early Christian church and sought to bring its principles and practices into the modern world. But they sought this goal by different paths, and some, such as Episcopal convert W. D. P. Bliss, combined their social concerns with a renewed emphasis on high-church ritual. Harold Frederic captured this angle neatly in *The Damnation of Theron Ware* when he depicted Theron peeking into a Catholic Mass for the first time and being swept away by the smell of incense, the sight of a priest in rich vestments, and the echoes of a haunting Latin chant. Anglican and Roman Catholic traditions offered a sense of mystery and wonder. Though the actual extent of Protestant conversion to Catholicism is unclear, medieval saints such as Francis of Assisi and Joan of Arc began to enjoy cult status in literature and art. Medievalism drew deeply on the era's wellspring of spiritual need: the search for a profound and authentic faith in a world ruled by material values.

In emphasizing Christians' work in the world, some Catholics met Social Gospel Protestants on middle ground. One of the most prominent was Father John Ryan, a Minnesota farmer's son who became a leading figure at the St. Paul Seminary and in 1906 wrote the influential progressive text *A Living Wage*. Ryan drew on Catholic doctrine as well as other sources to argue that every breadwinner should earn enough money to provide basic shelter, food, and security for his family. Such arguments were part of a broader struggle to claim a place for Catholics in modernizing America. The number of Catholics in the United States doubled between 1870 and 1900; by the latter year they constituted 20 percent of the population. Even the most prejudiced Protestants could not fail to note the significance of Catholicism, while the Vatican could no longer overlook the power and size of its church in the United States.

American Catholics were made up of a diverse mix of peoples, including eastern Europeans, Italians, French Canadians, and Mexicans as well as the more established Irish and Germans who dominated the church hierarchy. Lay Catholicism was often strong in areas where church infrastructure was weak. Though most Mexicans in the Southwest lived far from the nearest priest (who, when he visited, often spoke no Spanish) they carefully tended family altars, celebrated holy days, and each December mounted elaborate productions of the Spanish drama *Los Pastores* (the shepherds), a Christmas story that spoke to the circumstances of their daily lives. Similarly, immigrants from southern Italy brought rituals and beliefs surrounding a beloved image of the Virgin Mary, the Madonna del Carmine. In Italian Harlem each July, the *festa* of the Madonna brought Italians together to give thanks and petition for healing. Some Americanized Catholics were embarrassed by the public procession to the church, which included barefoot penitents with bloodied faces and women who crawled on hands and knees and expressed their devotion to Mary by dragging their tongues along the stones of the church floor as they approached the altar.

From the 1880s onward, the American Catholic church was riven by conflict between traditionalists and so-called Americanists who sought to raise the church's stature in the United States through assimilation. The Vatican did little to help Americanists and much to undercut them. In 1870 the First Vatican Council announced the doctrine of papal infallibility, a bulwark against lay dissent and secularism. In 1896, when Father John Zahm tried to reconcile Darwinian science and Catholic faith in a popular series of lectures under the title *Evolution and Dogma*, he met intense criticism and censorship from the Vatican, as did the American Sulpician priests Francis Gigot and John Hogan when they proposed that modern scientific ideas be included in Catholic seminary education. The Vatican's crowning statement of orthodoxy was Leo XIII's *Testem Benevolentiae* in 1899, which warned against "theological Americanism," or excessive accommodation to the forces of modernity and religious relativism. "There are some among you," Leo warned, "who conceive of and desire a church in America different from that which is in the rest of the world." This the Vatican could not tolerate.

Leo XIII handed one clear victory to Catholic liberals. In his 1891 statement *Rerum Novarum*, an encyclical on the relations of capital and labor, he critiqued industrial capitalism and issued a clarification on Catholic membership in labor unions, an issue hotly disputed among U.S. bishops. *Rerum Novarum* gave Catholics the pope's explicit permission to join worker brotherhoods such as the Knights of Labor. Though he condemned socialism and ruled private property to be "in accordance with the law of nature," Pope Leo also criticized industrialization, arguing that "working men have been surrendered, isolated and helpless, to the hardheartedness of employers and the greed of unchecked competition." He noted the disparity between the super-rich and "the utter poverty of the masses" and described some wage earners as under "a yoke little better than that of slavery." *Rerum Novarum* thus opened avenues for American Catholic reformers such as John Ryan to speak out on questions of economic justice.

In the meantime, one of the greatest areas of conflict between Protestants and Catholics, as well as among Catholics themselves, was schooling. Catholic conservatives feared Americanization, believing it would lead immigrants and their children (like Celia Madden in *The Damnation of Theron Ware*) into the temptations of secularism. They argued for separate Catholic schools where students could be taught in immigrant languages because "language saves faith." In Wisconsin an 1889 law requiring all school instruction to be in English precipitated a furor among German speakers, including Lutherans and especially Catholics who had 40,000 children in the state's parochial schools. Catholic liberals, while distressed by Protestant prejudice, believed that the solution lay in English-language schooling that would integrate Catholic immigrants into the mainstream. The Vatican tolerated a brief effort by Archbishop John Ireland of St. Paul, a leading Americanist, to operate joint public-Catholic schools in two Minnesota districts, but such experiments were rare. Most of the energy of priests and lay leaders went toward parochial education, based on the mandate of the First Vatican Council that Catholics around the world should help to create and maintain local Catholic schools.

American Jews faced a number of problems similar to those of Catholics. Like Irish and German Catholics who had emigrated in large numbers before the Civil War, German Jews had prospered in America for a generation. In the late nineteenth century, both assimilated groups watched with dismay as waves of newcomers altered the face of their religions. Most eastern European Jews, like Italian and eastern European Catholics, arrived poor and clung to the bottom rungs of the economic ladder. Their poverty and alien customs seemed to heighten Protestant prejudices, and they swamped existing structures of worship and social services. Though many immigrant Jews attended services only a few times each year, makeshift arrangements had to be made for open-air services on the High Holy Days, which were attended in New York by as many as 164,000 people.

Before the 1880s American Judaism was led by figures such as Rabbi I. M. Wise of Cincinnati, who sought to adapt his faith to a climate of relative religious freedom in the United States. Wise helped establish what is known today as Reform Judaism, but he gave it the name *American Judaism*. He instituted such reforms as seating men and women together in synagogue, providing religious education for girls as well as boys, having music sung by mixed choirs, and even using organ music. By 1880 Wise had created a nationwide Union of American Hebrew Congregations and a seminary, Cincinnati's Hebrew Union College. Yet the use of the term *union* masked debates and disagreements among those who considered themselves Reform, American, or modern Jews. Should American Jews keep kosher, or was that a superstitious form of "kitchen Judaism," as Wise once called it? How much Hebrew and Talmudic education should boys receive—and how about girls? To what extent should American Jews think of themselves as a separate nation or people? In assimilating, were they losing their identity and faith?

Eastern Europeans complicated these questions by bringing a very different kind of Judaism to the United States. While some were secular in outlook, many others arrived with a heightened sense of tradition in light of the brutal anti-Semitism from which they had fled. The first great influx from Russia occurred in 1882, after the assassination of Czar Alexander II, when government officials and the press blamed Russia's Jews as a convenient scapegoat and touched off rounds of violence. An even deadlier wave of pogroms began in 1903. During both decades synagogues and Jewish homes were set on fire, women raped, Jews beaten to death and burned alive in their homes, and small children thrown out of windows. Harsh laws followed, expelling Jews from towns and cities and restricting their employments and access to education. One Jewish veteran of the Russian Army, decorated for his heroism on the battlefield, was stunned to find himself expelled from Moscow. He decided he had "only one exit, to seek my fortune in America."

By the mid-1880s the increasing diversity of American Jews was already precipitating conflicts. Hungarian Rabbi Alexander Kohut, arriving in the United States at the invitation of traditionalists, declared that American Reform Judaism had gone too far from the "Mosaic-rabbinical tradition. . . . It is suicide; and suicide is not reform." Reform Jews responded vigorously, calling a conference in Pittsburgh to formulate a clear statement of their views. They shared two goals with the traditionalists: they considered Judaism "the central religious truth for the human race," and they sought to combat indifference and secularism among the American Jewish masses. But taking a historical perspective, they argued that most biblical laws had stemmed from the "primitive ideas" of ancient times, and they argued that modern Judaism should be rooted in progressive ideals and Enlightenment rationalism. The Pittsburgh Platform called for women's religious equality and mission work among the poor. It also declared that American Jews "consider ourselves no longer a nation, but a religious community." This controversial statement, which distanced Reform

Judaism from Zionism and the quest for a Jewish state in Palestine, stood for fifty years.

The Pittsburgh Platform was a rallying point for progressives, but it hardly created unity among Jews, especially with the steady increase of new arrivals from eastern Europe. While there had been only about twenty Orthodox synagogues in the United States in 1880, by 1910 there were nearly 2,000. By that date Orthodox congregations constituted 90 percent of all American synagogues and served more than two million people. Yiddish-speaking communities sprang up in the large cities of the Northeast—especially New York—and built rich traditions of worship, literature, theater and political activism. Many new immigrants joined *lands-smanshaftn*, clubs made up of people from a particular village for the purpose of maintaining home ties and sending aid in time of crisis.

But traditional Jews confronted some of the same problems as did Reform leaders. Religious practice was compromised by the conditions of American life, especially in a commercial metropolis such as New York. Poverty-stricken immigrants endured long hours of work, often on Saturday, the Jewish Sabbath. The majority of children received little religious or Hebrew teaching. Jews were, in their own ways, susceptible to the same forces that worked on Theron Ware: the promise of material plenty and religious relativism in a pluralist society. Like Protestants and Catholics, they struggled in various ways to blend old and new. Jewish women, for example, traditionally excluded from religious leadership and learning, took on prominent roles in American Judaism through nationwide women's organizations and local sisterhoods. Ray Frank of Oregon, an inspiring speaker, represented the tensions between tradition and modernity when she went on the lecture circuit urging women to help men uphold Jewish tradition.

Through projects to revitalize and adapt Judaism in the United States, a range of traditions developed between the poles of Orthodoxy and Reform. Rabbi Solomon Schechter, who arrived in 1902 to become leader of the Jewish Theological Seminary in New York, challenged Reform principles while at the same time speaking of "Catholic Israel," the unity of all Jews. Schechter succeeded no better than his predecessor, Isaac Wise, in bringing all American Jews under one spiritual umbrella. Instead, the term *Conservative Judaism* came into use to describe his particular blend of tradition and modernity. Eventually, Jewish synagogues in the United States fell roughly into the categories Orthodox, Conservative, and Reform, but all differed markedly from European tradition. In the most prominent Orthodox synagogues of Boston and New York, men and women worshipped (separately) in quiet surroundings, according to prevailing American tastes rather than eastern European custom. They vied to hire the most talented cantors, and they sat beneath spectacular chandeliers on velvet cushions, as proud of these material manifestations of faith as were prosperous urban Protestants and Catholics, sitting in their grand urban churches and cathedrals.

The adaptability and creativity of religious faith was illustrated even more dramatically by religious liberals and by those who did not fit clearly on a continuum between the traditional and modern. Orthodox Jews pointed in horror to

Felix Adler's Society for Ethical Culture, which carried Reform Judaism past its furthest limits and remade it into an essentially secular form of moral inquiry. Movements such as Theosophy and Christian Science also carried Americans into new spiritual territory. Experimental colonies abounded, from the Shiloh Movement in Durham, Maine, to the *bruderhof* colonies of Hutterites, who emigrated from the Ukraine to South Dakota in 1874. The Koreshan Unity Movement, followers of a Union veteran and medical doctor who in 1869 experienced a celestial vision of himself as a messiah, became established in Chicago, San Francisco, and other cities. In 1895 Elizabeth Cady Stanton and a group of feminist theologians published *The Woman's Bible*, challenging the idea that the Bible called for women's subordination. The project was so controversial that it cost Stanton her position as head of the National American Woman Suffrage Association, where a rising generation of young leaders wanted to appear more mainstream.

Meanwhile, in Belton, Texas, a devout Methodist housewife named Martha McWhirter founded a sort of Protestant convent. Grieving over the deaths of two children, McWhirter attended a revival meeting in 1869 and heard the voice of God urging her to bring women together. She and other Belton women (including at least five who had suffered domestic violence) declared themselves celibate, left their husbands, and created the Sanctified Sisters. They supported themselves with a cooperative hotel and farm, organizing their work so efficiently that no one labored more than five hours a day. The Sanctified Sisters moved to Washington, D.C., in 1898, renamed themselves the Woman's Commonwealth, and flourished well into the twentieth century. The extraordinary diversity of experiments such as these showed the extent of the challenges that traditional religion faced; they also suggested that Americans responded to modernity not only with secularism and skepticism, but with creative forms of religious practice.

NATURE AND FAITH

In 1902 Dakota Sioux author Zitkala-Sa published a bold declaration to the Christian world that she remained unconverted. "When the spirit swells my breast," she wrote in *Atlantic Monthly*, "I love to roam leisurely among the green hills; or sometimes, sitting on the brink of the murmuring Missouri, I marvel at the great blue overhead." The shape of a prominent rock reminded her of the "subtle knowledge of the native folk which enable[s] them to recognize a kinship to any and all parts of this vast universe." Visited by missionaries and converts among her own people, Zitkala-Sa rejected their beliefs. She wrote, "I prefer to their dogma my excursions into the natural gardens where the voice of the Great Spirit is heard in the twittering of birds, the rippling of mighty waters, and the sweet breathing of flowers. If this is Paganism, then at present, at least, I am a Pagan."

For centuries American Indians like Zitkala-Sa had listened politely to Christian missionaries and gone off to continue their own religious practices, but before 1902 none had explained his or her rejection of Christianity to a nationwide audience in *Atlantic Monthly*. Even more important, some readers of *Atlantic* began to accept her views and even share them. Zitkala-Sa was meeting Christians on a spiritual middle ground. In the same year she published "Why I Am a Pagan," Anglo author Mary Austin put the finishing touches on *Land of Little Rain*, destined to become famous for its melding of Christian and native traditions in a tribute to the desert. Austin, who moved to a ranch in the Owens Valley of Southern California with her husband in 1892, had grown up a devout Methodist in rural Illinois. Pressed by her grandfather to learn large parts of the Bible by heart, she experienced revelations as a young child but found herself dissatisfied with the limits of Christianity. In the desert Austin undertook a religious quest, studying Paiute and Shoshone beliefs and prophecies. Among her characters in *Land of Little Rain* were Seyavi, a Paiute basket weaver, and Winnenap, a Shoshone healer, both based on neighbors who taught Austin that God could be found in reverence for the earth.

Americans had good reason to discover such reverence at the turn of the twentieth century. Like Austin, who grieved over the sale and development of grasslands near her ranch, Americans had witnessed an immense push to clear forests, drain swamps and deltas, mine, and farm. The landscapes left in the wake of these enterprises were ugly: burned-over clear-cuts, fields stripped of topsoil, hillsides littered with oil derricks, and noxious piles of mine tailings. Those very landscapes helped bring forth an ethos of respect for the untouched places that remained, and from that impulse emerged a loosely organized but popular movement of nature worship, often blended with Christianity and other traditional faiths but sometimes supplanting them. At the same time, railroads and resort hotels made it easier for Americans to visit remote locations and contemplate awe-inspiring vistas. The old contrast between the dangerous backwoods and the safety of human settlements was reversed, and the wildest spots on the continent became places of refuge from the ills of a human-dominated continent. Nature, as *Outlook* magazine observed, was coming to be seen as "the playground of the soul."

Love of nature took many spiritual forms. Magazines such as *Outing* (launched in 1885) and *Outdoor Life* (1897) not only dispensed practical travel advice but also celebrated the awe and peace that nature could impart. Many Protestants relaxed old prohibitions on Sunday recreation, arguing that fresh air and exercise were appropriate for the Lord's Day. "The Puritan Sabbath has been definitely renounced," wrote a minister in 1900, endorsing Sunday afternoon golf. Landscape architect Frederick Law Olmsted designed urban parks as well as walkways and landscapes at sites such as Yosemite and Niagara Falls. Yosemite, he wrote, represented "the union of the deepest sublimity with the deepest beauty."

Congress set aside Yosemite for the state of California in 1864, specifying that it be preserved for "public use, resort, and recreation." Yellowstone became the first national park in the world in 1872, followed by Yosemite, which returned to federal ownership in 1890; Sequoia in the same year; Mt. Rainier in 1899; Crater Lake in 1902; and South Dakota's Wind Cave in 1903. "You think of the civilization you have left behind," wrote one journalist of such sites. "Seen through the eyes of the wilderness, how stupid and insane it all seems. The mad eagerness of money-seeking men, the sham pleasures of conventional society, the insistence upon the importance of being in earnest over trifles, pall on you when you think of them. Your blood clarifies; your brain becomes active. You get a new view of life."

For the era's greatest advocate of wilderness preservation, John Muir, nature worship served as a replacement for Christian faith. Born in Scotland and raised in Wisconsin, Muir suffered brutal beatings and overwork at the hands of a harsh Presbyterian father. Like Mary Austin, he learned to recite large portions of the Bible by heart, though in Muir's case he recalled learning his verses through "sore flesh." From an early age Muir found solace in the natural world. Handy with tools, he presented some of his inventions at the Wisconsin State Fair when he was twenty-two; an impressed onlooker encouraged him to attend college. At the state university in Madison, he fell in love with botany and came to question his father's austere doctrines. Fleeing to Canada to escape the Union draft during the Civil War, Muir experienced a spiritual revelation when he found two rare orchids growing beside a stream. "I never before saw a plant so full of life; so perfectly spiritual, it seemed pure enough for the throne of its Creator," Muir wrote. "I felt as if I were in the presence of superior beings who loved me and beckoned me to come. I sat down beside them and wept for joy."

Muir carried this feeling on a long trek from Kentucky to Florida in 1867, the journal of which was published after his death a half-century later. Inside the front cover of his notebook, the author signed himself "John Muir, Earth-planet, Universe."

Winslow Homer, *An Adirondack Lake*, 1870. Homer painted many tranquil scenes in the Adirondacks, capturing the appeal of wilderness in an increasingly urban, industrialized, fast-paced society. Courtesy Henry Gallery, University of Washington, Horace C. Henry Collection, 26.71.

Frank Jay Haynes. Old Faithful Geyser, Yellowstone National Park, 1880s. Yellowstone and other national parks served a growing tourist industry. Visitors like these could contemplate sublime landscapes while also enjoying the comforts of modern hotels built by the railroad companies. Courtesy Frances Lehman Loeb Art Center, Vassar College.

In Kentucky he recorded an encounter with a blacksmith who criticized Muir for roaming the country looking at flowers instead of doing a man's work. Well prepared by his youthful training, Muir offered a biblical response. "Do you not remember," he asked, "that Christ told his disciples to 'consider the lilies how they grow,' and compared their beauty with Solomon in all his glory? Now whose advice am I to take, yours or Christ's?" The blacksmith "acknowledged that he had never thought of blossoms that way before." "From the dust of the earth," Muir wrote, "from the common elementary fund, the Creator has made *Homo sapiens.* From the same material he has made every other creature, however noxious and insignificant to us. They are earth-born companions and our fellow mortals."

In the 1870s Muir began publishing his writings in leading magazines, and he headed to California for what became a world-famous residence at Yosemite. Rambling through the valley, he proved to be an astute scientific observer who solved the mystery of Yosemite's glacial origins at a time when professional experts offered other explanations. But Muir became more famous for spiritual explorations than for scientific ones. He argued that plants, animals, and the universe had purposes distinct from those of humans, and awe-inspiring in their own right. In one article he described how he climbed an immense evergreen in the Yuma Valley during a thunderstorm to see how it felt to be a tree in the wind. "It never occurred to me until this storm-day," he reported, "that trees are travelers, in the ordinary sense.

They make many journeys, not very extensive ones, it is true; but our own little comes and goes are only little more than tree-wavings—many of them not so much."

Muir shared his love of great trees and natural wonders with influential contemporaries, and it led him into political activism. In 1892 Muir and Robert Johnson, his editor at *Century* magazine, founded an "association for preserving California's monuments and natural wonders." That association, the Sierra Club, became Muir's great life work, despite his fear that he had "no genius for managing societies." The club lobbied for preservation of old-growth forests and wilderness sites, and after 1901 it sponsored outings in the backcountry led by Muir himself. By this point its members were making common cause with nature lovers across the United States. The Appalachian Mountain Club persuaded New York to designate part of the Adirondacks "forever wild." To protect wildlife, especially birds, northeasterners had founded several state chapters of the Audubon Society. Between 1901 and 1905—just when Zitkala-Sa and Mary Austin published their ritings—the Audubon Society became a nationwide organization.

Environmental conservation was not wholly a spiritual affair. Some of its earliest successes stemmed from economic concerns. In 1891, for example, Congress gave the president power to set aside federal forests to protect watersheds and topsoil, and both Benjamin Harrison and Grover Cleveland set aside millions of acres. Enforcement arrived in 1897, when the secretary of the Interior was given the right to regulate use of such lands. President Theodore Roosevelt, who expanded this initiative into the U.S. Forest Service in 1905, had in some ways a more pragmatic vision of conservation than did men such as Muir, advocating "wise use" rather than pristine preservation. But Roosevelt in his own way shared Muir's spiritual values. That was evident in 1903 when Muir welcomed the president on a tour of the Sierras. Recalling the massive sequoias that surrounded him as he camped with Muir, Roosevelt wrote that "the majestic trunks, beautiful in color and in symmetry, rose round us like the pillars of a mightier cathedral than was ever conceived by any human architect."

While sublime monuments such as Yosemite won preservation, less spectacular environments did not. Gene Stratton Porter, who grew up in Indiana, lost her mother at age eleven and found the same kind of spiritual solace in the vast Limberlost Swamp, near her home, as Muir at Yosemite. Stratton Porter wrote a series of novels mythologizing the Limberlost, beginning with *The Song of the Cardinal* in 1903. But her swamp, unlike western geysers and sequoia groves, did not meet contemporary definitions of sublimity. Before Stratton Porter's books appeared, much of the Limberlost had already been drained and converted to farmland, and only recently have wetland projects re-created a small portion of what was destroyed.

Still, seeds of spiritual renewal began slowly emerging from the drained, mined, and burned-over soil. Writers such as John Muir, Mary Austin, Zitkala-Sa, and Gene Stratton Porter paved the way for a new environmentalist faith, seeing in nature not cause for terror or conquest but opportunities for contemplation and renewal. They created, in effect, a new and popular American religion, one whose place of worship was not in a church or synagogue but in nature itself, in "cathedrals," as Roosevelt put it, greater than those of any human architect. By the 1930s one could look back and trace a spiritual revolution that had taken place between the end of the Civil War and the first decade of the twentieth century. In *A Sand County Almanac* naturalist Aldo Leopold told that history backward, marking it along the rings of a giant oak tree that had been struck by lightning on his Wisconsin farm. As Leopold was keenly aware, his farm lay next door to the county in which John Muir had grown up. Sawing, with his neighbor, through the outer rings of the trunk, Leopold recalled recent struggles against waste and conquest. Then he sawed deeper, back into the rings of an earlier era.

> We cut 1906, when the first state forester took office, and fires burned 17,000 acres in these sand counties. . . . We cut 1892, another year of fires; 1891, a low in the grouse cycle. . . . It was likewise in 1890 that the largest pine rafts in history slipped down the Wisconsin River in full view of my oak, to build an empire of red barns for the cows of the prairie states. . . .

> Now our saw bites the 1870s, the decade of Wisconsin's carousal in wheat. . . . In 1873 one Chicago firm received and marketed 25,000 prairie chickens. The Chicago trade collectively bought 600,000 at $3.25 per dozen. In 1872 the last wild Wisconsin turkey was killed, two counties to the southwest. . . . In 1871, within a fifty-mile triangle spreading northwestward from my oak, 136 million pigeons are estimated to have nested, and some may have nested in it, for it was then a thrifty sapling 20 feet tall. Pigeon hunters by scores plied their trade with net and gun, club and salt lick, and trainloads of prospective pigeon pie moved southward and eastward toward the cities. It was the last big nesting in Wisconsin, and nearly the last in any state.

> The same year brought other evidence of the march of empire: the Peshtigo Fire, which cleared a couple of counties of trees and soil. . . . In 1870 a market gunner boasted in the *American Sportsman* of killing 6,000 ducks in one season.

Cutting to the heart of his oak, Leopold calculated that it had emerged from its acorn in the same year when John Muir had first conceived the idea of a wilderness refuge. In 1865, the year that had brought emancipation and peace, Muir had asked his brother to sell him a piece of land to create a wildflower sanctuary. "His brother declined to part with the land," Leopold reported, "but he could not suppress the idea." Muir would have approved of Leopold's conclusion: "1865 still stands in Wisconsin history as the birth-year of mercy for things natural, wild and free."

FOR FURTHER READING

On the World's Parliament of Religions, in addition to the original report of the organizers, see Richard H. Seager, *The World's Parliament of Religions* (Bloomington, IN, 1995). On encounters between Europe and Asia see Stephen R. Prothero, *The White Buddhist* (Bloomington, IN, 1996), and Amiya Sen, *Swami Vivekananda* (New York, 2000). On Protestant missions, both domestic and foreign, the best recent scholarship focuses on women; see Patricia Hill, *The World Their Household* (Ann Arbor, MI, 1985), Jane Hunter, *The Gospel of Gentility* (New Haven, CT, 1984), Maina Chawla Singh, *Gender, Religion, and "Heathen Lands"* (New York, 2000), and Peggy Pascoe, *Relations of Rescue*, cited in Chapter 6. See also the essays in *Black Americans and the Missionary Movement in Africa*, ed. Sylvia M. Jacobs (Westport, CT, 1982), as well as George M. Frederickson's *Black Liberation* (New York, 1995). On women's roles in African-American churches see Evelyn Brooks Higginbotham, *Righteous Discontent* (Cambridge, MA, 1993). The quotation about "a nation within a nation," from sociologist E. Franklin Frazier, is on page 11 of Higginbotham's book.

On Protestantism generally and the emerging split between liberals and fundamentalists, I have relied heavily throughout this chapter on George M. Marsden, *Fundamentalism and American Culture* (New York, 1980). On the Salvation Army see Diane H. Winston, *Red Hot and Righteous* (Cambridge, MA, 1999), and on liberal Protestantism, Robert T. Handy, *The Social Gospel in America, 1870–1920* (New York, 1966), and Henry F. May, *Protestant Churches and Industrial America* (New York, 1949). On medievalism as a response to modernity see T. J. Jackson Lears, *No Place of Grace* (Chicago, 1981).

On Catholicism I rely on Patrick W. Carey, *The Roman Catholics in America* (Westport, CT, 1996), and on specific Catholic communities, Arnoldo De León, *The Tejano Community*, cited in Chapter 3, and Robert Anthony Orsi, *The Madonna of 115th Street* (New Haven, CT, 1985). On parochial school controversies in politics see Richard E. Jensen, *The Winning of the Midwest* (Chicago, 1971). On Father Ryan I am grateful to Robert Prasch, Department of Economics, Middlebury College, for "Father John Ryan and *A Living Wage*," manuscript in author's possession. On Judaism I rely largely on Jonathan D. Sarna, *American Judaism* (New Haven, CT, 2004); see also Hasia Diner, *A New Promised Land* (New York, 2003), and Gerald Sorin, *Tradition Transformed* (Baltimore, 1997). On events in Russia see Stephen M. Berk, *Year of Crisis, Year of Hope* (Westport, CT, 1985), and on the origins of the National Council of Jewish Women, Faith Rogow, *Gone to Another Meeting* (Tuscaloosa, AL, 1993). For background on various experimental communities, see Donald E. Pitzer, ed., *America's Communal Utopias* (Chapel Hill, NC, 1997), as well as Wendy E. Chmielewski, "Heaven on Earth: The Woman's Commonwealth, 1867–1983," in *Women in Spiritual and Communitarian Societies in the United States*, ed. Wendy E. Chmielewski et al. (Syracuse, NY, 1993), 52–67.

On American Indians, in addition to works cited in other chapters, two starting points are Omer C. Stewart, *Peyote Religion* (Norman, OK, 1987), and for native influences on Mary Austin, Mark T. Hoyer's *Dancing Ghosts* (Reno, NV, 1998). On religion and the outdoors see Clifford Putney, *Muscular Christianity* (Cambridge, MA, 2001). On Olmsted see Anne Whiston Spirn, "Constructing Nature," in *Uncommon Ground*, ed. William Cronon (New York, 1996), 91–112. Also very influential to this section of the chapter is Cronon's provocative essay "The Trouble with Nature: On Getting Back to the Wrong Wilderness," in the same volume, 69–90. For an innovative look at the "trouble with nature" in national parks, see Mark David Spence, *Dispossessing the Wilderness* (New York, 1999). My thanks go also to the Vassar graduate Emily Avery-Miller for her research and our conversations in History 367. Stephen Fox, *The American Conservation Movement* (Madison, WI, 1981), is my key source on Muir and the early Sierra Club in addition to Muir's own writings. I am also grateful to the historian Adam Rome for his observations on the Christian roots of Muir's thought. On conservation generally, a good starting point is Ted Steinberg's environmental history of the United States, *Down to Earth* (New York, 2002). "Good Oak" appears in Aldo Leopold's *A Sand County Almanac* (New York, 1949), 6–17.

PART III

The Fires

At the age of twenty-four, José Martí, born in Havana in 1853, had already joined the movement for Cuban independence from Spanish rule and been convicted of treason by Spanish authorities. He had served part of a six-year sentence at hard labor, had the sentence commuted to exile, and lived by turns in Spain, Mexico, and Guatemala. Not long afterward he moved to the United States, where he wrote for a number of North American and Latin American newspapers. In the late 1880s and early 1890s, convinced that peaceful methods would never succeed against Spain, Martí helped plan and lead the Cuban Revolution. He died on a Cuban beach in 1895, as he and his compatriots launched their rebellion.

In the meantime, Martí reported for Argentina's *La Nación* on the funeral of four anarchists who were hanged in Chicago in 1886 after allegedly throwing a bomb in Haymarket Square. Martí argued that the anarchists had been wrong to advocate violent revolution in a democracy, but he was fascinated by their rhetoric. He compared them to volcanoes erupting from an underground reservoir of molten rock—the working class in the new economy. The United States, he observed, "is terrified by the increased organization among the lower classes. . . . Therefore the Republic decided, by tacit agreement resembling complicity, to use a crime born of its own transgressions as much as of the fanaticism of the criminals in order to strike terror by holding them up as an example."

The anarchists, Martí wrote, "come from hell; what language must they speak but the language of hell?" He was less worried about their influence than he was about what he saw happening more broadly in the United States. Earlier in the nineteenth century, he argued, European immigrants had found in America

> a republican form of government [that] enabled the recent arrival to earn his bread and lay aside a portion of his earnings for his old age, and in his own house. But then came the corrupting war and the habit of authority and domination which is its bitter aftereffect. Then came the credit that stimulated the creation of colossal fortunes and the disorderly foreign influx. . . . The Republic changed from a wonderfully desirable village to a monarchy in disguise.

The United States, Martí concluded, "because of its unconscionable cult of wealth, and lacking any of the shackles of tradition, . . . has fallen into monarchical inequality, injustice, and violence."

Martí, like many Latin Americans, had long hoped the United States would serve as a model republic and defend the rights of other American nations to resist European aggression. During the years he lived in the United States, Martí did come to see parallels between it and Latin America, but they were not such flattering ones. Noting that Anglo Americans thought of their country as more rational, civilized, and orderly than its southern neighbors, he saw instead "the crude, uneven, and decadent character of the United States, and the continuous existence there of all the violence, discord, immorality and disorder [that North Americans] blamed upon the peoples of Spanish America." By the early 1890s Martí warned that the United States, was likely to develop its own imperial ambitions. His prediction proved accurate. The United States "helped" Cuba win independence and then asserted its own forms of control over the island.

U.S. intervention in Cuba was in some ways an extension of the conflict Martí had observed in Chicago. Post–Civil War America was a tremendously violent place, and by the 1890s the domestic conflicts generated by rapid transformation spilled over into other parts of the world. American policy makers sought overseas markets for U.S. products to ensure domestic stability and deflect the prospect of "socialistic" solutions. Chapter 9 of *New Spirits* examines various wars of incorporation that raged within the boundaries of the United States over lands in the West and control of labor. Workers of all classes and trades, as well as the landscape itself and the people who had lived on it for centuries, were integrated into a hierarchical corporate and political order, managed from urban centers of financial power. Chapter 10 describes a series of creative nonviolent responses that arose in the face of these conflicts. Chapter 11 explores how, in the wake of a massive depression in the 1890s, such projects were postponed or transformed, paving the way for long-term changes in the twentieth century but also defeating the most radical options and setting narrower limits on Americans' reform vision.

Reactions to the depression included a hardening of class and racial lines, and they ended with the consolidation of new powers both in Washington, D.C., and in corporate boardrooms. Those powers are the subject of Chapter 11, and they included the building of an overseas commercial and military empire. Justifications for new military exploits ran along racial lines, and here the continuities between domestic and foreign policies were also strong. Having rejected the legacy of Reconstruction, shunted American Indians onto reservations, and passed an Exclusion Act barring Chinese workers from the United States, Americans had laid the groundwork for offering second-class citizenship to Cubans and Filipinos. José Martí was right: the United States had changed. The fires of incorporation, both at home and abroad, left future generations a legacy of material progress and hope, but also violence and confusion.

CHAPTER 9

A State of War

If the club of the policeman, knocking out the brains of the
rioter, will answer, then well and good; but if it does not
promptly meet the exigency, then [use] bullets and bayonets.
. . . Napoleon was right when he said that the way to deal with
a mob was to exterminate it.

—THE INDEPENDENT, NEW YORK

[The propertied classes] everywhere and always fall back upon
the use of force. . . . In the midst of such a struggle, to
talk of peace and peaceful methods . . . is blasphemous and
exasperating to the last degree.

—THE ALARM, CHICAGO

For Europe's most powerful nations, the 1870s and 1880s were an era of high imperialism. Britain crowned Queen Victoria empress of India. France laid claim to Indochina. Germany, Belgium, and Italy joined them in carving up coastal China into spheres of influence, and the Great Powers divided eleven million square miles of Africa into colonial territories. The United States took a different path in these decades. It had already claimed an empire in the West, contiguous to existing states; while Europeans sought colonies overseas, Americans waged ferocious battles for control and development of what the nation had already claimed. The two-million-square-mile West yielded most of the raw materials European powers sought abroad: gold, silver, copper, coal, oil, old-growth timber, and diverse lands that could support cattle, sheep, grain, and semitropical crops.

In 1893 historian Frederick Jackson Turner famously described the American frontier as a zone of "free land," but in fact, the process of wresting it from people who already lived there was bloody, complicated, and costly. Subjugation of western tribes brought little peace in its wake, since conquering whites clashed with Mexicans, Chinese immigrants, and one another. Among the most famous of dozens of violent incidents was California farmers' war against the Southern Pacific Railroad, which Karl Marx followed with interest in the London papers and which became the basis for Frank Norris's novel *The Octopus*. The conflict centered on Mussel Slough, a patch of land thirty miles south of Fresno where homestead-ers and the Southern Pacific held conflicting claims. In 1880 a judge who was a close friend of the railroad's leading shareholders ruled in favor of the road. When the Southern Pacific sent an armed posse to evict farmers, the resulting gun battle left seven dead. Daring train robbers later carried out a three-year crime spree against the Southern Pacific, during which many farmers cheered for the outlaws.

In the meantime, western mining and railroad workers organized thousands of strikes, shutdowns, and even acts of sabotage. Corporate managers fought back by calling in armed detectives, state militias, and the U.S. Army. Conflict was espe-cially violent in the mining industry. In 1892 six men died in clashes at Idaho's Coeur d'Alene mines, whose owners ultimately destroyed the local affiliate of the Western Federation of Miners (WFM). A few years later Idaho's ex-governor was assassinated in a revenge killing orchestrated by leaders of the WFM. In Colorado conflict between owners and miners was so bloody and constant that historians have dubbed it the Thirty Years' War. At one point vigilante businessmen in Cripple Creek forced the pro-labor sheriff to resign at gunpoint. In 1914 at Ludlow, Colorado, state militia and local deputies killed thirty-nine people in a camp of striking coal miners. Among the dead were two miners' wives and eleven children, whose tents were set on fire by the attack.

As violent as the West became, labor conflict was equally fierce in many other parts of the country. Pennsylvania miners waged the same kinds of fights against employers as their compatriots in Colorado and Idaho, including several assassi-nations carried out in the 1870s by a secret cadre of Irish-born workers known as the Molly Maguires. Whether protests were peaceful or not, eastern employers struck back with the same repressive measures as they did in the West, often esca-lating strikes into full-scale war. The Great Railroad Strike of 1877, centered in Pittsburgh and other eastern cities, resulted in ten times more deaths than the shootout at Mussel Slough in the so-called Wild West. The new economy also brought violence to the South. In Appalachia the famous Hatfield-McCoy feud resulted partly from the rising value of Hatfield land, as railroads and coal compa-nies undertook large-scale operations. The folktales surrounding "Railroad Bill," a famous black train robber in Alabama, had much in common with those attached to Jesse James's gang and the California bandits who attacked the trains of the Southern Pacific. Bill won admiration from both whites and blacks who resented the wealth and power that railroads represented. Long after Bill was shot dead by an Alabama sheriff, blues songs celebrated him (inaccurately, it appears) as a man who stole from the rich and gave to the hungry.

So vicious and continuous were the battles of these decades that we might call them "wars of incorporation," a second Civil War that persisted into the twentieth century. Incorporation was a geographic process, consolidating networks of con-trol across the continent; it also consolidated power in the hands of a few.

About the best that can be said for the violent processes of incorporation is that they produced results that were more democratic—by some measures, at least—than similar conflicts in other parts of the world. The Australian Outback ended up even more dominated by big landholders than did the American West. In the conquest of the Argentine pampas, which took place in the same years, native peoples were hunted to extinction like the wild ostriches, while Argentina's dictator handed over enormous tracts of land to his cronies. Considering the unspeakable atrocities that occurred in the African Congo under the sponsorship of Belgium's King Leopold, the wars of incorporation in the United States look relatively mild. Yet what happened in Europe and America (for example, the arrival of bicycles and automobiles with rubber tires) was inextricably bound to what happened in the cruelest corners of the Congo and Peru (rubber harvesting). Confronted with violence and dislocation on a global scale, many came to agree with Social Gospel minister Washington Gladden: the new economy brought with it a "state of war."

INCORPORATION IN THE WEST

The most famous of America's violent struggles in the post–Civil War years was not new: it was the final stage in a three-century-long conquest that dispossessed American Indians of their land. Consolidation of the continent seemed inevitable to most observers; an army that had just defeated the Confederacy could surely subdue small bands of nomads, even if the latter had intimate knowledge of their home terrain. By 1870 the federal government had created reservations for almost every surviving Indian nation, and President U. S. Grant proclaimed a "Peace Policy" focused on education and assimilation rather than military campaigns. But conquest looked far from inevitable to Indians themselves. "All the land south of the Arkansas belongs to the Kiowas and Comanches, and I don't want to give away any of it," Kiowa chief White Bear informed treaty commissioners in 1869 in a speech that brought shouts of support from men standing behind him. Comanche chief Ten Bears explained that his people had no interest in white customs. "I want to live and die as I was brought up," he declared. "I love the open prairie." What followed were a series of conflicts that one historian has ironically dubbed "the Wars of the Peace Policy."

In these wars the U.S. Army bore responsibility for a long string of atrocities. Men such as General Philip Sheridan, sent west after the Civil War, ruthlessly punished Indians who left reservations or attacked invading settlers. In January 1870, after a series of murders and revenge killings by white ranchers and Blackfeet warriors in Montana, Sheridan ordered a strike on the camp of a resisting chief. With the band's warriors away hunting, U.S. troops opened fire and set lodges ablaze in a surprise dawn attack beside the Marias River. Bear Head, a young boy at the time, heard the screams of women and children as burning lodge covers collapsed around them (a scene eerily similar to the militia attack on miners at Ludlow, Colorado, forty-four years later, though the casualties at the Marias were far higher). "I sat before the ruin of my lodge and felt sick," Bear Head remembered. "I wished that the seizers had killed me, too. . . . I could not pull up the lodge-skin and look under it. I could not bear to see my mother." At least 173 people died. They turned out to be members of a friendly band whom the army had attacked by mistake.

In other acts of violence, though, U.S. troops were last on the scene. Unlike the Canadian West, where the Royal Mounted Police served as respected go-betweens and law enforcers, the American West was weak in federal authority. Disputes and revenge killings between Indians and local traders, ranchers, and farmers triggered escalating cycles of violence, with federal agents playing confused or secondary roles. Before the 1872 Modoc War on the Oregon-California border, the Modoc believed they had reached an agreement with U.S. negotiators on their future. But officials in Washington changed the terms, refusing to situate the tribe near their ancestral lands. One faction of Modoc, led by a chief named Kientpoos or "Captain Jack," resisted the move and stuck to the terms of the treaty they had signed. U.S. troops, accompanied by local armed whites, went to relocate them by force. They were shocked to find themselves beaten back. Captain Jack and his followers fled to nearby lava beds, where they hid out for months, eluding capture and killing many men sent after them. The U.S. Army defeated the rebels only with the help of other Modoc—including, ironically, men who had killed white settlers and persuaded the reluctant Captain Jack to launch a surprise attack on a U.S. peace commission. These Modoc were pardoned, while Jack and three others, none of whom had at first advocated violence against negotiators or civilians, were convicted and hanged.

Whether they won or lost a battle, the U.S. Army's role was almost always controversial. Bungled campaigns such as the Modoc War aroused the wrath of westerners at army incompetence, while incidents such as the slaughter on the Marias River provoked public outrage. The latter atrocity, in fact, persuaded Congress to reject a measure that would have transferred the Bureau of Indian Affairs back from the Interior Department (where it had been since 1849) to the War Department. Reformers in the Northeast clashed with western politicians who saw the "Indian problem" as their own affair. Congress and a succession of presidents fought over what policy to follow, and in the meantime local agents and missionaries pursued their own conflicting agendas. Kiowa chief Sitting Bear pointedly observed that he was tired of hearing contradictory pledges. "We do not break treaties," he said of his people. "We make but few contracts, and them we remember well. The whites make so many they are liable to forget them. The white chief seems not to be able to govern his braves." Chief Joseph of the Nez Percé voiced similar frustration. "I cannot understand why so many chiefs are allowed to talk so many different ways, and promise so many different things," he wrote. "It makes my heart sick when I remember all the good words and all the broken promises."

The first source of dispute was often, as in the Modoc War, the question of what was being given up. Some chiefs hoped to keep peace by sharing their territories with encroaching settlers; few believed they were consenting to be removed from ancestral homes. Some managed to stay: the Crow, for example, who allied with the United States in defense against their traditional Sioux and Cheyenne enemies, retained a portion of their lands for their reservation. The Crow cooperated with federal officials, Chief Plenty Coups said later, "not because we loved the white man who was already crowding other tribes into our country, . . . but because we plainly saw that this course was the only one which might save our beautiful country for us." Yet many other tribes were carted off to arid wastelands far from home. The Wichita, Osage, Cheyenne, Arapaho, Kiowa, and Comanche, all of whom lived on coveted lands, were deposited in Indian Territory (now Oklahoma), just as the Cherokee of Georgia had been during the 1830s "Trail of Tears."

Most of the era's Indian wars occurred *after* such removals, as peoples who had reluctantly moved to reservations found themselves subject to new forms of oppression. Appalling corruption among agents in the field exacerbated federal stinginess. Pensions, blankets, medical supplies, and rations never materialized or were skimmed off by agents while the intended recipients froze and starved. When the Ponca, a settled farming people in Nebraska, were shipped to Indian Territory, more than a third of the nation died of exhaustion, starvation, and contaminated water. "They took our reapers, mowers, hay rakes, spades, ploughs, bedsteads, stoves, cupboards, everything we had on our farms," remembered Chief Standing Bear. "After we reached the new land, all my horses died. The water was very bad." Standing Bear led repeated escape attempts, in one case taking the body of his son back to his homeland for secret burial.

Similar conditions led to the last major Indian war, fought by the Mimbre and Chiricahua Apache in the 1880s. Despite promises to the contrary, these Apache were forced onto a consolidated reservation at San Carlos, along Arizona's Gila River, in brutally hot country rife with malaria. "There was nothing but cactus, heat, rattlesnakes, rocks, and insects," one man remembered. "No game; no edible plants. Many, many of our people died." After a two-year struggle to live under these conditions or negotiate a move, the Apache revolted. Mimbre leader Victorio led the first fight, eventually crossing into Mexico, where he and seventy-seven warriors were killed in a battle with Mexican soldiers in 1880. A year later Chiricahua leaders Juh and Geronimo also abandoned San Carlos and engaged in a rebellion that lasted six years. When Geronimo finally surrendered, the federal decision to imprison 300 Apache at Fort Marion, Florida, seemed an exercise in randomness as capricious as the hanging of the Modoc Captain Jack. The prisoners included not only Geronimo but also scouts who had fought with U.S. forces *against* him as well as a number of men who had never left the reservation at all.

Many Americans were distressed by these events. A San Francisco newspaper judged the government "murderous," calling the country's Indian policy "a miserable one and a failure." President Rutherford B. Hayes bluntly stated in a message to Congress that "many, if not most, of our Indian wars have had their origins in broken promises and acts of injustice on our part." Helen Hunt Jackson's *A Century*

Frank Leslie's Illustrated Newspaper, 10 November 1877. "Not Much! Uncle Sam to Sitting Bull—If you will come back peaceably, we will forgive you the Custer matter, and give you everything you ask for.' Sitting Bull to Uncle Sam—'Don't trouble me. You have lied to us before. You have more lies now. I shall stay here with my White Mother. Go home by easy stages—and don't come back.'" This cartoon was published when Sitting Bull had led his Hunkpapa band and other Lakota into Canada (under the protection of Queen Victoria, the "White Mother"), after defeating General George A. Custer at the Battle of the Little Big Horn. Sitting Bull is not depicted very sympathetically, but the image is far more friendly than many ugly caricatures of native peoples sketched at the time. Note the reasons for conflict that the cartoonist has written on papers scattered across the ground: "corrupt traders," "false friends," "bad faith," "knavish settlers," "lying agents," "broken contracts," and "reservation swindles."   Courtesy Rutherford B. Hayes Presidential Center.

of Dishonor, which was published in 1881 and remains one of the most damning accounts of U.S. Indian policy ever written, won widespread praise, and its author hoped it would serve as another *Uncle Tom's Cabin* to sear the national conscience. But the abolition of slavery had been synonymous with progress and uplift, while few Americans—even Jackson herself—could imagine letting "primitives" live in traditional ways. As Theodore Roosevelt put it crudely in his book *The Winning of the West*, "The Indians never had any real title to the soil. . . . This great continent could not have been kept as nothing but a game preserve for squalid savages." The federal courts ruled in *Standing Bear v. Crook* that the U.S. government could

Cohoe, *War Dance at Fort Marion*, circa 1875–77. A Cheyenne taken as a prisoner of war, Cohoe was held for several years at Fort Marion, Florida. In this sketch from one of several notebooks left by Fort Marion prisoners, Cohoe records a dance performed by prisoners for tourists. The detail with which Cohoe renders the tourists' clothing and accessories suggests that the prisoners observed the visitors at least as carefully as tourists watched them. From *A Cheyenne Sketchbook* (Norman, OK, 1964), 83. Courtesy University of Oklahoma Press.

not treat Indians as permanent noncitizens, but they did not set a clear limit or deadline on this "temporary" status.

The "Wars of the Peace Policy" launched a new attempt to replace armed conflict with Indian assimilation and citizenship. The crux of the plan was to divide reservations into individual parcels for families to farm, a goal set forth in the Dawes Severalty Act of 1887. Ownership of private property, the bill's sponsors believed, would motivate Indians to follow white ways. They demanded acceptance of this system as a precondition for citizenship. In many ways the Dawes Act finished the job that violent removal had begun. Under the allotment system, Indian peoples lost enormous swaths of their remaining lands to intruders. A few agricultural peoples who, like the Ponca, kept or regained part of their traditional lands fared decently under the system, and some large nations such as the Navajo and Cherokee held on to significant resources. But most tribes entered a nether region between citizenship and dependency. Catastrophic losses of land continued until the New Deal of the 1930s. Allotment also divided tribes. When the Choctaw nation in Indian Territory was given a choice of adopting or rejecting the new land system, the election created a rift. "There was bitter feeling on both sides and even some killing," remembered one council member. A similar decision split the Hopi pueblo of Oraibi. The winning assimilationists forced 400 traditionalists to leave the village and go into exile, taking only what they could carry. The refugees formed the new town of Hotevilla.

Despite severe hardship, Indians found ways to resist. Indeed, within a decade of Geronimo's surrender, young men and women such as Dr. Charles Eastman and Zitkala-Sa were exploring new avenues for cultural survival, while Indian leaders mounted legal challenges over land and human rights. Sacred dances and feasts continued secretly, while grandparents passed down legends in the traditional tongues. Well aware that census-takers thought they all looked alike, people on the Lakota reservation in South Dakota filed by the census table multiple times to raise their official count and thus their rations. On the second and third time through the line, they quietly registered their contempt by submitting names that translated into obscenities such as "Shit Head." In Indian Territory, the Creek writer Alexander Posey used the same kind of biting satire to critique federal policy, referring to Theodore Roosevelt as "President Rooster Feather" and the local Indian agent, a Mr. Shoenfelt, as "Sho-am-fat."

On some reservations Indians who accepted white ways found themselves ostracized. Laura Pedrick, one of the first full-blooded Indians appointed a field matron among her own people, exposed the performance of secret dances and feasts to reservation authorities. She found herself under pressure as Kiowa, Comanche, and Apache on the reservation told authorities they found Pedrick "objectionable." Other native leaders skillfully blended old and new. Local agents considered William Wash of the White River Ute to be "pro-white"; when the tribe debated the land allotment system, he accepted it, prospering afterward as a rancher and farmer. Yet Walsh used his power to advocate on behalf of all Ute, and he shared much of his prosperity with less fortunate neighbors, building community ties in the fashion of a traditional chief.

In the decades when the United States quelled the last armed Indian resistance, wars of incorporation were also waged over Mexican-American ranches and farms in the Southwest. At issue were property titles in the Mexican cession, lands the United States had seized in 1848 after the Mexican-American War. The lives of Mexicans living in remote parts of Texas, New Mexico, and Arizona had been largely undisturbed for decades afterward, and these rural outposts—as well as small cities such as Tucson and Santa Fe—remained overwhelmingly Mexican. But after the Civil War, white ranchers and developers began moving in to stake their claims. As in the Indian wars, some used violence and intimidation to get what they wanted. Faustino Morales, a cowboy employed on a giant Texas ranch, described the process there. "There were many small ranches belonging to Mexicans, but then the Americans came in and drove the Mexicans out. . . . After that they fenced the ranches."

Some Mexicans fought back, especially in New Mexico and south Texas, where their communities were strong. Men such as Juan Patrón and Juan Gonzalez, a county clerk and deputy sheriff in New Mexico's Pecos Valley, tried to protect neighbors during waves of violent land seizures, in this case instigated in the 1870s by invading Texans. The resulting Lincoln County War temporarily stalled the newcomers. New Mexico Territorial Governor Edmund G. Ross, sympathetic to his state's Mexican residents, wrote to one cattle company in indignation. "I understand very well," he wrote, "and so do you, what a cowboy or cattle herder with a brace of pistols at his belt and a Winchester in his hands, means when he 'asks' a sheepherder to leave a given range. It means instant compliance or very unpleasant consequences to the herder and his flock." Ross denounced the company for setting "these men and your cattle upon a quarter of the public domain that has been occupied exclusively by these Mexican sheep herders for a generation or more." But officials more friendly to white interests soon replaced men like Ross.

When intimidation did not work, property rights could be manipulated. With taxes overdue on one coveted Mexican ranch in Hidalgo County, Texas, during the depression of the 1870s, the sheriff sold all 3,000 acres to an associate for $15. More often, powerful business interests hired teams of lawyers to contest Mexican land titles, most of which were communally held, poorly documented, and decades or even centuries old. In New Mexico, leaders of the notorious Santa Fe Ring got immensely rich through such litigation. Lawyers played both sides of the fence, working for corporate investors but also offering to defend Mexican land titles in exchange for a portion of the estate as their fee. By these methods, as well as armed occupation of several parts of the territory, Santa Fe attorney Thomas Catron came to possess nearly two million acres of land.

Because property claims in the Mexican cession were so tangled, Congress set up a federal Court of Private Land Claims in 1891 to sort them out. The results were dramatic: the court recognized almost no Mexican *ejidos*, or traditional communal properties, returning only 5 percent of the thirty-five million disputed acres to Mexicans living there. The court awarded most of the other acres to another kind of collective owner: corporations, who consolidated their landholdings and undertook ranching, lumbering, and mining on a grand scale. Some of the court's rulings precipitated protracted battles on the Maxwell Land Grant in northern New Mexico and southern Colorado. This tract was occupied by villages of Mexican farmers who held their land by informal recognition from large landholders. The grant had also attracted Anglos such as Richard and Marian Russell, a Union veteran and his wife, who staked a claim in a Colorado valley where they built a ranch, dug a small lake, planted an orchard, and raised six children. When Lucien and Luz Maxwell, brothers who owned the "two million acres more or less" of the Maxwell Grant, sold out to a consortium of European investors, a lengthy and violent conflict ensued. As early as 1875 a Methodist minister who opposed corporate takeover was found dead in a canyon near Cimarron, New Mexico. The conflict escalated after 1882, when the Supreme Court ruled that the grant belonged to the consortium. Investors proceeded to "clear the grant"; they wanted it empty to begin a vast cattle ranching operation of their own.

The consortium's agents employed a divide-and-conquer policy, brokering deals with individual residents and isolating those who tried to hold out. Pressured by the agents, county sheriffs all over the grant undertook eviction procedures. They met stiff resistance. In Raton, New Mexico, armed men defended the property of outspoken editor O. P. McMains. Along the Vermejo River farmer Jacinto Santistevan and his sons led their neighbors in a decade of stubborn refusal to leave. Farther south, along the Poñil, the killing of rancher Julio Martínez by two deputies triggered a wave of shootouts. But ultimately, across the grant, the consortium prevailed. One of the last episodes of protest took place on Main Street in Stonewall, Colorado, where farmers and ranchers barricaded corporate agents inside the local hotel. In the shootout that followed, homesteader Richard Russell watched as two of his neighbors, "Frenchy" Giradet and Rafael Valerio, were gunned down. Russell himself was shot. He died five days later at home. Though his wife pursued her legal right to hold on to the family's land, she, too, was forced to leave.

On the Maxwell Grant some white and Mexican-American farmers worked together to resist eviction, but such cross-racial cooperation was more often the exception than the rule. Americans had always been divided along ethnic and racial lines, and the upheavals of incorporation intensified long-standing hatreds and precipitated new ones, not only among whites, Indians, and Mexicans but even more against immigrants from China. Some Chinese had entered California as early as the Gold Rush in 1849, but starting in the 1870s employers pinned their hopes on a much larger supply of cheap Asian labor. In several parts of the South, planters sought (unsuccessfully) to replace militant freedmen with Chinese workers. In 1870 shoe manufacturer Calvin Sampson shipped seventy-five Chinese workers into Massachusetts to replace French Canadians and Irish who were out on strike. His maneuver forced the strikers back to work with a 10 percent pay cut, fomenting bitter resentment against the Chinese. Around the same time, the owner of a large steam laundry in South Belleville, New Jersey, recruited Chinese men to replace Irish-American women. In almost every case the goal was to cut wages, though the long-term results were mixed. As soon as they could, many Chinese quit low-paid jobs and set up small businesses of their own.

Thus, the Chinese, like blacks in the South, confounded the stereotype that they were pliant and obedient employees. During anti-Asian violence in San Francisco, Chinese business leaders wrote to the mayor warning that if attacks continued they had "neither the power nor disposition to restrain our countrymen from defending themselves to the last extremity and selling their lives as dearly as possible." Having endured a winter of avalanches and subzero temperatures in the Sierra Nevada, 5,000 Chinese construction workers on the Central Pacific Railroad struck in the spring of 1867. They asked for wages of $45 a month (the company offered $31) and showed keen awareness of the national campaign for an eight-hour workday. "Eight hours a day good for white men," they declared, "all the same good for Chinamen." Bosses cut off food to the camps and wired New York about the possibility of importing 10,000 blacks as replacements. The strikers held out a week before they surrendered.

Despite evidence that they shared common goals with the Chinese, some leaders of the American labor movement devoted more energy to anti-Chinese agitation than they did to more constructive goals. The most notorious was Dennis Kearney, head of San Francisco's Workingmen's Party, who denounced Chinese immigrants as "almond-eyed lepers" and promoted the slogan "The Chinese must GO!" During one boycott of businesses in San Francisco that employed Chinese, a group of Chinese workers at one of the boycotted firms went on strike for higher wages. Instead of seeing them as potential allies, white workers announced they were exempting that employer from the boycott, on the grounds that if the Chinese disliked him, he must be OK. Kearney stirred up a public that was already deeply anti-Asian. Chinese faced hostility not only because they worked for low wages but also because they were not from Europe and for the most part not Christians. A typical article in the *New York Tribune* denounced Chinese immigrants as "utter heathens, treacherous, sensual, cowardly and cruel."

In the West, hatred of the Chinese fueled brutal violence. Mobs in San Francisco went on a three-day rampage in July 1877, burning and looting Chinatown and beating up residents. Eight years later in Rock Springs, Wyoming, vigilantes burned to death twenty-eight Chinese men in one of dozens of incidents in which Chinese were lynched or driven out of mining camps and towns across the West. One of the first activities of the Knights of Labor in Wichita, Kansas, was to organize a boycott of Chinese laundries. African-American women who resented competition had already forced Chinese laundrymen out of Galveston, Texas. Even in the absence of large-scale violence, Chinese faced steady harassment. "We kept indoors after dark for fear of being shot in the back," recalled one man. "Children spit upon us as we passed by and called us rats." Chinese-American workers had to negotiate between two worlds. Family and friends at home in China might think a man was happily collecting riches in "Gold Mountain," while he actually found himself living as a pariah, sometimes in fear of his life. Maintaining their pride, some immigrants told relatives in China that they were "clothing entrepreneurs" to hide the fact that they worked in sweaty laundries.

Hostility toward the Chinese expressed itself in two federal laws of pathbreaking significance. The first, the 1875 Page Act, subjected all female Chinese immigrants to interrogation and exclusion as potential prostitutes. Rigid enforcement denied entry to almost all Chinese women, even wives seeking to join their husbands. Since the early Chinese population in the United States, like that of many other immigrant groups, was overwhelmingly male, the Page Act kept the gender ratio skewed. It thus had the opposite of its intended effect, perpetuating prostitution while also sustaining hostile stereotypes about Asians' supposed inability to sustain proper family life. As late as 1900, less than 5 percent of all Chinese in the United States were women. Though a few worked as cooks and seamstresses, most were indeed prostitutes: in a community of single men and others with families thousands of miles away, they aptly fulfilled the Chinese name for their work, *baak haak chai*, or "hundred-men's wife."

In the meantime, the Chinese Exclusion Act of 1882 barred all poor Chinese laborers from entry into the United States. In an era of unrestricted immigration, this was an unprecedented measure to bar newcomers of a single nationality. It was extremely popular with voters, but never as effective as supporters claimed. Though immigration became more difficult, Chinese men found ways to get in and out of the country—and powerful business interests helped see to it that they did. Indeed, both the Chinese and U.S. governments estimated after the act's passage that nine out of ten Chinese men in America had entered illegally. Some disguised themselves as Mexicans and crossed through the desert from Mexico, a dangerous journey that regularly claimed lives. Others arrived as stowaways on cargo ships or, in the Pacific Northwest, on local ferries from Canada. Many others, known as "paper sons," established false identities based on fictitious relationships with Chinese who were already in America and permitted to bring their children. Border officials kept extensive records and interrogated newcomers, but their screening procedures proved ineffectual.

The Chinese thus became the nation's first illegal immigrants. As Congress tried to ratchet up enforcement, the issue remained a focus of public anger for three decades, especially in the West, while the Exclusion Act remained a sore point in U.S.-Chinese relations until its repeal in 1943, when the two nations allied during World War II. China set up a permanent consulate in San Francisco, and its representatives protested that Chinese should have the right to enter the United States on the same basis as everyone else. Chinese Americans also protested their treatment. "The Chinese must stay," asserted journalist Yan Phon Lee, contradicting Dennis Kearney's rallying cry. He noted that "it was by the application of Chinese 'cheap labor' to the building of railroads, the reclamation of swamp-lands, to mining, fruit culture, and manufacturing, that an immense vista of employment was opened up for Caucasians, and that millions now are enabled to live in comfort and luxury. Besides," he added, "are you sure that Chinese laborers would not ask more if they dared, or take more if they could get it?" While defending themselves from racism, Chinese spokesmen sometimes revealed prejudices of their own. Lai Chun-Chuen, a San Francisco merchant, bridled at being classed with "Indians and Negroes"—especially the former, whom he described as barbarians living naked in caves.

The Page and Chinese Exclusion acts had a profound long-term impact on immigration policy. As the first laws barring entry to people of a specific race or nationality, they served as models for twentieth-century immigration quotas. Follow-up legislation required Chinese immigrants to register with the government and carry identification cards. Chinese Americans put up vigorous legal challenges to these and other discriminatory laws. In the decade after 1882 they filed more than 7,000 habeas corpus petitions in northern California courts, and these helped shape definitions of U.S. citizenship. By the early twentieth century, the Supreme Court had confirmed that anyone born in the United States was a citizen, and judges had struck down a range of discriminatory laws. But the courts also granted the federal government broad leeway to naturalize or deport immigrants as it saw fit. Congress made increasing use of these powers, excluding polygamists in 1891, anarchists in 1903, and four years later, people suffering from tuberculosis, epilepsy, or physical disabilities. By the 1920s this evolved into a stringent quota system for immigrants from all parts of the world. Enforcement was, in the meantime, handed over to a Bureau of Immigration (later the Immigration and Naturalization Service), and those subject to deportation were denied access to the courts, even if they had evidence that they were U.S. citizens. "If the Commissioners [of Immigration]," remarked one federal judge, "wished to order an alien drawn, quartered, and chucked overboard they could do so without interference."

In every major case that denied due process to aliens, plaintiffs were Asian-born. Occasionally they were Japanese (as in the 1892 case *Nishimura Ekiu v. US*), but most often they were Chinese. It was thus hostility to Asians that fueled the rise of a Bureau of Immigration with unprecedented powers, and the definitions of legal and illegal immigrants have remained highly racialized ever since. As economic growth brought millions of Europeans into the harbors of New York, Philadelphia, and Boston and thousands of Mexicans across the unmarked and unguarded border into El Norte, anti-Asian prejudice laid the foundations for later policies that would shut those doors.

LABOR, RACE, AND VIOLENCE

The wars of incorporation were racial conflicts in at least some of their dimensions. In the West they pitted whites against American Indians and Mexican *ejidos*, in the South struggles between landowners and laborers often boiled down to white versus black, and across the country hostility toward the Chinese fueled violence and exclusion. One Massachusetts writer described French-Canadian workers as "the Chinese of the Eastern States." The leader of a Pennsylvania steelworkers' union voiced disgust at Italians, Hungarians, Bohemians, and Poles, whom he also compared to the Chinese. One Irish-American woman angrily told a visitor that there ought to be a law "to keep all them I-talians from comin' in and takin' the bread out of the mouths of honest people."

Such attitudes sprang in part from lived reality. Many of the new immigrants *did* work for lower pay and lived as cheaply as they could, saving to return home or send money back to families in poorer parts of the world. Employers exploited the divisions within the working class. Hawaiian sugar planters, for example, carefully maintained a one-half Chinese and one-half Japanese workforce, and when they suspected the two halves were beginning to cooperate, they imported Portuguese. Employers brought in Italians to break a strike in the New York construction trades in 1874. Italians arrived in Pennsylvania coalfields that same year as employers sought to cut local wages. Three were murdered in the ensuing conflict. A Vermont quarry owner, when Irish-American workers demanded union recognition and an eight-hour day, wrote to a steamship company and asked for 300 Swedes. Fifteen years later steamboat operators on the

Thomas Nast, "Sectarian Bitterness," detail from a political cartoon satirizing conflicts over school funding. In this schoolyard fight, Nast captures an array of prevailing stereotypes: against Jews and Irish (the central figures) and African and Chinese Americans (on the right). *Harper's Weekly*, 26 February 1870, 140. Courtesy Vassar College Library.

Mississippi also tried to recruit Swedes, in this case to replace blacks (though the new workers quit, having many other employment options). Discrimination did not always start at the top, but with white unions. "I was on the Southern Pacific Railway in 1884," recalled one black rail worker, "when 295 colored firemen and an equal number of brakemen were discharged. . . . I could name five more roads where colored men have been relieved by the request of the white brotherhoods."

Labor activism did occasionally cross ethnic and racial lines, especially at the local level. The labor movement was loose and decentralized, and most strikes began at the grassroots rather than with a decision by union leaders. Such "wildcat strikes" were most often prompted by a wage cut or another sudden injustice. An enormous number of such spontaneous protests—as many as 1,500 in a single year—took place in the late nineteenth century. At Montana's Gregory Consolidated mine in January 1887, company officials announced that they were closing down and workers would not receive pay for their previous two months' employment. After a hasty meeting, miners seized the town and took four company hostages. They then wired A. J. Seligman's New York banking firm, which held a large interest in the mine, and warned that they would not surrender until back pay arrived. They got their money right away. (Astutely, they had chosen as one of their hostages Jesse Seligman, the banker's son.)

The first nationwide upheaval was even more explosive, centering on that transformative enterprise, the railroad. The Great Railroad Strike jolted the nation for two weeks in July 1877. It began when managers of the four largest railroads met and agreed to slash wages, on top of a series of cuts already made over the previous three years. When the Baltimore & Ohio announced reductions of 10 percent, workers in West Virginia walked off the job, followed by railmen all over the East Coast and as far away as St. Louis and Chicago. Within days the strike shut down the transportation system. Ironworkers, dockworkers, and thousands of others gathered in the streets to join the revolt. In an indication of the breadth of

Police during the 1903 Chicago City Railway strike. In hundreds of late nineteenth and early twentieth-century conflicts between labor and capital, urban police played a decisive antilabor role. Courtesy Chicago Historical Society.

anger against the roads, those arrested for joining a militant crowd in Buffalo included masons, blacksmiths, clerks, merchants, and even a stove manufacturer.

As railroad officials pressured state governors to send in the militia, Republican president Rutherford B. Hayes declared the strike an "insurrection" and called up U.S. troops. The arrival of armed units with instructions to get the trains running, no matter what, transformed the walkout into a bloody fight. After a militia unit fired into a crowd in Baltimore, killing eleven, the mob went wild. In Chicago strikers clashed with police near the McCormick Reaper Works and the Burlington & Quincy roundhouse, where they destroyed two locomotives. The *Chicago Times* demanded in response that hand grenades be used against the "unwashed mob."

Two infantry regiments, two cavalry companies, and an artillery unit were called from the South Dakota Indian wars to patrol Chicago's streets. The struggle was equally dramatic in Pittsburgh, hub of the much-hated Pennsylvania Railroad. Knowing that most local residents sympathized with the strikers, the railroad's president called up militia units from other parts of the state. "My troops," he declared, "will see that the trains pass." Met by an angry mob, the militia killed twenty people with random rifle fire. Infuriated workers then looted and set fire to the Pennsylvania rail yard, leaving behind the charred hulks of freight cars and engines. By the time federal troops suppressed the strike in Pittsburgh, forty-five people were dead.

The 1877 strike exposed a widening chasm between affluent Americans and those who identified with the working classes. Many of the former—and most of the press—considered the strike itself illegitimate. No matter how much strikers disciplined their ranks and how many deaths were caused by militia rifles, protesters were depicted as disruptive and violent thugs. Spectacular strikes brought visibility and mass solidarity, but they also provoked backlash as prosperous Americans became panicked by labor militancy. Small wonder that labor leader Terence Powderly struggled desperately to *prevent* strikes.

Powderly led the most visionary labor organization of the era, the Knights of Labor. Its growth depended in part on a successful 1885 strike against Jay Gould's Southwestern Railroad, begun at the grassroots by workers who had not yet joined the union. The Knights sought to bring under their umbrella skilled and unskilled workers of all races and backgrounds, whether rural or urban, male or female, immigrant or native-born. (They made one crucial and predictable exception: they denounced the Chinese and refused to accept them even when they applied to join.) " 'Each for himself' is the bosses' plea," proclaimed a sign carried by Knights members in a Detroit parade; "Union for all will make you free." Or as a Boston man explained, the Knights' strength came from "the fact that the whole life of the community is drawn into it, that people of all kinds are together, . . . and that they all get directly the sense of each others' needs."

Knights were visible across the country. St. Louis and Cleveland workers founded one hundred assemblies each, and twice that number were established in Brooklyn. Philadelphia, where garment cutters had first founded the order in 1869, boasted almost 300 locals. Knights in Omaha, Nebraska, organized grocery clerks, mattress makers, and musicians. The Arkansas Knights boasted locals in forty-eight counties, including coal miners, cotton mill workers, and farmhands. At one point a strike by Knights telegraphers in the ex-Confederacy halted communications in Atlanta, Montgomery, Charleston, Jacksonville, and Wilmington. In Pensacola, Florida, lumbermen and stevedores joined the Knights in 1886, followed by laundrywomen and housekeepers. The Knights boasted all-black, all-German, all-Jewish, and all-Italian locals; some women formed their own separate assemblies, while others joined clubs along with men. In San Miguel County, New Mexico, the Knights organizer Juan José Herrera and his brothers Pablo and Nicanor organized secret midnight raids. Calling themselves Las Gorras Blancas, or "White Hats," they cut barbed-wire fences and burned railroad bridges to protest Anglo intrusion. "There is a wide difference between New Mexico's 'law' and 'justice,' " Las Gorras Blancas declared in their 1890 manifesto (signed "1,500 Strong and Growing Daily"). "Justice is God's law, and that we must have at all hazards."

Law and politics eventually defeated the Knights after other tactics did not, as events illustrated in the town of Rutland, Vermont. Rutland's marble quarries employed large numbers of Irish and French-Canadian immigrants. Under the banner of the United Labor Party in 1886, such workers and their allies swept a full slate of Knights candidates into office. But well-connected quarry owners pressured the state legislature to divide Rutland. They then unseated a newly elected judge and fifteen justices of the peace on grounds that they had no jurisdiction in the three newly created districts; they also demanded that each local official post an expensive $1,000 bond. As a historian of the incident writes, "It was as if [the Knights] had sat down to dinner only to discover that the main course had just been removed." The new town of Proctor (named after the leading quarry owner) became staunchly Republican; West Rutland, saddled with debts by the reorganization, fell back in the hands of old-line Democrats. Only in the third district, the now much smaller town of Rutland, did the Knights of Labor continue to hold sway.

At the time of the Rutland election, the Knights, with nationwide membership peaking at 750,000, were suffering from repercussions from an infamous episode of violence that shaped the course of American labor relations. During a strike at the McCormick reaper plant in Chicago, police killed several protesters. Leaders of Chicago's militant anarchist movement called for a protest rally the following day at Haymarket Square. On May 4, 1886, as teamster and labor leader Samuel Fielden addressed a sparse crowd, someone threw a bomb that killed a policeman and wounded dozens more. In the chaos that followed, several more officers and three bystanders died from police gunfire.

Amid public hysteria, blame for the violence was quickly pinned on anarchists. Police found bomb-making equipment in the possession of one anarchist leader, Louis Lingg. Forensics experts at the trial testified to similarities between Lingg's bombs and fragments of the one that had killed Officer Mathias Degan, whose murder was charged against eight anarchists who stood trial. But even today, having reexamined the forensic evidence, historians are not sure who made the bomb thrown at Haymarket Square, nor who threw it. The eight anarchists were convicted largely because they advocated violent overthrow of the U.S. government and refused to renounce those views.

Among the eight men who stood trial for the incident was Albert Parsons, a charismatic anarchist who had grown up in Texas and fought in a Confederate regiment at age fourteen. As active Republicans during Reconstruction, Parsons and his wife, Lucy, had been harassed because of their politics and their interracial marriage (Lucy was of mixed Mexican and African-American descent) and had moved to Chicago, where they joined the anarchist cause. Knowing police wanted him for questioning, Parsons fled into hiding in Wisconsin, but on the first day of the Haymarket trial he created a sensation by walking into the courtroom and asking to be tried along with the defendants. "As in former times," Parsons declared in a public statement, "a privileged class never surrendered its tyranny, neither can it be expected that the capitalists of this age will give up their rulership without being forced to do it. . . . There remains but one resource—FORCE! Our forefathers have not only told us that against despots force is justifiable, because it is the only means, but they themselves have set the immortal example." Lingg, a twenty-two-year-old immigrant carpenter, put it more bluntly in his final statement. "I do not recognize your law, jumbled together as it is by the nobodies of bygone centuries, and I do not recognize the decision of the court," Lingg said. "I am the enemy of the 'order' of today."

In the small number of lives lost, the violence at Haymarket paled in comparison to that of many other clashes of incorporation, but its influence on public opinion was profound. A jury convicted all eight defendants of conspiracy and sentenced four to death. Despite a nationwide petition campaign, Parsons and three others were hanged, while Lingg killed himself in his cell to resist execution by the state. Across the nation the labor movement divided over how to respond. Knights of Labor leader Powderly distanced himself from the defendants, declaring that he would rather see the hanging of "seven times seven" innocent men than show any sympathy for anarchism. Powderly even viciously slandered Parsons's wife as a "woman of bad reputation." After Haymarket, in fact, Powderly became obsessed with purging the Knights of dissenters. Divided and discredited, the Knights lost two-thirds of their members within a year. Meanwhile, some Americans were shocked at the unfair convictions, and the anarchists became known as the "Haymarket martyrs." Journalist Henry Demarest Lloyd feared the results portended "government by police," a massive erosion of the rights of free speech and fair trial. Novelist William Dean Howells called the executions, an "atrocious piece of frenzy and cruelty, for which we must stand ashamed forever before history."

But Lloyd and Howells were in the distinct minority among the country's prosperous and intellectual classes. Both faced social ostracism because of their stand, as public sentiment turned against the entire labor movement. In what has been called the nation's first "Red Scare," Chicago police helped feed the hysteria. Captain Michael Schaack and Inspector John Bonfield, in particular, used Haymarket as a career-making opportunity. They and other police arrested hundreds of Chicagoans, mostly without warrants, and alternately beat and bribed many to extract confessions. For weeks they issued almost daily warnings of imminent danger, suggesting they were uncovering an immense nationwide anarchist conspiracy. Newspapers reprinted these reports under banner headlines. "[Captain Schaack] saw more anarchists than vast hell could hold," one commentator wrote later. One of Schaack's superior officers admitted later that the captain "wanted bombs to be found here, there, all around, everywhere" and sought to "keep himself prominent before the public." Nonetheless, the damage was done. Editors denounced all labor leaders as the "scum and offal of Europe," "long-haired, wild-eyed, bad-smelling, atheistic, reckless foreign wretches." In the wake of Haymarket, many Americans concluded that the whole movement for worker rights and an eight-hour workday was a violent, antidemocratic conspiracy.

Employers used the opportunity provided by Haymarket to roll back the labor movement. Before the end of 1886, 100,000 workers had been locked out and replaced. Strikes across the country were crushed, including protests by packing-house workers in Chicago and laundry workers in Troy, New York. The following year, striking under the banner of the Knights of Labor, African-American sugar-cane cutters in Thibadaux, Louisiana, were mown down by field artillery and a Gatling gun wielded by state militia and local sheriffs' posses. These defeats further divided a labor movement whose more conservative leaders were already so fixated on distancing themselves from radicalism that they rejected May Day—the labor holiday recognized in other industrialized countries—and invented a separate Labor Day in September. (Already, the year before Haymarket, Chicago union leaders had banned any red flags or socialist symbols from their Labor Day parade.) Haymarket intensified the predicament that labor editor John Swinton had described three years earlier: "We have openly arrayed against us," he wrote, "the powers of the world, most of the intelligence, all the wealth, and even law itself."

Economic incorporation, then, brought violence not just to the Reconstruction South and the western frontier but also to the entire nation. The single year of 1877, for example, witnessed not only the Great Railroad Strike but also the Combahee rice workers' strike in South Carolina (discussed in Chapter 1); in the same year the National Guard was created to respond to domestic unrest, partly because the understaffed army was fully occupied fighting Indians in a series of battles including Wolf Mountain in Montana and Clearwater in Idaho. In the very same year, anti-Chinese demagogues were inciting riots in San Francisco, while Jesse James was still at large somewhere in Missouri (or perhaps Nebraska), and the Santa Fe ring was wrapping up the first phase of its consolidation of property in New Mexico.

In most of these conflicts, public opinion, as reflected in both popular culture and the mainstream press, projected violence onto the victims (who were, them-selves, not always inclined toward peaceable self-defense). Not only did Anglos widely accept stereotypes of bloody-minded Indians, cruel Mexicans, and treacher-ous Chinese immigrants, similar stereotypes applied to labor activists. A New York newspaper called the Haymarket defendants "foreign savages . . . as much apart from the rest of the people of this country as the Apaches of the plains." John Hay, later secretary of state under William McKinley and Theodore Roosevelt, anony-mously published a novel on the same theme. The hero of Hay's *The Breadwinners* fought in the Black Hills against the Sioux and then came east to suppress the Great Railroad Strike in Chicago.

Western artist Frederic Remington was one of the most extreme proponents of this view. Remington, in fact, expressed more admiration for Indian warriors than for strikers, though in his increasingly racist rants he did not differentiate groups with a great deal of clarity. At one point he referred to the Sioux War as a "jihad" against the United States, and in private correspondence he expressed hatred toward all non-Anglos. "Jews, Injuns, Chinamen, Italians, Huns,—the rubbish of the earth I hate," Remington wrote. "I've got some Winchesters and when the massacring begins, I can get my share of 'em, and what's more, I will." Though few Americans expressed views as crude as Remington's, many shared them in part. Across the country, middle-class whites looked down on Indians, Mexicans, African Americans, and strikers for similar reasons: all were supposedly dirty, violent, and unwilling to accommodate themselves to the "natural" order of the new economy.

Such judgments were changing and unstable; the categories of "colored" and "working class" were not the same, and sometimes popular commentary pitted one against the other. In 1879, when thousands of blacks migrated out of the South into Kansas to seek a better life, observers compared these earnest "Exodusters" favorably with strikers in the Northeast. An Anglo in the Southwest might characterize a pious Mexican housekeeper, with her flower garden and well-scrubbed children, as a "Spanish woman"; her husband, brothers, and sons, resisting Anglo encroachment on their grazing lands or striking with a mineworkers' union, were more likely to be classed as "greasers" or "Indians." Hardworking people received praise from antilabor conservatives when they "knew their place," but in episodes of protest and conflict the same people became "indolent, bigoted, cheating, dirty, cowardly."

In this reading of the world, up was down and down was up. New systems of corporate capital and labor relations, which were causing immense disruption and dislocation, were seen as agents of order and civilization. Gold-seekers who encroached on Indian lands were, if Indians retaliated, innocent victims. Militia units that fired into unarmed crowds were preservers of the peace. This explains why the term *riot* became mysteriously affixed to various confrontations such the "Haymarket riot" and a long series of "race riots" in the South, which, in fact, were carefully planned military attacks. In a "riot" the exact source of violence became fuzzy and could be shifted about. Despite considerable evidence to the contrary, comfortable Americans needed to believe that the sources of violence were meeting defeat.

Above all, Americans needed to believe that incorporation was a form of progress. Politicians and editors often expressed this view, and it also circulated through paintings and sketches such as Remington's as well as in popular novels. Starting in the 1860s, an avid public bought thousands of dime westerns that told the tales of "savage redskins, vicious greasers, or heathen Chinee" who met their defeat at the hands of manly white heroes. Books such as *Diamond Dick's Decoy Duck* and *Out with the Apache Kid* typically featured the rescue of a white maiden from the clutches of a dark-skinned captor (though working girls relished dozens of stories in which frontier heroines defended themselves). Some dime novels celebrated real incorporators such as Buffalo Bill Cody, who had started his career as a bison hunter feeding railroad construction crews. By the time of his death, Bill had been featured in more than 1,700 dime novels.

Buffalo Bill himself was one of the most successful salesmen for incorporation. His Wild West made a huge splash at the Chicago World's Fair and toured Europe before immense crowds. As the show began, small herds of bison thundered into the arena pursued by skilled Sioux and Pawnee riders (whom Bill, to his credit, treated as respected employees). Bill claimed to display more buffalo in his arena than remained wild "on the whole American continent," a claim that was, sadly, off by only a few hundred or so. The climax of the Wild West was a re-creation of the famous killing of George Armstrong Custer by Sioux and Cheyenne warriors at Little Big Horn in 1876, one of the few battles incorporators had lost. Americans dwelled almost obsessively on this incident; by depicting the tragedy and heroism of "Custer's Last Stand," they reassured themselves that the Indian wars had been a necessary fight against a ruthless and savage foe.

Buffalo Bill suggested such a lesson when he strode into the arena to reenact his killing of a Cheyenne warrior in a sequence called "First Scalp for Custer." These scenes became such a popular part of the Wild West that the Anheuser-Busch brewing company, seeking a promotional angle for Budweiser beer, commissioned a lithograph of Custer's Last Stand on the twentieth anniversary of the battle. (Borrowing from a book on South Africa, it depicted Custer's attackers carrying Zulu shields.) Reprinted many times, the lithograph hung for decades in saloons across the United States. Neither Buffalo Bill nor Anheuser-Busch had much interest in the complexity of the events they depicted—but they were hardly alone. The first reports of Custer's death had been filed by a man who falsely claimed to have been at the battle and built a lucrative career out of his "eyewitness" account. Buffalo Bill carried on the tradition when he brought on tour with him the real scalp of Cheyenne warrior Yellow Hand, without explaining that he had orchestrated the encounter in anticipation of selling the story. (Nor did Bill ponder, apparently, the irony of taking a scalp on behalf of civilization.)

Significantly, by the 1890s Buffalo Bill's Wild West began to draw connections between conflicts in the West and those emerging overseas. After an international coalition, including 5,000 U.S. troops, suppressed the Boxer Rebellion in China in 1899, the Wild West introduced "Buffalo Bill's New and Greatest Military Spectacle: The Rescue at Pekin[g]." (Sioux and Cheyenne employees of the Wild West donned pigtails to play the Chinese.) Popular narratives of incorporation, like incorporation itself, were already assuming international dimensions. Mythologizers like Buffalo Bill found large and enthusiastic audiences for their message that violent conquest was inevitable and brought political, economic, and cultural progress to all the races of humanity. Among peoples subject to such conquest, responses were as varied elsewhere as in North America. But to many observers, the presumed triumph of civilization was a matter of serious doubt.

FOR FURTHER READING

My analysis in this chapter draws first of all on Richard Maxwell Brown's essay "Violence," in the *Oxford History of the American West* (cited in Chapter 2; 803–34). In *The*

Incorporation of America, Alan Trachtenberg also uses the term *incorporation* in both geographic and hierarchical senses to describe consolidations of power. In analyzing the international dimensions of such conflicts, Walter LaFeber's *The American Search for Opportunity, 1865–1913* (New York, 1993) has been immensely helpful here as well as in Chapter 11. For international comparisons see Walter T. K. Nugent, "Comparing Wests and Frontiers," also in the *Oxford History of the American West*, 393–425. On conflict in the South see Altina Waller, *Feud* (Chapel Hill, NC, 1988), Gordon McKinney, "Industrialization and Violence in Appalachia in the 1890s," in *An Appalachian Symposium*, ed. Joel W. Williamson (Boone, NC, 1977), 131–44, and Burgin Mathews, "Looking for Railroad Bill," *Southern Cultures*, 9.3 (Fall 2003): 66–88.

Patricia Nelson Limerick, "Haunted America," in her collection of essays *Something in the Soil* (New York, 2000), 33–73, is quite possibly the most eloquent forty pages ever written about the so-called western Indian wars; I borrow from her analysis here. For Plains Indian viewpoints see Colin G. Calloway, ed., *Our Hearts Fell to the Ground* (Boston, 1996). "Wars of the Peace Policy" is the title of Chapter 6 in Robert M. Utley's *The Indian Frontier of the American West, 1846–1890* (Albuquerque, NM, 1984). On assimilation policy see Frederick E. Hoxie, *A Final Promise*, cited in Chapter 5. Material on Native Americans here is also drawn from the articles by Thomas Biolsi, Lisa E. Emmerich, and David Rich Lewis in *American Nations*, ed. Frederick E. Hoxie, Peter C. Mancall, and James H. Merrell (New York, 2001). On Posey see Betty Booth Donohue, "Alexander Posey," in *Native American Writers of the United States*, ed. Kenneth M. Roemer (Detroit, MI, 1997), 233–41.

For conflicts over the Mexican cession I depend on six books: Howard R. Lamar, *The Far Southwest, 1846–1912* (New Haven, CT, 1966), Robert J. Rosenbaum, *Mexicano Resistance in the Southwest* (Austin, TX, 1981), David Montejano, *Anglos and Mexicans in the Making of Texas, 1836–1986* (Austin, TX, 1987), Richard White, *'It's Your Misfortune and None of My Own'*, and Richard G. de Castillo, *La Familia*, both cited earlier, and most of all, María E. Montoya's study of conflict on the Maxwell Grant, *Translating Property* (Berkeley, CA, 2002). See also Sarah Deutsch, *No Separate Refuge* (New York, 1987). On conflict over the arrival of new immigrants see works on immigration cited in Chapter 2, as well as Gwendolyn Mink, *Old Labor and New Immigrants in American Political Development* (Ithaca, NY, 1986). On anti-Chinese agitation and violence see in addition James W. Loewen, *The Mississippi Chinese* (Cambridge, MA, 1971), Robert G. Lee, *Orientals* (Philadelphia, 1999), John Kuo Wei Tchen, *New York Before Chinatown* (Baltimore, 1999), and Patricia Nelson Limerick, "Disorientation and Reorientation in the American West," in her book *Something in the Soil*, cited earlier, 186–213. On Chinese exclusion see Erika Lee, *At America's Gates* (Chapel Hill, NC, 2003), the essays in Sucheng Chan, ed., *Entry Denied* (Philadelphia, 1991), and Charles J. McClain, *In Search of Equality*, cited in Chapter 5.

On labor organizing and labor conflicts, in addition to works cited in Chapter 3, see John Higham's *Strangers in the Land* (New Brunswick, NJ, 1955), Leon Fink's *In Search of the Working Class* (Urbana, IL, 1994), and Robert M. Fogelson, *America's Armories* (Cambridge, MA, 1989). On the Knights of Labor see Melton McLaurin, *The Knights of Labor in the South* (Westport, CT, 1978), Jonathan Garlock, *Guide to the Local Assemblies of the Knights of Labor* (Westport, CT, 1982), and Rosenbaum, *Mexicano Resistance*, cited earlier. On the Southwest see also Juan Gómez-Quiñones, *The Roots of Chicano Politics, 1600–1940* (Albuquerque, NM, 1994). For the great 1877 strike see Robert V. Bruce, *1877* (Chicago, 1959), David O. Stowell, *Streets, Railroads, and the Great Strike of 1877* (Chicago, 1999), and David Roediger, "Not Only the Ruling Classes to Overcome, But Also the So-Called Mob," *Journal of Social History* 19 (Winter 1985): 213–39. The best general source on Haymarket is Paul Avrich, *The Haymarket Tragedy* (Princeton, NJ, 1984); see also Carl S. Smith, *Urban Disorder and the Shape of Belief* (Chicago, 1995). For new forensics research see Timothy Messer-Kruse, James O. Eckert, Jr., Pannee Burckel, and Jeffrey Dunn, "The Haymarket Bomb: Reassessing the Evidence," *Labor: Studies in Working-Class History of the Americas* 2 (2005): 39–51.

On the popular mythology of the frontier see two massive studies by Richard Slotkin, *Fatal Environment* (New York, 1985) and *Gunfighter Nation* (New York, 1992), as well as Joy S. Kasson, *Buffalo Bill's Wild West* (New York, 2000), and Janet M. Davis, *The Circus Age*, cited in Chapter 4.

CHAPTER 10

Cooperative Dreams

I am for development and progress along social and spiritual
lines, rather than those of commerce, nationalism, or material
efficiency.
—Dr. Charles Eastman (Ohiyesa), Santee Sioux

In 1885 a former surveyor from Chester, Pennsylvania, set out to build a spectacular city on the Pacific coast of Mexico. While touring there, Alfred Kimsey
Owen had glimpsed paradise north of Mazatlán at a site called Topolobampo Bay.
He published a book, *Integral Cooperation*, to describe his proposed project. Pacific
City would guarantee each shareholder a home and job. Its internal economy
would work on the principle of cooperative exchange, and colonists could choose
to build private homes or live in cooperative hotels that would feature restaurants,
libraries, and day care centers. Twenty-five-acre parks would be scattered through
the city. Homes and businesses would have electric light and the latest sanitary
plumbing. Public schools would educate each citizen free to the age of twenty, after
which he or she would work eight hours a day, six days a week, for thirty years and
then retire to enjoy the balmy climate. Pacific City would have no taxes, no rents,
no prostitution, no saloons, and very little crime. With such encouragements to
family life, Owen believed few residents would be single for long. To avoid religious conflicts he planned to allow no churches, but he said individual residents
could preach whatever they chose. Pacific City would be modern, scientific, and
harmonious in every detail.

Unfortunately, the future of Pacific City depended on Owen's related plan to
build a railroad from Topolobampo to the U.S.-Mexican border, where he hoped
his rail connections would create a "Great Southern" stretching all the way from
his colony to Norfolk, Virginia. The dream of such a road was the chief reason that
Mexican president Porfirio Díaz permitted Owen to try his cooperative experiment. But building across the Mexican Sierras would have been a spectacular feat,
and Owen, in the end, had neither the money nor the engineers to pull it off. In the
meantime, dozens of enthusiastic colonists arrived before Owen was ready for

them; few had useful skills, and many wrangled over the harsh conditions they found at the site. Utopian author Marie Howland created a scandal by bathing nude in the ocean and conducting an affair with a businessman from Enterprise, Kansas, who had emigrated with his family. Owen himself proved short-tempered and autocratic under stress. About 200 colonists managed to set up houses and schools, dig irrigation canals, start farms, and sustain themselves for a decade, but Pacific City never materialized. In fact, it was the Mexican government, after the revolution of the 1910s, that eventually achieved two of Owen's goals. In the 1930s it nationalized the old Topolobampo property (which had fallen into the hands of a wealthy U.S. sugar planter) and gave it back to local farmers as *ejidos*, village allotments that were communally held. Thus, Topolobampo became a co-operative farming community for Mexicans. In 1961 the Mexican government also undertook one of the great engineering feats of the twentieth century and completed a railroad over the Sierras.

Owen's Pacific City experiment was one of dozens of utopian schemes and communities created by Americans in the post–Civil War decades, an era marked by the watchword *cooperation*. After Emancipation some freedmen and freedwomen created economic cooperatives to work the land. Two decades later Jews arriving from Russia created agricultural colonies in seventeen states, ranging from Arkansas to New Jersey. A leader at a socialist colony in Tennessee proudly told a reporter that "in our new cooperative kitchen the people can be fed at a cost of eighty cents to one dollar a week, a great saving upon the individualistic plan of single homes." A host of projects like Topolobampo could be found all over the United States: the single-tax Fairhope Colony in Alabama, the Kaweah Cooperative Commonwealth in California, and the Niksur Cooperative Colony in Minnesota, for example. The list was particularly long in Washington Territory, where the Puget Sound Cooperative evolved into the city of Port Angeles.

Millions of Americans who did not move to utopian colonies partook of a spirit of hopeful cooperation. Urban women's groups formed shopping cooperatives and exchanges to sell female handicrafts. There were cooperative boardinghouses and kindergartens and farmers' cooperative stores. Workers and farmers paid dues to cooperative insurance ventures such as the Farmers' Mutual Benefit Association. Across the country Americans founded alliances, unions, commonwealths, sisterhoods, and brotherhoods. Such projects took many troubling forms. Leading industrialists, for example, spoke directly of the benefits of cooperation when they created corporate pools and trusts. Even members of the Ku Klux Klan saw themselves as a cooperative brotherhood banding together to protect white supremacy, just as vigilante lynchers in the West claimed to represent the collective voice of their communities. In racial terms, one American's utopia could be another's nightmare. To its founders Washington's Puget Sound Cooperative was an experiment in harmony, but to Chinese workers it was just another hostile venture, one that emerged out of a spate of anti-Chinese protests in Seattle.

Utopia, then, was in the eye of the beholder. Which, for example, was the truest cooperative experiment in Chicago: was it the company town of Pullman, founded as a supposed worker paradise by manufacturer George Pullman? Or was it the beautiful suburb of Riverside, designed by Frederick Law Olmsted as a place where prosperous families could escape urban noise and crime? Or was it Eugene Debs's Social Democracy of America, a union-led cooperative launched in Chicago a quarter-century later? Cooperation could serve purposes of exclusion and social control, it could bridge class and racial divides, or it could accomplish a little of both. Various impulses competed with each other as Americans sought to reorder their lives in a tumultuous era.

Many of the more radical experiments in collective living were inspired by books such as *The Cooperative Commonwealth*, published in 1885 by Danish immigrant Laurence Gronlund, who argued that socialism would arrive in America through gradual change rather than the violence predicted by Karl Marx. Evolution, rather than revolution, reflected Americans' trust in democracy, their religious faith, and their hope of scientific progress. But the cooperative dreams of the post–Civil War years were shaken to their foundations by an earthshaking crisis in the 1890s. Confronted by a massive economic depression and unprecedented upheaval, many Americans wondered how to move their democracy forward, or whether progress was possible at all.

THE OTHER HALF

Over the course of the nineteenth century, prosperous Americans took advantage of new opportunities to set themselves apart. In the decades before the Civil War, as cities grew, middle-class and professional families had begun withdrawing into distinct residential neighborhoods. That process accelerated in the postwar years, aided by commuter railroads that fueled the growth of suburbs. As early as the 1870s, a key marker of success was to move to a place such as Riverside. Sited on a major rail line eleven miles from downtown Chicago, it was far enough away that the annual cost of commuting excluded all but professionals and businessmen and their families. Olmsted envisioned Riverside as a place of "healthfulness and permanent rural beauty." Arguing that "the essential qualification of a suburb is domesticity," he provided playgrounds and meandering parkways along the Des Plains River. Almost half of Riverside's land was set aside for parks. A more exclusive expression of the desire for shelter and security was the town of Tuxedo Park in Orange County, New York (two of whose founders introduced a new type of men's formal wear without tails that took the name *tuxedo*). Developed by the heir to a tobacco fortune and built by a crew of 1,800 Italian and Slovak immigrants, Tuxedo Park featured a clubhouse, hotel, commuter rail station, and three fishing lakes as well as homes and shops. It seems to have been America's first gated community. Following the tradition of aristocratic estates, a stone wall surrounded the resort, and visitors entered through a staffed gatehouse.

Along with the exclusive suburb came the country club, a well-recognized institution by the 1890s. Country clubs offered members the pleasures of boating, swimming, fox hunting, clay-pigeon shooting, tennis, and golf. In Philadelphia polo was the craze. The Elkridge Fox-Hunting Club outside Baltimore was noted for its fine chef. Country clubs offered the assurance that fellow members were the "right sort," protecting women and children, especially, when they went out for pleasure or exercise. Henry James, who waxed rhapsodic over country clubs on his 1905 visit to the United States, noted their centrality to elite domestic life. He wrote that in the country club—as opposed to the traditional gentlemen's club—one saw "everything staked [on] the active Family as a final social fact." Within the enclave of the club, an elite family could withdraw from the public eye.

One did not have to move to the suburbs to see many forms of such segregation. Visitors to a port city such as New York or Baltimore could wander through large slum districts where poverty was the norm. Even in an inland city such as Detroit, cross-class ethnic neighborhoods faded, and rich and poor increasingly went the rounds of daily life without encountering each other. Public celebrations as well as residential space diverged. By the 1880s citizens in the factory town of Worcester, Massachusetts, held an array of distinct Fourth of July gatherings. Working-class Irishmen gathered for firecrackers, music, and drinking at a picnic sponsored by an Irish fraternal order. Swedish workers marched from church to their own picnic grounds, while French Canadians gathered in family enclaves for "pique-niques," as did Welsh, Finns, Armenians, and Jews. In the evening many working-class groups mingled at a nearby lake and amusement park, but native-born Protestants retreated for the holiday to private clubs and summer resorts away from town.

Segregation was equally obvious in hundreds of other factory and mining towns, where wage workers and immigrants were nearly synonymous categories. In Clifton, Arizona, copper mine managers built their homes and country club in North Clifton, while Mexican residents were shunted into polluted districts along the narrow canyon of Chase Creek. In Los Angeles, burgeoning numbers of Mexican-American residents were increasingly segregated into separate *barrios*, creating by 1900 the foundations of East Los Angeles.

Journalists ventured into tenements and slums to report with pen and camera on what they saw. The most famous was Jacob Riis, a Danish working-class immigrant who became a police reporter for the *New York Tribune*. Persuading friends to help him experiment with new flash photography equipment, Riis published the results in his 1890 book *How the Other Half Lives*. He charged that "the half that was on top cared little for the struggles, and less for the fate of those who were underneath, so long as it was able to hold them there and keep its own seat." Riis took middle-class readers on a tour through the streets of "Jewtown" and "The Bend," interiors of stifling tenements and sweatshops, cellars where immigrant workers slept for 5¢, and heating grates where homeless children huddled against the cold. Riis blamed "wealthy absentee landlords," and being pessimistic about the prospects of government action, he suggested instead that private investors buy and improve notorious slums. His book attracted the attention of prominent reformers such as Theodore Roosevelt while stimulating a much broader debate over urban poverty.

Children on the playground at the Webster School, Chicago, 1902. Across the United States, settlement workers and other civic activists worked to beautify city neighborhoods, improve health practices and combat disease, and build schools, day care centers, and safe play spaces for children. Courtesy Chicago Historical Society.

Riis was not the pioneer of this form of journalism, though he made it vivid through photography. Among his notable predecessors was Helen Campbell, also a writer for the *New York Tribune*, who in the 1880s published exposés such as *Studies in the Slums* and *Prisoners of Poverty*. Campbell considered herself an instructor in "survival economics" who brought the latest findings in sanitation, diet, nutrition, health care, and budgeting to the poor. As an investigator she conducted interviews and published detailed statistics on women's wages, working hours, and the effects of layoffs and injuries. Far more sweeping than Riis in her vision, Campbell advocated equal pay for women, labor organizing, abolition of sweatshops, appointment of factory inspectors, and more educational opportunities for the next generation.

An influential group of young reformers proposed that middle-class people not just read about the slums but connect themselves directly to the poor by living among them. The settlement movement began in London in the mid-1880s, but idealistic Americans soon brought the idea across the Atlantic. The first U.S. settlement began in 1886 on New York's Lower East Side, founded by a group of young men influenced by Felix Adler's Society of Ethical Culture. It was followed a year later by a coalition of Smith graduates led by the Wellesley instructor Vida Scudder, whose College Settlement Association drew interested members from northeastern women's colleges and beyond. The movement grew rapidly. In 1891 there

Virginia Day Nursery, East Fifth Street, New York City, 1906. Founded in 1879, the nursery cared for the children of working mothers on the Lower East Side. It is still in operation today. Courtesy Museum of the City of New York. The Byron Collection.

were 6 settlements in the United States; by 1905 there were 200, and five years later, 200 more.

The movement brought together professionals from the new social sciences, advocates of the Social Gospel, and most of all energetic, educated young people. Almost all settlement founders and participants were young, and four-fifths were recent college graduates. The most famous was Jane Addams, who founded Chicago's Hull House in 1889 at the age of twenty-nine. A graduate of Rockford Female Seminary in Illinois, Addams experienced a crisis when she left school. Addams quoted a young woman from a wealthy family who met her on a European tour: "'I am simply smothered and sickened with advantages. It is like eating a sweet dessert the first thing in the morning.' This then, was the difficulty," Addams wrote, "the assumption that the sheltered, educated girl has nothing to do with the bitter poverty and the social maladjustment which is all about her, and which, after all, cannot be concealed, for it breaks through poetry and literature in a burning tide which overwhelms her; it peers at her in the form of heavy-laden market women and underpaid street laborers, gibing her with a sense of her uselessness."

Addams suffered special griefs, having lost her mother when she was a young child and her father only six weeks after she graduated from college. But she shared her passionate need for a life of moral purpose with other young women who held college degrees and had no clear sense of what profession they might follow. (Belle Kearney, from a wealthy Mississippi family, felt similarly paralyzed after she left an Ohio boarding school. "If my life had to be spent on the plantation," she wondered, "what was the use of reading, of trying to cultivate my mind, when it would have the effect of making me more miserable?" Kearney added, "In those days I died ten thousand deaths. I died to God and to humanity. . . . A deadness settled upon my soul . . . for ten dreary agonizing years." She eventually built a career as an advocate of temperance and women's suffrage.) Addams borrowed the phrase "the snare of preparation" from Russian writer and pacifist Leo Tolstoy. That snare, she wrote, was the education "we spread before the feet of young people, hopelessly entangling them in a curious inactivity at the very period of life when they are longing to construct the world anew and to conform it to their own ideals."

Despite Addams's grief over the death of her father, his will provided her with the opportunity she craved by leaving her independently wealthy. After years of travel and indecision, she moved to Chicago with several close friends and purchased a run-down mansion in one of the city's poorest immigrant districts, formerly the property of Charles J. Hull. Like many other settlement workers, those at Hull House sought, at first, to provide "uplift" to the poor through concerts, art exhibits, and classes in literature and history. With humor and self-deprecation, Addams later described these early efforts as naïve. The programs of many settlement houses fit the satirical description of novelist Sinclair Lewis, who claimed they offered to the downtrodden lectures on "trout fishing, exploring Tibet, pacifism, sea shell collecting, the eating of bran, and the geography of Charlemagne's Empire."

But culture was not always alien to poor immigrants: settlement founders discovered many who were delighted to study history, gain access to a piano, or gather for readings of poetry from their home country. A fruit vendor from Athens beamed when he found a picture of the Acropolis at Hull House. He told Addams that he had talked to thousands of Chicagoans and never yet found one interested in the glory of classical Greece. At the same time, wise settlement workers such as Addams learned much from their new neighbors about the urgent problems of urban poverty. Within a few years Hull House, like many other settlements, was building safe play spaces for children and tackling the urban crises in housing, medical care, and garbage collection. A mere five years after Hull House opened, Addams was serving as a citywide mediator in tense Chicago strikes and lobbying for the appointment of Illinois factory inspectors. The first such appointee, Florence Kelley, was a Hull House resident whose socialist views influenced Addams's outlook on labor and poverty. Still another Hull House luminary, Julia Lathrop, served on the State Board of Charities and helped design the nation's first juvenile court system.

Similar campaigns went on around the country. Boston settlements, for example, played a leading role in reducing the use of child labor and advocating public ownership of utilities. For its day, the settlement movement was remarkably diverse. Jamie Porter Barrett, an African-American graduate of the Hampton Institute, remained in Hampton and formed the Locust Street Settlement to provide work and child care training for troubled young women. The White Rose Mission, founded by African-American reformer Victoria Earle Matthews, helped blacks arriving in New York City from the South. Lillian Wald, founder of Henry Street Nurses' Settlement in New York, was a Jew who won the support of the city's leading Jewish charities. Her team of 175 nurses, including 25 African-American women, pioneered in healing the sick and teaching hygiene in the tenements. Settlement houses thus offered an array of public roles and professional careers for women. A reporter observed in the early 1900s that "twenty years ago . . . a young woman who was restless and yearned to sacrifice herself, would have become a missionary or married a drinking man in order to save him. Today she studies medicine or goes into settlement work." Even more important, settlement houses laid the groundwork for an array of twentieth-century public welfare projects.

At the same time settlements arose, another movement began to address some of the same economic and political ills, but it emerged from a very different sector of society. The Farmers' Alliance had been founded in Texas during the depression of the 1870s. In the 1880s, with cotton, corn, and wheat prices plunging to new lows and drought devastating the West, it supplanted the Grange and other farmers' groups in mobilizing rural people. Like these groups, the alliance brought farm families together for picnics, debates, and educational lectures. But it took self-help in bolder directions as its leaders, like other innovators of the day, hailed the benefits of cooperation. Texas alliance members formed cooperative stores, inviting members to pool their money to obtain bulk discounts from manufacturers. Alliance wheat farmers in South Dakota experimented with offering crop insurance and establishing direct links to British milling companies to eliminate middlemen and get a better price. Alliance leaders in North Carolina set up their own tobacco warehouse as an alternative to the American Tobacco Company's control of crop auctions. In the Deep South, alliance leaders organized a coordinated response after makers of jute, a wrapping for cotton bales, used their monopoly power to raise prices by 60 percent. The Farmers' Alliance persuaded millions of farmers to substitute cotton bagging, and this forced the "jute trust" to lower prices.

Cooperative organizing also pushed the alliance into electoral politics, since much of its agenda rested on government action. A looser money supply and more federal regulation of railroads—demands held over from the Greenback movement of the 1870s—topped the wish list. In addition, some alliance leaders endorsed a subtreasury plan, modeled on the national banking system, that would allow farmers to store crops in government-run warehouses so that they, rather than middlemen and futures traders, could benefit from seasonal price swings. Southern Farmers' Alliance members tried to work through the Democratic Party until 1892, when they became disillusioned with Democrats' conspicuous lack of action. In the meantime, Alliance farmers nationwide began to hope for partnership with the Knights of Labor, which was also turning its energies to politics. A gathering in St. Louis in February 1892 to create a new national party featured representatives from an array of groups. They included the various Farmers' Alliances; sympathetic middle-class reformers in the West who organized themselves as the Citizens' Alliance and the Women's Alliance; the Knights of Labor and a number of other unions; proponents of Henry George's single tax on land and of Edward Bellamy's Nationalist utopian ideas; and the economically progressive wing of the Prohibition Party, led by Frances Willard herself. It was one of the era's most diverse and radical gatherings.

The new People's Party (soon known as Populists) held a second convention to draft a platform and nominate national candidates. Their platform, adopted at Omaha, Nebraska, on July 4, 1892, called for federal expansion of the money supply, public ownership of railroad and telegraph networks, and a progressive income tax levied on the very rich. Among other proposals were laws enforcing the eight-hour workday and the establishment of public savings banks at the nation's post offices, where people could safely deposit small sums. The People's delegates offered a scathing assessment of the state of the union in their preamble:

> We meet in the midst of a nation brought to the verge of moral, political and material ruin.... The newspapers are largely subsidized or muzzled; public opinion silenced; business prostrated; our homes covered with mortgages; labor impoverished; and the land concentrating in the hands of capitalists. The urban workmen are denied the right of organization for self-protection; imported pauperized labor beats down their wages.... The fruits of the toil of millions are boldly stolen to build up colossal fortunes for a few, unprecedented in the history of mankind; and the possessors of these, in turn, despise the republic and endanger liberty. From the same prolific womb of governmental injustice we breed two great classes—tramps and millionaires.

In blaming "governmental injustice," Populists recognized the active role of state and federal policies that over the prior three decades had favored corporations over small business, investors over producers, and the Northeast over the West and South. Populists declared themselves not so much in favor of more government as of a different kind of government, one that served "'the plain people,' . . . to the end that oppression, injustice, and poverty shall eventually cease in the land."

With similar state platforms, the People's Party won considerable power in the West in the early 1890s, from Nebraska and Kansas through the Rocky Mountain states to Oregon and Washington. Nationwide their presidential ticket won a million votes in 1892, even though southern opponents engaged in fraud and acts of terror to keep power in Democratic hands. Few southern alliance members were racial egalitarians, but they did court black voters, denounce disfranchisement attempts, and cooperate with a separate Colored Farmers' Alliance that had organized its own cooperative experiments, such as a Norfolk, Virginia, cotton exchange. Democrats deeply feared an alliance of poor southerners that crossed racial lines, and while the People's Party never fully embodied this dream, it came closer to doing so than any other movement after Reconstruction's end.

Democrats, in response, refused to accept their opponents' legitimacy and justified any tactic to crush them. One Georgia Democrat, who assisted in an 1894 "recount" that turned a Populist victory into defeat, said later, "We had to do it! Those damned Populists would have ruined the Country." Where they could not win by such means, Democrats removed opponents from office in ways that harkened back to the overthrow of Reconstruction. Instigators described an 1898 coup in Wilmington, North Carolina, where Republicans and Populists had forged an effective coalition, as a "race riot." But in fact, it was a carefully planned attack by Democrats, who had maintained a vigilante presence throughout the preceding political campaign. (One observer wrote that it was "an awesome sight to drive through town in the dark and see synods of armed men standing at each corner.") The "race riot," carried out with a Gatling gun, resulted in not only the deaths of two dozen African Americans but also the resignation at gunpoint of local Populist and Republican officials.

The People's Party faced a number of other daunting challenges. Backed by relatively poor voters, it suffered from a chronic lack of cash. The mainstream press, centered in New York and Boston, ridiculed its leaders as hayseeds and wild-eyed fanatics, echoing the media hysteria over strikes and other protests by the working class. In addition, the U.S. winner-take-all political system and its complex set of checks and balances hampered the Populist cause. Kansas Populists won control of the lower house of the legislature in 1890, but since the Republican-dominated upper house did not face reelection until 1892, the result was deadlock and lost momentum. Colorado's Populist governor faced a hostile legislature backed by powerful mining corporations, which along with railroads spent liberally to defeat the new party. In states such as Iowa, savvy Democrats picked up aspects of the Populist agenda and prevented the new party from developing. In other states "fusion" arrangements (usually with Democrats in the West and Republicans in the South) watered down the party's program and led to infighting and disillusionment. Thus, the People's Party fell prey to some of the very conditions it arose to combat: the poverty of farmers, rifts within the American working class, the power of elite interests, and the entrenchment of Republicans and Democrats. Most of all, a national economic cataclysm spelled doom for the party as an institution, if not for some of its most enduring ideas.

DEPRESSION

Between 1890 and 1892 the success of the People's Party showed how seriously the rural economy had deteriorated in the South and West. Unluckily for Populists and for the nation as a whole, the situation got much worse. Even as Populists met in Omaha, railroad investment was slowing down. Early in 1893 the Philadelphia & Reading went bankrupt, and many businessmen began to feel uneasy. Then, on May 5, 1893, the storm broke: Philadelphia's National Cordage Company went under, taking with it two Chicago banks and three brokerages heavily invested in its stock. As in previous economic panics, during the era before federal deposit insurance, people who held savings in private banks risked losing every dime. Desperate financiers in the heartland began calling in their deposits from New York's national banks; by July 25 those banks partially "suspended," turning away depositors who wanted to withdraw funds. People began frantically hoarding cash. Manufacturers laid off workers. Railroads lost shipping revenue and began to go under. By the end of the summer, the country had slid into a deep depression that lasted until decade's end.

Once again it appeared that the nation was headed not toward lasting peace but into distress and turmoil. While J. P. Morgan and the Cleveland administration struggled to shore up the gold standard, unemployment in major cities rose to 20 or 25 percent. The resulting misery was starkly obvious to settlement workers such as Jane Addams, who nearly bankrupted herself keeping Hull House open to provide emergency aid. Walter Rauschenbusch, serving as a street minister in New York City's Hell's Kitchen during these years, wrote that "one could hear human virtues cracking and crumbling all around." Urban police, finding themselves over-whelmed, ended their long-standing practice of allowing homeless people to take shelter on station floors. Year-round, but especially during the terrible winters between 1893 and 1897, urban newspapers published a steady stream of reported deaths from starvation, freezing, and suicide.

The impact was as severe in small towns and the countryside as it was in the great cities. "Never in my life of forty-five years of responsible activity," wrote one Ohio congressman, "have I seen a time when in spite of the hardest labor, strictest temperance, plainest frugality, and closest economy, the 'average farmer' has grown so poorer." Camps of wanderers sprang up along railroad sidings. Tramps became a familiar sight at farmhouse doors, begging for work or food. In Wisconsin, business failures and bankruptcies triggered suicides and mental breakdowns. "Jan. 3, 1894," read a typical entry at the state insane asylum. "Town of Melrose. Norwegian. Age 27. Single. Farmer. Poor. . . . Deranged on the subject of finances. Disposed to injure others." A Nebraska banker wrote in January 1895 that it made him "heartsick to look at this once prosperous country. The suffering is terrible. . . . We have several families who for a month past have had nothing to eat but flour and water and they are very thankful to get that. Scores of women and children have to stay in their sod shanties bare-footed for the want of something to cover their feet. All this was brought on these people through no fault of theirs. They are hard working, industrious people."

The United States had suffered depressions before and would do so again. But by some measures, the crisis of the 1890s was larger even than the Great Depression of the 1930s, and it was accompanied by determined, collective protests that shocked the nation's elite. In 1892, the year before the depression hit with full force, Americans had already witnessed showdowns in the steel mills of Pennsylvania and the mines of Idaho, along with a general strike in New Orleans and smaller ones in such diverse locations as Buffalo, New York, and Tracy, Tennessee. The first full year of depression, 1894, brought two more large-scale labor conflicts. In April,

125,000 Pennsylvania coal miners walked off their jobs (the United Mine Workers' official membership rolls counted 20,000). The strike spread to mines in Illinois, West Virginia, Ohio, and elsewhere. Two months later the American Railway Union (ARU) announced that its members would no longer carry Pullman cars, in sympathy with workers at Pullman's Illinois plant who had walked out after wage cuts of 25 to 40 percent. (There had been no corresponding cut in their rents for company-owned housing, nor in shareholders' dividends.) Eugene Debs had purposely built the ARU as a broad-based, industrywide union, having witnessed past defeats when brakemen, switchmen, and engineers tried to negotiate separately. The strategy worked. On June 26, ARU workers all over the Midwest began shunting Pullman cars to the sidings. By the following day, traffic on twenty railroads had slowed to a near halt, and at passenger stations as far apart as Delaware and California, Pullman cars ceased to run.

While the Pullman boycott paralyzed parts of the country for a month, Americans were also astonished witnesses to a novel form of protest: the first march on Washington, undertaken by legions of unemployed men in an appeal for federal aid. The founders of this project called it the Commonweal of Christ, but the press dubbed it Coxey's Army after its leading spokesman, Ohio businessman Jacob Coxey. Coxey proposed an immense public works project to prevent starvation. Hundreds of thousands of Americans needed jobs and bread, he observed; at the same time, the nation's dirt roads were in terrible condition for wagons, bicycles, and automobiles. Coxey proposed that the federal government hire unemployed men to build good roads.

Only 122 men accompanied Coxey as he left Massillon, Ohio, on Easter Sunday morning in 1894, but the number swelled to more than 400 by the time they arrived on the outskirts of the District of Columbia. In addition, throughout spring and summer new "armies" organized across the West, with thousands setting out from Los Angeles, San Francisco, Portland, Tacoma, and many inland points. Crossing into the Midwest and Pennsylvania, appointed "generals" worked hard to keep marchers organized and prevent theft. Having reviewed the California army led by Charles T. Kelley, a manager of the Rock Island Railroad described them as "intelligent determined men. . . . Their leader is a man of brains and character and great determination. He is a religious man, too." The manager added that "it is a terrible thing, and it made me sad to find that there were sixteen hundred respectable, well-meaning men reduced to such desperate straits in this country."

The Commonweal of Christ prompted an outpouring of compassion. Chapters of the WCTU organized lunch stations to feed marchers along the route. People in dozens of cities and towns held mass meetings of welcome, and churches opened their sanctuaries and basements as sleeping quarters. In Omaha, where the People's Party had taken its stand, Mayor George Bemis and prominent merchant Emil Brandeis joined a crowd of 40,000 who greeted Kelley's marchers and helped raise money and gather supplies. The Populist governor of Kansas issued a statement of support. "I am in sympathy with these men," declared the sheriff of Council Bluffs, Iowa. "They are creatures of circumstances." But more ominously, the cities of Detroit and Cleveland offered a cold shoulder. As the armies traveled down rural roads and suburban streets, some citizens sat on their front porches cradling shotguns.

In the major protests of the early 1890s, as well as in the march of Coxey's Army, labor leaders tried to make sure their followers were law abiding. Officials of the ARU stressed again and again that participants must use "no threats" and "let liquor of all kinds alone." But hungry men walking across the continent got weary, and unemployed marchers "borrowed" at least fifty trains in various parts of the country, including some during the weeks when the Pullman boycott had already brought chaos on the railroads. Having walked all the way from San Francisco, Kelley's Army decided to speed things up in Council Bluffs. They flooded aboard an eastbound train that sympathetic local women were decorating with American flags. "Pop, you are our prisoner," a jobless railroadman informed the engineer as he took over the cab. In Montana Hogan's Army fired up the Northern Pacific's most powerful locomotive, attached it to empty coal cars to carry their men, loaded up three tons of food and supplies donated by Bozeman supporters, and ordered rail officials to clear the tracks. Furious, railroad managers complied, but they also telegraphed Washington. Hogan made it 300 miles east to Forsyth, where a superintendent spiked the switches and U.S. troops, under instructions from the attorney general, intercepted the train.

The wild ride of Hogan's Army highlighted two factors that ultimately defeated the protests of the 1890s. First, many Americans were terrified by such bold challenges to the established order. Newspapers and magazines played a major role in shaping public opinion, especially in the East. "This is no time to arbitrate," declared the *Christian Advocate*. "The battle of law and order must be fought to the end.... Despotism would settle this matter better than we can." The *Chicago Tribune* covered ARU activities under screeching headlines such as "Law Is Trampled On—Riotous Emissaries of Dictator Debs." "Chicago at the Mercy of the Incendiary's Torch," echoed the *Washington Post*. During Hogan's ride, when police deputies panicked and fired into a Billings crowd, headlines in the *New York Times* screamed "Blood Flows from Coxeyism" and "Battle Between Law and Anarchy." Many Americans remained firm in their conviction that striking and marching were illegitimate tactics; disrupting rail traffic and demanding government aid went beyond the pale.

The Pullman conflict proved especially bloody. While the Republican governors of Pennsylvania and Idaho called in state militia to Homestead and Coeur d'Alene, Illinois governor John Peter Altgeld chose not to do so in response to the ARU boycott. He observed that it was a peaceful stopping of trains and ruled that Illinois did not need any help from outside. Over his outraged protests, the U.S. attorney general sent federal troops to Illinois anyway. ARU leaders such as George Howard, a Union Army veteran, found themselves facing ranks of rifles. In a replay of the uprising of 1877, mobs joined in looting and rioting, with at least fifty-three killed in violence that, like the strike, radiated outward from Chicago to other locales. Angry crowds overturned trains, burned engines, and attacked rail stations and roundhouses, destroying millions of dollars worth of equipment.

It is not quite right to call these conflicts showdowns between labor and capital. Though labor relations were clearly at stake, it was government intervention on the side of capital that, as in the days of Reconstruction, decided the outcome. Thus, Pullman, Homestead, and the march of Coxey's Army can be described as three-way struggles in which government proved to be the critical corner of the triangle. U.S. troops halted both the Pullman strike and Coxey's marchers after courts granted injunctions ordering each protest to cease. In Washington officials prepared for Coxey's arrival by mobilizing the Secret Service and troops from surrounding states. With rumors circulating that Coxey's men intended to attack the Treasury, though they were armed only with white flags, department officials stockpiled weapons and ordered clerks to prepare for defense. After his parade into town, Coxey tried to stand on the Capitol steps to appeal for government aid. Police beat back the marchers, and Coxey was, to his shock, arrested, tried, and sentenced to twenty days in jail for the crime of trespassing on the Capitol grass.

The impulse for law and order in the mid-1890s accompanied a hardening of racial and religious antagonisms. During the 1890s Jews began to be systematically excluded from elite resorts and social institutions—even from New York's Union League Club, which Jews had helped establish during Reconstruction. The American Protective Association (APA), peaking at perhaps half a million members in 1894, campaigned against immigration and circulated fraudulent "proof" that the pope was instigating the murder of non-Catholics. The APA advised Protestants to boycott Catholic businesses and fire Catholic workers. Their agitation provoked at least three riots, partly because some APA members were, ironically, immigrant Protestant Orangemen who had brought sectarian hatreds with them from northern Ireland. Many Scandinavian and English immigrants also joined the APA's call to shut the door against new arrivals.

Meanwhile, in sports, the League of American Wheelmen excluded African Americans in 1894. Chicago's YMCA, one of a handful that was racially integrated, held out until 1900 before it segregated—the same year the South's last black congressman, George H. White of North Carolina, left office, and the ex-Confederacy's congressional delegation turned all-white for the next six decades. Meanwhile, 1898 was the last year any black player appeared in major- or minor-league baseball until Jackie Robinson joined the Brooklyn Dodgers in 1947. Separate Negro leagues began to arise in the face of exclusion. The same was true among women's literary and social clubs. The newly formed General Federation of Women's Clubs barred black clubs from joining, despite protests from the National Federation of Afro-American Women. Advocates of women's suffrage sailed with the prevailing tide. In a particularly nasty episode, Susan B. Anthony asked her elderly colleague Frederick Douglass, a longtime champion of women's rights, not to attend an 1894 suffrage convention in Atlanta because his presence might alienate white women in the South. Douglass stayed home. Southern suffragists argued that white women's votes would be "a means to the end of securing white supremacy."

In central Texas, as the turn of the century loomed, school segregation began extending to Mexican Americans as well as blacks, and a few districts in the South even forced Italian students into nonwhite schools. One group of Anglo Texans undertook a legal campaign to disfranchise all Mexican immigrants, though federal courts rejected their case in 1897. In New Mexico Territory, still predominantly Latino, the 1890s brought a transformation in attitudes toward the long-standing practice of bilingual schooling. By the early twentieth century, Anglos fought to conduct public schools on an English-only basis, and Congress rejected New Mexico statehood in 1902 on the grounds that too many of its residents were "alien" in language and custom.

Many racial animosities spilled over into violence. In the Deep South, Jews not only were targets of social discrimination, as in the North, but also had their farms and businesses attacked and burned. In the coal fields of western Pennsylvania, two dozen unarmed Polish and Hungarian miners were gunned down by police in one of many incidents stemming from suppression of strikes. (The United Mine Workers were by this point, wisely, bringing recent immigrants into the union fold.) Chinese farmworkers were beaten and driven out of California fields and orchards. Violence intensified most of all against blacks. During the 1890s lynchings occurred in almost every state outside New England, and the number of lynchings during the decade exceeded 1,500. Most of the victims were black men, but they included Mexican and Italian men and even some women.

While increasing in number, lynchings also became a public blood sport, with large crowds of white men and women gathering to watch for hours as victims were tortured and burned alive. Though such rituals of terror were most frequent in the former Confederacy, they also occurred in the West and Midwest. Newspapers advertised the places and times in advance, and photographers rushed to the scene to sell souvenir pictures. Two of the most notorious examples were the lynchings of Henry Smith in Paris, Texas, in 1893 and of Sam Hose in Newman, Georgia, in 1899. Both men were accused of the rape and murder of whites, but the charges later proved false. Investigators found that Hose, for instance, had been involved in a dispute with his employer. At the time, however, newspapers asserted that "the usual crime" had been committed, with the alleged rape victims cloistered from interviews. Smith, Hose, and others were slowly burned and cut to death, with railroads running excursion trains for those who wanted to watch. Afterward some onlookers hacked off victims' fingers and toes to keep as mementos.

Why did such a confluence of race hatreds take place in the 1890s? Or, to put it another way, why did Americans respond to economic crisis and social upheaval in racialized ways? As we have seen, they had long been conditioned to do so, and with a new century approaching it was clear that whites no longer securely dominated any part of the country, at least in numerical terms. An influx of Mexicans, Asians, and southern and eastern Europeans was remaking the national landscape; nervousness about their presence was openly expressed in calls for "Anglo-Saxon" rule. Southern whites also responded with fear and anger to the coming of age of the first freeborn generation, who in the late 1880s and 1890s were reaching adulthood. Writers noted that this generation had never known the submission of enslavement. Lynching victims were often described as "strange Negroes"— itinerant laborers in transit, men unknown in the community and thus suspect and vulnerable. But in a broader sense, by the 1890s all young African Americans were "strange" to whites, and those with education, property, and ambition were strangest of all. Three young men lynched in Memphis in 1891, for example, had committed the crime of opening a grocery store across the street from a white competitor. Their murder launched their friend Ida B. Wells on a distinguished but lonely career as an antilynching investigator.

A Texas lynching in 1901 prompted Mark Twain to write his powerful essay, "The United States of Lyncherdom." Twain quoted from a telegraph report on the lynching, which had been delayed for several hours after the victim was nearly hung: "It was suggested that the man ought not to die too quickly, and he was let down to the ground while a party went to Dexter, about two miles distant, to procure coal oil. This was thrown on the flames and the work completed." Noting that 203 lynchings had been carried out in the previous year, Twain asked his readers to

UNITED WE STAND, DIVIDED WE—FIGHT ONE ANOTHER.

"United we stand, divided we—fight one another." An 1892 People's Party cartoon envisioning cooperative political action by American farmers and working men. Those coming to the ballot box include a former northern Republican and former southern Democrat who have joined the Farmers' Alliance; a Colored Allianceman; and members of the Knights of Labor, the American Federation of Labor, and the Brotherhood of Locomotive Engineers. *Kansas Commoner*, 14 January 1892.

read that telegraph again, and yet again, and picture the scene in their minds. . . . Then multiply it by 115, add 88; place the 203 in a row, allowing 600 feet of space for each human torch, so that there may be viewing room around it for 5,000 Christian American men, women, and children, youths and maidens; make it night, for grim effect; have the show in a gradually rising plain and let the course of the stakes be uphill; the eye can take in the whole line of twenty-four miles of blood-and-flesh bonfires. . . . All being ready now, and the darkness opaque, the stillness impressive—for there should be no sound but the soft moaning of the night wind and the muffled sobbing of the sacrifices—let all the far stretch of kerosened pyres be touched off simultaneously and the glare and the shrieks and the agonies burst heavenward to the Throne.

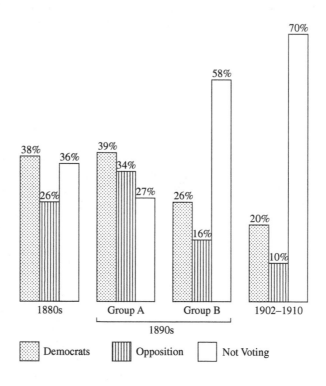

The impact of disfranchisement. Party politics remained competitive in the South during the 1880s; it remained so in the following decade wherever suffrage restrictions had not been passed (in the states of Group A, consisting of Alabama, Louisiana, North Carolina, Texas, and Virginia). In the states of Group B (Arkansas, Florida, Georgia, Mississippi, South Carolina, and Tennessee), poll taxes, grandfather clauses, and other restrictive measures were in place by 1894. Group A followed suit over the next decade. The results were dramatic. With Democrats fully ascendant, apathy and nonvoting set in even among those still eligible to go to the polls. From J. Morgan Kousser, *The Shaping of Southern Politics: Suffrage Restriction and the Establishment of the One-Party South, 1880–1910* (New Haven, CT, 1974), 225.

"O compassionate missionary," Twain concluded, "leave China! Come home and convert these Christians!"

If anyone had the authority to make Americans confront such hard truths, it was the beloved Mark Twain, who found himself a celebrity as far away as Cape Town and Calcutta. But Twain never published "The United States of Lyncherdom." He and his publisher worried that it would damage his reputation and sales in the South. "I shouldn't have even half a friend left down there," Twain wrote privately, "after it issued from the press." So he set aside the essay, which was found years later after his death, and turned his attention to a little parody of Sherlock Holmes.

REACTION AND REINVENTION

In all parts of the country, the depression of the 1890s provoked a sharp response at the ballot box. For the previous twenty years, since the midterm election of 1874, the national balance of power between Republicans and Democrats had been extremely close. A succession of presidents won narrowly, in three cases winning the electoral vote but not the popular vote; except for U. S. Grant, none served two terms. Control of both the Senate and the House changed multiple times. Bases of power in both chambers were also destabilized by the reentry of the South, rapid population growth, and the admittance of ten new western states. When U. S. Grant took office, there had been 68 senators and 226 representatives in Congress; by 1893 there were 88 and 356. In an era of close party competition, campaigns in key swing states such as Ohio and New York were hard-fought and exhausting. Close margins of victory prompted fraud and high-pressure tactics as each party struggled for advantage.

For a brief moment in 1889 and 1890, Republicans won control of both houses of Congress and the White House. Benjamin Harrison, the last Union general to serve as president, adhered to the issues of the Civil War: he ran on his military record and denounced the disfranchisement of southern blacks. Republican leaders, in what became known as the "Billion Dollar Congress" of 1890, passed a major new pension program for Union veterans, built up the navy, and renewed the high protective tariff. These measures proved unpopular: Democrats won control of the House in November 1890 and recaptured the Senate by a slim margin two years later as Democrat Grover Cleveland recaptured the presidency. But unfortunately for Democrats, these events put them fully in control when the United States was hit by the depression of 1893.

Voters apparently blamed the party in power for the economic cataclysm, and the election of 1894 brought overwhelming Republican victories. Across the North and West, Democrats were voted out; in the few western states where Populists had won control, they were also swept from office. Democrats, who had held the House of Representatives by a margin of 218 to 124 (with 2 Independent Democrats, 11 Populists, and 3 Silver Party members), now found themselves in the minority, 254 to 93 (with 9 Populists and 1 Silverite). Two years later William McKinley completed Republicans' national power with a decisive presidential victory. It became clear over the next few years that the era of close party competition had ended: after 1896, Republicans controlled the White House and both houses of Congress until 1910.

The Republican Party that came to power in 1894 and 1896 was very different from its predecessor of the Civil War era. Republicans had made their last effort to preserve a piece of Reconstruction during their active session in 1890, through a bill sponsored by Massachusetts senator Henry Cabot Lodge. The Lodge elections bill would have created a new federal board empowered to investigate any election when 100 or more citizens petitioned for aid. If passed, it would have provided ordinary citizens with a tool to push for fair elections. But the bill created an uproar in the South, where it was known as the "Force Bill" and generated hysterical warnings of "Negro supremacy." It also generated opposition in the West and among leaders and allies of urban political machines. Lodge's bill passed in the House, but it met defeat in the Senate by one vote.

The bill's failure had the worst possible results. It failed, and its failure persuaded Republicans to abandon any further effort to enforce fair elections in the South. At the same time, its near-passage galvanized southern Democrats, who worked to blunt the impact of any future such bill. In the 1890s they chose white supremacy as the banner under which to unite white voters and defeat southern Populism. Having taken power—in some cases through fraud or terror—southern Democrats secured their position. They passed disfranchisement laws that entrenched white supremacy for decades to come. Black voters were shut out almost completely. As poll taxes and new registration laws came into effect, the number of poor white voters also declined, as much as 46 percent in Louisiana and 48 percent in Virginia. It was "horrible," wrote an observer in Virginia's Appalachian districts, "to see the marks of humiliation and despair that were stamped on the faces of honest but poor white men who had been refused registration. . . . We saw them as they came from the presence of the registrars with bowed heads and agonized faces." The South, as one historian puts it, became less a democracy than "a broad-based oligarchy." This result had a profound impact beyond the South. In Washington, no one challenged southern states' right to continue using their total populations to calculate their electoral votes and congressional delegations. This gave the South's voting elite an extremely disproportionate share of national power.

Whites in other parts of the country acquiesced in disfranchisement, in part because they had come to share many of the views of southern white elites. Anglos in the West were fighting to control Asians and Mexicans. (It was no accident that the hero of Owen Wister's best-selling western novel, *The Virginian*, hailed from the South.) Commentators such as E. L. Godkin of the *Nation* heartily agreed with Virginia politician Carter Glass that "nothing can be more dangerous to our republican institutions than to see hordes of ignorant and worthless men marching to the polls." Meanwhile, as early as 1888 one critic noted that American literature was becoming "not only Southern in type, but distinctly Confederate in sympathy." Popular novelists such as Mrs. E.D.E.N. Southworth described the antebellum South as an idyllic place, where plantation families had dwelled in beauty and chivalry while contented slaves frolicked in the quarters. By 1900 professional scholars joined writers like Southworth and Thomas Dixon, author of virulently racist national best-sellers like *The Clansman*, in rewriting history. School textbooks reported that slavery had been benign or even beneficial to slaves, while Reconstruction had been an orgy of rape and arson instigated by northern carpetbaggers.

Such ideas were difficult to challenge anywhere in the United States by 1900; in the South the attempt could be perilous. A number of outstanding black and white southerners became exiles in the North—notably novelist George W. Cable, congressman George H. White of North Carolina, antilynching journalist Ida B. Wells, historian John Spencer Bassett, and Emory College professor Andrew Sledd. A degree of intellectual chill touched other regions of the country as well. University of Wisconsin economist Richard Ely, for example, faced pressure to resign after he wrote sympathetically about socialism.

It was a measure of the narrow, blinkered experience of prosperous Americans that many remembered the decade of depression as the "Gay Nineties—full of fun—while millions spent desperate years between 1893 and 1899 struggling to find work and food. Lecturing in eastern Pennsylvania, Nebraska Populist Cecilia O'Neill found that when she described the plight of farmers and the unemployed, she met "heartless indifference." Warned of "the dangers imminent from the unrest of the people," her listeners airily replied, "'O, that is only around the mines, the Army and our Militia will keep order there.' No one," O'Neill wrote, "can make the fortunate and comfortable comprehend that humanity around the mines is of the same nature as his own."

Amid hardship and political backlash, few cooperative dreams survived the 1890s in unaltered form. Instead, the theme was regrouping and retrenchment. "Oh I have been through the partisan battle," remarked a weary Susan B. Anthony, whose suffrage movement got caught in battles between western Republicans and Populists. The suffrage cause was a notable casualty of political realignment: it became associated with western Populists, who endorsed it, and was discredited after the party's defeat. With Populist support, Colorado women won full voting rights in 1893, and Idaho women in 1896. But after that, suffragists endured a "decade in the doldrums," as one later put it, winning no further victories for fourteen years. Antisuffrage writer Helen Kendrick Johnson claimed that female voters in Colorado had endorsed "Free Silver and Populism of the most extravagant type." In California, on the other hand, male voters had rejected a referendum for women's voting rights and at the same time elected Republicans, choosing "sound money against repudiation" and "authority against anarchy." Only in 1910, with the revival of close party competition and the rise of a pro-suffrage Progressive Party in the West, did the women's suffrage movement begin once again to achieve state victories.

After the Prohibition Party fragmented and declined, Frances Willard sadly dismissed parties as "of no more value than so many tin cans." With progressive

Illinois governor John Altgeld replaced by a conservative Republican, Hull House reformer Florence Kelley lost her post as a factory inspector to a pro-business successor. Numerous cooperative colonies and experiments failed in the economic crisis, and new ones focused on the cause of sheer survival. The Salvation Army created unemployment colonies in California, Colorado, and Ohio. One Maine activist proposed abandoning reform at the national level and moving radicals to a single western state, which he hoped to convert into a cooperative commonwealth. The plan, briefly supported by Eugene Debs and others, brought a series of socialist and anarchist colonies to Washington, but it did not ultimately succeed.

Other reformers suggested withdrawing from the United States altogether. Populist Henry Demarest Lloyd toured New Zealand, which had given women the vote and instituted a host of labor reforms; he returned on lecture tours to describe New Zealand's charms to disillusioned Americans. Among African Americans, interest in overseas colonization reached an unprecedented peak. AME bishop Henry McNeal Turner proposed establishing an African state whose "glory and influence will tell upon the destinies of the race from pole to pole." The International Migration Society carried several shiploads of migrants to Liberia, while several thousand more left the Gulf states and emigrated to a Mexican colony founded by black Texas businessman William Ellis.

But emigration schemes proved far less important and popular than other strategies for cooperation and self-defense. During the 1890s African Americans created a striking number of organizations for race pride and defense of human rights. Among them were the Afro-American League, formed in 1890 in Chicago, and the National Association of Colored Women, created in 1895 from the merger of several women's groups. A year later the American Negro Academy gathered intellectuals from across the nation for a convention in Chicago, which became an annual event, and Atlanta University began hosting an annual Conference on Negro Problems. Between 1900 and 1906 black leaders in a number of southern cities launched boycotts against segregated streetcars in a campaign that presaged the later strategies of the civil rights movement. The streetcar boycotts showed— like interest in emigration projects—that ordinary blacks in places such as Houston, Memphis, Pensacola, and Mobile held on to a strong collective dream of equal treatment under the law. Unfortunately, conditions were not ripe for sympathetic whites or the national press to offer a supportive response.

Nonetheless, in the summer of 1905, W. E. B. DuBois and other race leaders gathered near Niagara Falls to draft a statement of principles. Young and well-educated, the Niagara signers represented a new generation of leaders who were setting out to challenge Booker T. Washington's strategy of compromise and conciliation. They argued, instead, for the defense of voting rights, good schools, decent work and pay, and healthy housing and streets. They reminded Americans of the meaning of the Thirteenth, Fourteenth, and Fifteenth amendments— "articles of freedom" that Reconstruction had enshrined in the Constitution—and insisted that they be enforced. Follow-up meetings in 1906 and 1907 helped lay the foundations for the twentieth-century civil rights movement, and most immediately for creation of the NAACP (National Association for the Advancement of Colored People) in 1909.

In the same years, Mexican men in Arizona developed the Alianza Hispano-America, a mutual aid society that spread rapidly across the Southwest and became a vehicle for labor advocacy. The Texas equivalent was La Unión Occidental Mexicano, and Mexican-American women matched this with their own Sociedad Benificencia. Meanwhile, a coalition of American-born Chinese founded the Native Sons of the Golden State (later renamed the Chinese American Citizens' Alliance). The group's founders came from a generation of merchants' sons, often criticized by their Chinese-born elders for lacking seriousness and respect for tradition. But the Native Sons gained grudging admiration when they defended themselves from the virulently anti-Chinese Native Sons of the Golden West, who brought suit claiming that the term *native sons* was proprietary to their white group. The Chinese, to their great satisfaction, won the right to keep their name.

The obvious plight of the unemployed during the depression—and the bias of courts—began to provoke regret and reconsideration. Attorney General Richard Olney, for example, much hated for his central role in suppressing the Pullman and Coxey protests, found to his dismay that he had been duped by railroad executives. A commission investigating the Pullman conflict discovered that 3,600 of the U.S. marshals whom Olney had authorized in Chicago had been handpicked, armed, paid, and supervised by the railroads themselves. Olney also discovered that the railroads had deliberately attached Pullman passenger cars to U.S. mail trains in order to hinder those trains and provoke federal intervention. Confronted with these facts, Olney began to lean toward arbitration, seeing the need for government to take a more even-handed role in struggles between capital and labor.

In a broader sense, the massive depression began to slowly undermine affluent Americans' assumption that poverty and unemployment resulted from personal moral failings. Even earlier, amid the depression of the 1870s, the Massachusetts Bureau of Statistics and Labor had begun to use the term *unemployed* to describe those who wanted work and could not find it, rather than those who did not want to work. The noun *unemployment* made its debut in 1887 in one of the bureau's reports. By the 1890s, the New York Charity Organization Society, which had once warned that soup kitchens would damage the morals of the poor, changed its views. In 1898 it undertook a joint scientific study with social scientists from Columbia University and concluded that unemployment, illness, and disabling accidents were the overwhelming causes of poverty. One charity leader declared that such troubles were "as much beyond [workers'] power to avert as if they had been natural calamities of fire, flood, or storm." "Personal depravity," wrote another reformer, "is as foreign to any sound theory of the hardships of our modern poor as witchcraft or demonic possession."

Thrown out of power in the 1890s, Democrats began to gradually reshape their party, even as their southern leaders settled the "race question" (and the

Populist question) by securing power for the white elite. Democrats had mistrusted central authority and championed small government. But they began to argue that ordinary Americans needed government allies to counter the power of trusts and large corporations. As early as the late 1880s, Democrats provided key votes for regulatory measures like the Interstate Commerce Act. They began to champion a federal progressive income tax on the wealthiest Americans, a measure that passed the Democratic-controlled Congress in 1894 and received President Grover Cleveland's signature, only to be overturned by the Supreme Court.

Perhaps the most important figure in this transition was Nebraska Democrat William Jennings Bryan, whose presidential nomination stunned the country in 1896. Though Bryan lost the election, he inspired millions of Americans with his stump-speaking tours and his impassioned rhetoric. Nominated by his party again in 1900 and 1908, Bryan helped his party enter the modern age with a new agenda: fair labor laws, regulation of trusts, and government aid to farmers. By 1906 Bryan came out for government ownership of the nation's transportation system. The railroads, he declared, "must ultimately become public property and be managed by public officials in the interest of the whole community." Bryan and his followers helped put Democrats on a path that would lead to Franklin D. Roosevelt's New Deal in the 1930s. (An irate Herbert Hoover would dismiss the New Deal as "Bryanism under new words and methods.")

In fact almost all the major leaders of early twentieth-century progressive reform had arrived on the public stage by 1905. They ranged from Jane Addams at Hull House, to John Muir of the Sierra Club, to Carrie Nation and the Anti-Saloon League, which initiated a new high-profile antiliquor campaign that eventually carried the Prohibition movement to national victory. Investigative journalism was carried forward by the powerful documentary photographs of Lewis Hine, taken for the National Child Labor Committee. After witnessing the impact of the depression, Jane Addams's colleague Florence Kelley launched the national Consumers' League, which organized female shoppers to choose products made by workers who earned fair wages in decent working conditions. The Women's Trade Union League began to experiment with similar cooperative ventures that brought together women from the elite and the working class.

Having expanded their public roles over the previous four decades, women claimed a prominent place in much of the work that emerged during and after the 1890s. Women's literary and study clubs, which had flourished over the past two decades, began to turn their attention to education and civic reform. Joining settlement activists, professional nurses and social workers, and advocates of the Social Gospel, club women argued that they had a role to play in "municipal housekeeping," since forces outside the home were threatening their families' health and safety. "Very early," wrote an officer of the General Federation of Women's Clubs in 1906, "club women became unwilling to discuss Dante and Browning over the teacups in some lady's drawing room . . . while unsightly heaps of rubbish flanked the paths over which they had passed in their journey thither." Reformers in rural areas also undertook campaigns to improve education, housing, hygiene, and health care. Across the South, chapters of the WCTU and other groups worked across racial lines for prohibition and public health.

City governments, especially in the Midwest, underwent a new wave of innovation as dramatic as that which had followed the Civil War. Rebuilding after a horrific hurricane in 1900, Galveston, Texas, introduced the commissioner system of city government, copied soon afterward from Oakland to Buffalo. Samuel "Golden Rule" Jones of Toledo, Ohio, proved to be one of the nation's most inspiring mayors between 1897 and 1904. An industrialist who had prospered in the oil well business, Jones believed in treating workers as he would his kin. He established an eight-hour workday and a minimum wage for city workers, as he had in his company's plants, and he gained broad support for construction of better parks and schools. Mayor Tom Johnson of Cleveland offered similar social welfare programs beginning in 1901, while during the depression years Detroit mayor Hazen Pingree had already won nationwide praise by opening vacant lots for community gardens. Dubbed Pingree's Potato Patches, the gardens fed thousands of grateful residents and were copied as far away as the Netherlands.

In the meantime, ARU leader Eugene Debs, arrested for failure to heed the Pullman injunction, refused bail on principle and spent several weeks in the rat-infested Cook County Jail. His cell there overlooked the courtyard where the Haymarket anarchists had been hanged. Debs emerged from the experience as a socialist, and the new party he led became the first homegrown, English-language movement for socialist democracy in the United States. At once more narrow in its base and more radical than the People's Party, it nonetheless included practical municipal gas-and-water socialists such as Milwaukee's Victor Berger. While socialism grew in the heartland amid economic distress, the arrival of radical Russian Jews and "Red Finns" invigorated the ranks of the political left. Abraham Cahan's socialist *Jewish Daily Forward*, founded in the 1890s, soon had the largest circulation of any Yiddish newspaper in the world.

At the state level, Wisconsin's Republican governor "Fighting Bob" LaFollette carried forward such progressive reforms as higher corporate taxes and tougher railroad regulation. In 1900 Maryland became the first state to make employers compensate employees injured on the job, and western states such as Utah and Oregon were at the forefront in setting minimum wages and maximum working hours. State and local reforms were accompanied by federal initiatives such as antitrust and environmental conservation measures, marking the first great peak of progressive reform around 1906. Eventually, voters in the states that had given birth to Populism elected many of the congressmen who championed federal deposit insurance for investors, the Federal Trade Commission, the Federal Reserve, and the progressive income tax.

In the long run, then, even though the Populist Party and other cooperative dreams of the 1890s foundered, many of their ideas endured, though they did so in an altered political climate. Evolution away from capitalism had been at the core of utopian projects and books such as Owen's *Integral Cooperation* and Gronlund's *The Cooperative Commonwealth*. The slow transformation of that vision set crucial precedents for the future. Had Americans, for instance, nationalized their telegraph system during the late nineteenth century, a measure seriously debated by Congress at several junctures, that single reform would have had important implications for future generations. Accustomed to a public communication network, later Americans might have been more inclined to insist on public ownership of telephone lines, radio and television stations, cable bandwidths, cell phone frequencies, and Internet service. As one looks down such paths not taken, the scenery fades into the mists of uncertainty. To take just one example, a Populist proposal that *did* win later adoption, the federal income tax, was originally designed to tax only a small percentage of Americans, the very richest, and use the proceeds to help level the playing field for all. Over nine decades the program has mutated into something very different indeed.

In a similar way, the ideas advanced by utopian colonists, settlement workers, Populists, and other reformers and dreamers changed shape during the critical decade of economic depression. They established a lasting legacy in American politics, a deep well into which future progressives could dip their buckets. But America's immediate collective response to depression and crisis was grounded in experiences of conflict and privation. In her novel *A Lost Lady*, Willa Cather later wrote that the 1890s brought to the forefront "a generation of shrewd young men, trained to petty economies by hard times.... The space, the color, the princely carelessness of the pioneer they would destroy and cut up into profitable bits, as the match factory splinters the primeval forest." More than the frontier West was at stake. The 1890s also brought a consolidation of new powers by U.S. presidents and corporate leaders.

FOR FURTHER READING

Ray Reynolds tells the story of Topolobampo in *Catspaw Utopia*, 2nd ed. (San Bernardino, CA, 1996). A wonderful source on such projects generally is Donald E. Pitzer, ed., *America's Communal Utopias*, cited in Chapter 8; for another case study see W. Fitzhugh Brundage, *A Socialist Utopia in the New South* (Urbana, IL, 1996). On suburbanization see Stuart Blumin, *The Emergence of the Middle Class* (Cambridge, MA, 1989) and Kenneth T. Jackson, *Crabgrass Frontier* (New York, 1985); on urban segregation see Olivier Zunz, *The Changing Face of Inequality* (Chicago, 1982), and Roy Rosenzweig, *"Eight Hours for What We Will"* (Cambridge, MA, 1983). I have also relied on Nora E. Schlesinger, "Riverside, Illinois: Frederick Law Olmsted's Bourgeois Utopia," research paper, American Culture 250, Vassar College, fall 2003.

On settlement houses see Allen Davis, *Spearheads for Reform* (New York, 1967), and Victoria Bissell Brown's introduction to her edition of Jane Addams's *Twenty Years at Hull-House* (Boston, 1999). On Addams see Louise W. Knight, *Citizen* (Chicago, 2005). On Hull House see also Kathryn Kish Sklar, *Florence Kelley and the Nation's Work* (New Haven, CT, 1995). The best short overview of Populism is Robert McMath, *American Populism* (New York, 1993); see also the first two chapters of Michael Kazin, *The Populist Persuasion* (New York, 1995), as well as John D. Hicks, *The Populist Revolt* (Minneapolis, 1931), and Lawrence Goodwyn, *Democratic Promise* (New York, 1976). Also helpful here was Barbara

Fields, "Ideology and Race in American History," cited in Chapter 1, and Stephen Kantrowitz, *Ben Tillman and the Reconstruction of White Supremacy* (Chapel Hill, NC, 2000).

In *Protestant Churches and Industrial America*, cited in Chapter 8, Henry F. May uses the metaphor of "three earthquakes" that I borrow here. Also see Charles Hoffman, *The Depression of the Nineties* (Westport, CT, 1970), Kenneth L. Kusmer, *Down and Out, On the Road* (New York, 2002), H. Roger Grant, *Self-Help in the Depression of the 1890s* (Ames, IA, 1983), and Michael Lesy's nightmarish and disturbing *Wisconsin Death Trip* (New York, 1973). On Pullman see David Ray Papke, *The Pullman Case* (Lawrence, KS, 1999), and the essays in *The Pullman Strike and the Crisis of the 1890s*, ed. Richard Schneirov, Shelton Stromquist, and Nick Salvatore (Urbana, IL, 1999). The best account of the Commonweal of Christ is Carlos A. Schwantes, *Coxey's Army* (Moscow, ID, 1994).

For a broad analysis of the rise of "radical racism," see Joel Williamson, *The Crucible of Race* (New York, 1984). On various forms of heightened racial and ethnic segregation and animosity see also three works previously cited: John Higham, *Strangers in the Land*, Steven A. Riess, *Sport in Industrial America*, and Gerald Sorin, *Tradition Transformed*. In addition I have drawn on Rosalyn Terborg-Penn, *African American Women in the Struggle for the Vote, 1850–1920* (Bloomington, IN, 1998), and Marjorie Spruill Wheeler, "Race, Reform, and Reaction at the Turn of the Century," in *Votes for Women*, ed. Jean H. Baker (New York, 2002), 102–17. On Mexican Americans throughout this chapter, see four books on the Southwest that were cited earlier: Linda Gordon's *The Great Arizona Orphan Abduction*, Matt S. Meier and Feliciana Ribera's *Mexican Americans/American Mexicans*; Arnoldo De León, *The Tejano Community, 1836–1900*, and David Montejano, *Anglos and Mexicans in the Making of Texas*. Also helpful on New Mexico is Erlinda Gonzales-Berry, "Which Language Will Our Children Speak?" in *The Contested Homeland*, ed. Erlinda Gonzales-Berry and David Maciel (Albuquerque, NM, 2000), 169–89.

On lynching see James Allen's powerful book *Without Sanctuary* (Santa Fe, NM, 2000), W. Fitzhugh Brundage, *Lynching in the New South* (Urbana, IL, 1993), and for both lynchings and the broader pattern of political and racial conflict in the South, Edward L. Ayers, *The Promise of the New South*, cited in Chapter 1. A statistical summary is the NAACP's *Thirty Years of Lynching in the United States, 1889–1918* (originally 1919; reprinted New York, 1969). On Ida B. Wells's investigations see Patricia Schechter, *Ida B. Wells-Barnett and American Reform* (Chapel Hill, NC, 2001), as well as the introduction by Jacqueline Jones Royster in her edition of Wells's *Southern Horrors and Other Writings* (Boston, 1997).

On politics, see Charles Calhoun, *Conceiving a New Republic*, cited in Chapter 1, R. Hal Williams, *Years of Decision* (New York, 1978), and Samuel T. McSeveney, *The Politics of Depression* (New York, 1972). On western Populism and the structures of the political system see Peter H. Argersinger's two books, *Structure, Process and Party* (Armonk, NY, 1992), and *The Limits of Agrarian Radicalism* (Lawrence, KS, 1995), as well as Jeffrey Ostler, *Prairie Populism* (Lawrence, KS, 1993). On legacies of Populism see, in addition to McMath's *American Populism*, Elizabeth Sanders's impressive *Roots of Reform* (Chicago, 1999). On Bryan see Michael Kazin, *A Godly Hero: The Life of William Jennings Bryan* (New York, 2006). On disfranchisement in the South, see J. Morgan Kousser, *The Shaping of Southern Politics* (New Haven, CT, 1974); the quote on the rise of southern "oligarchy," from Walter Dean Burnham, appears on p. 224. On southern sympathies in literature and the chilling of the intellectual climate, see Nina Silber, *The Romance of Reunion* (Chapel Hill, NC, 1993), Ayers's *Promise of the New South*, cited earlier, and David W. Blight's *Race and Reunion*, cited in Chapter 1. On the case of Richard Ely, see Mary O. Furner, *Advocacy and Objectivity* (Lexington, KY, 1975).

For shifting responses to poverty amid the crisis of the 1890s, see Alexander Keyssar, *Out of Work* (Cambridge, MA, 1986), Walter I. Trattner, *From Poor Law to Welfare State*, cited in Chapter 1, Daniel T. Rogers, *Atlantic Crossings*, cited in Chapter 2, and Anne Firor Scott, *Natural Allies* (Urbana, IL, 1991), and Glenda Elizabeth Gilmore, *Gender and Jim Crow* (Chapel Hill, NC, 1996). On the rise of socialism, see Howard S. Quint, *The Forging of American Socialism* (Columbia, SC, 1953); on black nationalism and pan-Africanism, Edwin S. Redkey, *Black Exodus* (New Haven, CT, 1969); and on the Niagara movement, John Hope Franklin's *From Slavery to Freedom*, cited in Chapter 1. On the origins of the Chinese American Citizens' Alliance see Sue Fawn Chung's article in *Claiming America*, cited in Chapter 5, and on boycotts see August Meier and Elliott Rudwick, "The Boycott Movement Against Jim Crow Streetcars in the South, 1900–1906," *Journal of American History* 55 (1969): 756–75. Willa Cather's comment on the depression's impact is in *A Lost Lady* (New York, 1923), 90. For emphasis on positive long-term outcomes of the crisis of the 1890s, see Steven J. Diner, *A Very Different Age* (New York, 1998), and Michael McGerr, *A Fierce Discontent* (New York, 2003).

CHAPTER 11

Executive Powers

The world lies before us. It'll not be the same world when we get done with it.

—WALTER HINES PAGE

It is hard to pinpoint an exact date when the United States took over the Hawai'ian Islands. Protestant missionaries arrived in 1820, and over the decades that followed they converted the island's royal family. New laws in the 1840s, advocated by the missionaries, opened land for market purchase and resulted in rapid takeover by American-born landowners, at the same time that American whaling ships made Honolulu a key port and brought an influx of foreigners and trade. By the 1850s and 1860s, Hawai'i's legal code had been thoroughly transformed, and high-quality sugarcane was replacing whales as the most lucrative natural resource. Cane planters imported thousands of laborers from China, Japan, and Portugal, who soon made up a majority of Hawai'i's population. Rapid growth of the sugar industry created, in turn, momentum for U.S. political annexation. In 1887 militant planters forced King David Kalakaua to accept a constitution that brought "American-style democracy" to the islands. (Eligible voters included all whites, no Asians, and only some native Hawai'ians.) A coup by U.S.-born locals in 1893 against Kalakaua's successor, Queen Liliuokalani, when she tried to replace the 1887 constitution with a royal charter of her own, paved the way for Hawai'i to become a territory of the United States.

The conquest of Hawai'i illustrated in microcosm almost all the major themes of U.S. history in these years. Epidemic diseases—smallpox, typhoid, leprosy, syphilis—reduced the islands' native population from perhaps a half-million to 30,000, making resistance as difficult for Hawai'ians as it had been for native peoples on the North American continent. The land reforms of the 1840s offered lessons that the authors of Reconstruction should have heeded: missionaries hoped it would turn the peasantry into landowners, but instead 85 percent of the islands' land fell to outsiders, most of whom were elite men from the United States. No one wanted an Asian majority on the islands, but the interests of powerful sugar planters brought that about. The result was hysteria and violence against Chinese and Japanese cane workers. They, in turn, struck repeatedly for better wages and working conditions despite planters' attempts to keep the labor force racially divided.

Many planters opposed U.S. political annexation for many years, fearing that enforcement of the Chinese Exclusion Act would undercut their source of cheap labor.

But sugar planters had become enmeshed in American politics. In the coveted U.S. market they competed with Louisiana cane growers and western sugar beet farmers, whom Republicans protected with a high tariff. After an 1875 treaty placed Hawai'i inside the tariff barrier, the islands' sugar exports to the United States grew twentyfold in two decades. When the treaty came up for renewal in 1887, U.S. negotiators demanded exclusive naval rights to Pearl Harbor, and after some debate they received it. But in 1890, notwithstanding this concession, Congress lifted all tariffs on sugar in response to intense lobbying from beet growers and instead began paying a direct subsidy of 2¢ a pound to producers inside the United States. The result in Hawai'i was catastrophic. Sugar prices plummeted. Some smaller-scale planters went bankrupt, precipitating, in part, the final drive for annexation so that Hawai'i could claim a secure place in the U.S. economy.

The machinations of annexationists show that it was hardly inevitable as late as 1890. Officials repeatedly denied that they sought to conquer Hawai'i. U.S. diplomats who pulled strings in island politics often did so without help from Washington, or even against direct orders. But by the 1870s U.S. warships began to materialize offshore when business interests were at stake. After 1891 the U.S. consul-general in the islands, Republican appointee John L. Stevens, flouted diplomatic protocol by joining a secret Annexation Club that conspired to overthrow the queen. During the subsequent coup he called in U.S. Marines armed with Gatling guns, who stationed themselves near the royal palace to "watch" as the queen surrendered control. (The queen had ten Gatling guns herself and without direct U.S. intervention might well have fought to keep her throne.) Stevens recognized the new government before it had even secured control of Honolulu.

The coup leaders hoped the United States would immediately annex the islands, but that did not happen for five more years. In the intervening period, uncertain whether their political and economic system would even survive the crisis of the mid-1890s, policy makers in Washington undertook a massive quest for new foreign markets in which to sell U.S. products. This initiative helped lead to war in 1898 and the acquisition of not only Hawai'i but also the Philippines, both way stations for American ships headed to and from Asia. Soon afterward, in coastal China, the Caribbean, and Central America, U.S. policy makers made bold grabs for control.

Two critical configurations of power emerged clearly between 1896 and 1906. First was the growing dominance of the presidency in relation to Congress, so closely linked to the nation's rising power on the world stage that some historians describe William McKinley and Theodore Roosevelt as creators of an "imperial presidency." In many ways Roosevelt shared the worldview of Liberal Republicans such as E. L. Godkin of the *Nation*, who fiercely attacked "socialistic" ideas but wanted stronger forms of government administration and regulation—as long as government lay in the hands of experts and the elite.

Roosevelt, who came from a wealthy and privileged family, called for men of his class to reclaim political power from immigrants and men of "lesser breeding," and he saw his own career as an embodiment of that ideal. As president he pioneered overseas police actions and executive agreements, circumventing the constitutional rules that gave Congress authority over war making and required presidents to seek the Senate's consent for foreign treaties. In the domestic arena Roosevelt's expansion of presidential authority brought him head-to-head with another set of chief executives who wielded unprecedented power: leaders of multinational corporations. Through intervention in a 1902 coal strike and through vigorous Justice Department actions, Roosevelt's administration made some of the first federal attempts to block corporate monopolies and force CEOs to negotiate with workers. The imperial presidency, the multinational corporation, and the struggle between them left Americans a double legacy of consolidated power.

IMPERIAL CLAIMS

From the depression of the 1870s onward, intellectuals and policy makers in the United States, fearful of a rising tide of strikes and political protests, worried that the country would adopt "socialistic" measures. The brief success of the People's Party, which advocated just such measures, heightened their anxiety. The alternative, imperialists believed, was to secure overseas markets for American products, ensuring jobs and prosperity to ease domestic distress. The result was what some historians call "social imperialism," focused not on building a European-style administrative empire but on creating favorable conditions for commerce—but at gunpoint, if necessary.

Social imperialism stemmed directly from William Seward's vision of "the flag following trade." It was under way as early as 1879, when the United States and Germany muscled into the South Pacific kingdom of Samoa to claim rival harbors and coaling stations. By 1890 a Republican-controlled Congress appropriated funds for steel battleships to match those of Britain and Germany. Vermont senator Justin Morrill, arguing for aggressive trade policies and "enlargement of our Lilliputian Navy," noted that Russia, Germany, France, and Britain were already competing for economic supremacy. "To lag behind when all the world is on the move," he stated, "is to accept the fate of the decrepit and dull-pated bison who lingers on the prairie in the rear of the ongoing herd."

On the domestic front, commentators worried in the 1890s that workers were tending toward socialism or even revolution. Apocalyptic forecasts abounded, with one newspaper predicting that "fire and sword will devastate the country." Political thinker Brooks Adams, in his influential 1896 book *The Law of Civilization and Decay*, wrote that "the time has now come" when surplus American products "must be sold abroad," especially in the immense markets of Asia. Otherwise the United States "would be devoured by the gangrene which attacks every stagnant society and from which no patient recovers." Senator Henry Cabot Lodge of

Massachusetts argued that "we must have new markets . . . unless we would be visited by declines in wages and by great industrial disturbances, of which signs have not been lacking."

The elections of 1894 and 1896 brought to national power Republicans (and some Democrats, especially in the South) who were committed to solving domestic conflict by opening overseas markets. To implement this vision, American policy makers had to readjust their view of the country's role in the world. Many decades earlier, President James Monroe, in the Monroe Doctrine, had told Britain and Spain that the United States would come to the aid of any fellow republic in the Western Hemisphere that was threatened by European powers. The crisis of the 1890s culminated in 1904 with Theodore Roosevelt's Corollary to the Monroe Doctrine, which was, in fact, an entirely different doctrine. Roosevelt asserted that the United States had an exclusive right to intervene in other New World countries as it saw fit.

The war that brought the United States to power on the world stage and swept away the last vestige of Spain's New World empire started not in Washington, but with Cuban rebels such as José Martí. They conducted their revolution at a time when Cuba's sugar economy was suffering through the same crisis that hit the U.S. mainland. Cubans' fight for independence was widely popular in the United States. Men smoked Cuba Libre cigars, and editors sympathized with the plight of a people who, like the thirteen colonies of North America had in 1776, sought freedom from European monarchy. Newspaper magnates such as William Randolph Hearst used front-page headlines to trumpet Spanish atrocities. (They did not need to exaggerate much: rounding up Cubans into concentration camps and conducting a war of extermination, Spanish commanders unintentionally deepened resistance and spread the revolt across the island.) When the U.S. battleship *Maine* sank in Havana harbor, apparently due to a boiler explosion, Spain was instantly blamed, and President McKinley faced a surge of support for American troops to assist in making Cuba free.

Congress, through a law called the Teller Amendment, reassured Cubans that this was, in fact, their country's goal. It declared that the Cuban people "are, and of right ought to be, free and independent," and that the United States "disclaims any disposition or intention to exercise sovereignty, jurisdiction, or control over said island except for the pacification thereof." The resolution, one senator stated, ensured "the absolute and unqualified independence of the Cubans." But the actions of the McKinley administration suggest that its objectives were distinct from those of Congress and much of the American public. The *Maine* had been sitting in Havana harbor because administration officials (as well as jubilant Cubans) perceived that Spanish control was already collapsing. "Cuban independence is absolutely impossible," wrote McKinley's minister to Spain. State Department officials, explored the option of buying the island, since "some way must be found by which Spain can part with Cuba . . . with certainty of American control."

At the same time, the McKinley administration focused considerable attention on Spanish holdings in the Pacific. In Asia both American and European interests were facing sudden and aggressive competition from Japan, which had handily won a short war against China at mid-decade. "Japan has leaped, almost at one bound, to a place among the great nations of the earth," wrote the U.S. secretary of the navy. With China weakened, Germany had moved swiftly to seize a portion of Shandong province for a port and development of railroads. Britain, France, Russia, and Belgium then fought for their own pieces of the pie. Their combined invasions along the coast provoked an uprising of militant Chinese societies known in the West as "Boxers," who won the backing of dowager empress Cixi. In 1898 these patriotic groups began attacking Germans in Shandong, seeking to drive out the invaders. To American and European officials, much-coveted access to Asian markets seemed imperiled.

Thus, before the United States declared war against Spain in April 1898, the McKinley administration prepared carefully in the Pacific as well as the Caribbean. U.S. military forces actually launched attacks on the Wake Islands, the Philippine Islands, and Guam—all Spanish holdings in the Pacific—during April and May, well before they joined the Cuban revolutionary front in late June. With Spanish control already weakened by years of rebellion, the fighting in Cuba lasted only a few months. Spain formally withdrew its claims to Cuba, Puerto Rico, and an array of Pacific possessions before the end of the year. But the resulting pact differed sharply from the goals Congress had set forth in the Teller Amendment. The United States took Puerto Rico and the Philippines as "protectorates," and although negotiators acknowledged Cuban independence, they excluded Cubans themselves from negotiations with Spain. Two years later the Platt Amendment officially amended U.S. intentions. Congress and the president now asserted the right to intervene in Cuba whenever the United States deemed necessary. The United States set limits on Cuba's government budget, established a permanent naval base at Guantánamo Bay, and banned treaties between Cuba and any other power. Cuba, as one U.S. general wrote to Roosevelt after the amendment passed, had "little or no independence left."

In the war of 1898 the United States acquired, for the first time, territories with no apparent prospect of future statehood, though many Cubans and Puerto Ricans had hoped for U.S. statehood as a second-best outcome. Instead, the McKinley and later the Roosevelt administrations justified continued "protectorate" status on the grounds that the islands needed economic "stability." The United States could not leave Cuba, they argued, unless American business interests were fully secure. Given this opening, U.S. sugar interests tightened their hold over the plantation economy of Cuba and extended their reach in Puerto Rico and the Dominican Republic. By the early twentieth century these islands produced 1.6 million tons of sugar a year, with Hawai'ian and soon Philippine sugar added to this total. (Per capita consumption of sugar on the American mainland, not coincidentally, rose to 75 pounds a year in 1910, more than double what it had been on the eve of the Civil War.) In the Pacific, imperialists spoke of the Philippines as "our only safeguard for our trade interests in the East."

In explaining their policies to the American people, the architects of social imperialism appealed to the same racial thinking so evident in domestic affairs.

In both the Philippines and Cuba, the indigenous revolutionary movements that had challenged Spanish rule were overwhelmingly made up of non-whites. Local elites in both Cuba and the Philippines, threatened by popular uprisings, encouraged North Americans in the belief that the rebels were incompetent to govern and that race war would result if the United States did not remain in control. Officials in Washington needed little encouragement. "My own belief," Roosevelt wrote privately of the Filipinos, "is that there are not 100 men among them who comprehend what Anglo-Saxon self-government even means." "God has not been preparing the English-speaking and Teutonic peoples for a thousand years for nothing," declared influential senator Albert Beveridge of Indiana. "No! .... He has made us adept in government that we may administer government among savage and senile peoples."

Filipinos presented something of a complication to such views. Inhabitants of the islands were racially and linguistically diverse, indisputably Asian if one consulted a map, but including both Spanish-speaking Catholics and ethnic groups such as so-called Negritos, whom Americans saw as black. Many U.S. soldiers dismissed all Filipinos as "gu-gus" and "niggers" and compared the islands to the American South. But Indian wars served as the most convenient analogy for the conflict that ensued in the Philippines after the United States set itself to subdue the islands. Since Americans denied a voice in government to the Indian at home, asked Beveridge, "how dare you grant it to the Malay abroad? . . . There are people in the world who do not understand any form of government . . . [and] must be governed." If the United States was "morally bound to abandon the Philippines," declared Theodore Roosevelt, it was "also morally bound to abandon Arizona to the Apaches."

Such connections were more than rhetorical. Most military leaders in the Philippine war came directly from Indian-fighting (a few having detoured for riot control in Chicago). Even more important, the legal treatment of American Indians set the stage for annexing "dependent peoples." In 1871 the Supreme Court had ruled that Congress no longer had to negotiate treaties with Indian peoples but instead could enact legislation without their consent. In 1885 the Court gave the federal government jurisdiction over crimes on Indian reservations. American Indians belonged to a new category, "nationals," or "persons owing allegiance to the United States but without those privileges which go only with citizenship." The Court drew on these precedents in the *Insular Cases*, a series of rulings between 1901 and 1910 that relegated Filipinos and Puerto Ricans to the same category. Like American Indians, they were "nationals" without citizenship rights. The justices suggested that such a status could not be indefinite, but they did not set any deadlines on its use.

The anti-imperialist movement, meanwhile, suffered internal divisions. Most of the leading anti-imperialist spokespeople came from the white elite; their arguments ranged from humanitarian and democratic to openly racist, and since the latter struck a powerful chord, many rivaled the imperialists in championing Anglo-Saxon superiority. The *Nation* warned of the perils of admitting "alien, inferior, and mongrel races to our nationality." Senator Ben Tillman of South

Carolina drew explicit comparisons to white supremacy at home. Being from a state, he said, "with 750,000 colored population and only 500,000 whites, I realize what you [imperialists] are doing, while you don't; and I would save this country from the injection into it of another race question which can only breed bloodshed." Though there was considerable anti-imperialist sentiment among working-class immigrants and African Americans, arguments such as Tillman's hardly fostered alliances.

In the wake of the popular Cuban campaign, the McKinley administration moved swiftly to protect U.S. access to Asian markets. When Boxer revolutionaries in China reached Beijing, the United States sent a contingent to join Russian, British, French, German, and Japanese troops, who marched together on the capital. In August 1900 the combined expeditionary force took Beijing, engaging afterward in brutal acts of rape, looting, and indiscriminate murder. (German and Japanese soldiers were especially rapacious, but their allies made no efforts to stop

National Geographic, May 1903, 209. U.S. occupation of the Philippines brought a spate of reports about the islands in *National Geographic*. The images and language used in these articles suggest some of the ways in which scientific racism helped justify military conquest. Depictions of bare-chested women, a key marker of "primitivism," had only recently begun to appear in the magazine. "Adult Negrito woman, showing relative size," readers learned in the text accompanying this photograph. "The Negritos are physical and mental weaklings, and are rapidly disappearing." I am grateful to Vassar student Anna Kichorowsky, who located this image in her research.

them, and some joined the fray.) The Beijing expedition marked a crucial turning point in American foreign policy. For the first time since the American Revolution, U.S. troops joined those of other nations in a multinational force, and they fought side by side with European imperial powers.

Having participated in a rank campaign of conquest, the United States got its share of the spoils: 7 percent of a $333 million indemnity that China was forced to pay for its rebels' resistance. ("Poor China!" exclaimed Sarah Conger, wife of the U.S. minister in Beijing. "Why cannot foreigners let her alone with her own? China has been wronged, and in her desperation she has striven as best she could to stop the inroads." The United States later had second thoughts and returned the indemnity.) The United States and Britain enforced China's open door to foreign trade. As in Cuba and the Philippines, this entailed sharp restrictions on China's political and economic autonomy. Unlike Cuba and the Philippines, though, China fell under the sway of many competing powers rather than just one. Germany, France, Belgium, Russia, Japan, and the United States all pursued railroad contracts and access to Chinese markets.

As in China, upheavals arose in many parts of the world as the Western powers—including, now, the United States—made aggressive demands for empire and trade. Thus, while U.S. policy makers claimed to bring stability to turbulent parts of the world, in fact they helped precipitate the reverse. The decision to support or repress rebellion in a given place depended on what policy makers perceived American interests to be. In Panama, for example, U.S. warships intervened in 1901 to stop a popular uprising against Colombia, which had long claimed Panama as part of its territory. But in late 1903, when the Roosevelt administration felt ready to press a broader claim, the United States sent naval vessels to block Colombia from ending the Panama uprising, essentially backing a coup and violating a long-standing treaty. In exchange for abetting the Panamanian revolution, the United States demanded from the country's new government "titular sovereignty" over a strip of land on which it planned to build a canal, the long-yearned-for shortcut to Pacific trade.

The Philippines offered the greatest challenge to Americans' belief in their country's good intentions. Following a brief opening campaign in 1898 to take control of the islands after Spanish withdrawal, U.S. forces found themselves bogged down in a frustrating guerrilla conflict against Filipinos fighting for their independence. American military men quickly realized that they were not "liberating" a grateful people. Referring to Emilio Aguinaldo, the veteran leader of resistance to Spain who now led nationalist forces against the United States, General Arthur MacArthur wrote, "When I first started in against these rebels, I believed that Aguinaldo's troops represented only a faction. I did not like to believe that the whole population of Luzon . . . was opposed to us and our offers of aid and good government. But after having come this far, after having occupied several towns and cities in succession, . . . I have been reluctantly compelled to believe that the Filipino masses are loyal to Aguinaldo and the government which he heads." A sergeant in the 1st Nebraska Regiment put it more bluntly. "I am not

Life, 8 December 1898. This anti-imperialist cartoon questions Uncle Sam's "purchase" of the Philippines from Spain. Like many cartoons, both pro- and anti-imperialist, it depicts conquering Western powers as men and their new overseas territories as women—often young, beautiful, and exotic. Here, the woman's chains are a reminder of slavery in the United States. Courtesy Vassar College Library.

afraid, and am always ready to do my duty, but I would like someone to tell me what we are fighting for." "I deprecate this war," wrote an officer of the 13th Minnesota, "because it seems to me that we are doing something that is contrary to our principles in the past." Both Filipino and American critics of the war found it ironic when a U.S. commander in Manila seized copies of the U.S. Declaration of Independence that had been translated into Spanish, calling it "an incendiary document."

Many African-American soldiers found their loyalties conflicted. "The future of the Filipino, I fear," wrote a private in the 24th Infantry, "is that of the Negro in the South. Matters are almost to that condition in Manila now. No one (white) has any scruples respecting the rights of a Filipino. He is kicked and cuffed at will and he dare not remonstrate." Yet fighting with fellow Americans as proud volunteers, other black soldiers rejected any identification with the enemy. One described the slaughter of Filipinos in battle as "awful" but added simply, "it was fight or die with us." Thinking back later on his war service, another black veteran wrote, "I was filled with the spirit of adventure and also possessed a reasonable share of bigotry. It never occurred to my simple mind that there could be anything wrong, morally or otherwise, with any of our government's undertaking."

The guerilla war proved long and bloody. Most Filipino nationalists fought with bolo knives against U.S. troops armed with the latest Springfield and Norwegian-made Krag-Jørgensen rifles. With the fight hopelessly one-sided, the nationalists sought the advantage of stealth on home terrain and the shelter and aid of civilians. Americans found the bodies of fellow soldiers beaten to death or mutilated. Filipino women and children enlisted as spies or actively aided the fight, escalating American troops' hostility toward the civilians. Some U.S. commanders resorted to executing captured prisoners, and for interrogations they ordered the soon-infamous "water cure," forcing prisoners to drink water until their stomachs were distended and then punching, kicking, or jumping on them. Eventually, in some districts U.S. soldiers forced residents into concentration camps and treated the countryside as a free-fire zone, burning villages, destroying crops, and shooting anything that moved.

Even this did not fully defeat the rebel movement. At Balangiga on the island of Samar in September 1901, Filipino nationalists smuggled arms into a local church, hiding them inside a number of small coffins that, they told guards from the 9th Infantry, Company C, held the bodies of children who had died of cholera. (It was a measure of the war's devastating effects that the delivery of such coffins seemed routine.) The "women" who brought the coffins turned out to be men in disguise, and in a surprise dawn attack they killed fifty-nine U.S. soldiers and wounded twenty-three. Only six members of the company escaped unharmed.

News of the massacre jolted Americans, who thought that U.S. occupation was winning Filipinos' support. Denouncing the attack as "treacherous savagery," editors likened Balangiga to Custer's defeat at Little Big Horn and called for retaliation. They did not wait long. The commander of U.S. forces in the Philippines held a press conference to explain that Company C's officers had been guilty of "soft mollycoddling of treacherous natives." He sent in Brigadier General Jake Smith, a ruthless veteran of the Indian wars, to avenge the American dead. Smith ordered the immediate execution of any Filipino male in the area who was over age ten. "I want no prisoners," he instructed. "I wish you to kill and burn. . . . The interior of Samar must be made a howling wilderness." These written orders emerged later as evidence when one of Smith's subordinates faced court-martial for murder and argued—successfully—that he had just been following orders.

The result was a campaign of arson and slaughter that capped three years of bitter conflict. Investigating journalists soon discovered that a year earlier, Smith had ordered the execution of prisoners and held captured Filipinos in makeshift cages for weeks at a time, boasting to reporters of the resulting death rate. In a sensational trial Smith was court-martialed and found guilty (the first court-martial of a general in U.S. history), but he retained the loyalty of many soldiers, who believed that he was taking the fall for his own superiors. One Massachusetts volunteer wrote home that harsh measures were routine throughout the islands; he

"Things We Are Proud Of." William Walker, *Life*, 10 July 1902. This cartoon illustrates an array of America's unaddressed problems at the turn of the century. Walker suggests that it is hypocritical for the United States to offer itself as a role model for peoples elsewhere in the world, represented by the small, bemused Filipinos in the foreground. Courtesy Vassar College Library.

himself, he declared, had helped systematically execute 1,300 prisoners in Batangas, on Luzon, and had witnessed the hanging of the priest who had administered last rites to all those killed. In the meantime, returning general Fred Funston told Americans that excessive leniency was prolonging the war. He held anti-imperialists responsible for U.S. casualties and proposed that "the whole lot of them" be "hung for treason."

In the wake of Smith's scorched-earth tactics, fighting diminished, and on July 4, 1902, President Roosevelt declared the Philippines conquered. Thousands of troops came home, and though sporadic conflict continued on some islands for years afterward, the United States to a large extent settled into the business of administering its overseas "protectorate." The toll was high: more than 5,000 American soldiers were dead, as were at least 200,000 Filipinos, many of whom were displaced civilians (particularly children) killed by malnutrition and disease. Americans also sustained a serious blow to their national self-image, especially during 1902, when Smith's trial and several others brought daily revelations of torture and brutality. High casualties and the excesses of the "water cure" steered policy makers away from territorial acquisition and reconfirmed the benefits of pursuing commercial advantage without colonial rule.

Yet to a great extent, Americans' national optimism and sense of righteous mission survived the ferocity of the Philippine war intact. "The American public eats its breakfast and reads in its newspapers of our doings in the Philippines,"

"Ground Over Which the Montana Troops Advanced on Caloocan. Dead American Soldier in the Foreground." Caloocan was the first major battle of the opening stage of the Philippine War, in 1898. Modern standards of documentary photography had not yet emerged. Like his counterparts in the U.S. Civil War, this photographer may have repositioned the soldier's body to achieve the effect he desired. From Marrion Wilcox, *Harper's History of the War in the Philippines* (New York, 1900), 126.

anguished the anti-imperialist *New York World*, remarking on how little soul-searching Smith's trial provoked. "[It] takes another sip of its coffee and remarks, 'how very unpleasant!' . . . Where is that vast national outburst of astounded horror which an old-fashioned American would have predicted at reading such news? Is it lost somewhere in the 8,000 miles that divide us from these abominations?" President Roosevelt sent General Smith quietly into retirement, arguing that he had faced "well-nigh intolerable provocation" from savage foes. "I heartily approve of the employment of the sternest measures necessary," Roosevelt wrote, while skillfully dissociating himself from torture and military crimes. The president went on to crush his Democratic opponent in 1904, and his subsequent assertions of power in Panama, the Dominican Republic, and elsewhere seemed to enhance rather than dim his popularity.

McKinley's and Roosevelt's foreign exploits depended to a large extent on disjunctions between policy makers' public statements and their private calculations. Presidents who were ambitious for land and trade were not, in themselves, something new. In the 1840s James K. Polk had become perhaps the most successful imperialist in all U.S. history when he waged a popular war against Mexico. But Polk had made his objectives clear to voters, who elected him on a platform of annexation and, by implication, war. The new imperial presidency rested on a somewhat different relationship between Americans and their chief executive. McKinley and his successors expanded their powers by circumventing Congress and undercutting the Senate's role in foreign policy, which one imperialist dubbed "the constitutional lion in the path" blocking full presidential control.

Moves in this direction had taken place during the Civil War and in 1879, when the Hayes administration had negotiated an agreement with Samoa without bothering to ask for Senate approval. But it was Roosevelt who most expanded presidential authority, partly because anti-imperialists in Congress succeeded in blocking some of his early initiatives, and Roosevelt refused to recognize their right to do so. In 1905, after the Senate defeated a pact that would have put the United States in charge of customs revenues in the Dominican Republic, Roosevelt went ahead on his own to sign an "executive agreement" with the compliant Dominican government. (Roosevelt had already sent troops to protect U.S. sugar and shipping interests.) The president followed up with further executive agreements in Latin America and Asia, setting a precedent for enormous presidential authority in foreign policy. Already, during the wars of 1898, one English newspaper had observed that the U.S. presidency was becoming "neither more nor less than elective monarchy, limited as to duration, and regulated as to finance, but otherwise nearly unfettered." His remark echoed José Martí's claim that the United States was becoming a "monarchy in disguise."

McKinley and Roosevelt pioneered tools of executive power used by a succession of presidents in the decades since. Both were skillful managers of information and public opinion. They staged press conferences at locations ranging from the front porch of McKinley's home in Canton, Ohio, to wilderness settings where Roosevelt spoke of his support for conservation. Both kept tight control of news from overseas in order to accent positive reports. In elections they experimented with an array of modern techniques, from McKinley's expensive, sophisticated marketing campaigns to Roosevelt's forceful stump-speaking tours, which followed the precedent set by his archrival, Democrat William Jennings Bryan. But the imperial presidents were successful innovators, in part, because they operated in a different climate from that of their predecessors. The electorate had been considerably restricted, Republicans had secured dominance in Washington, and Democrats held the South.

Americans' support for a strong presidency resulted from a shadow of disorder that had international as well as domestic dimensions. Violent anarchists, in particular, provoked public fear. Anarchist assassins succeeded in killing the French president Carnot in 1894, a year when Americans were worrying about the Pullman boycott and the march of Coxey's Army. There followed, between 1897 and 1905 the assassinations of Spain's prime minister, the empress of Austria, King Umberto I of Italy (an assassination planned in Paterson, New Jersey), the king of Serbia, and two Russian ministers. In 1901, amid this string of European assassinations and several more botched attempts, an anarchist in the United States shot and killed President William McKinley. For those who believed European conditions might be emerging in the United States, McKinley's death offered grievous confirmation. It also marked the third assassination of a U.S. president since 1865, and though anarchists had had nothing to do with Lincoln or Garfield's deaths, public alarm ran high. In retrospect, violent anarchists were a tiny and politically isolated cadre, but at the time frightened Americans equated anarchists with all labor unions, European immigrants, and the entire political left. Before McKinley's assassination, and even more afterward, they accepted harsh measures to deal with the threat.

While projecting an aggressive image on the global stage, McKinley's successor proved willing to use his presidential powers at home for innovative ends. The Roosevelt administration launched key federal initiatives for environmental and consumer protection, creating the Food and Drug Administration in 1906, for example, to oversee food and medicine safety. Roosevelt even undertook efforts to reign in the power of corporations. During a 1902 Pennsylvania coal strike, he refused to follow his White House predecessors in sending troops to crush the protest. Instead, he insisted that mine owners hear the union's grievances, and when they refused to take arbitration seriously, he threatened to seize the mines and run them under federal authority. The owners hastily agreed to talk, and Roosevelt brokered a compromise. Two years later his Justice Department went to court to block an attempted merger of two giant railroads by J. P. Morgan and James J. Hill. In the resulting *Northern Securities* case, the Supreme Court upheld the government's right to prevent the merger under the Sherman Antitrust Act. The administration's crowning achievement was the 1906 Hepburn Act, which strengthened the Interstate Commerce Commission by giving it the right to set railroad rates, subject to court review.

While Roosevelt helped usher in the first wave of twentieth-century progressivism at home, other Americans were offsetting imperialism by joining international campaigns for human rights. Mark Twain criticized both the United States and the European powers for their conquests; his pamphlet "King Leopold's Soliloquy" was a devastating indictment of atrocities in Belgian Central Africa. The Ottoman massacre of thousands of Armenians in the mid-1890s provoked a humanitarian mobilization in the United States. Industrialists such as John D. Rockefeller, Sr., helped fund a National Armenian Relief Committee. The American Red Cross sent teams to help refugees, marking the organization's first work outside the United States. Congress's 1896 resolution condemning Sultan Abdul Hamid II for the murder of 100,000 Armenians marked the first U.S. resolution on international human rights. Four years later it was the farmers of Kansas, organized by People's Party leaders, who sent the first shipments of donated grain to India during a famine, and a pogrom against Russian Jews in Kishinev in 1903 provoked a series of public meetings in American cities to condemn czarist policies. "The most important fact in this new century," Charlotte Perkins Gilman wrote that year, "is the rapid kindling of the social consciousness." She hoped that

"America, with the blended blood of all peoples in her veins," would lead the civilized world in demanding "international law to restrain, prohibit, [and] punish; best of all, to prevent."

Thus, there were signs, even amid grim reports of U.S. atrocities in the Philippines, that Americans had the capacity to translate their democratic heritage into what Jane Addams called "an international patriotism." In a series of lectures given at the peak of U.S. imperialism around the turn of the century, Addams sought to articulate what that might mean. "Some of us", she told a Chicago audience, "were beginning to hope that we were getting away from the ideals set by the Civil War, that we had made all the presidents we could from men who had distinguished themselves in that war, and were coming to seek another type of man. That we were ready to accept the peace ideal, to be proud of our title as a peace nation. . . . Then came the Spanish war, with its gilt and lace and tinsel, and again the moral issues are confused with exhibitions of brutality." "Unless the present situation extends our nationalism into internationalism," she warned, "unless it has thrust forward our patriotism into humanitarianism, we cannot meet it."

Future reformers, intellectuals, and policy makers would answer Addams's call in a variety of ways. But American history books went on to describe the Philippine conquest as "benevolent" and the defeat of Aguinaldo's forces as a brief addendum to Americans' glorious liberation of Cuba. As the twentieth century unfolded, Americans largely forgot that the Philippine war had happened at all. When the United States granted Philippine independence in the wake of World War II, the turn-of-the-century war receded even further in American national memory. It was only in 1968, after U.S. troops perpetrated the My Lai massacre in Vietnam, that journalists went looking for elderly veterans who remembered the earlier conflict. Most expressed few regrets. They argued that harsher tactics should have been used earlier and even more ruthlessly in the Philippines; troops in Vietnam should beware, they said, of the treachery and cruelty of "Asiatics." Only a few looked back with doubt. One interviewee who had served on Samar, avenging the Balangiga massacre, remembered his platoon advancing through tall grass to make a stealth attack on a village of fishermen. "We opened fire and killed all but one," he recalled. "They were unarmed." There had been, this soldier remarked, "earlier My Lais." Veterans of an even earlier generation, who had witnessed General Sheridan's burning of a Blackfeet village on the Marias River back in 1870, or any number of other massacres inside the United States, could have said the same.

GLOBAL LEVIATHANS

By the early twentieth century, the United States was providing overseas missionaries and businessmen with military protection and aids to travel, such as the $720 million Panama Canal that U.S. engineers would complete in 1914. Control over Puerto Rico, Cuba, and the Dominican Republic secured access to the mouth of the canal, while the navy's Great White Fleet sailed the world to protect Americans and their property abroad. In domestic policy, also, despite Roosevelt's modest antitrust and pro-labor initiatives, Republicans in the main catered to corporate interests. They maintained protective tariffs and the gold standard, considerably benefiting manufacturers and investors.

The Supreme Court played a central role in protecting corporate power, as it struck down state and federal laws designed to protect workers and mitigate extremes of wealth. The Court had already showed such leanings in *Wabash v. Illinois* (1886) and the *Minnesota Rate* case (1890), which struck down regulatory laws of the 1870s and limited the ability of state legislatures to set shipping rates and counter the power of monopolies. In the Minnesota case the Court began to define property as not just land, buildings, and other possessions but as the "exchange value" of anything; regulation of rates was thus a theft of private property. In response to this weakening of state-level power, Congress passed the 1887 Interstate Commerce Act, creating an Interstate Commerce Commission for business oversight, and followed this three years later with the Sherman Antitrust Act, a vague law that made a first attempt to prohibit combinations "in restraint of trade." But in *United States v. E. C. Knight* (1895), the Court ruled that the Sherman Act gave the federal government no authority over manufacturing, even if the sugar refinery in question belonged to the American Sugar Refining Company, which controlled 98 percent of the national market.

The same year, 1895, brought other pivotal decisions, as the Court came under the sway of dogmatic Justice Stephen Field and his allies. In a case stemming from the Pullman affair, *In re Debs*, the justices upheld injunctions to halt strikes. Ironically, they based their opinion on the Sherman Antitrust Act, arguing that a boycott by a labor union, unlike a sugar refiner's bid for monopoly power, was an act "in restraint of trade." In *Pollock v. Farmers' Loan and Trust*, meanwhile, the Court struck down a federal income tax that Congress had passed in 1894. The Court argued that unless a constitutional amendment were enacted, such a tax must be apportioned on a state-by-state basis (a requirement that proved unworkable, leading eventually to passage of the Sixteenth Amendment for a federal income tax in 1913). The justices followed up these rulings with two more in 1897 that shaped the relationship between government and the economy. In *Smyth v. Ames* they declared that state regulators could set rates only according to guidelines written by the Court itself; in *ICC v. Cincinnati, New Orleans, and Texas Pacific Railroad*, they declared that the federal Interstate Commerce Commission had no power to set rates at all. As in the years of Reconstruction, a conservative Supreme Court effectively gutted the most progressive legislation that reformers had managed to obtain.

The justices did mitigate these decisions with some that recognized new government regulatory powers. In the 1899 case of *Addystone Pipe*, they ruled that price-fixing among corporations was illegal and upheld government sanctions against it. They also responded favorably to the Roosevelt administration's antitrust work and followed this up in *Swift and Company* (1905) by reconsidering the ruling in *E. C. Knight*, acknowledging to some extent that corporations engaged in interstate commerce fell under federal authority. By 1911 the justices would shift even further in this direction, upholding the U.S. government's right to break up a massive monopoly such as Standard Oil. Yet in cases relating to the states' police powers to protect the health, safety, and welfare of citizens, the Supreme Court proved hostile to reforms sought by labor advocates, a stance it maintained until the 1930s. The justices defined "police powers" by old-fashioned moral principles: laws to regulate or prohibit liquor met approval, as did bans on prostitution and gambling. In cases such as *Holden v. Hardy* (1898), they also allowed states to regulate working conditions and hours in certain dangerous industries, such as mining, and to end child labor. But they refused to let the states or Congress set minimum wages, and in most industries they struck down laws limiting working hours. The crowning case in this area was *Lochner v. New York* (1905), which overturned a New York law setting a sixty-hour workweek for bakers. Workers, the Court argued in essence, had the contractual right to labor as many hours as they chose. If they did not want to work more than sixty hours a week, they should look for a different employer.

The Court's juggernaut between 1890 and 1905—especially in cases related to unions, working hours, and wages—rivaled in significance its critical role in the collapse of Reconstruction. *In re Debs* had a long-term effect on the labor movement, paralleling in some ways the impact that *U.S. v. Cruikshank* and related cases had had on black voting rights. One historian estimates that between 1880 and 1930, state and federal courts issued more than 4,000 injunctions to stop strikes, almost always at the request of employers. By upholding this tactic (until Congress finally made the practice illegal in 1932), the Supreme Court tipped the odds in labor conflicts heavily in favor of employers, even before state militias or the U.S. Army intervened. It is hardly surprising that after the 1890s, trade unions such as the American Federation of Labor chose narrower and more limited goals.

The justices did not believe they were rolling out a red carpet for unrestrained corporate power. Instead, the aging judges on the court (Stephen Field, the oldest, had been born in 1816) reacted to another set of imperatives, similar to those felt by the era's natural scientists. Over their lifetimes the American judiciary had overturned English common law and systematized legal thought, creating elaborate theoretical categories. The justices believed such categories were scientific, universal, and immutable; their chief task was not to balance competing interests but to make expert rulings about the category into which a particular case fell. Judges, in other words, shared with many other professionals a serene confidence in the scientific basis of their enterprise. Believing themselves experts who were uncovering natural and universal laws, they prided themselves on dismissing the real-world impact of their decisions. This approach to law, which historians have called "legal formalism", reached its apex between 1894 and 1905 in some of the cases just noted.

Formalists were influenced by their conviction that the United States was a Christian nation, and that Christianity meant the defense of private property and public order. The Court's thinking was also rooted in anachronistic assumptions about government, labor, and capital. Their primary reference point for tyranny remained European-style monarchy, and the justices associated this with the power to tax. In decisions such as *Pollock*, they thus saw themselves as guardians of private property and the health of the republic, menaced by an overreaching Congress. In seeking to keep the playing field "level," they assumed businessmen and laborers contracted as equals and that government intervention on the side of labor would oppress business. The aging justices conceived of business as primarily the small-scale enterprise that had dominated the American economic landscape during their youth.

In this as in many other matters they were behind the times, and nothing showed this more clearly than their acquiescence on the issue of corporate personhood. As late as the early 1900s, the Court clung to an old definition of the corporation, assuming state governments were setting limits on what such entities could do. This had once been correct: as late as 1888 all states continued to set certain boundaries on corporate activity. But then New Jersey, seeking to attract enterprise, passed a revolutionary law inviting trusts, which were beset by legal challenges, to form "holding companies" under extremely lenient terms. The vast American Sugar Refining Company, with operations stretching from Cuba and Louisiana to California and Hawai'i, was among the first to take advantage of New Jersey's offer. Henry O. Havemeyer, a leader of the sugar trust in the 1880s, summed up the result of becoming a New Jersey holding company. "From being illegal as we were," he observed, "we are now legal as we are."

The result was a mass migration of corporations to New Jersey and later Delaware, after it also relaxed regulations. By 1904 all seven of the largest trusts, with a combined capitalization of $2.5 billion, operated under New Jersey charters. By 1905 the Supreme Court had essentially accepted New Jersey's definition of the corporation. In *Hale v. Henkel* it extended to corporations the Fourth Amendment right against self-incrimination, as if a corporation had a "self." In doing so the Court shifted from a definition of a corporation as a special entity, created by the state for public purposes, to the modern idea that it was the functional equivalent of an individual citizen (albeit one that existed in many places at once and could, in theory, live forever).

By the time Theodore Roosevelt and his successors bestirred themselves to limit the powers of these new leviathans and the Supreme Court began accepting their right to do so, corporate power had already undergone a dramatic concentration. New Jersey's and Delaware's laws, combined with the depression of the 1890s, enabled the largest trusts and holding companies to press their advantage against smaller competitors, many of which failed in the economic crisis. The depression also convinced businessmen in some sectors that they must merge to prevent price wars. Between 1895 and 1904, with a sharp peak at the depression's end in 1899, hundreds of American firms took this path, usually moving their headquarters to New Jersey or Delaware in the process. Almost 2,000 companies vanished, joining consolidated holding companies such as American Locomotive, DuPont, Eastman

Kodak, International Harvester, International Paper, Otis Elevator, and U.S. Gypsum, each of which controlled more than 70 percent of its product's national market share by the turn of the century. Laurence Gronlund had foreseen this development in *The Cooperative Commonwealth*. "These gentlemen," he wrote of the nation's leading executives, "have already found that while Competition is a very excellent weapon against their weaker rivals, Combination pays far better in relation to their peers."

Not all consolidations achieved such dominance, and not all businessmen found the strategy successful. But taken as a whole, the wave of mergers transformed the economy further in the direction of large-scale multinational enterprise. In the 1890s many of these consolidated companies won trademark protection through the courts, so that Ivory became synonymous with soap, Wrigley's with gum, and Gillette with razors. It is no accident that these names remain famous today. The most successful corporations became "first movers," taking a position of overwhelming dominance from which they could use their power (much as Republicans and southern Democrats were doing in politics) to shut out newcomers and rivals.

The result was an American economy even further integrated and financially centralized. A single national market in short-term credit linked the West Coast with the East by 1900. J. P. Morgan assumed control of the bankrupt Southern Railway (formerly thirty different companies), which gave his investors access to coal, iron, cotton, tobacco, lumber, sulphur, turpentine, and Florida fruit. The 1890s also saw a substantial movement of textile mills from New England to the low-wage South, starting with three Massachusetts firms that moved in 1895. At the behest of John D. Rockefeller, Sr., Henry Flagler opened a series of southern luxury resorts. "By 1896," wrote one historian, "palace cars from Bar Harbor and Newport could roll unimpeded through the poverty-littered Carolinas and all the way to Miami and its Royal Palm Hotel."

The most successful corporations emerged from the depression with multinational reach. Companies ranging from Borden to International Silver acquired factories in Canada. American Tobacco enlarged its empire with plants in Germany, Japan, and Australia. Behemoths such as United Fruit and U.S. Rubber regularly made purchasing and marketing decisions that impacted two or three continents. By 1897 U.S. direct investment overseas totaled $635 million, and in the next decade it rose to more than a billion and a half. By 1900 New York's most powerful financiers had intertwined their fortunes with those of the great industrialists, creating unprecedented centers of power. National City Bank, predecessor of today's Citigroup, counted among its directors not only John D. Rockefeller, Jr., and his brother William but also Henry Clay Frick of Carnegie Steel; Cleveland Dodge from the Phelps Dodge Corporation, one of the nation's largest mining concerns; reaper magnate Cyrus McCormick; railcar manufacturer George Pullman; and financier J. P. Morgan. National City Bank could by the first decade of the twentieth century exchange any currency into another in twenty-four hours and deliver it virtually anywhere in the world.

The bank knew what it was doing in choosing J. P. Morgan for its board. It was Morgan who had knocked Thomas Edison's name off Edison General Electric and taken it over in 1892. It was Morgan who had bailed out the gold standard during the Cleveland administration and in 1901 engineered the triumphant merger that created U.S. Steel, the first company in America with a billion-dollar valuation. Morgan's famous "Trio," consisting of himself and two close associates, provided links to investors and banks in Britain, France, Belgium, and Germany. The Trio, by this date, customarily swapped 15 percent shares in their U.S. and Mexican ventures for equivalent interests in Asian and African investments organized by their European partners. Association with the "House of Morgan" offered the most influential businessmen access to fabulous sums of investment capital and financial networks that stretched around the globe.

No one exemplified the new configuration of executive power better than Andrew Carnegie, who officially became the world's richest man when Morgan bought out his company. Carnegie Steel had thrived during the depression of the 1890s, largely through government contracts for the naval fleet that helped make America a world power. Back in 1886, when Carnegie had been approached about such contracts, he had lectured Grover Cleveland's secretary of the navy on the dangers of a military buildup, stating flatly that he was "opposed to every dollar spent by our Republic upon instruments of any kind for destructive purposes." Carnegie pointed out that Britain and Germany were unlikely to attack the United States, and he suggested that a naval arms race would increase rather than reduce the possibility of war. But on Christmas Eve 1886, Carnegie announced that a new open-hearth mill at Homestead would be built to roll out armor plates of the size the navy needed. "There may be millions for us in armor," he wrote privately.

The prices Carnegie charged the U.S. government for steel became the focus of repeated congressional investigations. Four former employees, embittered among other things by the defeat of the Amalgamated Steelworkers at Homestead, came forward in 1893 with persuasive evidence that the company had masked flaws and weakness in its armor. Carnegie was fined 10 percent on his current contracts, though officials to some extent hushed up the damage. Four years later Congress investigated allegations of overcharging. Carnegie, it turned out, was making profits of 30 percent or more on U.S. government contracts while selling similar steel to the Russian navy for a much lower price. "We are in the hands of this great steel combine," fumed Colorado senator Henry Teller. "The Republicans seem to have set their hearts upon giving to these people practically whatever they ask." Despite evidence that competing bids from smaller firms such as Midvale Steel were more cost-effective, Republicans handed most contracts to two big firms, Carnegie and Bethlehem. Carnegie then had the temerity to challenge the very policies that had made him rich. Amid debate over annexation of the Philippines, he offered to buy the islands outright from the United States for $20 million in order to give Filipinos their freedom. (The government declined.)

No incident was more telling than the moment in early 1897 when Grover Cleveland's secretary of the navy, Hilary Herbert, got fed up with the false information he was receiving from U.S. steel suppliers and boarded a ship to confer with European manufacturers. Herbert wanted to know what French and British steelmakers were charging their governments for naval steel, and he wanted to hear the answers directly from them. He made his trip top secret, but Carnegie, who had negotiated price-fixing agreements with Krups, Vickers, and other European steelmakers as well as with Bethlehem Steel, had agents in the administration who tipped him off. Unbeknownst to Herbert, the ship that carried him to Europe also carried a Carnegie employee who disembarked immediately and rushed to reaffirm the steelmakers' pact and warn of Herbert's visit. The secretary of the navy got vague answers on his tour and came home with little useful information. In the meantime, he and the French minister of marine commiserated with each other in Paris. Both governments, they felt sure, were at the mercy of steelmakers who were fixing prices and charging exorbitant rates, but neither man could prove it.

The late 1890s, then, at first glance marked the dawn of an era of fierce nationalism and unprecedented military escalation, in which the United States vied with European powers to amass battleships and claim overseas prizes, with each government eyeing the others suspiciously over the turrets. The U.S. government (as this story goes) had been weak in the Gilded Age but was now emerging as an invigorated global power, with Theodore Roosevelt equally aggressive in his policies abroad and his attack on trusts at home. There is some truth to this interpretation, as any Cuban or Filipino could attest. The significance of the imperial presidency can hardly be overstated.

Secretary Herbert's journey, however, offers a glimpse into a different reality. During the Civil War and its aftermath, the U.S. government had exercised immense powers and engaged in a series of bold experiments. But that war, along with the wars of incorporation that followed, had launched an economic revolution that left the authority of even the American president and the German kaiser humbled by that of Carnegie and his secret pool. Carnegie frequently argued that he placed his enterprise at the service of his country. (He went on to create the Carnegie Endowment for International Peace and fund construction of the Peace Palace in the Netherlands, home of today's World Court—while his company simultaneously forged the steel for dozens of warships.) But however much Carnegie did or did not serve his nation's interests, the reverse was clearly true: through its rising military expenditures, the U.S. government served the interests of Mr. Carnegie.

FOR FURTHER READING

An excellent short account of the U.S. conquest of Hawai'i is Scott B. Cook, "Islands of Manifest Destiny," in his book *Colonial Encounters in the Age of High Imperialism* (New York, 1996). See also Sylvester K. Stevens, *American Expansion in Hawaii, 1842–1898* (Harrisburg, PA, 1945), Merze Tate, *The United States and the Hawaiian Kingdom* (New Haven, CT, 1965), Gary Y. Okihiro, *Cane Fires* (Philadelphia, 1991), and Sally Engle Merry, *Colonizing Hawai'i* (Princeton, NJ, 2000).

My key sources on U.S. foreign relations throughout this chapter are Walter LaFeber, *The New Empire* (Ithaca, NY, 1963), and also his book *The American Search for Opportunity*, cited in Chapter 1; Louis A. Pérez, *The War of 1898* (Chapel Hill, NC, 1998); Thomas J. McCormick, *China Market* (Chicago, 1967); Dennis Merrill and Thomas G. Paterson, *Major Problems in American Foreign Relations to 1920*, 5th ed. (Boston, 2000); and Thomas Schoonover, *Uncle Sam's War of 1898 and the Origins of Globalization* (Lexington, KY, 2003). For excellent background on U.S. imperialism from 1782 onward, see Walter Nugent, *Habits of Empire: A History of American Expansion* (New York, 2008). Very helpful in placing foreign relations in cultural context is Matthew Frye Jacobson, *Barbarian Virtues* (New York, 2000). On the economic and cultural dimensions of expansion, see also Emily S. Rosenberg, *Spreading the American Dream* (New York, 1982), and for an environmental angle on U.S. consumption of tropical crops, Richard P. Tucker, *Insatiable Appetite* (Berkeley, CA, 2000).

Links between western frontier expansion and overseas imperialism are brilliantly analyzed in Walter L. Williams, "United States Indian Policy and the Debate over Philippine Annexation," *Journal of American History* 66 (1980): 810–31. On the perhaps underrecognized influence of Brooks Adams see William A. Williams, "Brooks Adams and American Expansion," *New England Quarterly* 25 (1952): 217–32. For alternative views of American imperialism see, for example, Ernest May's influential *Imperial Democracy* (New York, 1961), Kevin Phillips, *William McKinley* (New York, 2003), and James A. Field, Jr.'s provocative article, "American Imperialism: The Worst Chapter in Almost Any Book," *American Historical Review* 83 (1978): 644–68. On Jose Martí see the introduction by Deborah Shnookal and Mirta Muñiz in *The Jose Martí Reader* (Melbourne, Australia, 1999).

For the economic results of the 1898 wars in the Caribbean, see César J. Ayala, *American Sugar Kingdom* (Chapel Hill, NC, 1999). On the conflict in the Philippines I have drawn primarily on Paul A. Kramer, *The Blood of Government: Race, Empire, the United States, and the Philippines* (Chapel Hill, NC, 2006), on Stuart Creighton Miller, *"Benevolent Assimilation"* (New Haven, CT, 1982), and on black soldiers in the Philippines, Willard B. Gatewood, Jr., *"Smoked Yankees" and the Struggle for Empire* (Fayetteville, AR, 1987). On Americans' response to the massacre of Armenians, see Peter Balakian, *The Burning Tigris* (New York, 2003), and on Populist shipments of grain to India, Mike Davis, *Late Victorian Holocausts* (London, 2001).

My treatment of the U.S. Supreme Court draws primarily from Morton J. Horowitz, *The Transformation of American Law, 1870–1960* (New York, 1992), Owen M. Fiss, *The Troubled Beginnings of the Modern State, 1888–1910* (New York, 1993), and William E. Forbath, *Law and the Shaping of the American Labor Movement* (Cambridge, MA, 1991). On the importance of Christian faith, see Linda Przybyszewski, "Judicial Conservatism and Protestant Faith: The Case of Justice David J. Brewer," *Journal of American History* 91 (2004): 471–96. An overview of laissez-faire constitutional thought is Michael Les Benedict, "Laissez-Faire and Liberty," *Law and History Review* 3 (1985): 293–331. I also rely here once again on Richard F. Bensel, *The Political Economy of American Industrialization*, cited in Chapter 1, as well as on the following: Lawrence M. Friedman, *A History of American Law* (New York, 1985), Charles W. McCurdy, "The *Knight* Sugar Decision of 1895 and the Modernization of American Corporate Law, 1869–1903," *Business History Review* 53 (1979): 304–42, and Papke, *The Pullman Case*, cited in Chapter 10.

On the consolidation of power by multinational corporations see Naomi R. Lamoreaux, *The Great Merger Movement in American Business, 1895–1904* (Cambridge, MA, 1985), and

Walter Licht, *Industrializing America* and Mira Wilkins, *The Emergence of Multinational Enterprise*, both cited in Chapter 2. On credit markets see John A. James, "The Evolution of the National Money Market, 1888–1911," and "The Development of the National Money Market, 1893–1911," which appear respectively in *Journal of Economic History* 36 (1976): 271–75 and 878–97. On trademarks see Susan Strasser, *Satisfaction Guaranteed* (New York, 1989). The quotation on palace cars rolling through the Carolinas is from C. Vann Woodward, *Origins of the New South, 1877–1913* (Baton Rouge, LA, 1951), 297. The phrase *first movers* is drawn from Alfred D. Chandler's *Scale and Scope* (Cambridge, MA, 1990). On Mexico I return here to John M. Hart, *Empire and Revolution*, cited in Chapter 2. On Carnegie see Joseph Frazier Wall, Andrew Carnegie, and B. Franklin Cooling, *Gray Steel and Blue Water Navy*, both cited in previous chapters.

EPILOGUE

The Partridges
and the Hippopotamus

For America, if eligible at all to downfall and ruin, is eligible
within herself, not without.
—WALT WHITMAN, DEMOCRATIC VISTAS

During the hopeful years after the Civil War, Walt Whitman's essay "Democratic
Vistas" described his hopes for the triumph of American democracy. A visitor to
the St. Louis World's Fair of 1904, three and a half decades later, would have found
considerable evidence of fulfillment of Whitman's dream. Marking the centennial
of the Louisiana Purchase, which in 1803 had transformed the United States into a
continental power, the St. Louis exposition was the largest ever held. So vast were
its grounds and exhibits that medical experts urged patients with weak nerves not
to attend. The initial capitalization was $15 million, exactly the amount Thomas
Jefferson had persuaded Congress to pay for the whole purchase itself, and enthusiastic commentators spoke of the fair as a "coronation." "If all man's other works
were by some unspeakable catastrophe, blotted out," declared the chair of the
exposition board, "the records here established by the assembled nations would
offer all necessary standards for the rebuilding of our entire civilization."

If technology was the measure of progress, the fair offered plenty of it. With
officials counting almost twenty million visitors, St. Louis streetcars carried up to
120,000 passengers per hour to and from the site, while a double-track electric
trolley whisked visitors around the fair itself. On evening strolls along the exposition's pathways, visitors could bask in the soft glow of thousands of incandescent
lights. Technological marvels displayed at the fair ranged from the new wireless
radio to designs for future airships. A large exhibit heralded the "Era of the
Automobile." A somewhat less glamorous one hailed the "Age of Concrete."
An entire building was devoted to fossil fuels, and visitors could marvel at a
3,000-horsepower gasoline engine and a locomotive weighing 100 tons. (On the
Pike, equivalent to Chicago's Midway, St. Louis wisely reused Chicago's famous
Ferris wheel, whose enormous popularity had helped pull the 1893 exposition out
of debt.) One observer described what he had seen as "a succession of mental
shocks."

Those who needed a rest could enjoy the full range of urban amusements in St. Louis, famous for its ragtime scene. In clubs near the exposition, visitors could hear the great Scott Joplin perform his "Maple Leaf Rag" and "The Entertainer," the latter composed in honor of the fair itself. Baseball fans could go out for a Cardinals game, while movie palaces offered newsreels and dramatic thrillers such as *The Great Train Robbery*, a full eleven minutes long. St. Louis had proud new skyscrapers, including an 1892 Louis Sullivan masterpiece, the Wainwright Building. The vibrant features of the American city that had fascinated Whitman in his day were coming into full flower, their petals unmistakably flecked with commercial gold.

If social progress was the measure of democracy, then the fair offered evidence of that as well. An exhibit on U.S. settlement houses featured model playgrounds and reports on public health campaigns. The fair's Department of Physical Culture demonstrated exercises for pleasure and health. Government agencies proudly advertised their roles in improving citizens' lives. Germany's exhibit explained its new workingmen's insurance program, which would influence a similar U.S. program created four years later. The Smithsonian Institution showcased its recently built children's room. The U.S. Life-Saving Service gave daily demonstrations on a special lake, while elsewhere visitors could visit displays on Yellowstone Park. The overall design of the fair's "Forest City" showed, in fact, more than a glimmer of environmental consciousness. Situated in a hundred-acre woodland park, it featured naturalistic landscaping and soothing cascades.

Other signs would have pleased Walt Whitman. Thirty years earlier, all eyes had looked to London and Paris, but the United States now unmistakably asserted its own authentic culture. Educated European visitors probably knew the names of American writers such as William Dean Howells and Stephen Crane—certainly Mark Twain—as well as artists such as Winslow Homer, Thomas Eakins, James McNeill Whistler, and Mary Cassatt. Any English or Scottish tourist knew about evangelist Dwight Moody, while the name Othniel Marsh was familiar to devotees of Darwinian science. The fame of such figures both contributed to and resulted from a shifting flow of information. Back when Whitman had excoriated his countrymen for lack of cultural patriotism, far more Americans had subscribed to British journals and newspapers than the other way around. But by the 1890s American monthlies such as *Harper's* and *Century* began to outsell British monthlies—not only at home, but in England, too. One American editor noted that "a few British magazines and reviews continue to be imported into the United States, but they are very few indeed."

Forest City held irrefutable proof that the United States was becoming an economic, political, and cultural world power. Marks of militarism and empire were much in evidence. Along with models of the battleship USS *Missouri* and thirty other vessels, the Navy posted an immense map charting the locations of all its ships around the globe. The centerpiece of the fair, widely discussed and almost universally attended by visitors, was the so-called Philippine Reservation, an unabashed imperial display that cost more than $1 million. At its replica, school missionary teachers led classes in singing "My Country 'Tis of Thee," while in the plaza uniformed Filipino policemen and scouts (more than 600 of them, making up nearly half the reservation's population) conducted drills. Surrounding the plaza were ethnological villages displaying thirty-eight Bagobo "savages" and other representatives of Filipino tribes. The exhibit was considered so crucial as a public justification for U.S. occupation of the islands that President Roosevelt himself issued instructions on how to clothe the tribal peoples on display. If they seemed too primitive, officials worried, anti-imperialists might argue they were unfit to be Americans; if they seemed too civilized, that might fuel sympathy for Philippine independence.

Looking around the fair, one could find markers of the violence of incorporation at home as well as overseas. Apache leader Geronimo and Nez Percé Chief Joseph were "among the noted Indians on exhibition." To greet visitors at the entrance to the Pike, Frederic Remington sculpted *Cowboys Shooting Up a Western Town*, which one guidebook described as a "frolicsome" scene. Meanwhile, Chinese visitors were fingerprinted and forced to wear numbered tags as long as they remained in the United States, reassuring the American public that they would not remain after the fair was over. Japan, fresh from its stunning victory in the Russo-Japanese War, received more respectful treatment on the basis of its military might. Anthropologist W. J. McGee, who directed the fair's ethnological displays, explained that the Japanese were progressing because of their "complexity of blood," equivalent to that of Anglo-Saxons.

Few systems of racial categorization were ever presented with more confident assurance than McGee's, which turned the entire fair into an elaborate hierarchy of racial types designed to contrast "the barbarous and semi-barbarous peoples of the world" with the "full-blown enlightenment of America." McGee believed the keys to Anglo-Saxon superiority were cranial size and manual dexterity, as well as "sensitiveness to temperature, delicacy of touch and taste, [and] acuteness of vision and hearing." Even more obvious racial condescension emerged when a group of white St. Louis schoolteachers invited Filipino scouts to stroll with them through exposition grounds. The scouts were taunted with shouts of "nigger," beaten up by members of the fair's police force, and attacked by a group of marines who shot revolvers in the air and shouted "Let's clean the gu-gus off the earth!" A lynching was narrowly averted.

Such incidents suggested that Americans had not achieved all they claimed in civilization and progress. Much at the fair would have thrilled Walt Whitman, but much else would have grieved him deeply, and in retrospect it is hard to avoid the conclusion that Americans understood little about the world that their institutions and desires now played a key role in shaping. In the most generous possible reading of Americans' national mentality in 1904, they had fallen victim to a naïve misunderstanding of themselves. Philosopher William James captured this attitude and its consequences in a public letter denouncing the Philippine war. "Among the charming 'Fables' which the New York *World* printed many years ago," James wrote, "was one about a hippopotamus, which, walking one day in the forest, . . . scared a hen-partridge from her nest of new-hatched fledglings. Touched with compassion, the kind-hearted animal exclaimed: 'You poor, forsaken babes! Let me be a mother to you.' So she sat down upon the nest of little partridges."

James proposed that the United States resembled the kind hippopotamus. "Unquestionably the great heart of our people means well by the islanders," he wrote. "But what worse enemy to a situation of need can there be than dim, foggy, abstract good will, backed by energetic officiousness, and unillumined by any accurate perception?" He could have extended the point from the Philippines to the Caribbean, Central America, and China. As one historian has put it, America came onto the global stage with "a desperately parochial understanding" of the world outside its borders. It did so in part because geographic expansion on the North American continent—ending with the wars of incorporation—had already been romanticized. The public mythology surrounding conflicts within the borders of the United States provided a powerful template for the "schooling" and uplift of Cubans and Filipinos.

It would be wrong, however, to see the innocence of the hippopotamus as a personal failing on the part of individual Americans. Rather, the structures that now linked the United States to the rest of the world obstructed a clear view. The St. Louis World's Fair, which claimed to represent the objective truth about the world when in fact its exhibits were sponsored by corporations and powerful empires (as well as a deeply misguided anthropologist) was a prime example in itself. But larger and more subtle processes were at work. Americans were experiencing the world first and foremost as consumers. The very genius of corporate capitalism was to obscure the distant origins of rubber, sugar, and beef and whisk them to consumers as if by magic. To an unprecedented degree, Americans could enjoy the fruits of the global marketplace without guilt or thought. Just as state legislatures and courts had extended "limited liability" to investors and executives sued for acts committed by their corporations, manufacturers and advertisers offered a kind of psychic limited liability to consumers.

New political structures, like commercial ones, often obscured rather than clarified Americans' views of the world. In 1898 Americans had fought a war to free Cuba and found, in retrospect, they had conquered an overseas territory in the Pacific, a circumstance that was explained, like the failure of Reconstruction, by reference to the racial incapacity of the liberated people. The most powerful of all imperialist spokesmen, Theodore Roosevelt, had at the time of the St. Louis fair just been elected with an astonishing 57 percent of the popular vote, the highest any president had won since the 1820s. Roosevelt had watched William McKinley's campaign manager, Mark Hanna, market McKinley "as if he were a patent medicine," and Roosevelt in turn skillfully marketed himself as an embodiment of masculine vigor and who also spoke eloquently of the wonders of nature and the benefits of fair play.

Roosevelt's bellicose assertions of "Anglo-Saxon manhood" are all too easy to caricature. Other forms of racialized thinking were more complex. An Orientalist fad, evident at the St. Louis fair, captured many of the contradictions in Americans' racialized thinking. Englishman Edward Fitzgerald's loose translation of the *Rubáiyát* of Omar Khayyám, a twelfth-century Persian poem, came into vogue and Americans rushed to put "Turkish corners" in their parlors. As early as 1885 Gilbert and Sullivan's parody *The Mikado* started a rage for Japanese lanterns and kimonos. In the 1890s American artists had begun studying eighteenth-century Japanese prints and reflecting their influence in bold prints and posters. Japanese newspaper artist Beisen Kubota had visited the Chicago World's Fair, where he shaped the work of the young American artist John Sloan.

Perhaps the culminating moment of Orientalism was the publication of "Madame Butterfly," an 1898 short story by John Luther Long that playwright David Belasco borrowed two years later. "Madame Butterfly" reflected American racial condescension while at the same time critiquing it. The popular play centered on Cho-Cho-San (Butterfly), a Japanese woman who believes her lover, a U.S. Navy lieutenant, will return for her and their child. The lieutenant returns, but with his blonde American bride. He has no intention of marrying Butterfly and has written a revealing letter to a fellow officer about "that little Jap girl." "You won't believe it," he remarks, "but for two weeks after I sailed I was dotty in love with her." Cho-Cho-San wants to become an American but also retain her honor. Finding that her lover's betrayal prevents this, she commits suicide, placing in her baby's hand just before her death a little American flag. The play's critique of imperialism is complicated by the lieutenant's attempts to buy off Cho-Cho-San with "lots of money," as well as the presence of his new wife, Kate, who helps prompt Butterfly's suicide by telling her she will take away the child and raise him. "Let us think first of the child," she tells Butterfly. "For his own good . . . let me take him home to my country." Butterfly responds, "He not know then—me—his mother?" Kate responds, "It's hard, very hard, I know; but would it not be better?" The playwright clearly assumed audiences would agree.

In some ways "Madame Butterfly" is the story of three women, Cho-Cho-San, Kate, and Butterfly's wise maidservant, Suzuki, who tries to warn her mistress of the lieutenant's faithlessness. It is thus a critique of men's exploitation of women and perhaps of elite women's self-delusions as well as of racial prejudice. Yet in the United States, Cho-Cho-San was always played by white actresses. Blanche Bates, the most famous actress in the role, claimed she learned her Japanese mannerisms from family servants in San Francisco and from a personal maid, Suki, whom she employed in New York. Suki had a *real* tragic story: her fiancé in Japan, on the eve of boarding a steamship to join her in America, was murdered. To complicate things further, Belasco forced his heroine to speak broken English ("tha's mak' me mos' bes' happy female woman in Japan—mebby in that whole worl'—w'at you thing?"), verging on the exaggerated dialect that audiences of the time found cute and funny when attributed to blacks.

Butterfly's story had many meanings. She was an exotic, sexualized figure, and in light of U.S. marriage laws many Anglos surely rejected her aspirations to marry a white man. Yet her strong sense of honor highlighted the values of a feudalistic past in the days before money had meant everything, and her suicide was surely intended as a critique of Western imperial designs. Thus, racial condescension went hand in hand with admiration and desire, as non-Asians described (or invented) a version of Japanese culture useful to themselves.

The many calls to extend "Anglo-Saxon civilization" around the globe vied with the vision of Walt Whitman and his heirs of the United States as a crossroads of people from all continents. Humorist Finley Peter Dunne, who created the Irish-American character Mr. Dooley, addressed the problem when he had Mr. Dooley comment to a friend on race-based justifications for the war of 1898. Dooley, he averred, was a proud "Anglo-Saxon" name:

> They're a lot iv Anglo-Saxons in this country, Hinnissy. There must be as many as two in Boston. . . . Me ol' friend Domingo will march at the head of the Eyetalian Anglo-Saxons when th' time comes. There ar-re twinty thousan' Rooshian Jews in th' Sivinth Ward . . . [and] when th' sons iv Sweden, and th' Circle Francaize, an' th' Polacky Binivolent Society, an' th' Benny Brith, an' th' Afro-Americans an' th' other Anglo-Saxons begin f'r to raise their Anglo-Saxon battle cry, it'll be all done with th' eight or nine people in the wurruld that has th' misfortune iv not bein' brought up Anglo-Saxon.

Dunne captured with humor a fundamental contradiction between what the United States had become and what its elite leaders understood it to be.

The summer of 1904 waned into fall. Workers at the St. Louis fairgrounds disassembled the Ferris wheel and giant dynamos and tore down the grand façades. Fair managers totalled their profits and filed their official reports. Tourists, entrepreneurs, and the diverse people who had gathered went home (or in the case of some native peoples who had been put on display, struggled to raise funds to get home and ended up as wanderers). America's new wealth, military power, and economic reach—revealed through the fair as if through a fun-house mirror—endured.

On the morning after the fair closed, as the eastern sky lightened with dawn, thousands of Cuban, Puerto Rican, Filipino, and southern sugarcane workers headed out to the fields at harvest time; in Louisiana, scattered Italians and Portuguese trudged out among the black work crews. In Hawai'i, Chinese and Japanese women went out to labor beside the men, stripping dried leaves from the stalks as their husbands cut and loaded cane. Japanese women sang *hole hole bushi,* songs to match the rhythms of their work:

> *Worse than the birds crying*
> *Or the temple bell tolling*
> *Is the plantation bell*
> *Calling us to another day.*

Into San Francisco and New York harbors came the ships full of sugar: 400,000 tons from Hawai'i, 700,000 tons from Cuba, and more from Java, Mexico, and Brazil. In Louisiana 400,000 tons went into the refineries of the great sugar trust, while freight cars waited nearby to ship it nationwide.

New York cooked it into Tootsie Rolls. Farther upstate it found its way into boxes of Jell-O. Atlanta used it to sweeten Coca-Cola, and at the Wrigley's factory in Chicago it flavored Juicy Fruit and Spearmint gum. The New England Confectionary Company put it into gumballs, licorice, and Valentine conversation hearts. Whitman's Chocolate Company in Philadelphia blended it into that luscious nineteenth-century invention, milk chocolate, distributed through its new nationwide marketing channels. The factories of Derry Church, soon to be renamed Hershey, Pennsylvania, in honor of the local manufacturer, poured their supply of sugar into the great vats that brought forth nickel chocolate bars. All these fed into the great river of candy—$400 million worth—that Americans consumed that year.

And in New York City's Bowery district, Henry James sat in a darkened theater in December 1904 watching the audience around him eat candy. He searched their faces. He considered whether he himself, so long a wanderer abroad, belonged among them. He meditated on the United States they represented, so different from the nation of his childhood. He wondered what it all signified for the future of politics, business, and culture, and for the peoples of the world as they came to America's gates or found America at theirs. And while he thought, he munched his chocolate creams.

FOR FURTHER READING

All material on the Louisiana Purchase Exposition is drawn from Robert W. Rydell, *All the World's a Fair,* cited in Chapter 7, and from original guidebooks and reports. Especially helpful here is Matthew Frye Jacobson, *Barbarian Virtues* (New York, 2001); the quotation about Americans being "desperately provincial" is drawn from pp. 264–65. On other nations having to take the United States seriously, but not vice versa, I am grateful to Louis A. Pérez for ideas he presented in a lecture at Vassar College in April 2004. For the analysis here I am also grateful to Kristin Hoganson for her paper, "Girdling the Globe: US Women and the Fictive Travel Movement, 1880–1920," delivered at the American Historical Association, Washington, DC, in January 2004. The section on Orientalism draws on Mari Yoshihara, *Embracing the East* (New York, 2003). On sugar and candy I have drawn on Gary Okihiro's *Cane Fires* and César J. Ayala's *American Sugar Kingdom*, both cited in Chapter 11, as well as George Thomas Surface, *The Story of Sugar* (New York, 1910).

The lessons one draws from any period of history depend, to a large extent, on one's choice of beginning and ending points. Those interested in such questions (whether or not they like the choices of 1865 and 1905 that have been made in *New Spirits*) might appreciate William Cronon's essay "A Place for Stories: Nature, History, and Narrative," *Journal of American History 78* (1992): 1347–76.

Questions for Discussion

1. *New Spirits* tells, in brief, the stories of many famous and ordinary Americans who lived between 1865 and 1905. Identify two or three such individuals who strike you as interesting or compelling. What themes or ideas do their lives represent for you? Do they exemplify the era, and if so, how? Did you find any heroes in this book? If so, what qualities in them did you find heroic, and why?

2. The Civil War cast a long shadow over the decades that followed. Mark Twain called it an "ennobling war" (see the introduction), while José Martí described it as a "corrupting war" that bred a "habit of authority and domination" (see the introduction to Part III). To what extent do you think each of these views was accurate, and why? What legacies, both positive and negative, did the war leave for Americans who came of age after it ended?

3. Economic thinker Joseph Schumpeter famously described capitalism as a process of "creative destruction." In what ways did such processes operate in the United States between 1865 and 1905? How did they impact work and daily experience? Women's rights? Sexuality and family life? Religion and culture? Politics? In what ways do you see this "creative destruction" as having positive or negative consequences?

4. What kinds of violent conflict did Americans engage in between 1865 and 1905? What were the sources of this violence, and how did it shape relationships among Americans and between America and the world? (Note: A timeline of conflicts is posted at the *New Spirits* website, http://projects.vassar.edu/newspirits. It covers only public, large-scale episodes of violence; other forms, like domestic violence, were more hidden, but you may still want to take them into consideration.)

5. In the introduction, the author explains where the term *Gilded Age* came from and why she refrains from using it. Here and elsewhere she suggests alternatives, such as the "long Progressive Era" and the "paleotechnical era." She also employs several metaphors to describe the period, including fire in the

introduction; Henry George's wedge in the introduction to Part I; and the telephone exchange in the introduction to Part II. Which of these terms and metaphors seem most useful? What would *you* call this era, and why?

6. Thomas Frank is one of many American commentators who have described the 1990s and the first decade of the twenty-first century as a "new Gilded Age." Does such a comparison make sense to you? Why or why not? (You may see no parallels—or may see them in very different ways than Frank does— but for his comparison see "The New Gilded Age," in *Commodify Your Dissent*, ed. Thomas Frank and Matt Weiland [New York, 1997], 23–28.)

7. New *Spirits* emphasizes the racial and cultural diversity of the American working class, which was drawn from the Americas, Africa, Europe, and Asia and included people of many colors, religions, and languages. What were the consequences of this diversity for the labor movement, for the economy, and for society and culture? What are its legacies today? If you have an interest in world history, you might want to do some additional reading and compare societies where the workforce has been largely imported (for example, Brazil and the United States) with those having highly homogenous, indigenous populations (for example, Japan and Scandinavia). How has immigration— whether forced or voluntary, or both—or *lack* of immigration shaped the histories of these nations?

8. Former U.S. diplomat George Kennan, an iconoclastic thinker, has remarked that he has "a great distrust of the monster nations, where there is the exertion of political authority over millions of people from a given center. . . . I think they are dangerous to themselves, as well as to everybody else. . . . You lose all real, intimate connection between the source of national power and the people themselves. For this reason, I feel that our own country has to be decentralized." Kennan proposes that the United States be divided up into "something like a dozen constituent republics." ("The Provocateur," *New Yorker*, November 13, 2000, 100.) Using Kennan's idea, imagine a counter-history of the United States in which the Confederacy had maintained its independence and additional republics, perhaps starting in the West, had also broken away. Would the political, economic, and social results have been beneficial or harmful, and to whom? How might slavery have eventually ended? How might these "constituent republics" have responded to events in the twentieth century? What relations might they have with one another today?

Index